A PHILOSOPHY
OF THE
CHRISTIAN REVELATION

A
PHILOSOPHY
OF THE
CHRISTIAN REVELATION

by

EDWIN LEWIS

Professor of Systematic Theology
and the Philosophy of Religion
in Drew Theological Seminary

HARPER & BROTHERS PUBLISHERS
New York   London

Set in English Monotype Bell. Format by Faulkner Lewis.
Manufactured by The Haddon Craftsmen for the Publishers
Harper & Brothers

To

Louise Frost Lewis

*Who with no thought of personal achieve-
ment has yet achieved greatly in creating
and maintaining, by unobtrusive and
sacrificial toil, the conditions essential to
the achievements of others*

TABLE OF CONTENTS

FOREWORD

THE THEOLOGICAL BATTLE-FRONT SHIFTS CONTINUALLY. THERE IS every evidence that the question of Revelation is again becoming central. The proper logic of the humanistic emphasis, which was the retirement of all supernatural reference, has apparently run its course. The disappearance of the supernatural threatened to reduce religion to an ethic, and when religion, especially Christianity, becomes simply an ethic, it is no longer religion. "The Religion of Humanity" has proven itself as ineffective practically and as nonproductive spiritually as it was when Comte first projected it, a hundred years ago. Religion without God is something other than religion. And yet where shall God be found?

In any mood approaching the normal, men would fain be religious, which means that they would have a God. But the God which reason reads out of itself, and out of the course of events, is a God to whom so much uncertainty attaches, so much inconsistency. The evidence is so wavering. A conclusion which seems to be justifiable when looked at in the light of one feature of existence simply collapses before some other feature. It is evident that the best that is open to men is a guess. But is a guess enough? Indeed, have not the guesses become so numerous that many a modern mind has given up in despair?

It is this situation, the aftermath of a sterile humanism, which creates the new interest in the question of Revelation. Has the hidden God anywhere lifted the veil? Has he made himself known as to what he is, what his purposes are, and how his purposes are to be realized, and are we in possession of this knowledge?

The question has a Christian answer. There are other answers, in particular the Jewish, but the claim is made that the Christian answer subsumes all the rest and corrects them. In Jesus Christ, the very fact of him, the preparation for him, what he was, what he said, what he did, how he did it, together with all that comes to pass where this is taken for truth—in this, God stands self-disclosed. So runs the Christian claim.

The claim, just because it is so clearly central, has been unimportant at no time. Events have conspired together, however, to give it unusual relevance for the time through which we are now passing. It is becoming increasingly evident that Christianity stands or falls by the reality of its claim to be Revelation, that is, to bring to men a truth about themselves, and the whole order of things in which they are involved, which they could not otherwise know.

The following pages are devoted to a consideration of this claim. An attempt is made to set the question against the background of modern thinking in various fields. At some points, this thinking may be shown to be favorable to the issue. At other points, little insight is required to see that it is distinctly antagonistic.

The author makes no secret of his own personal convictions as to the question raised. He believes that the question is finally one of the right of men to take for truth that which makes life most meaningful, and that Christian truth has precisely this significance. It can make a place for every fact brought to light by patient investigation of the web of existence. Where it issues a challenge is not at the point of any indubitable fact. It challenges only when the fact is given an interpretation which invalidates Christian truth, especially that truth as it concerns God, man, and Jesus Christ himself.

The first part of the book endeavors to present the claim respecting Revelation. The claim is approached from the standpoint of "a philosophy of the word." All commerce of mind with mind is by way of "signs." Further light is held to fall on the claim from the fact of universal religion. There is a frank acceptance of all that modern scholarship has brought to light respecting the processes whereby the Old and New Testaments came to be. The function of these writings is held to be to bear witness to the Revelation. The way in which what is seen to be central in this witness is reflected and proclaimed in the fact of the Christian Church is treated as a vital element in the case for Revelation, if the case is to be fully stated.

The second part of the book considers the problems arising out of the general claim. Those problems are necessarily metaphysical, philosophical, epistemological, psychological, and, as respects the alleged Virgin Birth of Christ and his Resurrection, if nowhere else, scientific as well.

The third part considers to what extent the Revelation may be able to do what it has always done—maintain itself in an ever-changing scene; how the Divine Spirit which was responsible for it in the first place both guards it and perpetually renews it; what the evidence is to this process of renewal in our own time; and whether there is still any better or more effective way to present it to men, even to men of a scientific age like our own, than in those imaginative, emotional, and dramatic forms in which it was first clothed. It was clothed in these forms because, especially at the point of its consummation, the Revelation was itself conveyed in what can only be called the world's supreme drama, the drama of the Man Christ Jesus. But the drama has its full significance only if Jesus Christ is conceived as the form in which the Very God—"Think, Abib!"—came to a death-grapple with the hostile powers of existence, of his own and ours, reeled before their dreadful impact, and then in the Resurrection both signified his own victory and gave the certain assurance of a like victory for any man who would have it re-enacted in himself. This is more than mere subjectivism and emotionalism. That vast epic drama which was the nexus in the creative and redemptive conflict, a conflict implicit in the fundamental nature of existence itself, is so religiously adequate just because it is ontologically real.

Inevitably the preparation of books such as this has a by-product in the accumulation of numerous notes and references. What to do with them is always a problem. The average reader is annoyed by the presence of footnotes, and the professional student is likely to be annoyed by their absence. A not uncommon compromise has been adopted by retiring to the end of the volume a selection of references and explanatory notes deemed sufficient for the usual purposes. Foreign books are, with a few exceptions, referred to in their English translations, where these exist; quotations from them, again with occasional exceptions, are also in English.

The absence of any reference to a number of recent important books germane to the subjects discussed is regretted. The manuscript was finished in the spring of 1939, and was put into type during the following summer, but publication has been unavoidably delayed. Among the titles which could very well have been included in the references had circumstances permitted are the following: John Baillie, *Our Knowledge of God*; A. A. Bowman, *A Sacramental Universe*; John Burnaby, *Amor Dei*; A. H. Dakin, *Man the Measure*; W. G. de Burgh, *From Morality to Religion*; A. S. Eddington, *The Philosophy of Physical Science*; Nels F. S. Ferré, *Swedish Contributions to Modern Theology*; W. M. Urban, *Language and Reality*; and Charles Williams, *The Descent of the Dove*.

Dr. H. M. Taylor, jr., of the Department of Systematic Theology in Drew Theological Seminary, shared in the preparation of the index, and was of the greatest assistance in many other ways while the book was in process.

EDWIN LEWIS

Drew Forest,
Madison, New Jersey

PART I

REVELATION AND RECORD

CHAPTER 1

Summary at end

Signs, Symbols, and Meanings

JESUS CHRIST IS THE LIVING WORD OF GOD TO MEN. SO CHRISTIANITY claims. The claim is not made in any purely arbitrary way. It is based in history, fact, and experience, and is an interpretation of these which reason can justifiably make.

The claim in question is a claim of revelation. The fact of God, the meaning of God, the purpose of God, are held to be given in Christ as they are given nowhere else. Indeed, we shall see in due time that the Christian claim is that they are given here absolutely.

But if God is so revealed, it will follow that he is revealed elsewhere. Barth's attempt to limit revelation to Christ and the historical preparation for him is a profound mistake, even from the standpoint of Christian apologetics.[1] Of a God who reveals himself at only one point it may well be asked what good reason we can have for supposing that he is revealed even there. To ignore outside of one narrow stream the fact of creation, the fact of history, the fact of man's own distinctive nature, especially his reason and his conscience, the fact of ethical activity, and the fact of universal religion, is to weaken rather than to strengthen the case for revelation in Jesus Christ and in all that of which he was the climax.

In view of the widespread attempt of modern philosophy, and even, one fears, of much modern theology, to get rid altogether of the idea of "special" revelation, and to find revelation *only* in the total historical process, it is easy to understand the vigor and the passion with which the Barthian limitation has been presented. But to correct one error by falling into another will hardly promote the cause of truth. "God hath nowhere left himself without a witness." The witness may often be vague and of problematical import, but it were better to see in that the promise of a more certain word elsewhere than either to deny it altogether or to suppose that it is all

3

we may ever hope to have. Both alternatives have been adopted. If Barth represents an overly restricted view of revelation, there are those who represent an overly general view—a view so general, indeed, that it can nowhere find any clear standard of discrimination. Where all is equally revelation, who shall determine what is being said, and what, of all that is being said, is most important?

No recent writer has shown more clearly the insidious character of the attempt to get rid of "special" revelation by the use of the principles of speculative idealism than Emil Brunner, in *The Mediator*.[2] Brunner corrects Barth's one-sided emphasis on the scriptural and Christian revelation by showing that once we have this revelation, we are able to detect and to estimate its adumbrations elsewhere. The Spirit whose activity is intense at one time and place may carry on a less intense activity at other times and at other places. Either form of activity will throw light on the other. A true understanding of Christ becomes interpretive of *all* the ways of God. What is this but to say that all the ways of God are meaningful? If there is an ultimate divine Omega which is implicit in an original divine Alpha, then all that God does in the meantime has a significant relation to the purpose of the process. "Nothing walks with aimless feet." The God who reveals himself in Christ as Redeemer also reveals himself in Christ as Creator: wherefore creation, in its own way and kind, is revelation.

On the other hand, the denial of the redemptive significance of what is given in Christ in effect reduces revelation to what is yielded by creation alone, and this too Brunner has made indubitably clear. A God who speaks everywhere, but whose speech is baffling; a God who provides the key to the interpretation of his own speech; a God whose supreme Word throws its own meaning across all his lesser words—this is the situation according to the Christian view of things.[3]

In any consideration of the Christian view, it is obvious that we must choose a starting place. We could, of course, limit ourselves to a mere statement and elucidation of the Christian view itself. This may be helpful enough to those who have no difficulty with the view and simply desire to have it more fully explained. But that large number who feel that many things have conspired together to

bring the Christian view to-day into grave question have the right
to ask for more than simple elucidation. They have the right to ask
that the alleged Christian revelation be set against the background
of existence as a whole to ascertain to what extent it fits into that
background and to what extent it appears to be the proper issue of
all the rest. If it can be shown that the Christian revelation bears all
the marks of being the fulfillment of that which everything else
seems to be predicting, we can certainly claim to have a strong case,
even from the standpoint of reason alone.[4]

The question is where to begin. Would it be altogether arbitrary
to begin with the simple assertion that things are meaningful?
Some would say that it was, since the very question at issue is
whether we live in a purposive universe. Whether we do or not
must eventually be a matter of belief: it can hardly be called a
matter of knowledge. How much can be said for the belief has
recently been shown again with great clarity by Dean W. R.
Matthews in *The Purpose of God*,[5] and by D. S. Cairns in *The
Riddle of the World.* Yet the vogue of the novels and poems of
Thomas Hardy, the wide acclaim given to such books as Max Otto,
Things and Ideals, and Joseph Wood Krutch, *The Modern Temper*,
and the fact that Bertrand Russell, who wrote in *The Free Man's
Worship* that it is practically "beyond dispute" that the world as
presented by modern science is quite purposeless, void of meaning,
"the outcome of accidental collocations of atoms," justifying in
man nothing but the grim mood of "unyielding despair"—the fact
that Russell, who wrote this and much more like it, is regarded by
such great numbers to-day as an oracle, all shows that the belief in
a purposive universe is anything but general. Yet a non-purposive
universe and the Christian revelation are obviously two utter incompatibilities. For the person who accepts the revelation, the
purposiveness of all things else follows. The person who denies the
purposiveness will also necessarily deny the revelation. If a reasonable case is to be made for the revelation, therefore, it requires that
some good reasons shall be adduced for the belief that there is
meaning in things, and that this meaning, to some extent evident to
rational reflection, is augmented and clarified when seen in the
light of the revelation.

The simple truth is that we cannot carry on any kind of commerce with one another without the continual assumption of meaning in the things around us.[6] Some meanings, of course, we must recognize as assigned or imputed. This is true, for example, of a language, whether in its spoken or in its written form. With a few possible exceptions of the most rudimentary sounds and marks, written words and spoken words can be the conditions of intercourse only because of a prior agreement as to what each mark and sound, and the various groupings of marks and sounds, shall represent. But it would be quite wrong to suppose that these arbitrary or imputed meanings exhaust the possibilities. How could human intercourse ever have begun in the first place, and how could it begin even now, save as it took place in a common world whose features bore a common meaning which it belonged to minds mutually to understand? The significance of this commonness has been developed at great length into an "ontological" argument for God by W. E. Hocking, in *The Meaning of God in Human Experience.*[7] Even those who could not follow this argument could hardly deny the facts from which it proceeds. If a common world commonly experienced and understood is not the basis of all human fellowship, then what is? We cannot begin at zero. We are sharers from the beginning, and we are so constituted that the sharing is inevitable not only as to the fact of it but also as to the character of it. Within this common and inevitable meaningfulness we can build up many meaningful situations which call for more and more conscious and deliberate cooperation on the part of those concerned. What is important to observe, however, is that it belongs to men who know not a word of each other's language to find through a common experience of some fact of the objective world a path to each other's mind.

This possibility is fundamental to the argument of Rudolf Otto, in *The Idea of the Holy.* That power of response, even of inevitable response, which is the condition to what he calls the *mysterium tremendum*, is at least the evidence to the fact that men cannot but help find a meaning in things. That crude original response will later be subjected to all manner of criticism and refinement, and eventually may even be explained away. But what no man, not even the most sophisticated, can ever guarantee is that he will not again some day find himself making that same response.[8] *This* means *that*. It not only belongs to men to agree on meanings after due deliberation: it belongs to them to find meanings where there was no such preliminary agreement. What we may therefore call *interpretation* is native to man, spontaneous, something we cannot escape.

Mythology could very well be considered for its bearing on this fact. The Greek could not look anywhere without feeling that there was more than he saw. The dryad, the oread, the naiad, may easily enough be dismissed as mere creatures of fancy. To the unimaginative literalist, that is all that they are; but why suppose that minds pronounce most truly when they are most prosaic? A tree is—only a tree. But who says "only"? What does "only" mean in such a statement? The Greek did not say, "only" a tree, "only" a cloud, "only" a flower, "only" a bird, "only" a wave, "only" a breeze, "only" a reed. He saw a tree, and he bethought himself of Ceres and Erisichthon and Daphne; he watched a moving cloud, and it was as though divine Juno were approaching; a flower bent its head over a pool as though to see its own reflection and he said, "Narcissus"; he heard the nightingale, "the tawny-throated," and thinking of the pursuit by the murderous Tereus, he said, "Philomela"; the wave rose from the sea, and broke in a cerulean shower, and he said, "Proteus"; the breeze lightly touched him and passed —what was it but "Zephyrus"; and he heard the rustling of the reeds by the river's brink, and he said, "Syrinx."

Nobody will defend this for other than what it was. But then, what was it? Was it not seeing more than was evident to the eye, hearing more than was evident to the ear? To say that this "more" was not actually there, that it was due entirely to the imagination, is simply to reduce men to the status of mere impassive recording machines. It is to rob Noah of the rainbow, and Moses of the burning bush, and Elijah of the sound of a gentle stillness. It is to rob Jeremiah of his almond-rod, and Saul of Tarsus of his voice from heaven. It is to reduce to a mere gesture Gautama under the Bo-tree, and Augustine convinced he is to "take and read," and Mahomet undertaking his Hegira, and, shall we say, the claim of the Maid of France that the "voices" could not be withstood. It is not at all a question as to whether the meanings that were placed on facts and events were precisely what the facts and events existed to convey. "There are differences of interpretation." The question rather is whether we are ever justified in saying, "*This* means *that*." A given interpretation may be erroneous—*but is all interpretation always erroneous?* Can a thing mean nothing but itself? If it can mean nothing but itself, then there is no such thing as meaning, for to talk of meanings is to talk of symbols, to see the given as significant of what is not given, but is only implied or suggested.

In a word, to talk of meanings, and hence of symbols and signs, is to talk of revelation, and to talk of revelation is to talk of the conveyance of truth. Whether the truth shall actually be conveyed depends upon what is done by the mind which confronts the conveyance. There can be revelation only as there is response. Nevertheless, the *intent* of things, facts, and events to be meaningful, to say something, to be so many intelligible signs—this must be assumed even by those who deny it, for without this we are but as men beating the air.[9]

From the standpoint of the Christian revelation, even from the standpoint of a simple personal theism, there are many grave defects in the theological position of H. N. Wieman.[10] But for his steady insistence on the fact and centrality of meaning, we cannot be too grateful. Whether his metaphysic of meaning is as adequate as his psychology of it, is a serious question: in the opinion of the present writer, it is woefully inadequate. Without a doubt, Wieman is correct in his insistence that human experience is inseparable from meaningfulness, and that its value is to be judged by the extent to which there is growth of meaning. To define God, however, as "growth of meaning," which is what Wieman does, is to abandon altogether, so it would seem to many, the metaphysical basis of that very meaningfulness in which human experience is said to be so inextricably involved. That man has to do with meaning—yes; that the world is the arena in which meaning and man co-exist, and achieve what partnership they may—yes; that this is possible only because of some fundamental congruity between the very structure of mind and meaning-bearing situations—yes; but that a meaning-bearing situation is that only in relation to man, calling for no other great Reality of which the meaning-bearing situation is a "revelation"—*no!*

Perhaps a doubt concerning the adequacy of his own position is indicated in a parenthesis occurring in Wieman's section of *The Growth of Religion.* "Since God (or the work of God) is unlimited growth of meaning and value. . . ."[11] The parenthesis ought to be underscored. It is the absence of what it seems to indicate which has been one of the chief reasons for much of the criticism which Wieman's views have evoked. No special insight is called for to see that there is an incalculable difference between saying, "God is unlimited growth of meaning and value," and "The work of God is unlimited growth of meaning and value." In the first case, God would seem to be equated with the process, which leaves the process itself a quite inexplicable thing. In the second case, the process is the way—at least, *a* way—in which God is working: it therefore becomes a revelation of God, and a third term is introduced into the situation, without which the alleged situation cannot be accounted for. In a word, man as participant in meaning; the world as shot through with meaning-bearing facts and situations; these facts and situations as self-expressive of a greater Intelligence, to be called God, seeking in this way the realization of a purpose to which man is central—this is not only a fair reading of the situation: it is the most reasonable reading of it if the clew to the situation is held to lie, as Wieman insists it does, in the fact of meaning.

Whether or not the parenthesis referred to above was intended by the author to indicate as much as this, it still remains that what has just been written stands in the line of what is known as The Great Tradition. It may very well be called *the philosophy of the word.* In the ordinary sense, any word is a sign. It is a means whereby one mind holds commerce with another. All instrumentalities of minds may therefore be described as words. They are symbols of meaning. Their function is to say something. This is possible only if, so to speak, there is a mind on either side of them. Hocking says of all experience of nature that it is experience of Other Mind, and the capitalization is deliberate. It is not simply experience of other minds, although even this experience is possible only through a larger whole. Indeed, what ought to be said is that all experience of nature and all experience of other minds is at the same time experience of Other Mind. We are back with the familiar triad—the Mind of God, the mind of man, and those *media* of their relationship which in their totality constitute the world.

These *media* are functional besides factual. They vary in their meaning-bearing power. As existences, they issue not from man but from God, although man may do all sorts of things with them. He may misuse them, which is to say that he may misread them. Their true meaning he may entirely miss. Nevertheless, they remain as so many words of God. God is forever speaking, or, since deeds too are words, God is forever acting. Creation is his word, and the one word is compact of many lesser words. Creation is his deed, his purposeful deed which determines the countless lesser deeds which it comprehends.

What is this but the very essence of what Plato taught? Nobody has been able to show that Plato is completely consistent. That is hardly to be expected of any man who continued to write throughout many years. It must always be a question whether the "Godhead" of Plato is anything more than the totality of the Ideas conceived as organized under the supreme and controlling Idea of the Good.[12] If this represents the actual limit of his thought, then it must be held to fall something short of a true theism. But what can never be in doubt is that Plato was utterly unable to account for the temporal order save as a revelation of the eternal, it being the prerogative of man, whose true kinship was with the eternal and not with the temporal, to see in the temporal the means whereby he could regain the lost eternal.

The terminology of Plato is a small matter. The "mythic" forms which he employs are only so many evidences of the inadequacy of language. His thought is nowhere more truly expressed than it is in those very "myths" which are admittedly most imaginative—the myth of creation in the *Timaeus*; the myth of the struggling soul in the *Phaedrus*; the myth of the cave-dwellers in the *Republic*; the myth of the judgment in the *Gorgias*; the myths of the future abodes of men—the one narrated by Socrates at the close of the *Phaedo*, ending with the familiar words, "Glorious is the prize, and great the hope," and that of the soul of Er the Pamphylian which con-cludes the *Republic*. Of the Platonic myths, Westcott once wrote: "They are not, in essence, simply graceful embellishments of an argument, but venturous essays after truth, embodiments of defi-nite instincts, sensible representations of universal human thoughts, confessions of weakness, it may be, but no less bold claims to an inherent communion with a divine and suprasensuous world."[13]

Plato still holds his throne because men cannot escape the con-viction which, express it as he may, is central to all his thought. It is the conviction that *this* means *that*, and that the main concern of men is to find the *that* through the *this*. A world in space and time; man set in that world of space and time, yet transcending it, other than it, judging it, using it; a Reality above space and time which is everywhere reflected or revealed in the measurable and the ponderable, to the end that through the reflection man might come to know and lay hold upon that Reality—nothing other than this is what Plato is everywhere expounding. It is surely not with-out significance that modern minds of the first water—Cudworth and Whichcote, Schleiermacher and Hegel, Inge, Temple and Taylor, Shorey and More, Royce and Santayana, Unamuno and even Gentile—should have confessed their sympathy with the fundamental conception of Plato.

Nobody would want to claim that Spinoza was a Platonist. His inability to find any ultimate distinctions within the totality of existence is alone sufficient to preclude that. This, and his com-plete lack of any proper doctrine of creation, must always make him suspect to any thorough-going theism, in particular to Christian theism. De Burgh has recently offered an unusually understandable exposition of Spinoza, with enough of criticism to show that he realizes where Spinoza's deficiencies lie.[14] Yet he has no difficulty in showing that Spinoza sees man as engaged in a spiritual pilgrim-age beginning "like Plato's prisoners in the cave, shackled in a land of shadows," but seeking liberation through the successive steps of imagination, reason or scientific knowledge, and intuitive vision, this intuitive vision yielding *amor Dei intellectualis*. In this experience is man's complete liberation, the realization of "recip-rocal communion" between God and man. How "liberation" and "reciprocity" are possible on Spinoza's general principles is a question that might well be raised.[15] What is not disputable is that Spinoza sees the function of *natura* as *naturata* to make possible man's true relation to *natura* as *naturans*. In more simple language —although it is not possible to change the language without to some extent qualifying Spinoza's thought—the God who is manifested in the world is seeking through the manifestation to bring man, *himself a form of this very manifestation*, into harmonious fellowship with himself.

Admittedly this thought is placed in a baffling setting, but, as de Burgh very truly says, Spinoza's metaphysic has one basic assumption, an assumption which Spinoza admitted he must make, although he was quite unable to account for the operation with which it was concerned, namely, "that eternity must needs manifest itself, for man's inadequate apprehension, under the form of temporal duration."[16] What is this assumption but a way of saying, as respects the relation of the temporal and the eternal, *this* means *that*? Is the tree God? Spinoza would say, "No," since for him God is the sum total, including the tree, expressed in the tree, but still more than the tree. Then is not the tree, in common with every other "finite thing," a word of God? And while the question as stated may seem to have connotations to which Spinoza would object, nevertheless, in so far as it is asking whether the part does not *mean* a truth about the whole, it would be difficult to show that it must not be answered affirmatively.

If one other influential thinker may be named as representing this same central conviction, it could very well be Hegel. There are a score of aspects of the Hegelian philosophy which are as unacceptable as anything in Spinoza. Yet when we consider the illustrious group of British Idealists, from Wallace and Green to Bradley, Bosanquet, and Pringle-Pattison, to say nothing of other somewhat similar groups in Europe and America, it is difficult to suppose that Hegel, the progenitor of the line, was entirely wrong.[17] Perhaps we have to say that Hegel was most wrong at those points which were most peculiar to him, and most right at those points where he shared and perpetuated a conviction which in actual fact few men have ever been able entirely to escape.

Certainly, if ever a man, examining his world and seeking to account for it and to understand it, said, *"This* means *that,"* that man was Hegel. Let it be admitted that he talked much about the time-process being the process of the realization and fulfillment of the Absolute Idea. But it is just as true that the process of realization is also the process of revelation. "The things which are seen are temporal, but the things which are not seen are eternal," is a good Hegelian text. But how does one know that there is an unseen eternal? One knows it only because of the seen temporal, which has precisely the function—among others—of making known the fact of the unseen eternal. The Absolute Idea is known only in its un-folding, which is also its self-realization: so Hegel.[18] But since the Absolute Idea completely explicated, unfolded, realized, fulfilled, is God, there is nothing else that even Hegel could have said than that any given "moment of the process"—his own familiar phrase —was a word of God. Here some truth about God stands revealed, even if only momentarily, and even if in the very act of the affirma-tion the denial of it has begun.

It is easy enough to become fascinated by the Hegelian dialect: so facile it is that it allays suspicion. Only slowly does one begin to feel that anything so neat must somewhere be faulty. The system as a system is too "icily regular." The Demon gurgitates only to swallow again, the one example of that which feeds on itself and neither diminishes nor increases! But in Hegel if anywhere we have what was called above the philosophy of the word, and his numer-ous followers have been loyal to him at that point at least. The historical process as Greater Mind speaking as and in and to lesser mind—this certainly is central, even if it is not exhaustive, in the Hegelian view. We can regret the many unsatisfactory concomi-tants, as it would seem, of the view, especially as these have to do with the intrinsic nature of both God and man and of the relation in which they stand to each other, since in Hegel that relation is al-ways on the level of necessary existence, never on the level of per-sonal moral and spiritual reciprocity, this latter level being one for which Hegel can make no proper provision[19]—one can feel regret at these points, and still appreciate the fact that Hegel sees exist-ence as something to be read and man as designed to read it. What is readable is also meaningful. It proposes to lead the mind on beyond the reading to that which the things read serve to express.

Strictly speaking, there is nothing in the so-called modern view of the world which can properly be held to invalidate this philosophy of the word. The philosophy calls for man conceived as able to see meanings in the world of which he is a part, and to regard those meanings as evidence to the activity and purpose of Greater Mind. A person may feel that this is a reasonable philosophy, and at the same time be open to every scientific truth. In fact, he could say that science itself is one of the best supports of his philosophy, since what does science mean but the profound intelligibility of things?[20] That there is a universal relatedness, and that within this field of relatedness are fundamental differences—at least the difference between that which understands, or mind, and that which cannot understand but can only be understood—these are certainly integral elements of a modern view. A modern view also requires that man as an intelligent being shall be so integrated with the whole process of existence as that the hypothetical "beginning of things" was also the beginning of the process of securing man.

Naturalism takes this to mean that man is as he is because the world is as it is: *it* determines *him*. But that is because naturalism does not look beyond the process. Sufficient was said above to indicate the reasonableness of the view that the process itself needs explaining in terms of a still other Reality, in brief, God, whose activity the process then represents as it also reveals his nature and purposes. In that case, because conscious reciprocity with a meaningful world belongs only to man, who must therefore be regarded as the "end" of the process which makes him possible and which he in turn interprets, it becomes necessary, at least defensible, to make the daring claim not that the world has determined man but that man has determined the world. The claim may sound less drastic when it is restated to read that the creative activity of God has been determined by his purpose respecting man.

If, then, the world is a word of God comprising many lesser words, and this calls for a power somewhere of reading that word, and if that power is man, man himself becomes the most significant of all the divine words. If things mean God, and to some extent

reveal God, then nothing means God so much as does man himself.
The philosophy of the word must include that mind without which
no word could be a word because it could not evoke the intended
response. Man is therefore not only cosmic index, but divine index
as well. In the striking phrases of Francis Thompson, he is "cosmic
metonymy"; he is "bred o' the worm and Deity"; he is "equation
of creation"; he is "compost of Heaven and mire":

> "Great arm-fellow of God!
> To the ancestral clod
> Kin,
> And to cherubin."[21]

The more man is brought into the center of the stage of existence,
the more inevitable it becomes that so far from his being read in
the light of all the rest, as though he were merely one more item
in a collection of items, all the rest shall be read in the light of him.
To the casual view, man is contained within the world: he takes his
place in the total along with cloud and flower, along with fish and
bird and beast. But that is the casual view, and the casual view is
always superficial. To a deeper because a more prolonged and earnest view, the world is contained within man.[22] He experiences it,
he thinks it—and it is precisely as his experience, as his thought,
that it exists for him.

Admittedly this is not a self-evident truth, and it will be returned
to and elaborated at a later time. It is a truth, however, with a very
manifest bearing on the problem of revelation. The distinctiveness
of man must be treated as a fundamental postulate. His very power
of interpretation must be regarded as itself interpretive. It is interpretive of its own source. In a word, the step is not from man
to an impersonal *somewhat* called nature, as though this impersonal
nature were man's sole origin. The step rather is from man to God,
even if all that this permits us to say about God is that he is such a
One as is possessed of the very qualities distinctive of man himself. Let these qualities in man be reduced to two: reason and conscience, or the power of thought and the power of moral judgment.
A God *of this kind* may still be very much more than this, and he
may have ways of revealing this "more," but even a God of this

kind alone suffices to charge the fact of the world and the fact of man himself with a significance which can be secured on no other basis whatsoever.[23] What is more, this significance can be secured without the denial of a single known fact, either of the world or of man.

The philosophy of the word, therefore, which has now been briefly sketched, offers an explanation of the world and all its diversified forms, and it offers an explanation of man and his powers and relationships, and especially his power of interpretation, including as this does the power of moral judgment and evaluation, and it completes the explanation by referring both the world and man to the activity and purpose of a Greater Mind. If the world is a word, an organized body of symbols, there must be that which is able to read the word, or to interpret the symbols. To do this belongs preeminently to man.

But man is no more self-explaining than is the world. He, too, is a word, but a word of a peculiar kind. He has the power to read not only his world, but also *himself*. He is conscious of being a meaning-bearer. He is the seat of vast intimations. He can never be quite satisfied to think and to believe and to live below what he feels to be the best. This fact explains his history. It accounts equally for his social institutions, his political institutions, his cultural institutions. Above all, it accounts for his religion and all its diverse manifestations. It is in particular by his religion that man most indicates what he believes about himself, and about his world, and about his origin and destiny. Therefore it is in man as religious that most is revealed about the Source whence man issues. A man before an altar is man in his most significant attitude, for he is there intimating what he believes is the deepest truth not only of his own existence but of the totality of existence with which he is integrated. The praying man is the highest possible revelation of God within the circle of the natural.[24]

Our problem is to relate these considerations to the Christian revelation. The possibility of it is indicated in some of the greatest sayings occurring in the record of that revelation. One of the profoundest of them, which will be considered in due time in various ways, is in the Prologue of the Fourth Gospel: "In the beginning was the Word, and the Word was with God, and the Word was God. All things were made through him. The Word became flesh, and dwelt among us. No man hath seen God at any time. The only-begotten Son, Jesus Christ, who is the Word made flesh, he hath shown God to us in himself." If we accept this claim, then the revelation in creation, the revelation in human personality, the revelation in the whole fact of religion and especially in the fact of chosen men and perchance also in the fact of a chosen people, the revelation in the very experience of those men who have accepted the truth of God in so far as it was given to them to see it, all becomes intelligible. We see the imperfect in the light of the perfect, and we see the function of the imperfect to be preparatory to the coming of the perfect—"in the fulness of the time."

Before the Word could become flesh, it must utter itself in truth apprehended here by this man and there by that man, and must then be proclaimed as truth by these men to others. Before the Word could utter itself in such preparatory truth, it must utter itself in the whole fact of man with his gifts of reason and conscience. Before the Word could utter itself in man, it must utter itself in creation which is the abode and *milieu* of man. And before the Word could utter itself in creation, there must be that Word as a constituent element of the Godhead whereby the possibility exists of the purposes of God being given objective effectuation.

Always therefore we are driven back to God and the way God necessarily is. Always we see the divine activity as revelation of and by the Word. But always we see that only when the Word is completely uttered have we final evidence that there really is utterance elsewhere—utterance needing this perfect utterance for its proper understanding and interpretation.

Hence that profoundest of all Christian truths: "He that hath seen Me hath seen the Father."[25]

CHAPTER 2

Religion and Revelation

THE CONSIDERATIONS ALREADY ADVANCED CONCERNING MAN AND HIS relation to the rest of existence were seen to bear directly upon the fact of religion. Man's religion, quite irrespective of the form it may take, witnesses to his indestructible conviction of the mystery of things and of his own deep and perchance baffling significance. Only persons can be religious, because only persons can think about themselves in relation to a Higher and a Beyond.

There are ultimately only two views as to how persons could have come to be, and they have already been stated. One of them is that persons, with all their range of intellectual, moral, emotional and spiritual powers, are merely the issue of the vast natural process in the same fashion as any other living thing may be. Thus Shailer Mathews speaks of "the personality-producing activities of the universe."[1] The other view is that persons involve, in a way we are unable to describe, a specific form of the creative activity whereby their most distinctive characteristics are precisely those which have no discoverable antecedents in the natural process. In the second view, God is *totaliter aliter* ("totally other") respecting the universe. In the first view, God may or may not be recognized. If he is recognized, it is only as another way of referring to "personality-producing activities."

Whichever of these two views we adopt, we are still met with the empiric fact that the human being is religious, and that he only of all living things is religious, and that he is religious not by some arbitrary imposition, but because of his fundamental constitution. Of all the theories of the origin of religion, the most palpably absurd is the theory that religion is an invention of the priests.[2] It was Strauss who said that to get rid of mystery in religion, men must first get rid of the priests. They must do nothing of the kind. The

18

priest is because of the mystery, not the mystery because of the priest. A religion without the element of mystery would not be a religion at all.[3] It might be a useful individual or social ethic, but not a religion.

Religion looks Beyond and Within because to look Beyond and Within belongs to man as much as grace belongs to the flower or movement to the sea. There may be and there are countless numbers of irreligious men but no man is non-religious. The term "irreligious" connotes the more or less deliberate repudiation of an authoritative "otherness" which it was impossible not to recognize. The term "non-religious" connotes the impossibility of making such a recognition. Animals are non-religious; men are or may be irreligious. In basic idea and intention they are capable of entering into "over-natural" relationships, but they can refuse to do anything about this capacity except ignore it and keep it from expression. It is precisely in that that irreligiousness consists. So far as what it *indicates* about man is concerned, therefore, irreligion is as meaningful as religion.[4]

We have then here a fact—the inseparability of man and religion. This is just as much a fact as any of those countless other facts before which the scientist proposes to sit down, and, in the familiar phrase of Newton, "put questions." Not that religiousness is *only* a scientific fact, to be given *only* a scientific evaluation, but that it is indubitably factual, as much a part of the totality of existence as is anything that is measurable or ponderable. Nathaniel Schmidt did not say the last word about religion, nor yet lay bare, as he supposed he did, religion's lowest denominator, when he defined it as loyalty to a Cause;[5] but he comes very near to the root of the matter in his implication that no person is complete in himself, but has that in him which impels him to seek completion through relation with a larger whole. The title of Binder's book, *Religion As Man's Completion*, is suggestive enough.[6] Never, says Rossetti, is our actual horizon our potential limit.

> ". . . From this wave-washed mound
> Unto the furthest flood-brink look with me;
> Then reach on with thy thought till it be drowned.
> Miles and miles distant though the last line be,

And though thy soul sail leagues and leagues beyond—
Still, leagues beyond those leagues, there is still more sea."[7]

It is what Francis Thompson meant by his thought-packed line, "the limit limits not, but the desire."

Let "the larger whole" that man's very nature implies be called God, in the only true sense of the word as the Giver and Ruler and Lover of life, but let it also be admitted that men may seek the fulfillment of their incompleteness by relationship with "a larger whole" which is yet other than *this* God and less than *this* God, and we have the explanation of the fact that men may still live "the good life," may be very unselfish, devoted to a Cause, deeply moved by humanitarian impulses, and yet still fail of "fulness of life."[8] If there be in man that of which the correlate is God, and only God, then ever is man a broken arc if he does not find himself in God.

"Thou hast made me for thyself." Those are wrong who find the object of religious devotion in anything less than the Highest in Thought and Fact. The *fruit* of a true religion must indeed be in all those activities which seek to increase blessedness in other lives. But the religious man is not merely the socialized man. Socialization is inevitable, and religion must promote it. For all that, the great moments of the soul, and, if one may dare say so, the moments for whose sake primarily it exists, are those moments when all else is for the time being forgotten because God stands here self-disclosed, and the raptured soul knows it and rejoices in it and would fain build a tabernacle that would hold captive the divine presence forever—which thing still cannot be. The great moments are great only because they are *moments*. For God finds us only to commission us. Transfiguration to-day means conflict with evil forces to-morrow, and ever beyond that the haunting "terror of the shade." Plato's cave-dweller, having found for himself freedom and light, must seek the deliverance of those who are still blind and shackled. To break the manacles of ignorance only to keep to ourselves the emancipating knowledge—what is this but to

". . . wear the name of freedom
Graven on a heavier chain"?

The transfiguration experiences, however, evanescent though they must necessarily be at this stage of the human pilgrimage, impossible as it is to capture them in a permanent tabernacle whose impervious walls would open to no disturbing human cries from souls less richly blessed, are yet withal in God's good grace prophetic of that ultimate unbreakable fellowship of God and man which heaven is to be. These rare moments that save us from cold despair are analogous to those moments when the navigator, harassed all day by lowering clouds and at night by impenetrable darkness, concerned as to whether he is still holding his course, or instead is making for "some false, impossible shore," catches through a rift in the clouds a fleeting glimpse of sun or stars—and the glimpse suffices him. That light set in the unchanging heavens gives him again his direction, and to the anxious question, *Quo vadis?* he can answer with a serene confidence, *domum!*

> "Back flies the foam; the hoisted flag streams back;
> The long smoke wavers on the homeward track,
> Back fly with wings things which the winds obey,
> The strong ship follows its appointed way."[9]

Man has business with the things of time and space; he must cultivate relations with the here and now; nevertheless, these in themselves do not yield his full measure. He struggles with the temporal that he might learn the eternal. He looks at what is visibly set in space that so he might acquire power to "fetch his eye up to God's style, and manners of the sky." His full measure is yielded by the fact that he is so made that he can think God, be aware of God, yield to God, serve God, love God, find in God all the motive of his action, all the inspiration of his life. "As the hart panteth after the water-brooks, so panteth my soul after thee, O God." Here is the pole-star of the human spirit in its mysterious journeying through the mysterious time it as mysteriously creates. By this the course of life is to be set. Every other possibility of experience is to be adjudged according as it relates helpfully or disadvantageously to this. Herein lies the secret of all that "creative strife" which to a man like Berdyaev is the fundamental fact—that strife whose issue is the world and man in their interwoven and inseparable intimacy, and yet withal an intimacy whose meaning derives from man, who is therefore to remain what he has always been, the instrument whereby the still-continuing strife is to be directed to still higher ends.[10]

Dark indeed are many of the pages in which the story of religion lies written, as much "since Calvary" as before. How damagingly one may tell "The Natural History of Religion," let Hume's famous treatise be the attest. But the dark pages are only as they must be, since man has ever been but a creature in the making, and his religiousness has had coordinate expression with all his other powers. Of religion as of life it must be written that "the best is yet to be." For anything with which man has to do, the imperfect is the price of the perfect. "Strait is the gate, and narrow is the way." Many an altar had to reek with blood before it could possibly be seen that the one perfect sacrifice is the vicarious self-giving of the one perfect Priest, who is the perfect Priest able to make the perfect sacrifice just because himself needs no sacrifice. He for whose sins atonement must be made can make no atonement for the sins of others. Therefore is it written of Christ that "through his own blood he entered in *once for all* into the holy place, having obtained eternal redemption," and he could do that because, and only because, "through the eternal Spirit he offered himself without blemish unto God." Of this "once for all" the crudest religion, the weirdest rites, the most repulsive ceremonies, are prophetic anticipations.

What then is the story of religion, with all its complexities, but the evidence to that infinite mystery which is adumbrated in the human soul? Let those who wish to do so, see in the physical man, or the economic man, or the psychological man, or the social man, or the political man, "the measure of all things." Their conclusions will be deficient because their standard of judgment will be less than the highest. All that may be said about a man viewed under these various aspects may be true, but when it is offered as the final truth it becomes false. Without a body man is not man, yet is he more than body, else how could he even *think* that he was "only body"? Without the cooperation of his kind and with his kind, man is not man, yet is man more than a mere social unit.

There is only one view of society that is more false than the atomistic view, and that is the view that sees *nothing but* society and so never sees a man. Without continuous effort to subdue the earth to his purposes, obeying its insistent call to him—

"Yea, the rough rock, the dull earth, the wild sea's furying waters,
  All with ineffable longing are waiting their Invader,
  All, with one varying voice, call to him,
        Come and subdue!"[11]

—without this stooping to obey, that so he might enjoy and live by the fruits of the earth his very obedience conquers, man is not man; yet what does the response itself, and the diverse forms it takes, reveal but that man is more than an economic quantum with a measurable value in the world's markets? Without devising ever more perfect instrumentalities, Magna Chartas and Bills of Rights, democratic constitutions and untrammeled courts, whereby larger and larger groups are brought together, and the principles that promote the common good freely accepted—without this, man is not man. Yet is man more than Aristotle's "political animal."

Underlying all the undeniable truth that is present in these partial views is the deeper because ultimate truth that man is made for God. This God stands over against him, his Maker, his Judge, but his Goal. Even Rousseau saw that what made man man was the fact that on one side of his nature he was open to the infinite. God made this little bay, the soul of man, just that it might suffer him to pour into it the ocean of his love—yes, and that he, even he, might receive love in return. If there be any "proof" of God, where is it if not here? There can be no other "proof," because if what is here being said is not true, no postulate exists whence "proof" can proceed.

One dares to go farther, and to say that if man's religiousness does not in fact bespeak an "over-natural" reference and suffuse him with a light that never was on sea or land, then even "revelation" in the abrupt and apocalyptic fashion delineated by Kierkegaard and Karl Barth, becomes likewise utterly meaningless because impossible. If God speaks to me, it is because he has already made me with power to hear him. If God discloses himself in a human life, so that of that human life men in awed wonder exclaim, *God Incarnate!* it can only be because the power to become the vehicle of the divine self-disclosure is a fundamental human mark.

True, God is "the Wholly Other," but he is not therefore "the Wholly Different." Pringle-Pattison argues cogently, even though no mere *argument* can settle the question, that the more that naturalism insists that man, in all the range of his powers, is but the issue of the cosmic process, the more it becomes impossible to offer any explanation of that process save as the intended means whereby man should come to be as he is.[12] From which it follows that absorption in the non-personal phases of existence, justifiable though it is for certain purposes, can never yield the final meaning of that existence in its wholeness. Astronomy and geology may overwhelm us, but just what is astronomy without the astronomer, and just what is geology without the geologist, and just what is implied in the human possession of the sheer ability to forge and dwell upon conceptions of which the emotion of "over-whelmedness" is the concomitant?

Man therefore is more even than a "time-binder," although he is that, both climaxing and increasing all past time and perpetually making present all future time. But besides this, he is the "pointer-reading" which throws its clear interpreting light on all that concrete actuality which is time's content. Himself mystery, this strange creature man intensifies while also serving to reveal the mystery which lies across the whole face of existence. He is the key to the hieroglyphic scroll—or there is no key, nor ever can be one. He is kin, as Francis Thompson so characteristically expresses it, to both "the ancestral clod and to cherubin." Or, better still, he is

> "Swinging-wicket set
> Between
> The Unseen and the Seen."

Woven into the seamless robe of the universal life—yes! Nevertheless is there yet that within him which sets him apart: wherefore is the robe not seamless! He is an alien in the very universe which in certain moods he tries to convince himself produced him. He writes a canticle in praise of God for Brother Sun and Sister Moon, for Brother Fire and Sister Water, for Mother Earth and Sister Death, and very beautiful it is, and moving to the heart. Yet must the canticle be sung "with the understanding also," else is there danger of a false sentimentality as bad as Wordsworth at his worst.

For what is meant by brotherhood between man and all else, when only man can think brotherhood, know brotherhood, practice brotherhood? Brother Sun warms me, and I know it, but Brother Sun knows it not. Sister Water floats my frail bark and drowns my sailor-friend, and she knows nothing of the bark on her bosom or of the sailor in her unplumbed, salt, estranging depths. Let the gentle Francis sing his canticle and we will sing it with him, but while we sing we will also remember. For none of these "brothers" of his ever did as the singing monk did every day, and often every day, and as we may all do every day—it never withdrew into the "unleaguerable fortress" of its own inwardness, to find there an altar, and above it a Shekinah. "Brother man" to all else that lives he might be, yet he carries a secret which he cannot share with that which is less than he, as all these "brothers" are. It is the secret of another kinship, a kinship with the Eternal, and it sets him apart, and when he forgets it or ignores it or denies it, he becomes thereby an orphan, to remark sententiously to other like orphans, "You see, we have only ourselves."

On occasion this man is held by the inexpugnable conviction that only one thing ultimately matters among the thousand pressing concerns of life. So many things he wants, and life has so made him that he must want them; yet of them all there is only one whose complete abandonment makes of all the rest at last Dead Sea fruit. "I am he whom thou seekest": so speaks the Voice of the relentless pursuing Hound. Pascal, baffled at a thousand points, at last sees what the bafflement signifies, and he writes his imperishable thought, usually misquoted as "I should not seek thee, Lord, had I not already found thee."[13] Thomas Aquinas, thinking himself alone and unobserved before the crucifix, hears himself addressed by the Figure momentarily animate: "Thomas, thou hast written well of me: what wilt thou have!" Did he answer, as a selfless monk seemingly should, "I want—nothing"? He did not. Did he answer: "I want—

only a few things, such as befit a humble scholar"? He did not. He answered: "I want—everything!" Yes, he answered even that audaciously; for what he said was: "Lord, give me—*thyself!*" Repeating the familiar story, Chesterton is moved to the ironic comment that "there are some who feel that the audacity is softened by insisting that he said, '*only* thyself.'"[14] Not for nothing had the son of a noble line turned his back upon his ancestral castle, and betaken himself to the austerities of the scholar's cell. He had learned thereby that the life to which God gives himself—the God, that is to say, whose greatest deed is a Cross—finds that God gives other things in needful measure, but finds also that what God does not give is neither desired nor missed—nor needful.

Say not that utterances such as these, coined of the experience of too rare because saintly souls, are abnormal, anti-social, the unconscious rationalizations of perverted choice. Say rather that they represent that absolute norm from which any purposes less completely selfless and self-fulfilling are a deviation. "Earth changes, but thy soul and God stand sure." God smote himself a highway from There to Here, and though we call that highway the earth, and though we know that it is made only at last to be unmade, yet the Here and the There shall never pass, since strands more enduring than the perishable earth bind them together. For the Here is any place where a soul builds a Bethel, and any soul may build a Bethel anywhere and at any time, and Bethel marks the commingling of the soul and God. The restless search for Bethel—this is the history of religion, and the history of religion is integrated with the history of man—of man, whose history is likewise integrated with the history of all God's work.

And when every bit of religious symbolism, every obscure religious rite, every dogma and every chant, every institution and every creed—when all these are argued away as explicable in terms of an ever-changing historical situation, *the reason for them all still remains*, because that reason is in the very soul of man. Being left, it will manifest itself again. Because it cannot be destroyed so long as man is man, and because it is more potent than persecutions, inquisitions, intellectualisms, secularisms, philosophical and scientific naturalisms, economic absolutisms, dialectic materialisms, and all that ilk—themselves but the misengendered brood of the very spirit they deny. This being so, as often as the fruit of this indestructible root is cut down, it will fructify again, in new symbolisms and new rites, new institutions, new dogmas and new songs.

So once again it falls to be said that everything about a man spells "heritage." The ages incarnate themselves in him. The hissing fires of the cosmic furnace belched their fumes that his spirit might be distilled—the abiding fragrance of that which is perpetually being consumed. The only music of the spheres is the music which his soul but imperfectly yet prophetically makes. The labyrinthine ways of his mind are the slowly-built corridors down which a Voice—an awful Voice, a winsome Voice, at last a Voice of agonizing love—would utter at once its imperative command and its tender appeal. The arches of the years sustain the bridge that spans the otherwise dividing gulf, that so Creator and creature may hold their commerce. Herein lies that which constitutes man primarily and incurably and distinctively religious. He carries within himself a supernatural reference, and he cannot exscind it; or if excision there be, a scar is left, and the scar is testimony.

This supernatural reference permanently and embarrassingly challenges our naturalistic humanisms. When that reference is ignored or denied, while some of the social activities it properly calls for are still maintained, the movement has begun which ends in identifying religion with social behavior, and in limiting it to that.[15] These humanisms are right in their insistence that religion shall manifest itself in social concern. They are wrong in making such concern the real measure of religion. Religion is the intended means for bringing the more-than-human into the human sphere, to illuminate it, to redeem it, to sanctify it. In the proportion that the supernatural reference is denied, the human horizons become the more restricted, the human problem grows increasingly baffling, and the human task appears less and less joyful because its end is no longer discerned. If there is no "Higher Other" to whom we may look, and upon whom we may know we depend, and with whom we may enter into conscious fellowship, and from whom we may derive both power-to-be and power-to-do, then what earth's greatest souls have felt to be their deepest insights answer to no realities. We take thereby the mystery out of our life.

But do we? Do we not rather deepen the mystery, and leave it utterly without solution? Do we not rather create a riddle at which the very Sphinx can but gaze with uncomprehending eyes? That were little enough of gain! We get rid of God, it is true, and many in our day would seem to deem it desirable, but that is not all that we do. We also get rid of the One Fact from which shines light sufficient for us to walk by; and henceforth we stumble along through the darkling depths of a haunted wood—we call it life!— whose horrid shadows the fitful gleam of reason's uncertain light serves but to make more fearsome still.

Choose we must, and whatever choice we make is still but a choice among alternatives; but it is yet to be proven that they have made the less noble choice who make that choice which answers the most questions, gives rise to the most searching demands, creates the deepest peace while still most completely inspiring the will, and agrees most nearly with the wide range of human need.

Such a choice is a choice for that God whose glory is seen in the face of Jesus Christ. And what is being claimed here is that such a choice is also the ultimate logic of that whole process whereby man came to be what he is. Not that the logic is irrefutable. Not that logic alone will bring a man to Christ. *But Christ gives cogency to the logic!* As truly as man is seen to crown nature, so truly is Christ seen to crown man. When a man makes this choice, therefore— chooses Christ—he fulfills not merely the meaning of his own life: he fulfills the meaning of that total creative travail of which he is the supreme and predestined issue.

All else is as it is to make a man possible. On the upraised brow of this man is the mark of whence he came and of how he came and of why he came. The supreme affirmation of which he is capable— what is it but God, and how lower can he sink than by refusing to affirm him? Heir of all the ages! Offspring of the birth-throes of immeasurable time! Visible index of otherwise unimaginable invisibilities! No less than this is man—and more he could not endure to be, for to be this is to be but a little lower than God.

Then clearly he doth not live by bread alone. The hungers that

are in him are the hungers of one who by whatsoever long and
devious route he came, can claim a divine paternity. And if a son,
then an heir. Perchance he can present no unimpeachable evidence
of his sonship at the bar where with cold and critical air "bare
Reason" sits as judge. But what he cannot prove to the faintly
smiling sceptic he can still be sure of in himself. For he is religious,
is this man, and in his best moments he knows himself to be religious, indissolubly bound to an Other whose lure he feels and
whose rebuke he shuns. He is religious because he knows *nostalgia*.
Yes: religion is nostalgia; it is the homesickness of a pilgrim soul.
Lambent flames of strong desire leap from this creature seemingly
so earth-bound, and they give the lie to his crawling; they bespeak
a day when the clods shall fall from his feet; and they presage his
own ultimate flight to the bosom of "the God who is his home."

CHAPTER 3

The Old Testament and Revelation

CHRISTIANITY HAS TO DO WITH A KNOWLEDGE OF GOD AND OF HIS activities and purposes which it claims has been given by God himself in a special way. This claim is essential to the integrity of the entire Christian message. God has spoken, and because he has spoken we know what he is, and what he seeks, and by what means he seeks it. The process by which this has been accomplished, and still is being accomplished, we call revelation. Integrated with the process are the history of the Hebrew nation, the life, message, and work of Jesus Christ, and the origin and growth of the Christian Church. Our knowledge of the process up to the point at which the Church is well established is derived from the Hebrew and Christian Scriptures. These Scriptures exist precisely for this purpose. For this reason, they have a significance which belongs to no other body of literature, ancient or modern. Since the process of revelation covered many hundreds of years, and since it involved the activity of an almost infinite variety of men and women under most diverse circumstances and at many different stages of culture, we may expect the Scriptures to reflect the changes which necessarily characterized the revealing movement. We find this to be the case. Hence arises the problem of interpretation. The Word of God is given in the words of men, and who shall say which is which?[1]

The point at which the whole movement obviously culminates is Jesus Christ. It is therefore in his light that we are to understand all that goes before, just as it is in his light that we are to judge all that has followed since. This, however, requires a proper appreciation of Christ himself, not only as a historical figure, but also as a continuing reality. But if we depend exclusively upon Scripture for our knowledge of Christ, and then seek in his light to interpret Scripture, we simply move in a circle. The circle is broken by a proper appreciation of the significance of Christian experience, of the guidance of the Holy Spirit, and of the function of the Church. Christ can never be fully understood from the study of Scripture alone. Scripture gives us a body of indispensable fact and truth. But all this is intended to issue in an experience. Scripture is a means to an end. It is instrumental, not final. The end is utter surrender to the Christ who is here portrayed and whose work is here declared.

This surrender brings the surrendered life within the orbit of the illuminating, empowering, and sanctifying action of that same divine Spirit which guided the revealing, interpreting, and recording movement in the first place. Those who make this surrender and thereby experience this Spirit-action constitute, ideally, the Christian Church. In that aspect of it, therefore, in which the Church becomes the instrument of the Spirit because it has sought to give itself wholly to Christ, the Church is the final interpreter of the Word of God, and in particular is it the final interpreter of the relation in which Christ stands to its own life and action.[2]

This statement is offered as the gist of the Christian claim concerning revelation. That it leaves many questions open is obvious. But it is intended to do that. What is important, in the present state of thought, is the general truth itself. There is really only one fundamental question, and that is whether God actually has spoken in suchwise as is claimed in Christianity, and whether in what he has said there is "enough light for us in the dark to rise by." Failing this, no other question about revelation, especially critical questions in connection with the documents and their history, profoundly matters. If the central claim is admitted, then these questions become vital for their bearing on interpretation; but not otherwise.

Doubtless Matthew Arnold rendered a great and necessary service in his time by his insistence that the Bible is to be read as literature, not as dogma; but anyone who will take the trouble to read his book will speedily realize that Arnold not only shows a curious blindness to that deeper movement which was the only reason for the literature in the first place, but also approaches the literature in a spirit which is by no means without its own dogmatism.[3] What matters the steady output of books on the literary values of the

English Bible, if the implicit assumption is that it is the style of the book and the rich variety of its contents which give it its importance? The book would, indeed, have a significance even as only "one more collection of ancient writings." But it would be a significance arising from its contribution to the history of culture and of institutions. Valuable as such a contribution would be—and actually is—it still remains that this is incidental to the main purpose of the book itself.

The Bible came into being because of a movement that was taking place in the lives of men over a long period of time. The movement was essentially religious. God was involved in it to an extent in which, judged by any available evidence, he was involved in no other movement elsewhere. The movement slowly brought to light great truths about human life, which were always held to be inseparably connected with great truths about God, so much so that neither body of truths could long continue without the other, which is but to say that the Bible has finally but one theme—*God and his purpose with men.* It requires all the Bible to present that theme in its entirety, yet there is no part of the Bible, even the most dull and prosaic part, where the influence of the theme is not felt. Let the fact of this all-pervasive theme be granted, and let it further be granted that the steady although often irregular development of the theme is nurtured, in such ways as the nature of the human instruments makes possible, by the Spirit of that same God with whom the theme itself is concerned, and complete freedom as to every other aspect of the record is left to the investigator.[4]

At the risk of seemingly tiresome repetition, it must again be insisted on that unless this theme and this control of it be admitted to be central, the Bible is taken from its pinnacle. It may still be placed on some other pinnacle, but any other pinnacle on which it is placed it will be found to be sharing with other writings. In the nature of the case, there can be only one final revelation of God, and the Christian claim is that that comes to us through the Bible. Here is "The Supreme Book of Mankind," not only, as McClure has so ably shown, in respect of the influence of its English translation, but also, and primarily, in respect of the message it conveys; and that message is still conveyed no matter what the tongue employed, no matter how restricted the literary range, no matter how crude the translation.[5] In the porch which leads to the excavations which laid bare what is believed to be the Pool of Bethesda in Jerusalem, one may read in scores of different languages the account in the fifth chapter of the Fourth Gospel of how Jesus healed there the lame man. Whatever the language, the story is the same story, the meaning is the same meaning, the truth concerning the sympathy and power of the Son of God is the same truth. It is said that before the invention of printing, the Bible was found in thirty-three different languages. To-day, it is printed, in whole or in part, in over a thousand different languages and dialects. But always it is the same book, and always its message is the same message.[6]

The Bible is a linguistic vehicle which may be changed, as to its form, in innumerable ways, but this in nowise affects what is conveyed, and it is with this, the vital content, that the case for revelation finally stands or falls. Carlyle's argument in *Sartor Resartus* could very well be applied here. Clothing may make the man for certain social purposes, as being symbolic of status and responsibility. Thus clothing may indicate to the world the difference between the convict and the judge, but underlying these differences there is still an identity of the essential manhood. "The rank is but the guinea stamp."

The numerous contemporary English translations of the Bible reveal many differences of style, and here and there even of thought. A familiar example is Romans 12. 11, "Be fervent in spirit," which Moffatt renders, "Maintain the spiritual glow." Another is Isaiah 7. 9, "If ye will not believe, surely ye shall not be established," the paronomasia of which in the Hebrew is preserved in the translation of George Adam Smith: "If ye will not have faith, ye shall not have staith" (cf. Luther's, *Glaubet ihr nicht, so bleibet ihr nicht*). In each case, the new rendering is attractive, but the meaning persists unaltered; the rendering is, in actual fact, merely instrumental. The long dispute on how יהוה should be translated—whether as *The Lord* in the King James version, or as *Jehovah* in the American Standard version, or as a simple transliterated *Yahwe* in individual versions—has a certain scholarly interest, but the differences of rendering leave quite unaffected the basic idea, GOD, understood as the source of truth and authority. For reasons of sentiment, to say nothing of the rhythm, most people would prefer not to change "The Lord" to "Jehovah" in the moving words of the stricken Job: "The Lord gave, and the Lord hath taken away; blessed be the name of the Lord." But even if the substitution be made, the brave utterance of a submissive faith which is also a sure source of strength, remains unaffected thereby.

What is true in matters of detail like these is equally true of those more complicated questions which have to do with the origin, formation, and relationships of various groups of writings in the Bible. For the most part, the reverberations of the bitter controversy over the so-called Documentary Hypothesis of the Pentateuch have died down, but there are men still living who suffered greatly for the part they took in it. The symbols J, E, D, and P, which stood for the various earlier writings whose presence scholars believed they could detect in the Pentateuch in its present form, became symbolic of very much more than their original intent. That chapter in the history of criticism may now be regarded as closed, and it would be difficult to-day, in even the most conservative quarters, to revive the feeling that once raged around the question.[7]

What complicated matters was the fact that the theory was held to have a vital bearing on the inspiration and authority of Scripture. The Church had unfortunately committed itself to a type of verbalism which gave color to the claim. As things have turned out, the controversy over the theory is now seen to have contributed very largely to the breaking of the stranglehold of this verbalism. The claim of revelation has been released from the burden of much unnecessary baggage. It has become possible to distinguish between the Pentateuch as a record, and the emerging truth about God and his purposes with men which was making itself felt in human life, which truth alone gives the record any more than a merely historical and cultural significance. The amazing variety of the Pentateuch is apparent to the most casual reader, but a golden thread runs through it all, and gives it a unity. That golden thread is the message about God, presented as coming from him himself. How mixed-up the message is with transient and purely human elements can hardly be denied except by a doctrinaire who persists in closing his eyes to facts. God was carrying out his purpose in the situation as it actually obtained, and the situation was in the main provided by a nomad clan, its development under changing experiences, its contact with other peoples who had their own distinctive traditions, convictions, and outlook, and its growth in the apprehension of all that seemed to be implied in an original "covenant" with the God it held to be its own.[8]

The so-called historical books of the Old Testament, especially Judges, First and Second Samuel, and First and Second Kings, are related to revelation chiefly for the light they throw on the long-drawn-out struggle between the conception of God associated traditionally with the name of Moses and what is ordinarily called Canaanitish Baalism. That the tribes who spread slowly through Canaan under the leadership of Joshua brought their own religion with them, and that this religion centered in Yahwe, who was still thought of as having his abode in that Sinaitic region where Moses received his commission, and that they had a sharply-defined cult through which they maintained relationship with this their God— these are historical facts with ample attestation. How closely this cult came to being assimilated with those of the neighbors, and how a few brave spirits—Samuel, Nathan, David, Elijah, Elisha, Micaiah, and perhaps groups like the Nazirites and the Rechabites —fought the battle, often facing almost overwhelming odds, for the older heritage against the beguiling and degraded nature-worships and idolatries that were practiced all around them, even by their own people with the connivance of the court, is a story rising at times to the height of titanic drama.

One who reads the story feels as though he were watching a powerful swimmer struggling forward against threatening rapids. Again and again the swimmer is thrown back; often he disappears entirely from sight; the torrent seems on occasion to take on a demonic purpose to hurl the brave invader to destruction; but not-withstanding all obstacles he makes his way, and at last reaches the point where he is secure.[9] The history of the revelation of God from the period of the judges to the time when the great prophets of the eighth century B. C. burst upon the life of Israel, is something like that. It is the history of a great truth apparently fighting for its very existence, yet becoming clarified and strengthened by the struggle itself.

The records which deal with this struggle are faithful records. It is clear that they were more or less "edited," as the term goes, in the interest of later parties, in some cases the "prophetic," in some cases the "priestly." Especially is the priestly influence apparent if we extend our survey to include First and Second Chronicles. There are two quite different accounts of Samuel's attitude toward the people's demand for a king and toward the selection of Saul for that purpose (First Samuel 8–10); and he would be a bold man who should say that the David represented in the Books of Samuel agrees in all points with the David represented in the Books of Chronicles. The priestly influence is the evident cause of the differences. The reforms of Josiah may very well have been inspired by Deuteronomic and prophetic ideals, but the influence of the priestly cult on the account of these reforms is manifest (Second Kings 22 and 23).[10]

The modern historian would say that all this means that the records lack objectivity: they were prepared in order to support a point of view. This would have to be conceded, although the fact is nothing strange in ancient documents. But our thesis is not only not weakened by these considerations: it is strengthened by them. It would not be strengthened if the Bible, especially the historical books of the Old Testament, were held to be authoritative in the measure of its detailed historicity. But its authority does not lie at that point at all. For certain historical purposes, it would be interesting for us to have the exact truth about the reigns of the various kings of Israel and of Judah. But the real importance of these reigns is in the way in which they illustrate the persistence and application of a great truth. The integrity of the revelation does not stand or fall by the wrappings.

The compilers of the Books of Samuel, Kings, and Chronicles were undoubtedly conscientious and industrious men, and the man who was finally responsible for the account of the "outlaw" period of the career of David was a historian of the first class, but it is to be questioned if these men realized the full significance of what they were doing. We certainly do not need to invoke "inspiration" for their mere compiling activity. We must seek that inspiration rather in what was more and more coming to light in individual and collective experience as the result of the clash of antagonistic forces. These compilers could have had no proper consciousness of the part they were playing in the long movement whereby men were at last to see God fully self-disclosed. They tell as much of the story as it was given them to know or to believe, but we cannot appraise their part in the story unless we recognize all the elements in what they wrote.

The career of David is fascinating enough. From one point of view, we may read it as we read one of the "lives" of Plutarch.[11] In a score of ways, it reflects the beliefs, superstitions, customs, and outlook of the times. In his outlaw days, David led a band of very doubtful characters; he gave as one reason for desiring to return to Israelite territory the fact that his God could be worshipped only there—he could not be worshipped in Philistine territory where David then was, since *cuius regio, eius religio;* and he showed no scruples about marrying Abigail, although he had already married Saul's daughter Michal, to whose love and loyalty he owed his life.[12] To make such facts an intrinsic part of binding authority for the Christian mind obviously involves a perfectly incredible *tour de force.*

Then does David mean nothing to us, after all? Anything but that. We have still to keep in mind the process whereby he became king, first of Judah, and later of the other tribes; the insight which led him to seize Jerusalem, the Jebusite stronghold, and make it first the political and then the religious capital of the nation, circumstances whose influence is still operative in the world; and the military and diplomatic skill which thrust out the bounds of the nation until his rulership was acknowledged from the Orontes in the north almost to the River of Egypt in the south, and from the Mediterranean Sea to the Euphrates. It was then that the theocratic ideal became firmly established in Israel, and it is not difficult to understand how, as Edghill so plainly showed in *The Evidential Value of Prophecy,* the character and the reign of David should have been increasingly looked back to by a later age as the type of the Messianic King and Kingdom.[13]

It is in the facts of David's reign, and in the interpretation which came to be put upon it, rather than in the mere record of events, that we are to understand how the revelation of God was proceeding. The record itself could have been written by anyone who was familiar with the events, but the deepening religious outlook, and the relation in which this stood to all that had gone before and to all that was to follow after, is of such a character that the claim that the God whom it was serving to bring increasingly to light was the God who was using the events for just this purpose, takes on an increasing verisimilitude.

In ways such as have been but briefly indicated, the foundations were laid for the work of that line of prophets of whom Amos was the first. These prophets are unique in the history of religion. Other religions have had their shamans, their oracles, their sufis, their wise men, their teachers, but no religion can show a group of men in anywise comparable to the Hebrew prophets. Usually it is said that they were "preachers of righteousness." That is true enough, but it is not the whole truth. What they said about righteousness—always with a definite ethical and social content— was inseparably connected with their understanding of God.[14] The real problem, therefore, concerns the means by which they came to this understanding, and whether God actually was what they declared him to be.

As to this, they themselves had no doubt. They believed that the God in whose name they spoke was the God who had always been working in the life of the nation. But they went beyond that: they proclaimed him the God of the whole earth. This universalism is definitely marked in Amos, and in no prophet is it wanting, although it is more pronounced in some than in others.

But the prophets also have something to say about the *character* of God. They see him as in himself utterly without flaw or imperfection. The word "holy" is still perhaps the best word for expressing their thought. There was, indeed, a priestly conception of holiness which stressed primarily God's transcendence and remoteness, but was sometimes defective on the ethical side: at least, those who dwelt upon it and inculcated it were often themselves without too much ethical concern. The situation is nowhere better described than in the first chapter of Isaiah. In the true prophetic doctrine, "the Holy One of Israel" was the God who had called and used and instructed the nation, but he was also the God upon whose will all things depended, Creator of the universe, with a purpose for all mankind, a purpose to which Israel was instrumental, a God of judgment in respect of sin, sin being understood as a violation of his will and an opposition to his purpose, and yet withal a God of unfailing mercy, who will give of himself to the uttermost in order to establish among all the peoples of the earth the reign of peace, brotherhood, righteousness, and love.

This prophetic message as to God and his purpose has its own varying concomitants. We must remember that we are dealing with the work of human beings, who lived at definite times and in definite places, who had their own personal idiosyncrasies, who differed in their social status, who had varying gifts of utterance, who could ascribe their own prejudices and dislikes to their God, and who reveal in what they say the influence of all these factors. In a word, these men were not mere automata, and we are not to charge directly to the Spirit of God all that they said and did. God was, indeed, using them, but he was using them according to how it naturally belonged to them to be used.

Micah the farmer and Isaiah the courtier; Amos the fig-dresser and Ezekiel the ecstatic ritualist; the Unknown Prophet of the Exile, incomparable in his eloquence, whose moving periods, as in Isaiah 40 and 53 and 56, have power to charm even the dullest ear and thrust back the horizons of the most unimaginative mind; and that tragic Jeremiah, by every instinct of his nature a dreamer and a poet, yet compelled by the circumstances of his time, which begot in his bones a burning fire he could not constrain, to become the stern-visaged prophet of his nation's woe—Shelley's skylark playing the part of Poe's raven—these men write and speak according to the gifts that were in them. Their words were their own words: nevertheless, through these words the Word of God was getting itself more and more clearly expressed, as we, observing the place of the prophets in the whole revealing movement, cannot but see.

Speaking generally, we are therefore justified in saying that the earlier books of the Old Testament show us the truth about God in process of being originated in the life of a people; the historical books which deal with the experience of this people after their settlement in Canaan show us that truth becoming secured under great difficulties, chiefly difficulties arising from contacts with other cultures and a widespread disposition to accept their easier ways; and that the prophetical books show us how this truth of God was elaborated, deepened, universalized, and more completely ethicized, and then unflinchingly applied to human affairs, not only the affairs of the particular people through whom the truth had come, but the affairs of all mankind.

This is not intended as a complete survey of the Old Testament, but only as a suggestion as to how the thesis—the emergence in history and experience of the truth of God and his purpose with men—may be illustrated. A more exhaustive treatment would need to consider the significance of the Psalter, of the so-called Wisdom Literature, especially Job, of the moral and legal codes, of the cult practices, and in particular of the later priestly institutional development, reflected most clearly in Ezra-Nehemiah, which led to Judaism in the proper sense. Such a consideration, however, would only serve to substantiate the thesis. A movement which necessarily involved men, but whose full significance the men of the time could not wholly realize—this is what, from our vantage-point, we could see was taking place, just as we can see how it came to its great consummation.

And God was in it. He was in it in such a way as was compatible at once with human freedom and his own purpose. He himself inspires the movement which is to bring him at last unmistakably because personally into the world. The Old Testament has its being in the fact of that movement, and has the function to record its progress, together with the situation, individual, social, cultural, political, within which the movement was taking place. The Old Testament is as much a slow growth as was the movement itself. In its formation it served as a means for producing and nurturing the very movement which it was also to preserve and propagate. To say that the Old Testament in its totality is inspired is to create almost insuperable difficulties for our mind. To say that it preserves to all mankind the knowledge of a religious movement which God by his own Spirit was fostering and using, so that by it he is more and more revealed both as to what he is in himself and as to what he purposes for mankind—this is to say what every feature of the record, every aspect of the experience of the people chiefly responsible for it, and the actual pragmatic function of the record itself as it has spread through the world, serve amply to attest.

The central claim, that God really is such a God as this, and that his purpose really is such a purpose as this, is in the nature of the case one that cannot be completely demonstrated. The truth of the record bespeaks the truth of the movement, but neither the truth of the record nor the truth of the movement can bespeak incontestably the truth of that claim as to God and his purpose which is the only reason for the record and the movement alike. The movement itself was finally *a movement in the realm of belief and faith.* Revelation on the part of God involved response on the part of men. Without the response there could be no revelation: blind men do not see nor do deaf men hear. Response is a human act, with all the potential uncertainty which goes with that. Those who responded came into an experience which for them was the sufficient authentication of the truth of that to which they responded. This does not necessarily authenticate all their corollaries, and it certainly does not commit us to the acceptance of all those applications of the believed truth which plainly bear the marks of the contemporary and can be accounted for thereby. A movement which called for faith in its inception, ongoing, and consummation, calls for faith in its acceptance by others.[15]

God was revealing himself. Here is the story of how he did it. By means of the story we can see what God was revealing himself to be and what purpose he was seeking. Either we believe the revelation or we do not. We do not believe it merely as something which men were saying about God on their own account. If all that we have is a human speculation—well, that is all that we have, and our light is still but darkness. Instead, we believe it as something which God, "by divers portions and in divers manners," was *saying about himself.*

This is the real issue. It is that or nothing. If what is given to us here as the truth of God—that he is Creator, that he is a Spiritual Being able to enter into personal relations with men and desiring so to do, that in him, in his power, in his wisdom, in his moral nature, is not one flaw, that infinite resources are behind his gracious purpose, that he pursues this purpose with patience because he would have men be willing sons and not driven slaves, and that he will yet make one supreme effort of self-disclosure which will explain all the past and set the standard for all the future—if this is not in actual fact the truth of God, then is there no such truth. But whether we shall so accept it must depend in the end upon ourselves.

But the Old Testament does not give us everything. It does not give us everything because the revelation was not yet complete. The Old Testament is a book of *hope:* its face is toward the future. How sadly this aspect of it has been abused hardly needs to be said. There is without doubt a predictive element in the Old Testament, but the prediction falls primarily in the field of the operation and application of truth already possessed rather than in the field of specific detail. The Suffering Servant Songs of the Second Isaiah may be regarded as predictive, at least in part, but they are to be understood chiefly for their connection with the ongoing and perhaps consummation of God's gracious and saving purpose for mankind. We can better understand these Songs, especially the one in Isaiah 53, in the light of future events than the future events in the light of these Songs, although the relation is still reciprocal. That God will yet "make bare his mighty arm," speak as he has never yet spoken, act as he has never yet acted, and put the seal on all that he has ever done before, is what the Old Testament finally means, and without the consummation the book is but a torso.[16]

The Word of God insinuating itself into the life of a nation, finding expression now in this way and now in that, making alliances which often seem unnatural, opposed at one point to move forward at another, creating here a cult and its institutions and there such a depth of conviction in a human soul as must burst out in mighty-mouthed harmonies of sound—a Shepherd Psalm, an Amos discourse at Bethel, a Habakkuk prayer from the watch tower, a Joel proclamation of an outpouring of the Spirit, a Nahum cry that arrogance such as Nineveh's cannot permanently defy God—the Word of God in all these ways and many more like them comes to clearer and clearer utterance. Sometimes it is heard in a dramatic incident like that of which Elijah was the center on Mount Carmel, although it was later to come more distinctly in "the sound of a gentle stillness." Sometimes it is heard in events which disrupt a kingdom, and sometimes in that clash of warring forces amid which Jerusalem virtually ceased to be—for surely it was nothing less than a true Word of God which Jeremiah spoke when he declared that the destruction of Jerusalem not only could not destroy God's purpose but would become a means of furthering it, since now faith would have to be divorced from all merely external supports and find its strength in "a new covenant written on the heart." What cannot live by virtue of its own internal vitality and its complete regnancy in the human heart has not yet come to its full fruition.[17]

Sometimes the Word of God is heard in a solemn ritual like that of the Day of Atonement, which speaks of both judgment and mercy, or like that of the Feast of the Passover, which speaks of a deliverance which is also a promise of a greater deliverance still. Sometimes it is heard in ways more indirect, as when some unknown man, observing with sorrow how Nehemiah, when he had achieved the great task of re-building the walls of Jerusalem after they had long lain in ruins, promulgated the cruel decree that any Jew who had married a foreign wife should send her and her children away, since Jerusalem was David's city and therefore intended for only David's people, quietly went to the archives and verified David's ancestry. Then he wrote that most charming story of the Old Testament, the story of Ruth the Moabitess, daughter-in-law of Naomi and the dead Elimelech, and herself a widow, becoming by a levirate marriage the wife of her Hebrew husband's kinsman Boaz, lest the line of Naomi and Elimelech should die out. "So Boaz took Ruth, and she became his wife, and she bare a son. And the women said unto Naomi, Blessed be Jehovah, who hath not left thee this day without a near kinsman; and let his name be famous in Israel." Was the pious wish fulfilled? Hear the rest of the story! "And the women her neighbors said, There is a son born to

Naomi; and they called his name Obed; he is the father of Jesse, *the father of David"* (Ruth 4.17). What a wealth of meaning is there! But for that levirate marriage, not only the history of Israel, but, humanly speaking, the history of the whole world, would have been different. Yet here was Nehemiah, enforcing a decree which would have kept David out of the very city which he had originally built, and which bore his name![18]

If the Word of God does not speak in the book of Ruth, with its assurance that none are excluded from the scope of God's loving purpose on account of race or clan, then we listen for it elsewhere in vain. The little book connects directly with one of the great utterances of the New Testament: "As many as received him, to them gave he the right to become children of God, even to them that believe on his name: who were born, not of blood, nor of the will of the flesh, nor of the will of man, but of God" (John 1. 12, 13).

Somewhat less indirectly, perhaps, the Word of God is conveyed through the most abused book of the Old Testament which yet, in reality, is the book in which a true catholicity receives its most dramatic expression—the book of Jonah. By what incredible blindness are the eyes of men held that they are aware of nothing more important here than the problem of "the great fish"? The one thing that matters about this book is not the truth of its *form* but the truth of its *idea*. What is Jonah but the type of that narrow nationalism which characterized the Judaism of the third and fourth centuries B.C.? What is Nineveh but the type of that world beyond Judaism which was regarded as utterly alien to God and his purpose, existing only at last to feel the weight of his terrible judgment? And what was the message which Jonah was charged to go to Nineveh and proclaim but an indication of someone's belief that God, although he came in judgment, yet lingers in mercy, and that in this respect he bears himself the same to all mankind, even to hateful and wicked Nineveh, since he is "longsuffering, not wishing that any should perish, but that all should come to repentance."[19]

What if there were actually no such man as Jonah? What if the city of Nineveh had been virtually destroyed long before this story was written, and that there is no evidence of such a turning to God as is here described? What if "the great fish" is but a dramatic device for changing the direction of a messenger who would fain go west against the will of a God who had commanded him to go east? These are purely incidental matters. The Word of God is not *they*, but the great truth which they, the words of men, are used to clothe and to convey. He who cannot see that can never hope to understand the process of revelation. That a man remained alive for "three days and three nights" inside a great fish—this is the words of men. That there are no people beyond the reach of the divine purpose, and that those who know what that purpose is are under an imperative command to make it known—this is the Word of God. It took God a long time to get that Word uttered, and longer still to get it accepted. Indeed, few be they who hear it even yet, and fewer still they who live by it.

Such a book, with such a history, such a widening sweep, such a purpose, such a manifest forward look, is the Old Testament. All manner of men are involved in its composition, just as it was through the experiences of all manner of men that the truth it ultimately conveys was finding its way. Its inspiration is at the point of that truth, its origin, its clarification, its preservation, its application. There too is its authority, and there too its infallibility. The inspiration, the authority, the infallibility belong not to the words of men, except indirectly and inferentially, but to the Word of God as that Word, "by divers portions and in divers manners," could find expression through the words of men.

It was by the Spirit that the divine Word made its way. It was by the Spirit that it was saved from extinction. It was by the Spirit that men were led into its deeper understanding. It was by the Spirit that they were moved to embody and declare and perpetuate it in institutional, social, and linguistic forms. It was by the Spirit that men of a later time came to such an appreciation of what this book brought to them that they treasured it as that whose price was above rubies. And it is under the guidance of that same Spirit by which the book was thus given and preserved that the truth of God and his purpose which it conveys is to be ascertained and appropriated.

Revelation comes not through documents, since revelation must precede any record of it, but it comes in life and experience according to the will of God and the response which he is able to evoke. It then becomes the function of documents to be the witness to the revelation and the means whereby it was secured. According as the witness is pondered by other minds, they too may come to possess and to be possessed by the truth which is witnessed, and to enter thereby into an experience sufficiently self-authenticating. But a revelation which still looks forward is by that much incomplete. The logic of anticipation is completion. The logic of a Word of God more or less obscured because of its necessary articulation with the words of imperfect men—what is it? *Is it not a Word given in a life of such a quality that the life is the perfect equation of the Word?* In such a Word would not all other Words receive their vindication, their correction, their fulfillment, and their interpretation?

And so it is written: "When the fulness of the time came, God sent forth his Son, whom he appointed heir of all things, that we might receive the adoption of sons. And this Son was the Word made flesh, who dwelt among us, the only-begotten from the Father, and he hath declared unto us that God whom no man hath seen at any time."[20]

CHAPTER 4

The New Testament and Revelation

PRACTICALLY ALL THAT HAS BEEN SAID ABOUT THE CONNECTION BE-
tween revelation, experience, and writing in respect of the Old
Testament holds good also of the New Testament. Each book is a
witness. Neither would have existed but for the prior fact, truth, and
experience to which the witness is borne. God working in life and
history is the postulate of the Old Testament. God working in life
and history is the postulate of the New Testament. One and the
same movement therefore underlies both sets of writings. Wherefore while we have many books, we have but one Book—the Bible.
It has a common theme, God and his purpose, although the theme
has many variations.

In the New Testament we are faced with the completion of that
whose earlier process is to be discerned in the Old. Without the
Old Testament and what it represents, the New Testament and
what it represents could not have been. On the other hand, without
the truth and experience which created the New Testament, the
truth and experience witnessed by the Old fail of the fulfillment of
their own promise. Christianity gladly recognizes that the Old
Testament is a production of the Jewish people: nevertheless, it
does not hesitate to speak of "The Christian Scriptures of the Old
and New Testaments." It believes that the most tragic fact in
Jewish history was the repudiation of Jesus Christ as promised
Saviour and Lord, and it believes that that unhappy people can
never fulfill its destiny until it takes to its own heart and mind him
who was "great David's greater Son."[1]

The central fact in the New Testament witness is Jesus Christ
himself. According to that witness, he roots in the past and he fulfills the past. But that fulfillment is not the result of a mere normal
process of evolution. Something new appears with him, so new

47

that it has no historical antecedent adequate to account for it. He is "from above." He who comes "of the flesh" comes also of the direct action of God. The Consummator is also an Invader. He is the final bursting through of the divine into the stream of history. He does not come to reveal God in the sense that he will tell men some more truth about God, but he is himself God self-revealed in just this fashion as a man. To know him is to know God in the way God desires to be known. What befell him at the hands of men, in particular his crucifixion, is a part of that humiliation which his whole career involved.

The startling fact of his resurrection is offered as the undeniable evidence that One had been dwelling among men to whom belonged a significance never to be attached to any other. A faith in him was engendered which led to a type of experience of a revolutionary kind. In the light of this experience, still more sweeping statements were made about the Christ who was the vital center of it. He was seen as redemptively significant not only, but also as racially significant, and finally as cosmically significant. Such claims are presented as implicit in the revealing process. The God who "sent his Son into the world" did, by the same Spirit which had been operative in the long centuries of preparation, assure that men should truly know who he was who had come and tabernacled among them, what he had come to do, how the work he had done was to bear upon human life, and how it was to create that fellowship between man and God and between man and man which was already adumbrated in that Church of which his first followers were the nucleus.[2]

This, in brief, is the witness of the New Testament. The meaning of it all is nowhere more cogently expressed than in the brief statement of the Fourth Gospel: *"The Word became flesh."* "Word" points to something integral in the very nature of God; "flesh" points to the truly human conditions within which the Word appeared and functioned; "became" points to the series of acts which together make the one act long known as Incarnation. Revelation, which always involves the Word of God in various forms of utterance, is therefore no longer indirect, but direct. This Man in his totality, in what he says, in what he does, in how he suffers, in how he bears himself, in all the means required to secure him, in the climactic event of resurrection, in his power to create among men a new life and experience—this Man, in all this range of being and action, of power and promise, *is* the Word of God.[3]

That one may find parts of the New Testament where all this is not expressly being declared is true enough. All that is here being claimed is that this is what accounts for the New Testament as a whole. To say that we get the entire Christian revelation in Mark's Gospel is no more true than it would be to say that we get it in the Epistle to the Romans. Yet without the Christian revelation we should have had neither of these writings. The writings are the creation of a prior fact, and are so many attempts to describe, preserve, proclaim, and interpret the fact. Thus any one writing of the New Testament gives us its own witness, but for the total witness we need the total writings. Yet when we get the total, we find that no single writing denies the witness of the whole. It may omit something, but the omissions are supplied by what is said elsewhere. The presence of seven separate portraits of Christ in the New Testament has been contended for.[4] But each deals with the same Original. Each adds to the witness. Each serves to elucidate the Word made flesh. Each is the gift of the Spirit to the Church. Each is a human product with the marks of its creator upon it. Each comes by the words of men. But each has the same purpose: *to set forth Christ.*

If, therefore, we must do with the New Testament as we do with the Old, and recognize groups of writings—the Synoptic group, the Johannine group, the Pauline group, the Petrine group, and the like—we must still recognize that the different groups are dealing with the same fact, prompted by the same faith, seeking the elucidation of the same truth. *God in Christ for the salvation of the world:* this is what we meet everywhere in this book, and all the admitted and explicable differences must not be allowed to turn the attention from that fact. The various theories as to the origin and relationships of the Synoptic Gospels are all interesting enough, and for the painstaking work of many scholars in this field we cannot be too grateful.[5] Yet it still remains that these Gospels assume a faith and a Church, that they are written to set forth the factual and historical bases of this faith and this Church, that they were jealously guarded by those who shared the faith and knew the fellowship of the Church, and that they were used as means alike of defense, instruction, and expansion. Endless questions of detail about this and that may properly be asked, but no difficulties arising because of these questions should be allowed to obscure the fact that the purpose of the Synoptic Gospels was to justify the faith of the Church as then existing by telling the story of the life and work of Jesus.

What that faith was, there can be no manner of doubt: he was at once the fulfillment of the past and the gift of God, who so lived, so taught, so acted, so suffered and died, so conquered at last even death itself, so continued as an active reality in the experience of those who believed in him, that nothing else could be said of him than that he was the son of God and the promised Redeemer of the world, veritably the Mediator to men of all the wealth and wonder of the Infinite Love.

In the Johannine writings, and in the writings of Paul, Peter and others, what have we but this same truth set forth, elaborated, illustrated, and declared in a typical variety of ways? Here as elsewhere the Word of God reaches us through the words of men. To ignore the individuality of the various writers is fatal. Christ is being "evidently published," and that each should publish in his own way and according to his own immediate situation and purpose, is nothing strange. Anything different would be a violation of that method of the Spirit which meets us in the Old Testament. A great conviction about Christ, his relation to God, his relation to that whole movement of the past whereby God's Word was being increasingly given, his relation to all that sin which disrupts the true fellowship of God and man and of man and man—in a word, a great conviction about the foreordained and decisive relation of Jesus Christ to the whole fact and purpose of the world and of human life, is the ultimate reason for the New Testament as it was the ultimate explanation of that Church whose testimony the New Testament contains.

We may accept this central testimony or we may refuse it, but we cannot deny what it was intended to be. God is represented as having at last uttered himself in such fashion, in and as such a life,

such a passion, such a triumph, as that those who accept the revelation, or, better still, the self-disclosure, know that they hold in
their hands the one key which unlocks the door to man's destined
life. He who comes to see and to accept and to possess that which
the New Testament in its entirety *means* can say humbly, rever-
ently, gladly, indubitably, *This is why I am.* To which he perforce
will add, *And this is why every other man is.*

Admittedly it is a faith. If as a faith it is indeed true, true in the
sense that this represents and fulfills the will and purpose of God
"from the beginning," we have the standard by which all else is
to be judged. But if it is *only* a faith, man-made and therefore illusory, if the case is not actually as presented, if the truth belongs
rather to its denial, if the Christian Gospel is utterly unrelated to
the realities of existence and therefore nothing but "an idle tale,"
then are we as weary and tongue-parched travelers who see their
oasis vanish into thin air, a tantalizing, unsubstantial, and mocking
mirage. This is "the choice before us," and it ought not to be difficult to choose.

In the light of John's statement concerning Jesus Christ, that he
was "the Word become flesh," everything else in the New Testament falls into understandable place. We see why it was that his
Birth was not regarded as the birth of just one more human babe,
nor his Death as the death of just one more man. Something was
true about the coming and going of this Man which was not true
about the coming and going of any other man. This was because
something was true about the Man himself which was not true of
any other man before him and will never be true of any other man
after him. He is a pivotal Man, an epochal Man. To make his coming possible, God did something which has no parallel. The Word
become flesh is a new type, a new pattern, standing solitary among
men, while yet he is to be the Head of a new humanity. He is to be
"the first-born of many brethren," but not one of these "brethren"
is to be accounted for as is he himself. The second-born, and the
third-born, and the fourth-born, and so on indefinitely, are all to
be possible because of the first-born, but the first-born himself—
what makes *him* possible?

John and Peter and Paul, and a great multitude of others whom no man can number, fall to be explained by the Word become flesh, but how is the Source of this great brotherhood to be explained? To him there belongs an originative power, and that is being demonstrated just as truly to-day as it was in the primitive Church. He has his antecedents in time and history, but he is presented as more than the sum of these antecedents, just as, shall we say, the first truly human life on the earth was more than the sum of its supposed ancestry. God waited for the time, and in various ways he prepared for the time, but when that time came there was a new creative act, as original as the first creative fiat, as original as the first man, as original as the illumination which came to the soul of some chosen and responsive man whereby he added something to the increasing sum of the Word of God. Thus appeared a Life which connects with God on the one hand, and with man on the other, in a new and unique and miraculous way. The Eternal Word appears as the Word in time. God is known for what he really is. The truth of God and the truth of man are equally declared, and they are declared in one and the self-same life.[6]

All this will be called by some speculation from the human side rather than revelation from the side of God. The point will be returned to at a later time, and more will be said as to its significance. It suffices to say now that this is what actually is to be read out of the New Testament. The question is not whether this is flatly asserted in the Synoptic Gospels, but whether anything less than this does justice to the total New Testament witness, a witness, let it be said again, to that faith concerning Jesus Christ which characterized the Church at the earliest known moment of its existence.

In our consideration of revelation and the Old Testament, we saw that the Word of God was conditioned in a variety of ways. The means by which it was apprehended and expressed often served to conceal much more than to disclose. God was using men, but he was sorely hindered by the chosen instruments. It was the price to be paid for a process of revelation worthy of both himself and man.

We must recognize the influence of similar conditioning factors in the Word become flesh, in the various descriptions we have of the Life—the life of Jesus Christ—which ensued from this, and in the interpretations, explanations, and illustrations of its meaning which meet us in the New Testament. The New Testament is not a mechanically perfect transcript, but a product which bears on every page of it the stamp of its human authors. The New Testament is as much the words of men as is the Old Testament, but again like the Old Testament it is everywhere concerned to disclose the Word of God—and that Word of God is Christ.

When the Word which, as John says, is eternally of God, becomes humanly incarnate, it is conditioned by the very means of its appearance. In what other way than as a Man could the Word stand completely declared? And when the Word is declared in and as a Man, all the distinctive qualities of man set the conditions of the declaration. The Eternal Word as undeclared, and the Eternal Word as declared, are ontologically identical, but there are experiential differences. It is the fact of these differences which Paul is stating in the Kenosis passage in Philippians 2. 5–11.[7] How that which is of the very nature of the divine can be humanly expressed in its essential perfection, may be and indeed is beyond us to grasp wholly, but we can at least see what it entails. It entails that there shall be a genuine historical reality, a genuine human fact. Thus the Life which is portrayed in the Gospels is a human life in every proper sense, but it is a human life whose ultimate subject is the Eternal Word, which is to say that the same set of experiences have a double meaning, a meaning for God and a meaning for man.

Hence there is birth, and infancy, and childhood, and youth, and manhood. Hence there is the necessity of learning step by step, with the possibility of error. Hence there is the necessity of temptation, with the possibility of failure. Hence there is the necessity of acquiring knowledge and belief according to what was known and believed at the time. If the Word genuinely becomes flesh, that is, man, all the processes that go with being man, including hunger, thirst, pain, weariness, work, rest, companionship, moral struggle, faith, religious aspiration, and the like, must be endured. Hence there were some things this Man could not know, and there were some things he could not do, and there were some experiences he could not have. Humanity and omniscience; humanity and omnipotence; humanity and independence of space and time; humanity and freedom from all pain, effort, and temptation—these are not only incompatibilities: they are flat contradictions.

The New Testament is the portrait of a *man*. The Manhood, notwithstanding the overwhelming significance ascribed to it, the assertion as to how such a Man came to be and of what he was here to do and of how he did it, is indubitably real. The New Testament has nowhere the least touch of Docetism. "He was made like unto his brethren in all things." The Creed expresses exactly the burden of the record: "He came down and was made Man." The Word that was eternally of and with God is the Word among men, but as the Word among men he is no mere spectator: rather is he "bone of our bone and flesh of our flesh." He is "like as we are." The revelation is a revelation in human conditions and so far forth by human facts.

There is a further important conditioning to be considered. Not only is the Word humanly *conveyed*: the Word as thus conveyed is also humanly *described*. Let us again remind ourselves of our thesis, namely, that Scripture is a witness to the revelation of the Word of God, that the revelation came in various ways through life and experience, and that it came at last *as* Jesus Christ. He, the Person, *is* the revelation at its height, because he, the Person, *is* the Word —the Word become flesh. But how do we know about this? We know about this through a record. The involution of the record with the testimony of the Church will be considered later. Jesus Christ belongs in that total history which created Scripture. The New Testament, or, if one must be meticulous, the Gospel story, is the medium through which we see the Word—at least, in his "state of humiliation."

The Gospel story, however, was written by men, and whatever men write—let it be said once again—is conditioned both by what they have the ability to see and to understand, and by whatever power of expression they already have. The reality of the guidance of the Spirit as they searched and thought and wrote is not for a moment being questioned: indeed, precisely this is the basis of any claim that is finally to be made as to the integrity of what is witnessed to in the record. Nevertheless, these men are free men. The characteristics of the Synoptic *writers* come out in the Synoptic *writ-*

ings. Many (not all) of the differences in the Gospels which greatly trouble so many people are to be attributed to differences in the writers. Even if there be some doubt as to whether the right name is attached to "Matthew's" Gospel and to "Mark's" Gospel and to "John's" Gospel, it is a comparatively simple matter to deduce from each of the Gospels the manner of man the writer or compiler was.[8] What each had come to know and to believe about that Living Word who was Christ, he records in ways peculiar to himself. It is quite certain that "Matthew" deliberately omitted some things which he found in "Mark," and deliberately changed some others, and that he deliberately made additions on his own account.[9] This is why it was necessary to say above that the written word is not an exact transcript of the Living Word. Even here, the Word of God *stimulates* the words of men, but we are not to identify the two. The written words have the function to help those who ponder them in the Spirit come more and more to lay hold upon the Living Word but for whom the words would never have been written.

The Gospels are therefore biographies, but they are biographies written from a very definite point of view—the point of view of an established faith concerning the subject. This fact has led R. H. Lightfoot to quite unnecessarily sceptical conclusions.[10] The Figure which inspired these writings is unmistakably clear. To make absolute "inerrancy" at every point of the record the condition to believing in the reality of that Figure is unreasonable on the part of the sceptic who lays down the condition, and it is incredible fatuity on the part of the literalist who insists that the condition actually exists.[11] Surely the endless questions raised by Christian scholars as to sources, methods of compilation, parallels, repetitions, omissions, inconsistencies, revisions, modifications, adaptations, and the like, are not imaginary! The questions grow naturally and inevitably out of the records themselves.

Wrede's claim that it is impossible to construct a critically tenable view of the life of Jesus may be true enough on his definition of "critically untenable," but he is entirely wrong if he means us to conclude that the records are worthless for the purpose for which they were first written, namely, to help the world to "see Jesus."[12]

With a full realization of all the critical difficulties connected with the Synoptic Gospels—and the Fourth Gospel may be added—one may still claim that the reading of these Gospels yields a clear and convincing picture of a Man who in his speech, in his action, in his character, in his relation to other men, in his whole bearing, in all that radiates from him of moral and spiritual power, makes God indubitably real.

It is here—in this Living Word of God—that we find the authority. If one so wish, one may say that the Gospels are a sufficiently reliable record of an authoritative Word. It is Christ who mediates God, and the Gospels help us to see him. If we see *only* the record, if we contend for *only* the record, if we judge other men's devotion to Christ *only* by the extent to which they mechanize and literalize the record, then we stop at the vestibule of the temple, but never have sight of the Holy of Holies. We confuse the instrument with the end. We put the witness above him to whom the witness is borne. It is obvious that we need the witness. To believe in a historical reality to which there was no historical testimony would be the height of credulity. What is being contended for here is not that the witness is not essential, but that the witness is intended to help us to apprehend the living reality, Christ, in precisely the fashion in which he had been apprehended by those responsible for the witness.

How they so apprehended him is clear beyond any doubt. It is attested by the New Testament as a whole. It is attested by the very fact of the early Church. It is attested by every shred of evidence we can gather about the primitive Christian faith. That faith was centered in Christ as the very gift of the love of God, like unto his brethren but Lord of his brethren, bearer of infinite grace, crucified for the sins of the world, raised again in testimony of who he was and what he had accomplished, alive forevermore, and able perpetually to manifest himself to the believing soul.[13]

This faith is what gave us the Gospels, which therefore point beyond themselves to Christ. When they have helped us to share the faith which inspired them, they have accomplished their ultimate aim. The utmost freedom in the historical and literary criticism of the Gospels themselves may then be claimed and indulged

in, and their essential worth remains unimpaired. The words are
but so many varied and perchance even imperfect reflectors of the
Word, the Living Word, even Christ. It is *Christ* who is the Truth;
it is *Christ* who is the Way; it is *Christ* who is the Life. Do we see
him through these written *media*? If we do, it is well. If we do not,
no slavish devotion to the *media* as such will ever give us a living
faith or make us participators in the revelation.[14]

The New Testament, however, contains besides the Gospels
other groups of writings by various hands. These are to be regarded in general as interpretive. They testify to the same faith to
which the Gospels testify, but the testimony takes a different direction because it has a different purpose. Not a single one of the
letters of the New Testament, nor yet the Acts of the Apostles or
the Apocalypse of John, would ever have been written but for something which was believed to be true before any of the writing was
done. These writings do not *begin* something: they testify to something which is already extant, and which they are concerned to
amplify, interpret, expound, defend, and apply.

The variety that we have, therefore, is only what we should
expect, and this variety is apparent even in the writings of one and
the same man, Paul. There is evidence even that Paul changed his
mind at certain points, for example, eschatology,[15] but there is no
least evidence that Paul ever changed his mind on the central issue
of the Christian faith, that Jesus Christ came into the world in fulfillment of the eternal purpose of God to bring all men into sonship,
and that those are the sons of God, irrespective of race, location,
backgrounds, or social status, who believe in God through this
same Christ, and who therefore bring under the control of Christ
as the most real fact of their experience all their thinking about
God and life and the world, all their own distinctive powers and
capacities, all their relationships to other men, all their daily walk
and conversation. This is just as central in anything ever written
by "John"—including the Fourth Gospel and the Apocalypse—or
by Peter, or by the author of the Epistle to the Hebrews, as it is
central in the whole story told in the Acts of the Apostles.

But unity at the center is compatible with variety in a hundred
other ways. Even when God at last revealed himself, completely

and finally, "in a Son," the revelation had to become dominant in human lives before it could achieve its purpose, and then these had to talk about it and write about it and proclaim it in every other possible way if others were to know it as they knew it.

Just here we find another conditioning of the revelation. The writers of the New Testament, dominated by the revelation, under an irresistible impulse to preserve, propagate, and perpetuate it, were still men, "free men," and none the less free because they were "filled with the Spirit." We may very well insist that the Spirit guarantees the truth of the revelation and even the truth of the exposition; what we have no right to insist upon is that the Spirit destroyed the writers' individuality, dispensed with the necessity of their thinking and writing each in his own way and according to his own natural gifts, and created a book which is to be treated with the same rigid exactitude with which one treats the table of logarithms. The New Testament is not a text-book of logic; it is not a precisely-worded legal code. Instead, it is the natural expression, sometimes passionate and sometimes restrained, sometimes logical and sometimes poetical, sometimes polemic and sometimes expository, sometimes theoretical and sometimes practical, of a living faith as to Jesus Christ and of a related experience deemed to be so self-authenticating that no doubt concerning it was even possible.[16]

It is thus that these writings have to be considered and treated. In no other way can we be delivered from a deadening and superficial literalism. Even the meticulous scholar is in danger of falling into the same error of which he accuses a crude fundamentalism. It is well that we study the New Testament *linguistically*: what is not well is that the linguistic study should become an end in itself. Free men are writing under a double constraint—the constraint of a great faith as to Jesus Christ, understood by them as the focal point of divine-human relationships, and the constraint of the divine Spirit as they seek to amplify, expound, and apply their faith. That double constraint gives us the writings, but it still leaves the writings with all the characteristics upon them of the writers.

But it does something else besides: *it leaves us with a problem—* the problem of ascertaining the relation between the faith and the writing; the problem of what in the writing had only temporary significance and expressed only the author's idiosyncrasies; and the problem of determining what is of permanent significance because it is a principle of the central faith itself, and being permanent is also pertinent to our own experience and to the situation in our own time. Paul wrote the Epistle to the Galatians to meet a particular situation. The situation *in that form* is hardly existent to-day, but who would dare say that it does not exist in *any* form? The real theme of Galatians is that of "The Freedom of the Christian Man." Change some of the phraseology of the epistle, some of the illustrations, some of the allusions, and the epistle becomes as relevant to the modern situation as any writing in the New Testament.[17]

The little Epistle to Philemon has not ceased to be meaningful because slavery is no longer recognized. "Treat Onesimus as a brother beloved" is what Paul urges upon Philemon as the true Christian treatment for the runaway slave. That request is presented as simply the logic of the Gospel—and let who will consider in his heart whether the Gospel which has this for its logic is not the most revolutionary fact in the world, the one promise of that without which the world must perish. For remember that Paul makes this request because of "the faith which Philemon has toward the Lord Jesus"—not the faith which he has toward John the Baptist, or Paul, or Peter, or any other apostle or one of the Hebrew prophets, or one of the Greek philosophers, not even the greatest of them, but the faith which he has *toward Christ*, of whom, in a letter written at almost the same time as this one to Philemon, Paul writes, that "in him we have our redemption, the forgiveness of our sins; who is the image of the invisible God, the firstborn of all creation; for in him were all things created . . . and he is before all things, and in him all things consist. . . . For it was the good pleasure of the Father that in him should all the fulness dwell; and through him to reconcile all things unto himself" (Colossians 1. 14–16, 19, 20). God is not reconciled so long as there are animosities of men to God or of men to men, and Christ is his own ordained means of destroying these animosities. What is Paul's letter to Philemon but a specific application of this tremendous truth? And who cannot think of a hundred different ways in which at this very moment the application could be made? But who has any hope of the application in the absence of the original creative faith of which Paul writes?

We have been saying that the Eternal Word of God, which appears in various ways in the Old Testament, came at last "in the fulness of the time" as Jesus Christ; that the Word was necessarily conditioned by the reality of the manhood which conveyed it; that there was a further conditioning of it by the fact that "the Word become flesh" was humanly apprehended and described; and that there was a still further conditioning of it by the fact that faith in the Living Word gave rise to a Church, composed of free men and women, to some of whom it was given to set forth under the Spirit's guidance their faith and experience in ways that we meet in the New Testament.

It is claimed that such a view does justice to all the facts in the case, so far as we are able to ascertain them. There is complete loyalty to the reality of God's historical self-revelation, consummating in Jesus Christ as the Incarnate and Living Word, together with a frank recognition of the various conditions under which the revelation was made, apprehended, expressed, and recorded. The eternal and the temporal, the divine and the human, the truth and the record, are everywhere in the closest involution, but they are nowhere to be completely equated or identified. The temporal, the human, the record, are vehicular; the eternal, the divine, the truth —these are what is being conveyed. Our primary concern is with what is being conveyed—the revelation proper. All else is means to this end. The means were such as the Spirit could make use of. And it is still the function of the Spirit to use these various means in suchwise as to create in other souls the faith which inspired and created them.

There are those who try to use the New Testament to break down that but for which the New Testament would never have come into existence. This is sometimes called critical scholarship. It may be scholarship, but it is not truly critical, since it settles by *the mere presupposition of impossibility* the most serious question men have ever been asked to consider.[18] Only that scholarship is truly critical which recognizes that the Scriptures, Old and New Testaments alike, are the creation of a faith concerning God and his purpose which those who shared the faith believed was divinely-given. The *truth* of this faith may be denied, but it can never be denied by critical scholarship working on the records. It can only be denied on *assumed grounds* of what could or could not be.

This is only to say that in the end faith or non-faith must be a choice. Has God spoken? Is this what he has said? Is his Word sufficiently clear that none need mistake it? Does its acceptance— the acceptance of Christ as the self-activity of God in the arena of history for the purpose of securing that fellowship between himself and men and between men and men, which was his creative goal— does this acceptance lead to a self-authenticating experience? Does it appear as both the promise and the power of a universal salvation? And are this faith and its experiential issue of such a character that the related questions concerning Jesus Christ—his pre-existence with the Father, his miraculous birth, his ministry of mighty works, his sinlessness, his resurrection, his present activity through the Spirit[19]—are seen to call for just those answers which the Scriptures themselves give, and to which the Church from the beginning has been committed?

This is where the real issue lies, and not at the point of some documentary infallibility. When the character of the revelation itself is properly understood, and when the necessarily contingent character of the witness to it is properly understood, then the most free act of which any man is capable will be in his assent to the revelation.

But it is a free act which will bind him as he is bound by nothing else.

CHAPTER 5

The Church and Revelation

WE HAVE DESCRIBED THE FUNCTION OF THE SCRIPTURES AS BEING TO acquaint men with that revelation of God in life and experience which is the only reason why the Scriptures themselves ever came into existence to begin with. This revelation came to its climax in the whole fact of Christ, and this is the especial concern of the New Testament.

But if this was the case, then we are faced with another consideration. The influence of Jesus Christ had begun to be exerted upon men before there was any such record as we now have. The New Testament may be called written testimony, but personal testimony necessarily preceded it. Christianity was originally propagated without any written records, just as it still often is in mission lands to-day. Albert Schweitzer and the work he is doing in Africa—this is a Christian sermon which those for whom the work is done cannot possibly miss, even although Schweitzer could not speak a word of their language and even although they had no books to explain why he was doing it. Personal testimony is the fundamental testimony.

Personal testimony, however, assumes some kind of personal experience. So far as the writers of the New Testament are concerned, we have their own word for it as to what the experience was. For some of them it was experience of the historical Jesus, and for all of them it was experience, based upon the direct or indirect knowledge of the historical Jesus, of the risen Christ and of the Spirit.[1] Without these it becomes impossible to account for the record, either the Gospels or the Epistles or any other writing, because it becomes impossible to account for that vital and dynamic faith which is the essential thing in the record.

The ultimate impact of the Eternal Word upon the world—so

we have been saying—was made in the form of a human personality. One moved among men in whom the very nature of God was given and in whom the will of God for men was fulfilled. The ancient dream and promise of *Immanuel* was realized. It was realized in the one only way which the nature of the case permitted, in a Life, or, better, *as* a Life, a Human Life.

How that Life was for the most part treated, we know. It met endless hostility, but it also met some appreciation and love. Yet even those who did appreciate it never saw its entire meaning. "He came unto his own, and his own received him not." Even those who gave love for love were sufficiently wavering in their love to make the Gospel story of their relationship essentially tragic. The rebuke to Peter, "Get thee behind me, Satan: thou art a stumbling-block unto me: for thou mindest not the things of God, but the things of men," is one of the saddest utterances in the New Testament.[2] It should be put alongside that word as to what followed the arrest in Gethsemane: "Then they—the men with whom but an hour or two before he had shared the symbolic and prophetic bread and wine—all forsook him and fled." He died in utter loneliness, according to each of the writers, Matthew, Mark, and Luke, even the faithful women standing "afar off";[3] which makes it appear as though John narrated the story of the dying Jesus' request to "the beloved disciple" out of sheer shame that such abandonment could have been so. The divine had tabernacled among the human, and the human had not recognized the Heavenly Guest. There were some who understood much, but there was not one who understood all. The words of Jesus at the feet-washing had many other applications: "What I do, thou knowest not now; but thou shalt understand hereafter."

From the standpoint of anything that had occurred up to the moment of the Crucifixion, God had spoken the most meaningful word, had performed the most meaningful deed, of which until that time even he was capable, and he had spoken and acted in vain. The Word was not truly heard. The Deed was not truly understood. At least, it was in vain if all that he was seeking was to speak so finally to men, so convincingly, so undeniably, as to secure a response, immediate, appropriate, inevitable.

In actual fact, God was in Christ not only doing something for men: he was also doing something for himself. God does not utter himself just in order to be heard: he utters himself as the skylark sings—out of an impulse that cannot be restrained. Divine creativity, said Thomas Aquinas, was the overflow of the superabounding love of the divine life;[4] the passion of the Most Blessed, said Lotze, to share his blessedness and thereby increase the sum-total of blessedness;[5] the desire of God to give, said Coleridge, in order that he might be asked for more, because to give, and ever to give, is his perfect joy.[6] Apart from anything that it might mean for men, God, in the gift of Christ, was expressing and satisfying his own infinite love, meeting the demand of his own nature on his own action. That fundamental satisfaction, so clearly set forth in modern theology by Horace Bushnell, William Newton Clarke, John Scott Lidgett, Hastings Rashdall, W. Fearon Halliday, H. H. Farmer, W. S. Franks, and many others, would have remained even although not a single human soul had ever responded to it. God's love is primarily not a response to man's love, but an appeal to it.

For all that, God made this sacrificial expression of his love in order also that a new life might be made possible to men. Nothing is more certain than that that purpose was not achieved during the earthly career of Jesus. The Eternal Word made his impact upon the world as a Life perfect in holy love and self-forgetting service, and the response to that impact was hostility by the many, the wavering loyalty of a few friends who in their best moments were puzzled by what he said and did, and at last crucifixion.

But that same Eternal Word that is revealed as the historical Jesus is revealed once again, and this time as the Risen and Living Christ. The historical Jesus and the Risen Christ root in one and the same ultimate fact—the Eternal Word: this is the burden of the New Testament, and nothing can make the New Testament mean otherwise. Precisely because of that common rootage, we have continuity—genuine ontological continuity—between the historical Jesus and the Risen Christ. The Resurrection is understandable only on the ground that it is an event in the experience of the Eternal Word, which is to say that it involves the action of God.

This is exactly what the New Testament offers it as being. "Whom God raised up."

The Resurrection does not mean that a dead man came to life again. We are not faced here with a simple problem in resuscitation. Resuscitation is not resurrection, since resuscitation never reaches beyond the natural. The Resurrection means that the Eternal Word who manifested himself in the form of the human—"and was made man"—to acquire all the meaning and all the experience of a human life, and to be the means whereby God comes personally within the orbit of humanity as redeeming power, now manifests himself, or is manifested, in still another form. The Resurrection narratives are hopelessly confused on the supposition that they described the activities of a dead man restored to life again.[7] Even on the most literalistic view of the story of Lazarus, it bears a radically different meaning from the accounts of the Risen Christ. A new experience of a familiar Reality manifested under a quite new form —this, from the standpoint of the disciples, is what was taking place. The conviction became irresistible: *this* means *that*. He who was once known "after the flesh" is now known "after the Spirit." The crucified Jesus is read afresh in the light of the new experience. That which evokes the experience becomes *a new Word of God*, a deed whose vast meaning could not be escaped. It was Resurrection, and what did Resurrection mean but victory over death and therefore victory over sin and therefore the evidence of a new power at work in the world and therefore the opening of the gates of new life?

More will be said later on this question. It suffices now to say that the creation of these convictions and of these experiences was at the same time the creation of the Church. The idea of the Church as a corporate life is to-day being earnestly re-considered for the light it throws on the purpose of God in Christ. Those who are familiar with what is happening in the Church in our time find their imaginations quickened at the very mention of such names as Jerusalem, Stockholm, Lausanne, Edinburgh, Oxford, Madras. The re-union of Christendom is being envisaged as not impossible, even although it may be remote. A divided world is seen more and more to call for a united Church if the hurt of that world is to be healed.

It is hardly possible to attach too much significance to such recent publications as the eleven *Oxford Conference Books,* edited by J. H. Oldham, the two volumes on *The Union of Christendom,* edited by Kenneth Mackenzie, Bishop of Brechin, and the symposium on *The Ministry and the Sacraments,* edited by Principal Dunkerley and the Bishop of Gloucester in the interests of the Faith and Order Movement. These volumes represent the convictions of scores of recognized leaders of the various Christian communions. A statement by the Bishop of Brechin in his Foreword shows how widely the term "re-union" may be construed: "Re-union would be compatible with much variation in the manner of worship, with considerable latitude in religious opinion, with far-reaching differences in organization." Yet he recognizes that it is at the points of doctrine, worship, and the ministry and its powers, that the real difficulties exist.

It would be difficult to find a saner consideration of the question of the Church within the chosen limits than in the recent volume of R. Newton Flew, *Jesus and His Church.* Dr. Flew asks: "May it not be the next step toward the fulfillment of the cherished hope [of a restored unity], for the great Christian communities which share in the Faith and Order Movement to make a venture in fellowship on the basis of the New Testament idea of the Ecclesia, to acknowledge one another gladly and frankly as within the one Ecclesia of God on earth, to refrain from any condemnation of the ministries and sacraments which are regarded by any modern Church as God's gift, and to join repeatedly, and as fully as may be, in united worship?"[8] A more admirable Christian temper could hardly be displayed. The New Testament Church, however, while it clearly expressed, *as a Community,* the purpose of Christ, also must be conceded to have had its origin in a certain faith in Christ. This faith necessarily determined also the message of the Church. As to this, Dr. Flew finds himself in complete agreement with C. H. Dodd, who in *The Apostolic Preaching and Its Developments* insists that central to the message and so to the very life of the Church was faith in the crucified and risen Christ as God's instrument for the creation of "a new Israel," the *Ecclesia,* of which he was therefore the head, and who sent forth into the *Ecclesia* his Spirit as the power to its greater and greater glory. If only the Church of to-day could plough down through all the things that divide it, and recover this original and creative faith, and make that and that only the essential consideration, it would become evidence that the Church in this sense was veritably *a Word of God*, still another form of that same Eternal Word whose diverse activities constitute the history of revelation, and challenging the modern world in a way which could not be gainsaid.

In the light of these general considerations, we are to say concerning the Church—not the Church merely in the sense of an organization, this being incidental because consequential, but the Church in the sense of that which is organized—that it involves (1) belief, (2) fellowship, (3) new life, (4) testimony, and (5) instrumentality.

(1) The Church rests upon a belief. This is not to say that all the various creedal statements which have been constructed from time to time are alike binding on the Christian conscience. If, as respects the Scriptures, we may make the distinction between the Word of God and the words of men, so, as respects creedal statement, we may make a distinction between the Christian Creed and the numerous historical creeds.[9] There may very well be a difference between what a given church requires as a condition to membership in it and what is required as a condition to being a Christian. That is made clear every time two different communions unite in a common worship. Few persons to-day would say to another that he could not be a Christian unless he were a member of *their* church and subscribed to all *their* requirements.

It would be difficult enough, perhaps impossible, to put the Christian Creed into language which would include all that was essential and exclude all that was incidental. One of the most successful attempts to do it was made by James Denney a generation ago, when he suggested that the symbol of the Church's unity might be expressed as follows: "I believe in God through Jesus Christ his only Son, our Lord and Saviour."[10] The symbol was criticized at the time as being susceptible of most diverse interpretations. Denney's own exposition of it, however, makes perfectly explicit what he himself meant it to express. The term "Son," as applied to Christ, he would define according to his offices of Lord and Saviour, and these obviously could be significant only where there was some actual personal experience of them. "God" he would define—if that is the proper word to use—in the light of Christ as this kind of Son doing for men this kind of work, and as a God who sent Christ into the world for just this purpose.

The point is one on which it would be difficult to be dogmatic. A Christian who still claimed that he could not accept all that was stated or implied in Denney's symbol would certainly have derived his understanding of Christianity from something other than the New Testament. If, as stated above, the Church was of the purpose of Christ but at the same time was the creation of faith in him, then that creative faith was at the same time the Christian Creed. The evidence is indisputable that the faith was centered in Christ Cruci-fied and Christ Risen, the Revealer of God in a new and overwhelm-ing way, Redeemer from the power of sin and death, Originator through the Spirit of a new life and experience, Founder and Head of a community of re-born men.

To say that faith and belief are two different things is in part cor-rect. Faith is trust, and it is therefore primarily volitional and emotional. Belief, on the other hand, is primarily intellectual: it is the assent of the mind. But while belief is not itself faith, faith where there is no belief is something quite impossible. One may assent to the Christian Creed intellectually, and still not trust one's whole life to that which is believed. It is therefore true to say that while the Church is the creation of a faith, the faith is inseparable from those definite and positive beliefs about Christ, and about God as revealed in Christ, which alone can save faith from being the most indefensible credulity. Sever faith from historical fact and ex-periential truth justifiably believed to be so, and all that issues from such faith will be illusory just because it is detached from reality.

There are Christians enough who are on the outer edges of the Church. The Church owes little to them, but they owe much to the Church. It is not by them that the Church in its true sense is to be judged. Whether or not they believe as the Church believes, and whether or not they live as such believers should, it still remains that there is a Christian Creed which attests itself in a Christian way of life. This creed cannot be less than that which first of all brought the Church into existence, and whose content the Church set itself more sharply to define and to explicate. The Church did not come into being because of the belief that Christ was the perfect Teacher, or even that he was the perfect Example, but because of the belief that he had been proven the Son of God with power by virtue of his resurrection from the dead. Wherefore it followed that the defeat of his crucifixion had been transformed into a victory of the grace of God, and that just such a God ruled over the affairs of men, and that just such a Christ—a Christ whom not even death could destroy—was for evermore the Mediator between God and men.

The Church began as a Christ-centered Church, and the Christ who was its center was not the Christ whose legacy to the world was the tragedy of the Cross, but the Christ whose legacy to the world was the glory of Resurrection. Not despair, but hope, is final. The Resurrection was veritably *a Word of God*. It was saying that the doom of ultimate defeat lay upon all the dark forces of evil and sin and death, and that victory belonged to that perfection of self-forgetting love which the whole life of Christ—another *Word of God*—so unfailingly and unmistakably exemplified. Against a Church so created and so committed, even as Jesus himself had said, the gates of Hades shall not prevail—and there is good evidence that the words he actually used meant "the violent floods of Death," that is, the most dreadful and unrestrained manifestations of that malign power which seeks only to destroy.[11]

(2) The Church functions as a fellowship. In any field, a common belief acts upon men as a common bond. The bond makes for intimacy according to the nature of the belief. The original Christian belief was of a character that bound the believers together in an intimacy of a peculiar kind. They were "brothers." The metaphors describing their community were drawn chiefly from the family. In idea, at least, it was a *koinonia* of the most perfect kind. How this fellowship functioned in the first flush of the new faith and experience is evident in the Acts of the Apostles. "Singleness of heart" was the characteristic of the early Christian community. One of the pathetic features of the Church of our time is the spasmodic attempt to recover the early fellowship and commonalty *in*

separation from the faith which alone accounted for it. We are "one body," wrote Paul to the Corinthians; we "partake of the one bread"; the body is animated by "the one Spirit"; and this body is "the body of Christ."

This fellowship set off from the rest of the world those who were embraced in it. It brought upon them ridicule, which often passed over into aggressive hostility. It carried its own obligations, but with it went also quite peculiar satisfactions. There was a joy and a confidence and an inspiration and an exaltation about that early Christian fellowship which breathes all through the New Testament, which has again and again been re-captured in times of religious revival, and which we sorely need to re-capture again to-day. "The fellowship of kindred minds" can be only a pious phrase conventionally repeated, or it may represent the deepest reality of Christian experience.

In recent years it has become customary to offer a sociological explanation of the original Christian movement.[12] The attempt is of a piece with that of a generation ago to account for Christianity as one more of the Mystery Religions. It is obvious that there are sociological factors in any movement affecting numbers of human beings. No group can be entirely without relationships with its time and place, any more than those who compose the group can be unaffected by each other's presence and activities. It goes without saying that the Christian movement was a sociological fact of tremendous power and significance. Appearing in a despised corner of the Roman Empire, winning many of its adherents to begin with from the lower social strata, it was yet destined to outlive the Empire itself and even to play no little part in its disintegration. But to see in the early Church nothing but "one more social grouping" is to miss entirely all that we know about its origin and about the faith of those who composed it.

The Christian fellowship is utterly unintelligible apart from a supernatural reference. Irrespective of what any detached scientific investigator may think, the belief of the Church as to what brought it into being is undeniable. The Church may have accounted for itself in the wrong way, but this was still the way in which it accounted for itself—this, and no other. This fellowship had its origin not in race factors nor in cultural factors nor in economic factors, although such factors naturally affected its development, once it was in existence. The early Christian institutions, the early formulations of Christian truth, bear, as has often been pointed out, the marks of contemporary influences.[13] But what the institutions were concerned *about*, what the formulations were an attempt to *deal with* —these bear precisely that original character which revelation alone is held to be sufficient to account for. The Church originated in a *given*: when that is granted, all reasonable concession can be made to the social matrix within which its development occurred, although it would be fatal to lose sight of the fact that the Church as growing life *exerted* even more than it *received* influence.

In a word, the fellowship of the Church, speaking ideally, is the fellowship of kindred minds which are held by a kindred faith and know a kindred experience and seek a kindred purpose. Christ as the Son of God who lived and suffered and died and rose again for the world's salvation is the object of the faith. A new relation to God because of the faith, a new quality of life, a sense of inner peace and power—these are the characteristics of the experience. The nourishing of this faith and experience and its spread to all other men, with the far-reaching moral, social, economic and political changes which are their proper fruit, is the purpose of the fellowship.

The Church has a right, even an obligation, to consider every question which has to do with human welfare. The so-called "other-worldliness" of the Pietistic and other similar groups, with their indifference to secular affairs, involved a profound misapprehension of the true nature of the Church. But the Church considers such questions, or should do so, in the capacity of the representative here and now of Jesus Christ, the Incarnate Word of God. For that reason, as Brunner claims so earnestly, although in contradiction to a widespread present tendency, the Church cannot *identify* itself with any political party or with any social theory or with any natural group of any kind.[14] *Securus, judicat orbis terrarum:* the famous judgment of Augustine still stands. The Church is "a colony of heaven." It is "in the world, but not of it." It draws its life from above. It sees things *sub specie aeternitatis*. The sphere of its action is the natural, but the source of its power is in the supernatural.

(3) The Church means a new life—perhaps we should say a new way of life. There must be somewhere a difference of standards as between those who accept the Christian belief and who share in the Christian fellowship, and those who do not. We must be willing to recognize the truth in the common criticism that Christians often-times are not distinguishable in their lives from other people. Whether in such cases the term "Christian" even approaches a proper definition is, of course, a question. But even waiving that, we must certainly make a distinction between perfection as actually realized, and perfectibility as implicit in the origin and purpose of the Church, to say nothing of the other distinction, recognized generally throughout Christian history, between the Church as the body of Christ and the Church as "visibly organized."[15]

The Christian man even on the lowest level, however, represents a new type. He may not represent it in his own individual character, but he represents it as a member of the Church—of the Church, that is, understood as the continued incarnation of the Word.[16] The Roman Catholic theory of Church membership is at this point nearer the truth than the usual Protestant theory. Individual imperfection does not properly reflect on the Church in its ideal sense. One may charge to the externality what one may not charge to the internality. In so far as there is the least vestige of sincerity in a man's claim to hold the Christian belief and share in the Christian fellowship, he is both a fulfillment and a promise. He is a fulfillment of God's eternal purpose as revealed in Christ, and in that fulfillment there is a promise of a more complete fulfillment in days to come. Justification is "by faith," not "by perfection," else who can be saved? Christ's righteousness becomes a possession by "imputation," not by reproduction. Nevertheless, "to grow up into Christ, the living Head, in all things," remains the goal of the Christian faith, the end of the Christian's spiritual exercises, be they few and intermittent or be they many and continuous.

The purpose of God as revealed in Christ has to do not with complete freedom from all difficulties, but with holy living. It has to do not with the scientific conquest of nature, but with the conquest of sin in the human heart. It has to do not with the creation of a Utopia understood as a perfectly socialized state all of whose interests are horizontal, but with the realization of the Kingdom of God; and the Kingdom of God, if one dare say it in a day of social idealism like the present, is only secondarily in the organization and use of the material sources of existence; it is primarily in the subjection of the will of man in love and trust to the will of God as revealed in Christ. The phrase, "as revealed in Christ," is deeply significant here: indeed, it is every way crucial. If God really is as he is revealed in Christ, then what will be the will of such a God for those who believe in him, and what will it be for the world? Or if we call the Kingdom of God "the life of God in the soul of man," then it must be the life of that God whose most perfect utterance was Jesus Christ.

That "new life," therefore, which the Church represents, does not necessarily mean ease of circumstances; it does not necessarily mean economic security; it does not necessarily mean the attainment of the communistic or any other social ideal. It has social, economic, and political implications, and some of these are plainly stated in the New Testament itself, which, as Brunner says, is not merely a book of One Command but is also a book of many commandments which show how the One Command is to be carried out, but these implications are rather the fruit of the Kingdom, the evidence to its presence, than the Kingdom itself.[17]

There are hundreds of improvements in the human situation which may be thought of and carried through without a single reference to that "new life" which is presented in the New Testament as the Christian ideal. The Gospel of the grace of God means not simply better living conditions: it means a new quality in the life of men, new relationships, new experiences, new purposes, new motives, new sources of power, and this does not have to wait until the living conditions are the best that can be desired. As has so often been said before, a man can live in a mansion without a care in the world, and be a pagan; and he can live in a cottage, conscious of many a limitation, and be a Christian, with the peace of God in his heart, with fear put far away, with an inner joy which diffuses a glow over life's most drab and common tasks, and with a love for his fellows which destroys all bitterness, all animosity, all jealousy.

Perhaps one should apologize for repeating such obvious truths in a discussion of this sort, but just because they are so obvious is why they may need to be repeated. There are problems connected with the social and economic life of men which will yield to the application of human wisdom, and one may have this wisdom who makes no least pretence to the Christian faith. But there are other problems which will never be solved except by the wisdom and power which come from beyond the range of the human. It is that wisdom and that power which are represented in the Church of Christ, and which are there because of the relationship in which the Church stands to what came into the world with Jesus Christ.

(4) The Church is a voice for God. Like the Scriptures themselves, it is a witness. The imperfections of the Church men see can never change the fact that through it God is speaking to the world. The Church means a certain belief as to God; it means a certain belief as to Jesus Christ; it means a certain belief as to man; it means a certain belief as to the world itself. He who "belongs to the Church" in effect gives his assent to the Church's testimony. He declares himself.

But this self-identification with the Church is not his only declaration. That is more or less indirect. He is committed to make it direct. Just as truly as the Church is a voice for God, so truly must he, the believer, be a voice for the Church, since only so can he too be a voice for God. The testimony of the Church is so far forth in his keeping. The thought is solemn enough. If in his numerous journeys into Syria and Palestine the youthful Mahomet had encountered Christians *who were really Christians*, there might never have been the religion known as Mohammedanism—and one reflects on the thought with great soberness. A false Christian testimony at a crucial moment may change the history of the world!

The testimony of the Church is to the fact, first, that God is a God of holy love. The most effective testimony to love is love; but the weakness of the testifying love does not destroy the reality and power of the love that is testified to. The testimony of the Church is to the fact, second, that Christ gave himself for every man, so that every man by laying hold upon him may come to newness of life. With the fullest recognition of individual and even of collective failure at this point, we are still to say that the Church is the witness to the redeeming and transforming power of Jesus Christ. The testimony of the Church is to the fact, third, that a means has been created whereby the souls of men may be released from those numerous fears which rest upon life as a heavy burden. That many a Christian man and woman is still possessed by these fears must be admitted, a fact which gives much support to the Roman Catholic ethical theory of "degrees" on the one hand, and to the Reformation principle of "justification by faith alone" on the other hand. For all of that, what the Church testifies to is still a fact: to come under the control of the Incarnate Word who is forevermore the Living Christ is to find the secret of emancipation from the sin that stains and from the fears that bind.[18]

The Church as a witness is the Church in one of its most fundamental aspects. It is a new creation of the Creator of the world, and the fact that we can state the conditions of its origin and ongoing no more denies that divine creativity than it can be denied in the case of the world. The origin of the world and the origin of the Church are at one and the same ultimate point, and they look to one and the same ultimate purpose of God. A primal creative act brought the world into being. A second primal creative act brought the Church into being, for the Church is inexplicable apart from Christ, and Christ is inexplicable apart from God. The world as we know it in space and time is the continuation of that primal creative act: shall we say that it bears permanent witness to it? There could not be a series without a first member. In the same way, the Church as we know it is the continuation of that second creative act, and to that act it is similarly a permanent witness. It is what high churchmen like the late Charles Gore mean by "the Church as the extension of the Incarnation." The claim is defensible only as applied to the Church in its inner being, although it is to be admitted that men differ profoundly on what "the Church in its inner being" is held to mean and to include. Perhaps the true situation can best be indicated in the statement that the Church as organized in any and all of its historical forms may pass away: what will never pass away is the Church understood as that body of which Christ is at once the Head and the animating Spirit.

Briefly, then, the Church is a fact because the Incarnation of the Word is a fact, and its primary task is to be a witness to the power which created it. All its organization, procedures, orders, sacraments, definitions, pronouncements, are derivatives of its creative principle and purpose, and are to be judged as to their effectiveness accordingly. In a very real sense, the objective evidence to the Incarnate, Crucified, and Risen Christ is the Church: not some one particular communion, but the Church of which communions are so many forms. The churches presuppose the Church, and the Church presupposes Christ. But Christ how understood? Understood as himself the Eternal Word become flesh, who tasted death for every man, but whom God raised up both because it was not possible that death should hold him, and because only by means of the Living Christ could God carry on and realize the purpose for which all things are.

(5) The Church is therefore an instrument. To say this is simply to capture in one phrase all that has been expressed in more detail above. The Church is the instrument of God to achieve his vast creative designs as these have to do with men. *In* it the Gospel is made effective and alive, and *by* it the Gospel is to win its way in the world. The Eternal Word came as a Life—Jesus Christ. How else can that Life remain in the world save in and as other lives? Life is propagated through life. The Gospel is to be *preached* in the world: that is true. But it is also to be *demonstrated*. This demonstration must be not syllogistic but vital. God spoke as a Life and only by lives can he continue to speak the message spoken as a Life.

The Gospel means new life—and the Church exhibits it. The Gospel means fellowship—and the Church exhibits it. The Gospel means a new relation to God—and the Church exhibits it. The Gospel means salvation—and the Church exhibits it. Again it must be admitted that the reference is to the Church in its ideal sense. But the distinction between inner and outer as respects the Church is of the very nature of the case. Always the Word of God is conditioned by its medium, and the principle applies to the Church as a Word of God humanly operative. In any form of divine revelation, the *what* is of God, the *how* is of man.[19] The human reproduction of a divine utterance is never in all respects identical with the original. At the very heart of the Church are truth and power essentially divine. But the working of this truth and this power is conditioned by the human life in and through which it works. The Church is an instrument, but it is an instrument which necessarily articulates itself with men and women. This is why complete uniformity within the working Church is impossible. The Gospel functions as the Church, but the functioning is affected by a variety of factors. The Church as appearing in one land and in one age may differ in many respects from the Church as appearing in another land and in another age, yet is the Church one and the same. "We have this treasure in earthen vessels." The vessel is the Church as seen by the eyes of men; the treasure is the Church seen as only God can see it—the "substance" of which all other features are the "accidents."

Distinctions already made elsewhere may therefore be made here also. The Word and the words—the Gospel and the gospels—the Creed and the creeds—the Church and the churches—the Life and the lives: such manifestly valid distinctions alike indicate that while the *gift* is from God *the use of the gift* is in the hands of men.

PART II

EXPOSITION AND DEFENCE

CHAPTER 6

The Keeper of the Keys

MUCH THAT WAS SAID IN THE FIRST AND SECOND CHAPTERS IS ADMIT-
tedly of a speculative character. The considerations advanced in the
intervening chapters, however, indicate that what are only reasonable probabilities from the standpoint of speculation are converted
into certainties for any man who accepts the whole fact of Christ.
Christianity properly understood becomes an apologetic for even
the crudest of religions.

It is not that the Christian claim is to be regarded as self-evident:
Paul had something to say in this connection about "the wisdom of
men" and "the foolishness of God." Christianity is not a system of
irrefragable logic, which has but to be presented to the mind to
win an inevitable assent. Indeed, if it is only so presented and only
so assented to, then it is neither presented nor accepted in its deepest sense. Christianity is first and foremost a faith. Whether we
consider the conditions of its origin, or the conditions of its primary
acceptance by men, or the conditions of its expansion, or the conditions of its operation in a given life, always these conditions involve the act of faith. The very claim, made already, that life is intended to grow in precisely that direction along which Christianity
takes it is itself a claim which, reasonable though it can be shown to
be, can never make an absolute reply to every objection which "the
natural man" can conceivably lay against it.

In a way, the strength of naturalistic criticism is in this necessary
inability of what is after all "a faith" to build around itself a completely impenetrable fence of logic. A person can always find excellent reasons for not being a Christian—which does not preclude
that the reasons for being one are more excellent still.[1] Faith may
truly be called a higher rationality, but the very term "higher"
suggests a qualification as compared with the rationality of, say,
the mathematical schemata or the laboratory tests.[2]

81

Nevertheless, the claim in question is still made. The life of Christianity depends upon it. The moment Christianity is made secondary to anything else, it has ceased to be Christianity in any proper sense, and has become simply one more of a competing number of possible views of existence. Its absoluteness is its essence. Inscribed on its banner is "No Other Name."

This is not to imply that the acceptance of the Christian faith is to be a substitute for all the arts and graces of life. The common appeal, "Become a Christian, and nothing else matters," can easily be misunderstood. It were better to say, "Become a Christian, and you will then see truly in what sense other things—*all* other things —matter." How fruitful a mother the Christian faith has been of education, of music, of painting, of poetry, of architecture, history is a sufficient witness.[3] Brace and Glover and many others have written well of *Gesta Christi* ("The Deeds of Christ"), but no man is competent to tell all that story. John in his vision saw "a rainbow round about the throne," fit symbol of the grace that should ever be the aureole of holiness. Jerusalem and Athens are antagonistic only in respect of the claim to priority, not in respect of what each ideally embodies and represents.[4]

That a man may know the joy and power of the Gospel and at the same time be deprived of much that on any wholesome view of life must be held to be desirable, is simple truth. "I am come that they might have life, and that they might have it more abundantly." The abundant life does not mean *only* a life abounding in Christian piety, although without such piety no life is full. It is the very genius of Christianity to be the avowed enemy of everything that distorts life or prevents its intended fruition. The true Gospel is the friend of man because it sees in every man a fact of infinite value. For that reason, it is against poverty—save as poverty may be *chosen* for the sake of the Kingdom of God. For that reason, it is against disease—although it brings with it a power which can transform even physical distress into a servant of high ends. For that reason—its estimate of every man as an absolute—it is against degrading and unprofitable toil, and against everything else which is unworthy of the dignity of the children of God. How could we possibly talk about "revelation" and its significance without laying down the tremendous claim that the Christian faith, itself a heritage from one generation to another, carries with it the promise of the eventual realization by every man of his *total* rightful heritage in the things that God has provided for them that love him!

Nobody will claim that the Church has always *officially* taken this position.[5] But Christianity, and the Church as organized, have never yet been complete identities, and are not likely soon to be. The spirit of Judas and of Simon and of Ananias has proven itself perennial. "The Letters to the Seven Churches" were written in the first century: in what century have they been without point? The marks of human frailty are upon all the works of men, and the Church is not free of that frailty. "We look upon this visible church," wrote Samuel Rutherford, against those who would drive from the church all who were not perfect, "though black and spotted, as the hospital and guest-house of sick, halt, maimed, and withered, over which Christ is Lord, Physician, and Master: and we would wait upon those that are not yet in Christ, as our Lord waited upon us and you both."[6] But the imperfections of the church are not the imperfections of the faith. The Christian faith itself, imperfectly expressed though it has so often been, and still so often is, is not of the working of the mind of man: it is from above, a gift, a divine thrust down into the confusion of time to bring out of the confusion the peace of God.

All this is so. The abundant life is the life in which provision is made for the proper satisfaction of all the necessities, capacities, and aspirations of men. The Gospel is on the side of life so understood.

Nevertheless, it is still to be said that for the vast majority of men such satisfaction remains an ideal to be only imperfectly realized. It is of the very order of existence that there shall be differences among men. William James' well-known metaphor, that if there is to be wine there must also be lees, and that to some lives it is given to be the one, and to other lives it is given to be the other, is redeemed from its apparent harshness by his own noble declaration that he himself is willing to be lees if that be necessary to the larger good.[7] Christianity says of no man that he *ought* to be lees, but it can so transform a man's spirit as to make him *willing* to be lees. And a man who is willing to be lees is wine indeed!

Meanwhile, the Christian task is with men in the conditions that actually obtain. The Gospel does not have to withhold its ministration to a life until every desirable social good has been secured. There is here an urgency which cannot afford to wait for the realization of some Utopian dream. The City of Mansoul must be built even although the City of God still lingers. Indeed, it may be that the one lingers just because the other grows so slowly! In any event, immense variety in the range of the adornments of life is compatible with the experience of a common faith, a common love, a common joy, a common purpose. It is no proper implication of the relation in which human life stands to the whole movement of creation that every life shall be similarly endowed, similarly situated, and similarly employed. Rather is the implication the very reverse of this. *Variety* is the very essence of our human stuff. "There are diversities of gifts," even although all be animated by "the same spirit." The body has many members, and all members have not the same office, yet is each member, comely or uncomely, not without its own proper office and importance.

The attempt to impose *sameness* upon mankind from without must always fail. There are fundamental differences among men which no "planned economy" or any other kind of planning can ever destroy. The Christian faith can still accomplish its saving, transforming, and sanctifying ends even in the midst of all this variety, and not in spite of but *by means of* the variety; while at the same time it is operating to remove those many inequalities which, just because they are removable, are manifestly neither essential nor permanent in the structure of life. The vast conception which meets us again and again in the New Testament, and which is reflected in the ascending scale of Dante's *Paradiso*, and permanently symbolized in the integrated grace and strength of a Gothic cathedral wherein are silent invisibilities which alone make possible the visibilities and their message—the conception of a redeemed and perfected humanity in which differences among each serve the purposes of the whole because each is subjected to the same Spirit and bound to a central loyalty, is one which, so far from violating the logic of the whole movement of the universal life, richly and exactly fulfills it. One star differeth from another star in glory, but all take their place in the spacious firmament on high, and make it as it is.

As human beings, we are meant to be different, meant to supplement and serve each other by our differences, meant to be held in bondage to one great Power, meant to be swept by one common emotion, meant to be held at last in the security of one common and everlasting embrace. If Christ be not he by whom this our human meaning is to find fulfillment, then the fulfillment is nowhere promised. It is the Christian conviction that Christ was ordained for this very purpose from before the foundation of the world. He is therefore at once cosmic root, cosmic nexus, and cosmic crown, "the Alpha and the Omega," as much the Finisher as the Author, "of whom and through whom and for whom are all things." As he sees of the travail of his soul, he is satisfied, because creative love, which is the ultimate fact of existence, sees in that which comes to birth the fruit of its chosen agony. The purpose of our human existence as demonstrably woven into the very web of the fabric of the garment of God, and the purpose of the Gospel as given in Jesus Christ, are mutualities.[8] Each exists for the other. The glory of Christ waits upon a preparatory work, but the preparatory work comes to no consummation except Christ shall appear. God creates and God redeems, but it is by the Word that God creates and it is by the Word that God redeems, and this Word is Christ.

But clearly we cannot stop with this. If the Gospel is given this significance, then nothing else that may come to men out of life can take its place or compensate for its loss or rejection. The moment it is said that every life exists in order to become all that it would become as it falls under the complete domination of Jesus Christ, that moment the issue is drawn between the salvation that is of Christ and a salvation that is of any other means whatsoever.

There must be no misunderstanding of the sheer audacity of what is here being declared. *Christ and creation are inseparable.* Rich and deep and satisfying may be the experiences that come to men through devotion to other leaders, through prayers at other altars, through sacrifices at other shrines, yes, and through the pursuit of those vocations and the patient discharge of those obligations through which blessing is brought into the world. We do not need to degrade or to discount anything that is good in order to exalt the Christ. This is seen to be even more truly so when we bear in mind the significance of the Christian doctrine of the Holy Spirit, with its teaching that every good thing that a man does springs from an impulse of which the Spirit is the ultimate source.[9] All that is being said here is that no good can take the place of the absolute good, and that in our heritage of faith Christ is given as the absolute good, when he is properly understood, properly received, and properly placed.

That this lays a challenge against every other conception of "the absolute good" that has obtained among men, is evident; to say nothing of its bearing upon the common contemporary claim that no good can ever be absolute, since we live in a world of relativities and are ourselves but relative creatures. In the scheme of Plato, a good was a good only as it was properly related to *the* Good.[10] That is precisely the way it stands with respect to Jesus Christ. Substitute Plato's "supreme good"—or, for that matter, the "supreme good" as understood in any other system, ancient or modern—with Christ, and it will still be true, but in a sense never comprehended by Plato or any other, that every other good will be all that it might be only as it stands subservient to him.

To be specific, human love—of husband and wife, parent and child, friend and friend—that is consecrated in the love of Christ, takes on a quality which it cannot have, lacking that consecration. Physical well-being is an undeniable good, and there are those in our time to whom it is the only good that matters. But such a good is always in danger, and when it is lost, as it might be at any moment, the whole world collapses. Physical well-being, however, related to the ideal of Christ, is given its proper place in "the scale of goods," so that, whether it be kept or whether it be lost, the sense of life's worth continues. Art baptized into the spirit of Christ is saved from those degradations which seem to be permissible under the claim, "Art for art's sake." The one deficiency in the otherwise matchless Shakespeare lies in the failure to read, describe, and interpret the human scene in the light that Christ alone can shed upon it. It might be a literary heresy to say that: it would be heresy of a far deeper hue to say that there could be an accomplishment that suffered no defect through the absence of Christ and attained no increase in perfection through his presence. Great is the story of our human achievement in a thousand ways, but any achievement which Christ cannot bless or which love of him does not inspire is by that much less than it might have been.

One thinks of the artist who had used his gift to portray "the sensual and the dark" in such fashion as to make it attractive, lying in terror on his death-bed as he reviewed the course of his degradation, and from his awe-stricken friends around him exacting a promise that his pictures should be burned.[11] Would that have been the case had he consecrated his talent to "the beauty of holiness"? Would anything that was done "for Christ's sake" have been better done if Christ had had no place in the work? Who would dare to say that every scientific discovery or invention is *ipso facto* a human good? Who would dare to deny that it would become a human good if Christ could have his way with it?

Where Christ is glorified—this is the import of what has been written—there comes a new meaning to every fine human sentiment, a new power to every fine human purpose, a new supplement to every fine human effort. Strike Christ from his throne, and while the sentiment, the purpose, the effort, is still fine, it is still less than its own possible best. In him all things are meant to find their coherence, and, when they find it they make the perfect round. Where he is not, the best can never come. Therefore, where he is not, no life can come to its full stature. Christ is Saviour in the one true sense that he saves.

But let us not use the word "save" in any narrow and commonplace fashion. The Christian salvation seeks the perfecting of life. It would bring about the transformation of every single human activity. Every trade, every calling, every profession may be subject to the Christian salvation, and greatly needs to be. Notwithstanding that we set Christ and Caesar over against each other, as though there were some areas of life in which Christ need have no part, it remains that when business, industry, politics, recreation, education, and the like are under the exclusive control of Caesar, they by that much fail of what they should be. It is an inexcusably narrow view which sees, in the desire to have Christian business, Christian industry, Christian politics, Christian recreation, Christian education, an unfriendly invasion of Caesar's realm. The Christian who renders to Caesar a truly Christian loyalty achieves the paradox of being most loyal to Caesar when he is most loyal to Christ. He puts Christ first and Caesar second, but in putting Caesar second to Christ he most assures the integrity and the security of Caesar's realm. The world's Caesars have collapsed in proportion as their realms were wanting in that which only Christ can give. No force can meet his force, for "love never faileth." No rule can long defy his rule, for his rule is the rule of an Eternal Will, which may know postponement but never defeat. He is inseparable from the world's life, because he is inseparable from God, and what falls was already destined to fall because it was not in his keeping.

"For us men he came down." We do not like to say it, because we have been trained in a point of view which sees only a "coming up." What comes up has only a relative significance, and we can handle it—or we think we can. But what comes down is against the rule. It violates the order of things. It suggests the possibility that this is a lower realm under the control of a higher realm. It threatens us with an absolute. So we will have nothing to do with one who "came down," with one who burst into time from somewhere out of time—in a word, with one who was "conceived of the Holy Ghost and born of the Virgin Mary."

Yet the refusal only deepens our darkness and increases our perplexity because it leaves us without linkage to a greater than we are ourselves. If we would but believe it, we should see that the very fact that one could "come down" means that he who thus came did so "for us men and for our salvation," for whence can salvation come except "from above"? For who can lift us except be he above us, and how can he lift us except he connect with us?

"He descended into Hades." That too we do not like to say: indeed, we have long decided that we will say it no more. Our eyes are holden that we cannot see. Dull-witted as we are, we do not comprehend the marvel of this truth that he who "came down" as proof of his heavenly origin and to do on behalf of men that which, if not done, must but leave us to perish—that he who did this had done it in vain unless he did even more. He went deeper yet. "He tasted death for every man." That means for *all* men: and what is meant by "all men"? It means all who ever lived, for all who have ever lived have died. It means all who now live, for all who now live will die. It means all who are yet to live—"the innumerable caravan"—for all who are yet to live will also die. No soul can escape this "Tremendous Lover," not even though it make its bed in hell. The dark underworld takes on promise because he invades it. The spirits in prison are his deep concern.[12] Since the morning stars rejoiced together there has not been a pilgrim soul that did not exist for Christ and Christ for it.

And yet we hesitate to say, "He descended into Hades—into hell." Is it that we do not want to believe that he has a universal significance? Is it that we do not want to see in the story of the Wise Men and the Star anything more than an empty legend? Is it that we suppose that the Christian God is a God who had no deep concern for men until the sands of time had been running for, lo, uncounted years? Is it that we suppose that the presence of Moses and Elijah at that august moment on Mount Hermon, when he who had "come down" received divine authentication as to who and what and why he was—that this presence was but the fiction of heated brains? Is it that we suppose that there was no profound meaning in the announcement that "Abraham rejoiced to see that day"? And not Abraham only, but many others, of whom it stands written: "These all died in faith, not having received the promises, but having seen them and greeted them from afar, and having confessed that they were strangers and pilgrims on the earth. . . . And these all, having had witness borne to them through their faith, received not the promise, God having provided some better thing concerning us, that apart from us they should not be made perfect."

When all the Church of Christ everywhere had the courage and the faith to declare, "He descended into Hades," it was but a way of saying that all the dead equally with all the living were his concern. From the human standpoint, nothing is so final, so absolute, as death. But he who "came down" also "descended into Hades."

He tracked man's so victorious enemy to its last lair. He put himself under the law of sin and death. He bound the strong man that he might despoil him. Out of the very jaws of death he snatched life. The fantastic idea of the Fathers of the Early Church, that he put himself in the power of Satan on the condition that Satan would release men, and then himself escaped from Satan, God "having loosed the pangs of death, because it was not possible that he should be holden of it," is fantastic only because of its "ideologic" form. The truth that is in it we are only just now beginning to appreciate, namely, that the story of God's activities on behalf of men is told most effectively when it is told "dramatically," and what are these great declarations about the descent into Hades and the dethronement of Satan and the preaching to the spirits in prison and the taking the sting from death and robbing the grave of its victory, but so many dramatic delineations of the outworking of the divine purpose with men, and not with some men, a favored few, but with all men?[13]

For he who "came down," and who "descended into Hades," he also "ascended into heaven." That, too, we do not like to say, for it means resurrection, and how can one who was dead rise again? He could not, unless he were Lord even of death. He who became death's captive, as it would seem, at last led captivity captive, and gave gifts unto men, such gifts as no Roman general, riding in triumph with defeated kings tied to his chariot, ever dreamed of scattering to an acclaiming crowd. "He descended into Hades": that is the reach of his strong arm into the dark backward and abysm of time. "He ascended into heaven": that is the promise that that same strong arm will never fail, but will be outstretched in behalf of men *for ever!*

The individual soul is constituted with reference to Christ, and knows no rest until it finds rest in him. But more than that, the entire human race is constituted with reference to Christ, and knows no lasting good in that which denies him, and finds in its experience increasing confirmation that his law must be its law and his way the only way it can safely go. But more even than that, the entire creation is constituted with reference to Christ. What God began, he began in Christ; and what he carries on, he carries on in Christ; and what he is yet to accomplish, he will accomplish in Christ.

"He came down."
"He descended into Hades."
"He ascended into heaven."

Who did this? Christ. For whom? For us men. Why? For our salvation. Who then is excluded? Nobody.

"Unto me, who am less than the least of all saints, was this grace given, to preach unto the nations the unsearchable riches of Christ; and to make all men see what is the dispensation of the mystery which for ages hath been hid in God who created all things; to the intent that now unto the principalities and the powers in the heavenly places might be made known through the church the manifold wisdom of God, according to the eternal purpose which he purposed in Christ Jesus our Lord" (Ephesians 3. 8–11).

It is easy to dismiss all this as so much empty rhetoric. That, indeed, is what it is unless it is the utter truth of existence. It is no small matter to write what has here been written—and what is yet to follow—if it be not true. But by the same token, if it be true it is no small matter to wave it lightly aside. To turn from Christ may mean nothing much, or it may mean everything. That is the dreadful thing about the Christian faith. It is either wholly true or wholly false. If it has been given to us of God, then is it true. If it is nothing but a skillfully constructed fabric of wistful minds, then is it not true; for what men can devise other men can destroy. Empty rhetoric or solemn truth!

And which it shall be, no man may determine for another. I can say that it is not true, and for me it is then not true. And I can say that it is true, and my saying it, if I speak with complete sincerity— and how else dare I?—is precisely what makes it true, *for me!*

"Christ is the End, for Christ is the Beginning,
Christ the Beginning, for the end is Christ."

As for the rest, the sneer of the sceptic, the earnest reasoning of the philosopher, the airy refusal of the light of heart, even the sorrowful rejection of one who prefers his other riches—as for these, and they are legion, one can but say:

"Yea, with one voice, O world, though thou deniest,
Stand thou on that side, for on this am I!"

OVER

CHAPTER 7

The Creative and Redemptive Word

THE SIGNIFICANCE ASSIGNED TO CHRIST IN THE LAST CHAPTER CAN only mean that he is inseparably connected with the very springs of life itself, that is to say, with God. How audacious this claim is, when made of a historical figure, and, from the standpoint of bare reason, how incredible, has already been allowed.[1] Nevertheless, if the claim is surrendered, Christ is no longer the Figure which in the Christian tradition he has always been. We may talk all we like about the Jesus of history, but if in the Jesus of history we do not see at the same time a specific revelation of the nature and purposes of the Creator himself, and by consequence that absolute by which all history is to be judged, then no amount of sentiment poured out in honor of the historical Figure will avail to conserve and to perpetuate our heritage.

Certainly the Christian faith has to do with historical realities— with such realities as the birth, life, sufferings, death, and resurrection of Jesus Christ. Christianity is rooted, as the late H. R. Mackintosh so often said, in "the fruitful depths of history." We are not moving in a realm of fantasy and imagination. Historical research may have created various Synoptic problems: it has put beyond all doubt the historicity of the Subject of the Synoptic Portrait.[2] The history of our race includes "the man Christ Jesus," but it also includes, according to the Christian faith, a series of episodes connected with him which can no more be accounted for in terms of the normal laws of history than the origin of creation can be accounted for in terms of the laws which characterize its ongoing.

This reference to "the origin of creation" raises a question which is vital to Christianity in its largest sense. It has become customary to claim that the question of "the beginning of things" is irrelevant to any practical purpose, and, indeed, is quite unanswerable. Wie-

92

man, in keeping with his naturalism, flatly affirms this.[3] This in effect involves the frank abandonment of the whole idea of creation as involving an act of the will of a Creator. The usual reason given for the abandonment is the imaginative difficulty: we cannot possibly imagine how something could come to be where nothing was.

The objector quite overlooks the fact that *being* is just as inexplicable by us as *becoming*. We are "teased out of thought" as much by how anything can *actually exist* as by how anything could have *begun to exist*. We take time and its content for granted, as though that were something quite simple, but dismiss as utterly irrational the supposition that time and its content had a beginning. What this does is to make existence in time and space—including the human race—a necessity, not an option. This is certainly not the Christian view. The Christian view—which is to say the Biblical view—is that things are because God chooses that they shall be. Kraemer states the case with his accustomed clarity when he says that what "Biblical realism" calls for is the belief that "man, the world, nature, history are products and objects of God's will,"[4] although he makes some unnecessary concessions to the philosophical problem involved. But in his categorical statement: "God is the sovereign Creator of the world and of man: he is the Lord of history," he gives not merely the Christian position respecting God as Creator, but likewise the position by which every other great Christian belief stands or falls.

The "naturalistic theist" is entirely logical when, having rejected all belief in God the Creator, he goes on to reduce Christianity to a few simple ethical propositions. *The Christian faith calls for a God who chose to create.* The "how" or the "when" of the creative act is utterly inscrutable to us.[5] The processes being now operative, we can examine them and make deductions about them —not forgetting that these processes include also ourselves as intelligent and understanding beings. But there can naturally be no such thing as "a science of the beginning." Science always deals with something "given." Its interest is with existents and their laws. It is true that science deals with the origin of new forms, but always it assumes an antecedent environment whence these new forms "emerge." Science necessarily postulates "the frame of nature," and then devotes itself to an examination of what it has postulated and of whatever within that frame is susceptible of the sort of examination which it is the proper right of science to make —and that right certainly does not include *everything*.

But always the fact of the frame remains.[6] Philosophy has engaged in endless speculation about it, and perhaps its most characteristic conclusion is expressed in the dictum, *ex nihilo, nihil fit*. It is then supposed that the logic of that dictum is either some form of dualism, as in Aristotle;[7] or some form of eternal creation, as in Origen;[8] or some form of pantheism, as in Spinoza;[9] or some form of naturalism, as in men like the late S. Alexander.[10] But Christianity does not lead to any *ex nihilo, nihil fit*. Its doctrine of Creative Will implies a proper rationale of creation, namely, that it belongs to God to give his will objective effectuation in such a form as he shall choose, and existence in time and space is that form. Beyond that, Christianity does not need to go, and, indeed, is not able to go. It is satisfied to ground the very frame of nature in the will of God, and to see in the contents of that frame the progressive realization of the purpose inspiring the Creative Will.

Profoundly speaking, therefore, "I believe in God the Creator" must be and is the first article of the Christian creed. It offers no "explanation" of its affirmation, if by "explanation" is meant such a statement of the relation of dependence in which one thing stands to another as that the relation is clearly understood. The belief that the creation depends upon the will of the Creator, is all that Christianity commits us to. The Christian accepts it, not on speculative grounds, as is wrongly claimed by the naturalists, but as an element in a total body of revealed truth. "God spake, and it was done: he commanded, and the decree stood fast" (Psalm 33. 9). "Lift up your eyes on high, and see who hath created these, that bringeth out their host by number; he calleth them all by name; by the greatness of his might, and for that he is strong in power, not one is lacking"(Isaiah 40. 26). Every time we repeat the Lord's Prayer, we affirm our faith in the Creator: "Thine is the kingdom, and the power, and the glory, for ever." We can only say, therefore, that creation is primal miracle. The ways of God are past our finding out, but this is his way. We can but bow heart and mind, and exclaim: "In the beginning, God created the heavens and the earth."

But the creative act which is without understanding by us is not without reason for God, and sufficient of the reason has been made known to us. Divine activity is in pursuit of the divine purpose. According to the Christian revelation, that purpose is the glory of the Creator, for what can even God do greater than to give himself that something else might be, and Creation and that new creation which is Redemption are forms of God's self-giving. For in the Christian view, the fact of creation, and the purpose of creation, and the glory of the Creator, are alike so integrated with the fact of Christ that he becomes the nexus without which none of these had been possible.

We must still affirm that the "how" of creation is beyond us, but the Christian revelation has not left us wholly in the dark as to the constitution of the Creator whereby he can do as he does. We have had revealed to us not only the fact of God, but also the way he fundamentally and necessarily and eternally *is*. Intrinsic to the very being of God is that which in Scripture is sometimes called "the Word." It is by virtue of this Word not only that God is as he is but also that he can do as he does. His action springs out of his being, and a difference of being would involve a difference of action. God's will is not arbitrary. It is the will of such a God as he is, and his "is-ness" is not of his choice but of his necessity. Even God cannot choose to be other than he is. What he can do is to choose to act in such ways as his being makes possible. According to the Christian faith—which in its turn is Scripturally determined—God's being is not simple, but complex. He is compact of intrinsic differences which yet in nowise disturb his perfect oneness, but are rather the causes of it.

The primal miracle of creation is therefore not the act of a Being of absolute solitariness seeking something which he needs for himself: instead, it is the act of a Being in whom is a richness and versatility and completeness of experience such that *he needs nothing more*.[11]

The usual reply to this, that a Being so complete as this could not act, because he would have no motive for acting, arises from measuring God by human standards. We overlook the fact, however, that even among men the greatest acts are the most selfless acts, and that no act is so truly free as the act in which the doer seeks nothing for himself, but only the good of "otherness." It is the very perfection of God which makes his creative act so truly free. Were he less perfect than he is, his act would be by that much less free. His perfection is in the complete harmony of his interior life.

But it is the very conditions of that harmony which also provide the conditions of his creative act. That act—so it has been made known to us—is possible because of the Word. The case may be stated in somewhat formal fashion as follows: *The Word as intrinsic to the Divine Life constitutes the metaphysical basis of the process whereby that Life comes to objective self-expression in creation as we know it.* No Divine Word, no divine purpose—at least, not *this* purpose. No Divine Word, no divine creative act—at least, not *this* act. No Divine Word, no divine glory—at least, not *this* glory. Things could be different from what they are only if God were different from what he is, that is, ontologically different—and God could not be different! Creation is as it is because God is as he is; that is to say, because God is a Being able to plan, able to will, able to give his purpose objective effectuation, and because the ability to do this rests finally upon the fact that a constitutive element in the total nature of the creative God is the Word.

But the Word is no more to be "explained" than the sheer *existence* of God is to be explained. *That* God is—this is something "given" to us in the Christian faith; *how* God is—this too is something "given."[12] And it is enough.

Clearly such Christian belief is neither anti-rational nor anti-scientific. It has to do with a region which reason cannot penetrate and in which science as such has no interest. Once something has "begun" which includes in itself intelligence, philosophy and science become possible and have their field, and all that Christianity—which exists by virtue of the same conditions—asks of them is that they shall mind their business. The relation of the "beginning" to the "Beginner" beyond that of simple dependence; the conditions which make the "beginning" possible; the purpose for which the "beginning" was made; the ultimate end sought by the "Beginner" through the process which he initiated and continues to maintain—of all this the Christian flatly claims to "know" enough for the purposes of Christian living, centered as it is in faith in God. But he does not know it through "discovery," discovery being in the nature of the case excluded here, but he knows it through "revelation."

Such knowledge is evidently different from any other kind of knowledge. Some, indeed, would vehemently deny that it was knowledge at all, and the point could be conceded provided it were not then claimed that therefore it is *not true*. The obverse of knowledge may be ignorance, but ignorance does not necessarily mean the non-existent or the untrue. The correlate of revelation from the side of God is faith from the side of man. Man has a faculty of belief besides a faculty of knowledge, and existence answers to both. The faculty of knowledge implies something to be known, and faith in the knowing faculty is the prerequisite of all knowledge. In the same way, the faculty of believing implies something to be believed, else why the faculty.

Often enough men believe things to be so which are afterwards demonstrated not to have been so, but this does not imply that the believing faculty has no proper function. The Christian believes some things which can neither be "proved" to be so, or belief would not be needful, nor yet "proved" to be not so, or belief would not be defensible. He has reasons for his belief, good reasons, and he takes the reasons as sufficiently good to constitute a rock on which to build the structure of his life. He therefore has no quarrel with either philosophy or science, except when they proceed to make purely dogmatic denials of what to him is a reasonable faith. On the contrary, he would work with them for the more complete understanding of the processes which creation reveals. All he claims is that the primal creative act is neither a historical fact nor a scientific fact: instead, it is the presupposition of all history, conceived as the continuation of the act; and it is the presupposition of all science, conceived as the attempt to ascertain and state the laws that characterize the continuation.

Belief in God the Creator is therefore not the conclusion of a syllogism, but a faith. It is not a demonstration, but the free commitment of the mind to a body of truth offered as "revealed," one element of which is this truth of the Creative God who creates by virtue of the Word.

But if "God the Creator" is the first article of the Christian creed, the second article is "God the Re-Creator." Not only so, but just as creation was through the Word, so also was the re-creation. What Paul describes as "the old man" and "the new man" answers to two forms of the creative act and purpose of the one God. What is the whole meaning of the Christian faith but that the God from whom we derive our being is the God from whom we derive those spiritual resources, in particular that one great Spiritual Resource, which experience shows to be so necessary? The same Word through whom the creative God gave object effectuation to his creative purpose is the Word through whom he gave objective effectuation to his purpose to complete what he had begun. When we speak of the Divinity of Christ, applying the term to him considered as a historical figure, what we mean is the Divinity of the Word. In the same way, the eternity of Christ is the eternity of the Word; the power of Christ is the power of the Word.

That series of episodes, therefore, which marks the presence of Christ in the field of history is as inexplicable in terms of the processes of that history as the primal creative act is inexplicable in terms of the processes which characterize creation in its ongoing. Creativity is miracle, and Christ is miracle. In both cases, we have an absolute which is to be accepted as utterly original. But not therefore as self-originating. In the Christian view, creation and Christ alike are novel and inexplicable manifestations of one and the same ultimate reality, God, but of God existing in a certain way. The Word but for which creation could not have been is the Word but for which Christ, the historical figure, could not have been. The purpose of the primal creative act because of which all things could be as they are calls for that other creative act whose issue is that "Strange Man" whom we meet in the New Testament. Without the second the first remains, from any human point of view, sheerly tragic. It is the light that shines from "the Word made flesh" that diffuses with hope and with meaning the merely cosmic expression of that same Word. If we accept the Christian view, that the God because of whose will creation was is also the God because of whose will in a second creation Jesus Christ was, and that the purpose of the second creation was to redeem, transform, and sanctify the first creation,[13] then indeed are we as men who arise from the darkness in which they have been sitting because they have seen the light of life.

That this is as much a "faith-judgment" as belief in the God of the first creation is evident. The faith is not without its reasons, but what to most Christians is the most cogent of these reasons, namely, "the Christian experience," necessarily depends upon the faith itself having already been accepted. What certainty we claim to have grows out of acceptance, not acceptance out of certainty. To say that we will not accept until we have been made certain is as though a man in danger of drowning should refuse to grasp a rope thrown to him until he was assured it would bear his weight. He can prove the adequacy of the rope only by trusting himself to it. Christian truth, as has already been said, is not a syllogistic conclusion but an accepted postulate. We may reason back and forth about it all that we like. This, indeed, as Theodor Haecker has recently reminded us, is our obligation. Revealed religion, defined as dogma which embodies for both thought and thinker the spirit, will, and word of God, is "an incalculably fruitful field for dialectics because revealed truths which to human understanding contain insoluble contradictions and difficulties are found side by side."[14] Eventually, however, the situation narrows down to two alternatives. Either we accept such a God as God in Christ is seen to be, and we accept Christ as having this sole significance as a self-revelation of God in respect of his will and purpose for men and as the means of its realization—either we accept this, or we do not, and if we do not, then whatever we put in the place of this is something less than this, for something greater there could not be.

In a word, an act of faith on our part, answering to the act of revelation on the part of God, alone can place us within the circle of Christian truth and experience. Admittedly, much that is characteristic of Christianity may be enjoyed by men apart from this initial surrender of the mind and will. But it is still true that this enjoyment of the fruit by some is only possible because of the keeping alive of the roots by others.

The Christian heritage is therefore not merely a *heritage*, something that has come down to us from the past. It is also a heritage *of faith*, and what came of faith in the first place, and what has been held of faith by those who transmit it, can still only be held of faith by those who are called to receive it. Historical Christianity is authoritarian. The dogmatism of the Church has often enough been misdirected, but that its existence is dogmatically based is simple fact. The Church is a witness, and what it has to witness to is the truth in which it was founded. The Church has a teaching function, and the truth by which it lives is the truth it must teach to every man, woman, and child whom it receives. The Christian priest, the Christian minister, the Christian missionary, the Christian teacher of whatever sort, has this as his primary obligation.

What today we call "the Christian way of life" has only the most questionable pragmatic sanction unless it be in keeping with the truth of God—which is to say, the fundamental truth of existence itself. How questionable the pragmatism is is seen in the fact that on every hand today "the Christian way of life" is being challenged.[15] If those who are challenged cannot fall back on something absolute, how shall they stand? It is true that those who issue the challenge necessarily deny this absolute, but that does not disturb the believer, provided he is himself convinced of it.

Christianity is being confronted by new philosophies, new cults, new ideologies. If Christianity is to survive, it can only be on the condition that the Church shall both rediscover the basis of its message and its "way of life" in the very truth of God, and shall commit itself without reserve to the truth that worked through faith to create it. Of this truth we shall dare to say that it is so intellectually overwhelming, so ethically radical, so socially revolutionary, so spiritually adequate, so far beyond the power of the logical understanding either to prove or to disprove, and yet withal so responsive to the needs of our desperate human situation, that if this truth is not the key to the riddle of life, then is the riddle without any solution, and we shall but resume an unavailing search. Unavailing, because to our persistent "What?" "Whence?" "Why?" "Whither?" there will still come no satisfying answer, nothing but the faint and hopeless echoes of the questions themselves.

CHAPTER 8

Creation Without Redemption

WE HAVE ATTEMPTED TO SHOW THAT IN CHRISTIANITY, CREATION and redemption are linked together as parts of the same purpose and as arising from the action of the same Divine Word. It cannot be denied that this linkage throws a meaning over the whole which otherwise we do not find. For all that, there are many people who find it possible to believe in God the Creator, but who cannot at all bring themselves to believe in God the Redeemer. When they hear it said that in Jesus Christ there is just as novel and just as inexplicable an effectuation of the Divine Will as there was in the "Let there be!" which heralded and made possible creation's dawn, they protest as at some sheer incredibility.

But what shall be said of their own incredibility? Since when is it more reasonable to believe in a God who creates, and who *presumably* cares, but who gives no undeniable evidence of this care, than to believe in a God who creates and who most definitely does care because he gives evidence of that care in the most costly fashion that even he could conceive and carry out?[1] In actual fact, the man who accepts the whole of the Christian faith is far less open to the charge of credulity than is the man who accepts only half of it! This belief in a Creator held in separation from belief in a Redeemer justifies every pessimistic estimate of existence that has ever been sorrowfully or viciously proclaimed. For it is to believe in a God who willingly made possible this kind of world, who as willingly keeps it in being, and who does nothing more for it than *just that*.[2]

The problem would not be so acute if we could blot out of the picture the human side of it. Even with the human side out, however, the shadows are sometimes impenetrably dark. It is hardly necessary to repeat again the indictments of the cosmic equity which have been wrung from tortured souls these millenniums past as they have surveyed the spectacle of nature's redness in tooth and claw.[3]

Sunt lachrymae rerum, et mentem mortalia tangunt. Substitute *naturalia* for *mortalia* (if the Latin purist will permit!), and Virgil's unforgettable line will express what many feel about "the law of the jungle." Better to believe in no God at all than to believe in a God the measure of whose power and purpose is *this*. Even granting that much of the poignancy of the indictment has sprung from the fact that the spectator more or less unconsciously identifies himself with the spectacle, and feels about the sufferings which he beholds as he would have done had they been his own or those of one dear to him, it is still true that for the man who believes in simply God the Creator, creation in this aspect of it is much more an insoluble enigma than a plain evidence of goodness, wisdom, and power. David Hume has given classic expression to that enigma for all time.[4] But add to the natural scene the human scene—and we must do that, for the two are not separable—and the enigma becomes insoluble by simply that much more.

For now there comes into the picture not merely "a struggle for existence" which springs from the sheerly blind instinct to endure, and from which we may presume that deliberate purpose to inflict suffering is to be excluded. But there comes into the picture all the overwhelming evidence of deliberate wickedness and of *exultant joy in wickedness* which puts on human history the mark of Cain. All this is in addition to that inevitable suffering which enters into the lot of man equally with the lot of the beast. Sin and man are two inseparabilities, and that stands even if sin be defined in the very simple sense of one's knowingly doing what one knows ought not to have been done.

The spirit of moral anarchy, suppressed in one area only to break out in another, is as characteristic of man as is the power to think or the power to feel. You cannot be a man, and not find that again and again evil is occupying the saddle and riding you. For even if, with Paul, "I delight in the law of God after the inward man," also with Paul "I see a different law in my members, warring against the law of my mind, and bringing me into captivity under the law of sin which is in my members" (Romans 7. 22). It is the same dire truth which Plato has reference to in the *Phaedrus* in his metaphor of the charioteer and the two horses. No mind is adequate to conceive, nor pen to describe, the trail left behind by this spirit of moral anarchy as it has marched across the fields of time:

> "'God save thee, ancient Mariner,
> From the fiends that plague thee thus!
> Why look'st thou so?'—'With my cross-bow
> I shot the Albatross!'"

Coleridge at least was under no illusion as to the meaning of that remorse which at some time or another every man knows something about. Remorse is the concave of that arc of which the convex is deliberate wrong. "Out, out, damned spot!" and it will not out. Even if at one time we were in Eden, which is the symbol of innocence, we go to Eden no more. The flaming sword of an irrevocable choice flashes back and forth between us and the Garden we left, and we return if at all only in regretful fancy, never in actual fact.

In this respect, one man stands for every other man. That God should deal with us before we do as Adam did, as he dealt with Adam only after his fall, is no injustice, seeing that Adam did but make actual that which is potential in every man, and any other man would have done the same. Reading the dramatic record in the third chapter of Genesis, who is there but must say, "It is my story. My name is Adam. Put me there, and I should have done as he did. Indeed, I have done it!" No eugenics, no careful nurture begun even in infancy, no environment created according to the latest psychological pattern, can prevent the re-enactment of that primeval tragedy in every new life. The child sprung from pagan lust and the child of your own intelligent Christian love must alike, each in his own way, fight the moral battle and lose the first encounter and be constituted a sinner.

There is no such thing possible as eliminating moral tragedy from the human heritage. We may fall to rise, but we fall first, and to the certainty of that fall every man is born. Those who have supposed that this "radical evil," as Kant himself called it, which attends upon human nature, was destined to grow less and less by reason of the operation of some vast impersonal law of progress, have in our own time been once again disillusioned. We do not like the phrases, "original sin" and "natural depravity," but look out

over the human scene to-day, and then ask how else the spectacle
of rampant evil which everywhere meets the eye can be accounted
for save as the fruit of a root nourished from within the very depths
of human nature itself.[5] Men do not have to learn to be evil and to
do evil: they have to learn *not* to be evil and *not* to do it.

Even the good that one man may do may become a means of evil
for another man. The gentle Bishop received into his house as an
honored guest the recently liberated convict. Could fitter words
have been spoken than those words of welcome: "You need not
have told me who you were; this is not my house, but the house of
Christ. This door does not ask a man who enters whether he has a
name, but if he has a sorrow; you are suffering, you are hungry
and thirsty, and so be welcome." That night the guest, bound on
infamy, quietly entered the bedroom of the sleeping Bishop, and for
a moment the sight of "this unconsciously august man," on whose
forehead was "the inexpressible reflection of an invisible light,"
gave him pause. As though to make the pause a turning-point, a
moonbeam fell across the crucifix on the mantel-piece. But the
story continues: "All at once Jean Valjean put on his cap again,
then walked rapidly along the bed, without looking at the Bishop,
and went straight to the cupboard. He raised his crowbar to force
the lock, but as the key was in it, he opened it, and the first thing
he saw was the plate-basket, which he seized. He hurried across the
room, not caring for the noise he made, re-entered the oratory,
opened the window, seized his stick, put the silver in his pocket,
threw away the basket, leaped into the garden, bounded over the
wall like a tiger, and fled."

Was there a more Christlike deed than the Bishop's? Yet Jean
Valjean could pervert it into a means of evil. He could not have
stolen the Bishop's plate had the Bishop not trusted him as he did!
"Nothing whatever can be good without qualification," said Kant,
"except a good will." The Bishop's will was as near good as a will
could be—which only made blacker still the evil it made possible.
True, this is not the whole story. Jean Valjean's redemption started
when he touched this his nadir, but that does not change the fact of
the evil that comes with life. The good Bishop, too, belongs in the
story, but nobody supposes that he attained without great tribula-

tion that "luminous transparency" which even Jean Valjean in his darkest moment could not ignore.

Saints are not born; saints are grown. But how much more prolific the cosmic travail seems to be of "damaged souls" than of luminous saints! And the damage does not need to reveal itself in open and repulsive vice. It is just as actual in those refinements of self-regard which characterize our civilization as in the calculated cruelties of the naked aboriginal. Those very instruments whose conception and manufacture in our time have witnessed to man's intellectual power, and which it was supposed would increase his happiness and extend constructively his social sense—what have they turned out to be but means whereby he can make more effective still his primal will to destroy? Between the cave-man lashing a stone in a forked stick, with which he purposes to brain a neighbor whose food supply or mate he covets, and the modern aviator dropping gas bombs on a hospital, or a modern Lothario to whom no vows, his own or another's, have any slightest meaning, wherein is the difference in fundamental moral quality? In every case, the use of the best available means, mechanical or psychological, is inspired by the same complete disregard of the claims of "otherness." If there be any difference, it is that the disregard in the case of the cave-man is so much more understandable, and so much more excusable, than in the case of his modern successors.

The point need not be labored. It is so patent that man perpetually produces a kingdom of evil, and the man who produces evil has evil at the heart of him. He starts with a moral blight, and the blight manifests itself in the work of his hands. Augustine, with all his exaggeration, was much nearer the truth about man than was Pelagius.[6] Man is indeed salvable, which involves that there is that in him which can respond to the higher. What hope we have lies in that fact. Valjean could steal the silver plate of the sleeping Bishop who a few hours before had opened to him his home, but there was still in the soul of the convict a spark which the memory of the Bishop would some day fan into the white flame of a great and self-abnegating loyalty. All this is so, and we rejoice to know it. Yet it still remains that evil is a perennially fruitful principle in human life. So far from being modified and restrained by man's increasing mastery of the resources which nature provides, the evil principle is but brought to more dramatic and more devastating manifestation thereby.[7]

According to the believer in God the Creator, both the nature which is susceptible of such uses, and the man who in his callous and self-centered arrogance can so use it, are alike the creatures of this God. But God does nothing about it—except to perpetuate it! Perchance he maintains a causal order which brings it to pass that he who sows shall reap, and if he sow to the flesh of the flesh he shall reap corruption. But consequences are no guarantee that men will not again repeat the deeds that produce them. Sinai is as much a revelation of human impotence as of moral majesty. It is a simple matter for the Law to assert itself through a causal order. In that respect, the Law always speaks the last word, since its ultimate penalty is death.

But the death which bespeaks the power of the Law also bespeaks its helplessness. It smashes because it cannot win. "The wages of sin is death." That is the Law, and it is the height of the Law's triumph. To secure obedience is an infinitely greater victory than to administer penalty, but what is this penalty but a perpetual evidence to the conflict of Law and human nature?[8] If that is not the fundamental problem that Paul sets himself in Romans, what is? Paul has a solution of it, but that is because he believes in God the Redeemer as well as in God the Creator, and until he came to that belief he was as baffled by the moral problem as every other man is baffled by it in like conditions.

And this law of the harvest, which the mere theist depends upon as adequate, only adds to the problem because it works with such vast injustice. "Who sinned, this man or his parents, that he was born blind?" might have been at one time an excuse for much casuistry, which explains why Jesus pushed it aside as he did; yet it is solemn truth that most babies who are born blind *are* blind because of ancestral sin. It is a rare thing that the harvest of corruption is confined to those who did the sowing. Heritage has to do with evil just as much as with good. Again let it be said that the solidarity which spreads the harvest of evil also spreads the harvest of good. "The second Adam" answers to "the first Adam," and the principle which makes the one possible makes possible the other also. But the very necessity of "the second Adam" grows out of the permanent destructiveness of the principle of "the first Adam" when it is met by no check.[9]

This needful check can nowhere be found by the man who makes no place in his faith for God the Redeemer. What Saul of Tarsus could not do, in that he was weak through the flesh, no other man is likely to do! In a word, each successive generation of men re-enacts the moral tragedy—tragedy because it ends in defeat. The lessons of the past are palpable, and men would fain learn them, but the seeds of corruption are sown none the less, and none the less is the harvest reaped.

It has been the habit in many quarters in recent years to make merry over "the hoary dogma" of original sin. Readily enough one admits that many extravagances have been associated with the expression, interpretation, and application of the dogma, even to the point of graphic descriptions of hell as "paved" with the souls of unbaptized infants. The mediaeval theory of the *limbus infantum*, the abode of the infants, accepted even by Thomas Aquinas, at least has the merit of denying that unbaptized infants *consciously* suffered. One sometimes wishes that the impatient critics of the doctrine of "natural depravity" would take the trouble to acquaint themselves with what the doctrine really means.[10] Perhaps the same observation should be made of many of those who profess to *accept* the doctrine!

One may speak of "The Foredoomed Man" without thereby implying that man is fore-damned.[11] The fact that man is "doomed," by the very conditions of his existence, to sinfulness, does not carry with it as its proper corollary that he is "doomed to go to hell," whether he will or not. At least, it does not carry that corollary for those who believe in God the Redeemer. What those must say about it who believe only in God the Creator, and who must admit therefore that God simply creates and perpetuates sinful creatures, is for themselves to say. It is much to be hoped that somewhere along their line of reasoning they will be profoundly inconsistent!

Certainly if there is any one truth about man which is more

truly "empiric" than any other, it is just this truth of his fundamental moral anarchy—and what does "original sin" or "natural
depravity" mean but just this? "The heart of man is desperately
wicked." That *can* be nothing but an empty form of words. Or a
man, even a "good" man, may on occasion apply it to himself with
complete sincerity, especially when he realizes what evil thoughts
he is capable of entertaining and to what forbidden fruit he can turn
his longing eyes. "Man was born free," so runs Rousseau's famous
sentence, "and everywhere he is in chains." The chains, so far as
Rousseau himself is concerned, certainly do not need to be denied!
Of all the men who boasted of their freedom, he was one of the most
enchained. What he might better have written is: "Man was born
in chains, and his task is to find emancipation." Perhaps one of the
great ironies of our time is the fact that just as the theologians,
assisted by the educational theorists, had succeeded in ridding
theology of the alleged incubus of "natural depravity," the psychologists began to bring it back, and to bring it back with a lurid
descriptiveness which makes even the *Confessions* of Augustine appear commonplace. If the *libido* is really what it is said to be, then
of a truth, "there is none good, no, not one." Nevertheless, the
creationist must still affirm his creed: "Man is made in the image of
God."

He would be dull indeed who was conscious of no problem here.
One can easily understand the vogue of naturalism among those
who seek to ease its pressure. Get rid of God; surrender the whole
idea of purpose in creation; see man as simply the issue of a process
in itself inexplicable; account for every ethical conception as orig-
inating in a social necessity, and as having only social significance;
trace all moral struggle, all aspiration after "the better," to the
operation of impersonal natural law; explain all standards as
"ghosts," and all supposition of their authority as evidence of
"numinous fear"—do this, and the problem is enormously
simplified.

Sellars, arguing for the necessity the modern man is under of
giving up "a Cosmic Companion," meaning by that giving up God
as he has always been understood in Christianity, mentions as one
of the "compensations" of the loss that it "robs the universe of

some of the supernatural terrors which frightened men and women not so many years ago."[12] It is hardly fair to imply that this has been a chief result of the Christian belief in God; and in any event, how many passed beyond that terror into a strength of purpose, a reverence for truth, a devotion to other men, and a deep inward peace which they would not have known but for "the moral crisis" engendered of seeing themselves as sinful in the light of the Holy God.

Belief in the Holy God has not been sheer loss from *any* angle. From the angle of life as a serious business, shot through with great obligation, freighted with a more than temporal meaning, it has been exactly what the situation called for—and it would be difficult to show that where the belief in such a God has been surrendered, the situation is being met more effectively. But in so far as naturalism is able to retain the idea of "sin," it is as something merely anti-social, and the corollary follows that "the good life" is the life which has undergone the most complete social adjustment.[13] One wonders why it never occurs to the persons who take this position that the society to which the individual is to adjust himself may itself need adjustment. It is all very well to define goodness as communalism, but what about the communal ideals themselves? Are these to be held to be impeccable? Are they to be subject to no criticism? And if an individual arises who does subject to criticism his community, and who calls upon it to come into line with *his* insights, are these insights then to be esteemed anti-social and therefore destructive? Is it not a fact that it is always an individual who is the most effective community critic? Hocking's theory of the "recommender" as a product of society whereby society "lifts itself by its own bootstraps," shows his accustomed insight, but it still makes it impossible to find ultimate authority in any social group.[14] Yet when is society more impatient of criticism than when it has gotten rid of "supernatural sanctions," and set itself on the throne of the universe?

The modern emergence of nationalism as both a religion and a theory of state-absolutism is the proper logic of a naturalism which has abandoned all belief in a creative God. If the anti-social is the sinful then the good life is the life which uncritically submits itself to an arbitrarily imposed regimentation. Solve the moral problem by getting rid of God? But unfortunately those who make this proposal do not get rid of God at all. All they do is to exchange one God for another; and their new God proves to be much more arbitrary and much less adequate than the God whom they dethroned—and dethroned for no other reason than the desire to see "nature" as a process wholly self-contained, self-sufficient and self-explaining.

There are, however, those who do not solve the problem in this way. They do sincerely believe in God the Creator. They are aware of the difficulties for theistic belief arising from the dark facts we have been considering. They are under no illusion as to the reality of sin. But the whole idea of "revealed truth" impresses them as irrational. Even their belief in God to begin with is due to their reading of nature and history, and they read Scripture according to this other reading. That the whole scheme of things, and in particular the movement of life, has revelational significance— this they can believe. But just because they believe this, they see no ground for anything more. Both the history of the moral sentiments and the history of religion they regard as falling within the scope of that process whereby alone God can be made known.[15] They show a due appreciation of the great ethical teachers and the great religious geniuses of the race. They have no difficulty in including Jesus Christ in the number of these, perchance even esteeming him as the greatest. The incredibly patronizing rhapsody addressed by Renan to Jesus on the Cross, they could without difficulty approve.[16] But the tremendous claim which relates our Lord specifically to God the Creator as a new expression of the same Will which expressed itself in creation, and which affirms the purpose of the new creation to be the introduction into the old of precisely that power of re-creative and redemptive love which the old so demonstrably lacks—this claim, the very heart of Christianity, they reject.

The reasons for the rejection are various, but they spring in general from a pre-conceived philosophy in which such a claim can find no possible place. Once again, man makes himself "the meas-

ure of all things." What he can "understand"—this can be. What
he cannot "understand"—this cannot be.

This refusal, however, does very much more than simply dis-
integrate the Christian religion as historically understood. It
destroys all certainty respecting the character of God as a God of
Holy Love—and let us not forget that we are now referring to
those who claim to believe in just such a God as this. The Christian claim is that there is a point in our history possessed of absolute moral and religious value. It is the point at which are concen-
tered and made manifest in personal form, and that form Jesus
Christ, the ultimate character and the ultimate purpose of the
Creator. This is not merely a bare affirmation, with no experience
of any kind to support it, and with no good reasons which make it
intelligible. Some of these reasons have been stated already. As for
the rest, human experience sufficiently demonstrates that a miracle
of transformation, even of re-creation, does in fact occur in any life
which completely gives itself to this great truth of Christ, and to all
that it implies.

With this truth denied, however, mankind is still in the dark in
just those matters concerning which light is so ardently desired. It
is true that we still have the pronouncements of the prophets, the
insights of the seers, the intuitions of the mystics; but it is also true
that *these remain in the region of human guesses* apart from that authentication which they acquire from the fact that in Christ "the
Word became flesh." If there is no ultimate difference between
Jesus Christ and the great souls of our race, then we have no way
of validating human aspiration, and we have no sure ground for believing that the human story will ever be anything but tragic. It is
only when we make Christ more than others that we can make
these others what we would fain have them be—voices bespeaking
the one great authentic Voice.

What are all voices but voices crying in the wilderness unless the
heralded Lamb—"the Lamb of God that beareth and taketh away
the sin of the world"—become an actuality? In what way are Moses
or Isaiah or Socrates or Confucius or Gautama or Zarathustra degraded by being made inferior to Christ when the very superiority
that is assigned to him results not in making these others of no ac-

count, but rather in vindicating them as bearers of the truth? By being related to an actual Perfection, they are vindicated even in their imperfection. We see them as beams of that Eternal Beam whose fulness came in Christ and made him the Light of the World. In what other way can their vindication proceed? On what other ground can we possibly believe in alleged "revelations," even those conveyed in the Old Testament, much more those conveyed in the ethnic faiths, than on this ground—that we are confronted in Christ with one supreme and final Revelation? Secure him, and all else is secure. Deny him, and all else collapses. If we have no truth but relative truth, how are we to know that we have any truth at all? "Give me a place to rest my lever," cried Archimedes, "and I will move the world." Give us but one absolute standard of measurement, and we can measure every claimant for control over our life and thought.

> " 'Twas August, and the fierce sun overhead
> Smote on the squalid streets of Bethnal Green,
> And the pale weaver, through his windows seen
> In Spitalfields, look'd thrice dispirited.
> I met a preacher there I knew, and said:
> 'Ill and o'erworked, how fare you in this scene?'
> 'Bravely!' said he; 'for I of late have been
> Much cheered with thoughts of Christ, the living bread.'
> O human soul! as long as thou canst so
> Set up a mark of everlasting light,
> Above the howling senses' ebb and flow,
> To cheer thee, and to right thee if thou roam—
> Not with lost toil thou laborest through the night!
> Thou mak'st the heaven thou hop'st indeed thy home."

Matthew Arnold wrote that. It is not too clear that he had found for himself "a mark of everlasting light," but he at least recognized the human need for such a light—(who, indeed, better than he?)—and could pay fitting tribute to those who walked thereby, and became

> " . . . souls tempered with fire,
> Fervent, heroic, and good,
> Helpers and friends of mankind."

Let us but have Christ as he is presented in the Christian faith, and we have our "mark of everlasting light," our standard of judgment, our pointer set with undeviating stedfastness toward life's invisible but changeless north. Here is Holy Love in suffering but purifying contact with the world's deepest need. Here is a Power adequate to transform any human situation—not only in Bethnal Green, but in the Main Street of Middletown, in the East Side slum, in the Riverside mansion, in the college campus, in the drab mining village, in the halls of council. Here is a form of Personal Life against which the demonic forces of the world ranged themselves to destroy it—and out of the dreadful impact emerges the Cross, a monument to a Life that failed. But so also is there here a form of Personal Life which transformed the victory of these demonic forces into a victory for the Victim—and the Cross becomes the prelude to the majestic music of the Resurrection. And this Life which the Cross could not destroy but only authenticate, and whose indestructibility Resurrection does so astoundingly attest, is operative in untold ways in the world to-day, and we call it the Holy Spirit. That Life which was Christ is forever integrated with the structure of existence: wherefore, if Francis Thompson may be paraphrased, though this Life is Invisible, we see it; though it is Intangible, we touch it; though it is Unknowable, we know it; though it is Inapprehensible, we grasp it. Closer than our breathing; nearer than our hands and feet.

> " 'Tis ye, 'tis your estrangèd faces,
>   That miss the many-splendored thing."

Such a Life as is meant by the phrase, "the Living Christ," responds as surely to the venture of faith as light responds to the opening of the eye.

All about us is a world, but we become aware of it only because we meet the conditions which the world itself prescribes if it is to be known. Seeing comes of looking, and something to be seen is presupposed in the seeing. Hearing comes of listening, and something to be heard is presupposed in the hearing. Congruity is involved in all experience. There is necessary mutuality between experiencing subject and experienced fact. It is what Spinoza meant when he said that every *idea* has its *ideatum.* "Idea" involves something "ideated." When separate things are brought together in a unity, implied in the unity is the capacity of the separate things to be so united.[17] Did not even Schopenhauer realize that if it was true that the world was adapted to be the home of living creatures, these creatures were just as truly adapted to make the world their home? It is the tremendous fact of congruity, and it is basic to the ongoing of life.

But then, in the famous figure of Sir Thomas Browne, man is an "amphibium," adapted to more than one sort of world. "Thus is man that great and true Amphibium whose Nature is disposed to live, not only like other creatures, in diverse Elements, but in divided and distinguished worlds." Joseph Needham, quoting the words, comments that it belongs to us to live in different worlds at one time.[18] There is one world in respect of which man is a Machine. There is another world in respect of which man is an Organism or a Personality. There is a third world in respect of which man is "a Child of God and an Inheritor of the City of Heaven." Man is not each of these in turn, but at the same time. These three worlds do not exist successively: they co-exist. It is Sir Thomas Browne's notion of the "General Concourse." Existence has at least three patterns, the three just mentioned, and man is related to each of them: better still, he and they are "germane" to each other.

The great question for the Christian is as to whether there is between the human soul and the Living Christ a fundamental mutuality. That is to say, does Christ represent and embody that "third world" recognized by Needham? Is Christ "meant" for me? Am I "meant" for him? The Christian can give only one answer, and the answer is implied in Tertullian's saying, *Anima naturaliter Christiana.* There is a sense in which Christ is as real as the things we see, as real as the things we hear. "Each in his own order." Christianity stands or falls with the belief in "orders of reality" which, with all their differences, yet make up one "General Concourse," the whole finding its unity in the will and purpose of God on the one hand, and in the diverse capacities of man on the other.

In other words, "the testimony of Christian experience" is not to be lightly brushed aside as something having no objective reference, just because it can be "explained away" by the skillful psychologist. So far as that is concerned, psychology and philosophy can combine to reduce to illusion the deepest certainties of the souls of men. "Philosophy may clip an angel's wings," was the sad truth learned by Keats' "Youth of Corinth," as he watched the passing of his castle of dreams. It may do more than that: it may show that in actual fact there were no wings in the first place to clip. Man is a creature of earth, meant to crawl; not a fallen spirit meant to fly. If "wings at his shoulders seem to play" as he stands with Wordsworth "On an Evening of Extraordinary Splendor," and, while "the beamy radiance" seems to strike a highway from earth to heaven, feels the lure of

> "Those bright steps that heavenward raise
> Their practicable way."

—if this be so, that, he is assured by those whose main business is to make life drab, and to include even the rainbow in "the dull catalogue of common things," is only so much unrestrained and indefensible fancy. Not "clouds of glory" but mud-caked feet the better bespeak his origin—and his destiny! One feels sympathy with the mood of the youthful Clough:

> "Away, haunt thou not me,
> Thou vain Philosophy!
> Little hast thou bestead,
> Save to perplex the head,
> And leave the spirit dead.
> Unto thy broken cisterns wherefore go,
> While from the secret treasure-depths below,
> Fed by the skiey shower,
> And clouds that sink and rest on hill-tops high,
> Wisdom at once, and Power,
> Are welling, bubbling forth, unseen, incessantly?
> Why labor at the dull mechanic oar,
> When the fresh breeze is blowing,
> And the strong current flowing,
> Right onward to the Eternal Shore?"

That, happily, is not the whole truth about philosophy, although Clough's protest is well taken. The true philosopher is still, as Plato reminded the men of his day, "a lover of wisdom," and he only is truly wise to whom it has been given,

"Through love, through hope, and faith's transcendent dower,"

to feel and to make the rest of us feel "that we are greater than we know." When men, speaking in the name of philosophy, undertake to get rid of God, and of creative purpose, and of moral authority, and of Eternal Love, and of those noble dreams which serve to make tolerable the human lot, it does not at all follow that the case is closed. Other men, speaking in that same august name, may reasonably retain every one of these. Any authentic human experience is proper data for philosophy, and while the experience may in various ways be robbed of its significance, there will be those who, if the experience appears to be really authentic, will insist upon its voice being heard.

The claim here being made is that the Christian testimony is worth considering as offering a clue to the nature and purpose of human existence. Certainly there is a profound congruity between the Christian belief concerning Christ and the character of the experience which the belief creates. It is not so much that we would move from the experience to Christ, vindicating *him* through *it*, as that we would move from Christ to the experience, vindicating *it* through *him*. That is to say, that type of experience which calls for Christ as present fact is only possible to those who already believe about him what he is claimed to be in the Christian tradition.

This does not necessarily mean believing the dogmatic construction of which he has been the subject. But it does mean believing that about him which the dogmatic construction is an attempt to preserve. One of the great illusions of recent years, from which the so-called evangelical churches are just beginning to recover, is that there can be something called "Christian experience" existing in almost complete separation from any body of belief, and that this detached experience is self-authenticating.[19]

"So long as your experience is sound, it does not matter what you believe." But an experience which is not itself tied to truth and reality can be nothing but a form of self-hypnosis. Of course, if by "experience" is meant only a subjective state, all that is needed is a technique that induces it—and one wonders whether the renewed interest in ritual does not indicate just this. A man on a slowly-sinking ship may in complete disregard of the actual situation cultivate the "experience" of security, but his state of mind is not going to keep the ship afloat. A valid experience calls for relevant facts. A Christian experience which implies, shall we say, the love of God, and the reality of Jesus Christ, and the presence of the Holy Spirit, requires that these things shall be actually believed to be so.

But more than that, it requires that what is believed shall also be actual truth. It ought to be self-evident that *if what is believed is not so, then the experience arising from the belief has no ultimate validity.* The so-called "authority of experience" must rest finally on the validity of that which makes the experience possible. This means that there is a deeper authority than that of experience in the sense just indicated—the authority of the truth itself. To say that *all* truth comes by experience is simply not so. Some truth is "given," and then what experience does is to support the "given" truth. So far as the Christian faith is concerned, it rests itself on the authority of a truth which is offered to us as "revelation." If I accept the reality of God and the character of God and the purposes of God as these are made known in Scripture, and supremely in Jesus Christ, and as they are continued in the testimony of the Church to which they gave birth—if I do this, then it is clear that I have an experience in proportion to the sincerity and completeness of my acceptance of them. But it is also clear that my experience is real and illusory only in proportion to the truth of that to which I commit myself. The experience may indeed strengthen my conviction as to the truth of what I have accepted; but unless, so to speak, the truth is true already, true in its own right, true if no single person ever accepted it, then how can my experience of itself *make it true*?

Christian experience is dependable only in the measure of the dependability of the prior Christian truth. This truth, in the nature of the case, is not a human discovery, but a disclosure from God himself. On this single claim Christianity must eventually rest its case, if it is to be anything more than a temporary pragmatism in an arena of historical relativities. Briefly, the authority of Christian experience is the authority of Christian truth, and the authority of Christian truth is the authority of the Christian revelation.

The believer in God the Creator who "cannot" believe in God the Redeemer, and who by his unbelief of the one and his belief of the other, only deepens his perplexity in the face of a frank appraisal of the facts of life, may still hear a Voice which says: "I have set before thee an open door"—and this is the open door.

CHAPTER 9

The Spirit of Anti-Christ

"WE HAVE A GOODLY HERITAGE." HOW GOODLY, HAS ALREADY BEEN described. One has but to compare the Christian heritage in respect of the truth it brings concerning God, and the world, and man, with the heritage of belief where Christian truth has not penetrated, to realize to what high honor we have been all undeservedly "elected." The sense of destiny that characterized Jeremiah, and Paul, and Augustine, and John Calvin was due to their seeing in the events of their own lives the working of the will of God. They did not *begin* with the doctrine of Divine Sovereignty: they eventually *came upon it* as the only way of making intelligible their own experience. "Before thou camest forth out of the womb I sanctified thee" (Jeremiah 1. 5) would have expressed the conviction of them all.[1]

Such a judgment must necessarily be intensely personal: not something that one says about another (for that would imply a doctrine of fatalism), but something that one says about oneself. What did any one of us ever do to determine that from the moment of his birth he should be continually subject to the impact of a body of truth and of the social influences traceable to that truth which has served as a prophylactic against more evils than he can possibly imagine?

> "Thousands of heroes fought and fell
> That Homer in the end might tell."

What has it required just to make me possible—and you? If in the total "me" or "you" are included Christian belief and Christian experience, the question is still more one to be pondered.

There is no belief in God comparable to the Christian belief. There is no belief concerning the origin, the character, and the

purpose of the world comparable to the Christian belief. There is no
belief concerning man and his absolute value comparable to the
Christian belief.[2] Those of us who have been born into the circle of
Christianity, and who take for granted that which lies so close to
our hand, rarely if ever realize that we need a doctrine of election
and foreordination just as much as the Apostle Paul did when he
looked back over the course of his life.[3] "Life," said Pascal, "is an
incomprehensible mystery."

How can it be that I am at all, and that I am where I am and
what I am? The question is often asked by a meditative child: it is a
pity that as we grow older, sophistication is likely to destroy in us
this sense of wonder. We think we account for everything by the
ambiguous phrase, "the accidents of birth." But to the man who
has thoroughly Christianized his view of life, there is no such thing.
In the Christian view, the determining factor in all history is the
exigencies of the divine purpose. Aristotle saw the "end" as the
"final cause" of the process that led to it, and the principle cannot
be questioned.[4] Whatever freedom there is, is the freedom called
for by God's purpose. Whatever non-freedom there is—and there
is very much—is to be accounted for in the same way. No man
can use his freedom in suchwise that he finally defeats God. Even if
a soul should be at last "lost," it is lost because God's purpose
makes it possible. This is not to say that God *wills* that a soul shall
be lost. "He is not willing that any should perish, but that all
should come to repentance."[5] But it is to say that there can be no
result for which God has not provided, and lost souls are a possibility under conditions which God himself has laid down. Human
freedom is divinely determined both as to the *fact* of it, and as to
the *limits* of it, and also as to its *contributary significance* for the pro-
motion of God's ends.[6] It was not of one's freedom that one
entered into the possibility of enjoying the experience of the
Christian heritage, any more than it was of the freedom of one's
pagan brother on the other side of the world that he did not enter
into it. What one shall finally do with the possibility is, indeed,
a matter that is in one's own hands—at least, it is to some extent;
although it is useless for a man to suppose that the circumstance of
his having been born into a time and place in which Christian truth

was recognized and applied is a circumstance whose influence he can entirely escape.[7] How much does the avowed contemporary enemy of Christian truth owe to the truth he is attacking? The very university in which he was trained may well have been founded by the Christian Church, and its intellectual freedom and ethical idealism have been kept alive by the same influence. Any one of us is a point at which ten thousand lines converge. Among those converging lines is Christian truth and what it has accomplished in the past. Let us not be so arrogant as to deny that the fact has any connection with the purpose of God!

> "He fixed thee 'mid this dance
> Of plastic circumstance."

And if he fixed you *here*, then he fixed him *there*—and that holds if the "him" is the veriest pagan, and the "there" the most benighted spot on this earth. Nothing can be as it is save for the ultimate fact that makes all things possible. If this ultimate fact be a Living God such as is declared in the Christian faith, then there is always hope.

This whole question of his heritage, therefore, as has already been pointed out, is for the Christian a question of providence.[8] But it is more than that: it is a question also of obligation and responsibility. Of Sir Belvedere, weighted with the burden of the dying king, it was written,

> "He heard a deep behind him, and a cry before."[9]

Behind any man there is a "deep," the incalculable wealth of divine largess and of human achievement of which he is in greater or lesser measure (how often lesser!) the heir. Before any man there sounds a "cry," and he is as surely vassal to the future whence that cry arises as he is beneficiary of the past that makes him. How much more so if the man is a Christian!

> "What entered into thee,
> *That* was, is, and shall be:
> Time's wheel runs back or stops:
> Potter and clay endure."

If I am so bold as to say that it is of the purpose of God that I came into the Christian heritage of a great revelation, and if I am so bold as to say that it is of the purpose of God that others so far did not, I must also be so bold as to say that the heritage which has so richly blessed me is held in trust for as wide a dissemination as I can possibly bring about. God has done something for me which he has not yet done for many others, but he has done it for me in order that it might also be done for these others. These are not mere commonplace observations. They are the inescapable logic of Christian truth. They constitute the principle of the perpetuation and expansion of the Christian Church. Their practical application is the one sure guarantee of the only apostolic succession that profoundly matters.[10]

We can make no secret of the fact, however, that what has been set forth above as the body of revealed truth which is the essence of Christianity is to-day under persistent attack even in the lands where it is best known, and where in the past it has achieved its greatest triumphs. The confessed Christian may take his faith for granted: he is repeatedly made aware of the fact that all around him are many who do nothing of the sort. It is surely not without significance that a book can be written in our day entitled *The War Against God*—written by two devoted Churchmen who deplore the fact about which they write, but whose documentation of their thesis is devastating in what it indicates. Few will dispute the related claim made by Visser t'Hooft in *None Other Gods*, that in the Western world, once called Christendom, Christianity is rapidly becoming "a minority affair." The simple truth is that implicit in the fact of Christ is the fact of anti-Christ.[11] If, in view of what was said above, it be ironically suggested that even anti-Christ is of the purpose of God, the irony can be ignored, and the suggestion itself accepted as solemn truth.

"Why rush the discords in, but that harmony might prevail?"

The world is an arena wherein great forces contend for the mastery. It was into such an arena that God at divers times and in various manners slowly insinuated the truth about himself until "the fulness of the time was come," when, like a diviner Telemachus, he appeared in that arena in the person of his own Son, in a Life that was also a Word and a Deed, in a climactic episode that was Holy Love's incarnation, its tragic defeat, its glorious coronal. The Word was made flesh. The truth of God was embodied in a Life. In "a Face like to mine" the Face of God showed through the veil that time hangs over eternity, and the Face was marred, marred by hands that smote it. But infinitely more eloquent were those still deeper lines by which that Face expressed the holy and suffering love of the infinite heart of the God whose Face it was.

The truth that sets men free was no casual intrusion into a world taking its ease. The truth that sets men free was born of travail. The sword that pierced through Mary's heart was symbolic and prophetic.

> "The seven-thorned briar and the palm seven-leaved
> Are her great sorrow and her great reward."[12]

Symbolic and prophetic too were "the great drops of blood" that were for evermore to transform Gethsemane into what Robertson Nicoll once so aptly called "the Rose Garden of the Lord." One might almost say with the author of the Epistle to the Hebrews that "without the shedding of blood" nothing great comes and nothing great is kept. We can have no least reason for supposing that it was of the intent of God that the Christian heritage should automatically propagate and perpetuate itself. There can be no *laissez faire* where God's purposes are at stake. "My Father worketh hitherto, and I work"—and we must work, for the night cometh. When those who share in the heritage grow careless about it, by the amount of their carelessness the heritage is endangered. It is the law of the spiritual that we keep only as we give. By much tribulation did God enter the stream of our human life, to give its movement a new direction, and it is only by much tribulation that the new direction can be maintained.

For there is always an enemy. There is that in existence which is challenged to the death by Christian truth: wherefore is Christian truth also challenged to the death by this alien thing. It is what has already been referred to as anti-Christ. Bergson finds that life is always met by an opposing force which threatens life, would fain destroy it, and yet by the very opposition serves the purposes of life. It is true that Bergson offers this primarily as a metaphysical

theory, but the principle bears obviously on mankind's spiritual
progress, and this too Bergson recognizes. Berdyaev's view of
what he calls "meonic freedom," by which he means a primal
principle of opposition with which God has continually to reckon,
is definitely applied by him to man's moral problem—and, indeed,
to the work of Christ himself.[13] Anti-Christ is not a *being*, not even
a metaphysical entity, except in so far as the principle of negation
may be so described. The propriety, perhaps even the necessity, of
dramatizing the opposing power, and describing it under a personal
form, as is done so often in Scripture, and, indeed, throughout the
whole of Christian history—this is not to be questioned. It were
better that one believe tremendously in the Devil, and so keep
vivid before one's mind "the mystery of iniquity," than that one
should lightly wave the mystery aside by relegating the Devil to
the limbo of exploded myths. In the end, however, anti-Christ becomes effective by corrupting the hearts, perverting the wills,
and enchaining the minds of men.

This corruption and perversion is empiric fact, no matter how we
may seek to account for it. The modern re-discovery of the truth of
Original Sin has made us realize once again where the core of our
difficulty lies. We are all, says Jung, "statistical criminals," although the truth could better be expressed by the phrase "constitutionally sinful."[14] The difficulty lies with ourselves. It lies with the
manner of creatures we are. The great moralists have constructed
their systems on the assumption that the "ought" (the Moral
Law) and the "can" (the moral will) are equations. To the imperative and inevitable "Thou must" is made, with a like inevitability,
the reply "I can." A pure science of ethics could hardly take any
other ground than this. And yet in actual fact it is not so. Kant
himself insisted that man could be proper subject of a moral absolute only as it also belonged to him to be able to respond; but under
the sheer demand of human experience itself he admitted the presence of "a radical defect" in human nature which at one and the
same time left the moral absolute intact while yet making perfect
obedience to it impossible.[15]

Was there ever such a paradox? And is it not the very truth of
life? Every student knows by what painful and devious argument

Kant endeavored to extricate his moral idealism from this dilemma. *The reality of this dilemma is the great postulate of Christianity*. For it means original sin. It means that the heart which in the purpose of God is to become the throne of Christ is already the throne of anti-Christ. Adam lost his moral battle at the first encounter, and therein he is the type of us all. Christ never comes to a heart to find it swept and garnished—which is exactly why he needs to come! It is occupied before he gets there. He stands at the door, and knocks, and too often the knock is not heard because of the revelry within. "How can one enter into the house of the strong man, and spoil his goods, except he first bind the strong man? and then he will spoil his house" (Matthew 12. 29). The "strong man" (the power of evil) had been in possession of a human life, and Jesus had cast him out.

Always must there be a dispossession before there can be a new possession. The limitation on Tertullian's familiar saying, *Anima naturaliter Christiana*, has already been remarked. The soul is not naturally Christian save as one thinks in terms of the ideal. It is true that the Gospel of Christ and the human soul are mutualities. The Gospel is meant for man and man is meant for the Gospel. But what is this Gospel? It is a remedy, and a remedy implies disease. It is a life-line, and a life-line implies a soul in danger. "Original sin is foolishness to men," wrote Pascal, in one of his famous *Thoughts*, "but it is given out as such. You should not reproach me with the want of reason in this doctrine, since I give it out as being without reason. But this foolishness is wiser than all the wisdom of men, *sapientius est hominibus*. For without this, what will it be said that man is? His whole condition depends upon this imperceptible point. And how could he have discovered this by his reason, seeing that it is a thing above his reason, and that his reason, very far from discovering it by itself, revolts from it when it is presented to it? . . . For myself, I confess that as soon as the Christian religion discovers the principle that human nature is corrupted and fallen from God, this opens our eyes to see everywhere the character of this truth: for nature is such, that it everywhere indicates a God lost, both in man and out of man, and a corrupt nature."[16]

The Gospel speaks to a human situation whose very essence is

tragedy, although it at the same time reveals both the root whence
the tragedy springs and the means whereby it may be left behind.
That this tragedy may exist, and be known to exist, and yet create
no particular disturbance in a man's soul, is to be admitted. That
only shows how deep the tragedy is! "The carefree butterfly may
preach contentment to the writhing toad—which is evidence of the
butterfly's own tragedy! What greater tragedy than the tragedy of
not knowing how compact of the tragic life is and must be! The
publican at least knew the truth about himself, and so was by way of
moving 'beyond tragedy'; but the Pharisee, thanking God that he
was 'not as other men,' was only announcing how much like
other men he actually was."[17]

What can be more tragic than to look out upon the human scene
and observe only the comic? Nobody is going to be very much concerned about original sin or any other kind of sin until he sees
himself, in the words of Kierkegaard, "a solitary individual,"
standing over against the law of a Holy God. Conviction of sin is
not merely the painful awareness that I did this or that particular
thing and that I ought not to have done it. Conviction of sin is the
terrorizing realization that I did what I did because of a fundamental anarchism constitutive of my very being. Through me and
in me that which ought not to be has come to be. I create what I
hate.

That anarchism, however, may express itself otherwise than
in so many deeds. It may express itself in an intellectual pride and
in an assumed self-sufficiency which erect a barrier against Christian truth the most difficult it can be called upon to encounter. One
must not sit in judgment upon one's fellows. "One is your Judge,
even God," and that suffices. But it is nevertheless true that the unreserved acceptance of that truth of God which is enshrined in the
Christian revelation calls for an initial act of surrender which the
very constitution of human nature only serves to make difficult.

Those early Christian theologians who followed the Greek
tradition were wont to speak of the Gospel as the means whereby
"grace completed nature." Clement of Alexandria, in *The In-
structor*, frequently compares Christ to a physician, whose function it is to restore to health. "The Word has been called also the

Saviour, seeing he has found out for men those rational medicines which produce vigor of the senses and salvation; and devotes himself to watching for the favorable moment . . . supplying all the antidotes of salvation to those who are diseased."[18] In the same writing, Clement has much to say about the "reasonableness" of Christianity. "Christian conduct is the operation of the rational soul in accordance with a correct judgment and aspiration after the truth, which attains its destined end through the body, the soul's consort and ally. Virtue is a will in conformity to God and Christ in life, rightly adjusted to life everlasting. For the life of Christians, in which we are now trained, is a system of reasonable actions— that is, of those things taught by the Word—an unfailing energy which we have called faith. The system is the commandments of the Lord, which, being divine statues and spiritual counsels, have been written for ourselves, being adapted for ourselves and our neighbors."[19]

This is well enough, and, with proper reservations, could be accepted. But it still remains that one of the great problems respecting the moral life is *how to convince men that they need help*. Only the sick have need of a physician—but what if they will not admit the need? It also remains that only those who have already accepted the Christian faith realize in what sense it is "reasonable." Those on the outside find their chief objection to the faith at this very point: for them, its "reasonableness" is something yet to be "proved." What was called the "mutuality" of Christ and the human soul has already been set forth, and from this standpoint, grace does indeed "complete" nature. But no kind of reasoning can get around the initial difficulty—the fact that there is that in man which "disposes" him against the truth of Christianity. It is simply not so, that it is "easy to be a Christian," if by "easy" is meant something that comes to us "naturally." Involved here is something to be *believed*, something to be *accepted*, something to be *done*, something to *be*, and at every point there is that in us which creates a difficulty. What we so easily take for granted as seeming to be a part of the natural order stands in the way of what we are called upon to accept.

Clement is right in his thought that Christianity is directed to the restoration of our human nature, *but the very human nature which* *needs the restoration creates the obstacle to the restoration taking place.* Is it that the God who made us left something out of us, and that what he left out constitutes his defeat—and ours? But again is it that this is but the intended means to a still greater triumph for God— and for ourselves—if we will but have it so? The crux of the difficulty is in that "will." Suppose we will not! And if we will not, God cannot: by that much has God enlarged his own task. "He has made us for himself": so far we agree with Augustine. But he has also made us so that we may choose to dispense with him, as many do, and go on our way incomplete—"half men" for ever, because without God no man comes to his stature. Andrea del Sarto, "the faultless painter," contemplating the failure which he knows lies at the heart of his success like a worm in the bud, thus soliloquizes:

> "Incentives come from the soul's self:
> The rest avails not . . .
> In this world, who can do a thing, will not;
> And who would do it, cannot, I perceive:
> Yet the will's somewhat—somewhat, too, the power—
> And thus we half-men struggle."

God has made us for the enthronement of Christ, but anti-Christ— called by whatever other name one wishes—must first be dethroned.

But how came anti-Christ to be in possession? That is the question of questions. Did we ourselves admit him to that inner shrine which is life's central core? We did not. We found that he was already there! Grace completing nature? Shall we not rather say, grace reversing the very direction of nature? But that reversal can proceed only with our nature's consent—and how shall our nature consent to its own destruction, as it would seem! That in actual fact the destruction would not be destruction at all, but rather completion, is the blessed truth. But how shall that truth make its appeal and achieve its own vindication when the initial step which must be taken to make this possible is just the step which can most easily and most naturally and most plausibly be refused?

Nobody would deny that there is a quite general appreciation and acceptance of what might be called the by-products of Christianity, but Christianity cannot long live on its by-products. These by-products are not accidental: they spring from fundamental causes. The fruit of any tree is the evidence of its vitality, but the vitality must be maintained if the fruit is to continue. The Christian ethic grows out of the Christian Gospel, and the supposition that the ethic will continue after the creative Gospel itself shall have ceased to function is just one more of those optimisms by which men have ever been wont to deceive themselves. The heavier the Christian demand, the more imperative the need of an underlying Christian support.[20]

But such a support involves a belief, a belief about God and about Jesus Christ, the very belief which it is the chief business of the Christian Church to proclaim. It has already been shown how essential is this belief to any real Christian experience. Yet it is this belief that is increasingly the point of attack. May we state the case rather drastically, and say that from the standpoint of the claim that the Christian revelation is an absolute, so-called "original sin" has for one of its manifestations and evidences not only palpable moral failure here and there, but also an intellectual attitude which will not tolerate that truth which God has revealed to us about himself. In a word, anti-Christ is not only of the heart and will, but also—*and perhaps fundamentally*—of the mind.

There is much concern expressed to-day about the alleged impotence of the Christian Gospel. It is not the Christian Gospel that is impotent: in its entirety the Gospel is "the power of God." The impotence belongs to a Gospel that has been truncated, and it is truncated by men who say in effect that they will accept the Gospel only on their own terms. Such a spirit bespeaks anti-Christ regnant. Usually this spirit is said to arise from "the demands of reason." Perhaps so. But it may yet be true that reason's most rational act consists in a voluntary abdication at the behest of a truth whose majesty, once apprehended, admits of no denial. Faith is not reason, but only a rational being can exercize faith, and only a rational being can offer a rational vindication of that act which carries it beyond the discernible limits of reason itself. Every man has to make Christianity true *for himself* before he can see wherein its truth finally consists.

The intellectual atmosphere of our time, however, has created a tremendous presupposition against Christianity, *considered now as a body of belief*, being true. We have witnessed the birth of a new infallibility, the infallibility of human judgment—if, indeed, it is "new." Only that can be held to be true which can be demonstrated, and demonstration must follow a clearly-marked pattern. Judged by the standards of this new court of infallibility, the content of the Christian heritage in respect of definite declarations is ruled out. What is vaguely described as "the Christian spirit" is allowed to be worth some consideration, but the frame-work of truth in which that spirit has until now been set—this is palpably so much sheer credulity. Taking the Christian faith as our standard, therefore, we can but say that man's most distinctive endowment, his rational understanding, may prove to be his greatest enemy. Even reason must stoop to conquer, but it is not in the nature of reason to stoop. No handmaiden she, but rather the queen. But the essence of true queenliness is to retain its rank while still rendering service. Reason is given to sub-serve the ends of life.

What is the great end of the life of man? Does reason know? It does not. Then are we as men in the dark? We are not, unless we refuse to accept the proffered light. But this light, whence comes it? Is it discovery, or is it gift? *It is gift*, a gift to be received, and used, and in the receiving and the using to find—and to find there only— its abundant verification.

Then why not, as wise men, accept the gift? The answer is simple and direct: because everything about us makes the acceptance difficult. Surrender, surrender of mind and heart and will, is implicit in the enjoyment of the gift, but surrender of this kind is mankind's most difficult act. It is difficult just because man is man— made to "rise and stand upon his feet." But he does not stand securely until he has bowed, and he will not bow until he has seen a light from heaven and has heard a voice. And anti-Christ is that in man which holds him from bowing because it holds his eyes from seeing and his ears from hearing.

CHAPTER 10

Scepticism and Revelation

THE ULTIMATE AND PERHAPS INEVITABLE ISSUE OF THE SITUATION just considered is a flat rejection of the idea and fact of revelation. Quite apart from the question whether and in what way God may have spoken elsewhere, Christianity simply cannot maintain itself apart from its claim to represent the will and purpose of God not only uniquely, but also absolutely and finally. *Securus judicat orbis terrarum.* Here is that one form of divine speech and action with reference to which all other alleged forms of the divine speech and action are to be examined and appraised.

Many who are not willing to assent to this claim of what is usually called a "special" revelation are still not without sympathy with the idea of revelation in general. There are even earnest Christians who on philosophical grounds, and especially on the ground of the whole history of religion, find it increasingly difficult to keep the Christian revelation in its traditional centrality. They confess attraction to the claim of a certain speculative philosophy, itself not at all unfriendly to religion, that the movement of existence in space and time is the ongoing revelation of a reality not in space and time.[1] Nature is a word of God. History is a word of God. Conscience is a word of God. Reason is a word of God. All such statements seem to them to have the force almost of the self-evident. Then why ask for more? Why not give ourselves to the deciphering of these "words"? Why confuse the issue by the attempt to introduce some "special" word over and above what is so obvious and so normal?

Apparently it is easy to be a Platonist, and to see in the *Here* a reflection of the *Beyond*, as one sees the mountain summits reflected in the clear waters at their base. That is all simple enough. But it is much more difficult to be a Christian, because Christianity

132

presupposes that the reflection is not only not clear, but that it is confusing, and that if we would know what is so dimly and oftentimes so contradictorily reflected, it can be only on the condition that the veil of temporality be removed sufficiently to give us, for however brief a moment, a direct vision of the eternally Real. And Christianity claims that it is precisely this that has been done,[2] and offers as evidence of the claim Christ himself, with that by which he was adumbrated and that which the unreserved acceptance of him has brought to pass.

This, of course, involves that there has been a communication of truth to men over and above the intellectual, apprehensive, and interpretive processes which are the normal characteristics of human nature. It is declared by many, however, that everything we know about ourselves and our fellows, and about the course of events in the world, is against the probabilities of such a communication ever having been made. The abnormal or the supra-normal, call it which you will, is by that much suspect. A similar suspicion is held to attach to the content of that which is alleged to have come through revelational experience. Either the experience and the content must be held to be of the same general character as those similar claims to revelations which have been made by the oracle, the shaman, the seer, in all parts of the world and among all peoples, in which case the claim to distinctiveness must be surrendered; or, if the claim to distinctiveness is still insisted on, it must be allowed that the content is quite beyond all proof, since a truth that was accessible only to the man who proclaimed it is obviously beyond all verification. It depends on his word alone, and we know enough of the peculiarities of the human mind to be aware of the prevalence of self-hypnosis, self-deception, and the like.

Thus, while we do not need to doubt that Moses *believed* God was speaking to him out of the burning bush, this is no adequate reason why *we* should believe it, or why *we* should believe that what Moses then took God to be is what God actually is, to be accepted therefore on Moses' word alone. We do not need to doubt that the young Isaiah in the Temple at Jerusalem believed he had a vision of God as the Holy One, but the experience was purely psychic, and could have at the most only a personal value: it had its own antecedents, and followed its own proper laws; it entered into the continuing stream of Isaiah's life; but there is no more reason why we should believe in the intellectual content or the theological content that Isaiah read into his experience, as something binding upon our own minds to-day, than it is that we should do so in the case of the experience of Gautama under the Bo-tree or of Muhammed in the cave of Hira. Doubtless, too, the Hebrew people believed, and believed with complete sincerity, that it had been revealed to their remote ancestors that "in the beginning God created the heavens and the earth"; but there is nothing novel in this, since a creation-myth, in one form or another, is practically universal—to say nothing of the high probability that the Hebrew creation narrative was but a borrowing and re-vamping of the creation-myth of the Babylonians—or, as the more recent suggestion is, even of the Egyptians.

Nor do we need any longer to question—so the argument continues—that the New Testament represents the beliefs of the early Christian community—or communities! Very definite things were admittedly believed about Jesus Christ, such as that he was the gift of God; that he came into the world to save it from perishing; that the manner of his coming was miraculous; that mighty works equally with mighty words characterized his presence among men; that after his death he appeared again and again to those who had known him in the days of his flesh, and perchance even to those who had not so known him; that his life and death, read in the light of this fact of his re-appearance with its prior necessity of resurrection, were to be grounded in the very will and purpose of God; that Christ is therefore only properly described when he is called the veritable Son of God, Lord of Life, Mediator between God and men; that therefore even the Eternal God, never before fully self-disclosed, is laid bare to men by Christ as his absolute revelation, yes, even as his personal presence in our sinful world; and that this presence is still continued in the world, directly as the Holy Spirit in the life of the believers, indirectly in the Church conceived as "the extension of the Incarnation."

The informed modern critic no longer doubts that these were the sincere beliefs of the early Church. The evidence that it is so is admitted to be historically unimpeachable, but it is held that the origin and influence of such beliefs are perfectly explicable as so many psychological and sociological phenomena, following patterns whose laws are now well understood, and finding many parallels in the beliefs of religious communities in other parts of the world.[3]

Hence because men believed in the Virgin Birth of Christ; because they believed he wrought miracles; because they believed he rose again from the dead; because they believed that his death had expiatory significance, accomplishing equally something for God and something for men; because they believed that he was both the fulfillment of ancient hopes and dreams and the inexplicable but redemptive and recreative activity of the Holy Love of that same God in whose will all things had their origin—because, in a word, they believed, as the Church came finally to express it, that Jesus Christ was "Very God and Very Man," who came down and suffered and died and rose again for us men and for our salvation, can in nowise be held to bind the modern mind. All may be interesting enough as so many pages in the record of human history, and as so many illustrations of the growth of religious ideas and beliefs. But the claim that such ideas and beliefs must be true because they rest upon and indeed constitute a revelation—this is held to be a begging of the question, and the more so because the ideas and beliefs can be accounted for readily enough quite apart from any supposition of inspiration. Every alleged fact, truth, and belief of this sort must be examined. It must be examined in the light of the history of religion in general. It must be examined in the light of psychology, individual and social. Especially must it be examined in the light of our total body of scientific knowledge, as this has been patiently acquired by the greater and greater extension and application of the scientific method.

So speaks a scepticism which is undoubtedly in most cases honest —and honest any man must be, as much in his doubts and denials as in his confident affirmations. But the sceptic must face his own logic. Under such ruthless critical examination as he proposes, the great bulk of Christian belief, especially as it has to do with certain *events* and their alleged significance as revelations of truth not otherwise accessible to man, collapses. *It is judged by tests which are bound to issue in its rejection.*

God as he is proclaimed in Christianity, the creative God, the purposive God, the God of Holy Love, must be given up, to be replaced by whatever God the emancipated minds of men find themselves able to reconstruct. How fantastic some of these re-constructions are, any man knows who is familiar with the amazing variety of contemporary theistic theories.[4] Christ himself is also given a completely new description and evaluation, and it ranges all the way from "pious myth" to the presentation of him as the supreme "go-getter" of history.[5]

As for sin, understood in Christianity as a barrier between men and God, as a disease affecting all alike, as a dire reality about which God sacrificially did something under the impulse both of his holy nature and of his love for sinful men—this is no longer an intelligible conception: it must be replaced by an explanation cast in biological, psychological, and sociological terms, and when that is done, sin ceases to be an occasion for "supernatural terrors."[6] As though according to our growth in self-knowledge and our devising of a penology and criminology expressive of our psychological insights, the individual sense of inward insincerity and imperfection and demerit would disappear!

As for miracles, they simply "do not happen," indeed, *could not* happen, whether it be Virgin Birth or Resurrection, whether it be the healing of the blind or the cure of the paralytic: what we know about the rise of legends and the tendencies among men to exaggeration sufficiently accounts for all such features of the Gospel record. It should be added, however, that there is much less dogmatism to-day as to what could or could not "happen" than there was when Strauss, in his preface to his later *Life of Jesus*, wrote the famous words: "He who would drive the priest out of the Church must first of all drive the miracle out of religion." Especially is the doctrine of the Trinity held to be in a hopeless plight: it was only an "inference" in the first place, arising from accepted ideas about Christ and the Holy Spirit. Since these ideas are no longer valid, the "inference" ceases to hold—to say nothing of the intrinsic absurdity of the Triune conception even on simple mathematical grounds.[7]

The situation, therefore, as between those who assume the definitive significance of the categories of "modern thought," and those who believe that historical Christianity is compact of permanent truths, may be thus expressed from the standpoint of the former: "In the light of what we actually know about the structure of reality and the workings of the human mind, we do not see how the body of so-called Christian truth can possibly maintain itself: and because we can commit ourselves only to such truth as is capable of verification by approved methods, or to what is plainly in agreement with truth that is thus validated, we are therefore under necessity of regarding Christianity, at least in certain alleged factual and conceptual features of it, as a quite understandable but nevertheless quite indefensible superstition."[8]

As to this conclusion, it ought to be said at once that it destroys much more than the sceptic usually supposes. For it means that faith is to be entirely excluded as a means of apprehension or as a basis of valid experience. The place of tests in the ascertainment of truth is, of course, indisputable. But to limit truth to that which can meet tests scientifically devised is to endanger the very "values" which those who devise such tests may still be assumed to believe in, and to work for. The most indispensable bases for great living can never be established by the tests usually offered for determining "objective" truth.[9] If they are still accepted, it must be either because we ourselves "choose" them from a number of conflicting possibilities, or because we believe, on Christian grounds, that they represent for us the very will of God.

Those who take the second alternative at least know where they stand. They *have* their "objective" standard. But those who take the first alternative are clearly in a predicament. Their standard of judgment respecting alleged "values" must be purely subjective and relative. Any answer to a critic of these "values" must be based on subjective and relative considerations. If the critic should say, for example, that he preferred a life of sexual freedom to a life of sexual restraint, a life of pure self-regard to a life of other-regard, if, in a word, he should in Nietzschean fashion undertake a complete "transvaluation of values," there is no reply that can be made to the critic which is not just as much open to attack as the position the critic himself represents. Both are alike in having no absolute objective standard by which to determine the alleged values. One man says he intends to think only of himself. Another says he intends to think first of others. Who shall judge between them? Who shall say that it matters *profoundly* who is right? Then into the confusion there comes a Word of God *which settles the question* for whoever accepts it.

Whether it is a Word of God is, of course, the ultimate issue, never to be settled by any purely logical or scientific considerations. Its acceptance is necessarily an act of faith, but the act of faith is itself susceptible of the most complete rational defence, and the application of what one is committed to when the act of faith has to do with the Christian revelation is likewise such as can be amply defended by those who make it. Put side by side in imagination the world that would eventuate from the complete rejection of the Christian revelation and the world that would eventuate from its complete acceptance, and then add to the second the consideration that on the premises *that is the world that God intends and that he is working for,* and the case for faith can then certainly not be called a weak one, even from the standpoint of a boasted "reason."

Nor need the issue be confined to what may be "imagined." We have an abundance of concrete fact to go by. We can *see* on every hand what happens where what is held to be the Word of God is ignored, and what happens where it is accepted and applied. And those who want even a few of the things that the Word of God sets forth, but who seek to ground them in purely "human" considerations, must at least admit that their convictions and purposes would be enormously strengthened *if* they would bring to their humanism and humanitarianism the support of *God's revealed will.* Otherwise, the standard of "human good" alone remains, but in the situation then obtaining what is human good must be humanly determined, and how much confusion results from that hardly needs to be described. It at once becomes possible for every man to "do that which is right in his own eyes," and if a man can do that, so can the state. There is then no such thing at all as truth in respect of ultimate realities and of the fundamental issues of life.

In contrast to all baffling relativisms, the Christian faith announces to men a set of absolutes. It affirms God and what God is. It affirms what man is and what he is meant to be. It affirms what Christ is in relation alike to God and to man—the means whereby God would bring every man to fulness of life. It affirms the reality of sin, but at the same time sets forth how its power may be broken. It affirms the relation in which men should stand both to God and to their fellows. It affirms the priority of love, and the finality of that which love, and love alone, produces. It therefore offers a release from the vicious circle of subjectivism and relativism, presenting instead an authoritative truth, not as something "discovered" in the way in which other forms of truth may be discovered, but as directly made known or directly accomplished by God himself.[10]

According to Christianity, there is a truth of *being*, that is, a truth concerning the very nature and meaning of existence itself, and this truth God has either imparted directly to men or has led them in his own chosen way to apprehend. According to Christianity, there is a truth of certain *events* and of their meaning. These events are of two sorts, distinguishable as natural and miraculous. God is the ground of both, but in a different way, and both sorts have their meaning, which also God has declared. And according to Christianity, there is a truth of *relationships*, and this has to do with such vital questions as to what sin is and how it came to be and how it separates man from his true life and how it can be destroyed; as to what the sufferings and death of Christ accomplished, actually for God, potentially for man; as to perfect love, and how it results from a more and more complete surrender of the life to Jesus Christ; and as to the obligations, privileges, and purposes which are absolutely binding on the Christian man. When these various truths are clearly stated, they give us our standards, undemonstrable it is true just because of the claim that they are "revealed," but nevertheless of overwhelming significance in their application to human life, and, as stated above, of added force just because they are offered not as human discoveries but as divine disclosures.

These truths confront us not as candidates for our suffrages but as masters of our life. The Christian is the man who accepts them; who puts his mind, his heart, and his will under their complete control; who says that what denies them is untrue to the extent of the denial; and who in the spirit of "this one thing I do" brings all else to the test of his accepted absolute. He makes an initial acceptance which he frankly realizes is an act of faith.[11] The record from which he gathers his absolute is the Scriptures, and their fruitage in the life and experience of the Church. *He is a Biblicist,* and a Biblicist he must be in order to maintain his faith.

But he is not an uncritical Biblicist. He knows that the Word of God had to clothe itself in the words of men. He knows that he has his treasure in earthen vessels. He realizes therefore his need of a principle of discrimination. What is of the *form* of revelation, and what is of the *substance*? It may be that an infallibly exact criterion has not been given us. It may be that provision is made for the exercize, at the supremely crucial moment of decision, of that moral freedom which must never be entirely overwhelmed. It may be that wavering evidence is our divinely-given opportunity for self-assertion, so that when we do decide it is our deepest self that is uttered.

In the presence of two alternatives, which one do we vote for?— for in such a circumstance, vote we must. We have an *approximate criterion* in "the Mind of Christ" itself; in the collective judgment of the Church; and in the *testimonium Spiritus Sancti*. But this is not something offered to us ready-made. There is here no ruthless over-riding of individuality. When we surrender ourselves to what we take to be the criterion, so that henceforth we are as men under an authority, the surrender must be our own most free act. Thus when we find the authentication of "the Word as written" in the fact of "the Word made flesh," we are still not forgetting that our knowledge of "the Word made flesh" has reached us through "the words of men." But neither are we forgetting that if God is sufficiently concerned about us to speak to us clearly and definitively in a Life, he is also sufficiently concerned to see to it that the records which tell of that Life will not defeat the very purpose for which the Life was given. To that extent at least we shall insist on the "inspiration" of the record!

For the same reason we shall hold that if it was the purpose of God in speaking as "the Word made flesh" to get his will embodied in human life through the Church, then the pronouncements of that Church, whether contained in the New Testament or whether falling on later occasions, were likewise under a measure of divine control such as assures the truth of their root-meanings. And for the same reason we shall hold that the individual Christian who in complete sincerity seeks through the Scriptural record and through the judgments of the Church to know that truth about God and that truth about Christ and that truth about himself which God desires him to possess, will find himself being led into striking agreement with what may be called the general Christian mind. This is precisely what has happened on so many occasions that we might almost call it the law which illustrates the possibility of a complete conjunction of human freedom and divine authority. God speaks, but the hearing must be ours.[12] But there is a way of hearing so that what God actually speaks is what is also actually heard. Even in giving an absolute self-revelation, God respects and conserves the true dignity of the human as free, intelligent, and spiritual personality.

It is admitted that what has already been described as the content of the Christian revelation cuts drastically across our contemporary naturalisms, intellectualisms, relativisms, evolutionisms, and secularisms.[13] From one point of view, Christianity is a perpetual judgment on mankind: it is a light from whose remorseless glare no evil thing can be concealed. Turn the light of Christ on our modern world, and how stands it with that world, with its senseless competitions, its economic rivalries, its oppressions and persecutions, its superficialities and its pretences? But it is also to be admitted that great numbers of people in our time manifest no further interest in Christianity than to give it a complete dismissal, sometimes on the ground of its essential irrationality, sometimes on the ground of its impracticability, sometimes on the ground of its anti-naturalism, sometimes on the ground that those who follow it show a strange and inexcusable indifference to the pressing problems of the *here* and *now*.

Nevertheless, it is still here being declared that what has been written heretofore is what Christianity is, and whence it is, and what it means. The failure of too many Christians, perhaps of most Christians, perhaps of *all* Christians, is to be confessed with sadness, but that has no bearing on the central question. Wherefore it is again to be declared that while the fundamental fact is God and his purpose of love, there is yet that in the very stuff of existence by which God finds himself opposed. If Christ is the measure by which God desires that men shall understand him, then this opposition is of anti-Christ. In man, anti-Christ appears as that "original sin" which expresses itself as much in pride of intellect as in stubbornness of will and selfishness of heart and viciousness of action. It is also to be declared that in Jesus Christ the truth of God in its bearing on the recovery of man in both his individual and collective life is absolutely given: wherefore the measure in which the fulness of the divine revelation is rejected is to be regarded as the measure in which anti-Christ is in possession.

Herein is that "radical defect of our human nature" which God has set himself to remove, and yet which itself, in both its intellectual and its volitional effects, creates the most effective barrier to its own removal. "The War Against God" has its inception in the very means whereby God undertakes to realize his eternal purpose with men! The nature which God must give man in order that man might become what he wants him to be is precisely what makes it possible—shall we say "certain"?—for him to become other than what God wants. To endow finite and developing intelligence with the gift of freedom is to doom it, yet the doom must continue as the indispensable condition to its own eventual transformation![14] God *does* create us in order to put us under condemnation, and he *does* put us under condemnation in order to save us. "The law worketh wrath." "Law came that the offence might abound."

From the standpoint of God's purpose, man is constitutionally his own enemy. He is made so that he can believe, but just because he can believe he can also doubt. He is made so that he can be persuaded, as Irenaeus had it, but just because he can be persuaded he can also offer resistance. He is made so that he can choose the path that God marked for him as the way of life, but just because he can choose that path he can choose also another. In the qualities wherein lies the promise of his triumph lies also the promise of his defeat. *Scepticism is inseparable from the way we are*—as much so as are intellectual error and moral failure. Only through great tribulation, therefore, can God enter the kingdom of humanity. He has created his own difficulties with us, but he has also created the way out of them. There is a "corner" around which a man must painfully struggle before he sees full-orbed the glory of God in the face of Jesus Christ. He must "surrender," and everything in him is designed to make the surrender difficult.

But not impossible. Confronted with God, he can deny God just because God cannot meet the tests this man applies to him. Until suddenly one day the man sees that if God could meet these tests *he would not be God!* Confronted with Christ, he denies Christ, and again because Christ is equally unable to submit to the yardstick of familiar and otherwise reliable categories. Until once more the man realizes the true state of the case, and sees that *the greatest proof of Christ is that he cannot be proved.* Man's innate scepticism concerning the immeasurabilities of existence is the very condition to his rising to his supreme height of affirmation, and of self-commitment beyond the range of his mortal vision. The scepticism that repudiates revelation is what makes the eventual response to revelation intellectually splendid, spiritually satisfying, morally creative. Anti-Christ is originally enthroned that so the final enthronement of Christ may be man's supremely free and decisive act.

CHAPTER 11

Knowledge and Certainty

KNOWLEDGE AND CERTAINTY ARE OBVIOUSLY INSEPARABLE. WHEN WE say, "I know," we are also saying, "I am certain." We simply cannot know without at the same time being certain. It belongs to the very nature of the case. A situation in which we claim to know, but in which at the same time we confess to some uncertainty, must be described in some other way. We do *not* know, otherwise we should not confess uncertainty.

On the other hand, there can be certainty where there is not knowledge. The human mind is not exhausted by its knowing capacity.[1] It has likewise a capacity of belief. Belief and knowledge are inseparable but not identical. If we believe something, it is because we already know something, and if we know something it is because we already believe something.

For all that, we cannot say of the same thing that we both know it and believe it. I *know* that the pen with which I am now writing is a fountain pen of a certain style and make: I do not *believe* it. I *believe* that the person who presented the pen to me as a gift acquired it honestly: I do not *know* that he did. The knowledge gives me certainty. But the belief gives me certainty as well. The road to certainty in the two cases differs, but the ensuing state of my mind is in effect the same. In the first case, I am certain because there is no other possible alternative, unless I am to say that I never know, and that would be the end of everything. In the second case, I am certain not because there is no possibility that I am mistaken, but because I have sufficient reasons to convince me that I am not. We can distinguish the two types as respectively immediate certainty and mediate certainty.

The bearing of this on religion ought to be clear. Religion has to do with things that are known, and it also has to do with things

144

that are believed.[2] But there is a form of belief in relation to religion, or at least to the Christian religion, which is quite fundamental. It is what we mean by faith. Belief may be nothing at all but an assent of the mind. Faith includes this, but it goes beyond this to include also the free commitment of the whole life to what is believed. But no man has the right to commit his whole life to something he believes unless he can offer some rational vindication of what he believes. What this means for the question in hand is that Christian certainty is inseparable from the Christian revelation.

The reality of the revelation is therefore fundamental. Do we know that God has revealed himself in the way called Christian? We do not know it, but we believe it. But to believe in it in any vital way means also to have faith in it, and because of that faith there comes an immediate certainty that leaves the mind as much at rest as it is where there is knowledge in the proper sense. The acceptance of, shall we say, the objective world, is a matter of knowledge, and the certainty follows directly.[3] The acceptance of the Christian revelation is an act of faith, and the acceptance, if it be complete, is followed by a like direct certainty.

Have we good reasons for believing that God has spoken in this special way? It is clear that the question is crucial. Anyone who believes that God is himself a reality, and that he speaks in nature and in history, in reason and in conscience, has in that belief a presupposition that God speaks elsewhere. Because, as has already been shown, what God says in these other ways is not clear. It still leaves us in the dark on questions of great moment.[4] He who speaks obscurely may be expected to speak at last with undeniable clarity. Man is adapted, through his faculty of knowledge and of reason, to accept God's more uncertain speech. But he is adapted, through his faculty of belief and faith, to accept that other speech of God which is clear and explicit, but whose clarity and explicitness are not evident except as there are belief and faith.

There are therefore ways of revealing himself on the part of God, and corresponding ways of accepting the revelation on the part of man. The distinction secures the unity of God in his self-manifesting activity on the one hand, and on the other hand the unity of man in his apprehending activity. But God's self-manifestation is distinguishable as general and special. Reason in man answers to the general: there are things that we know. Faith in man answers to the special: there are things that we believe. Reason gives certainty. Faith also gives certainty. Paul's familiar words may be thus written: "I *know* whom I have *believed*; I have in *faith* entrusted my whole life to him; and I am *certain* that he will guard what I have put into his hands" (2 Timothy 1. 12).

What has been written above follows in general the treatment of the problem that was characteristic of the great Christian thinkers, in particular Thomas Aquinas, of the thirteenth century.[5] These thinkers, of course, had much to say about the corroboratory testimony of the Church, its councils, and its hierarchy, but the essence of the position may be stated without these additions, save that it must actually be the case that the creation of the Church in the first place was a direct outgrowth of the whole fact of Christ as crucified and risen. God as Creator and God as Redeemer; the God who acts through the order of nature and the God who acts through the order of grace; God in the Law and God in the Gospel—all are one and the same God. Man as rooted in nature and man as child of God; man as actual sinner and man as potential saint; man as able to know and man as able to believe; man exalted by the gift of reason which lifts him above every living thing, and man kept humble by the necessity of faith if he would complete what reason can only begin—these are one and the same man. And that God and this man are united in a living fellowship by the one Mediator, Jesus Christ, himself Son of God and Son of Man. It is as he himself prayed that it might be: "And the glory which thou hast given me I have given unto them; that they may be one, even as we are one; I in them, and thou in me, that they may be perfected into one" (John 17. 22, 23). Or as it was expressed by Paul: "Till we all attain unto the unity of the faith, and of the knowledge of the Son of God, unto a full-grown man, unto the measure of the stature of the fulness of Christ" (Ephesians 4. 13).

There is, however, a type of philosophy which precludes religious faith in any distinctive sense. It allows for belief, but only for belief that is unimpeachable rational inference from what we absolutely know. Direct knowledge, and what reason can show is justified by that knowledge—these are held to be the limits within which the human mind must confine itself. This is known as rationalism. Its motto may be said to be: "Prove all that you believe by what you indubitably know."⁶

That we should believe nothing without good reasons is clear enough. That we should begin with things we know is equally clear. Our approach to reality is admittedly by way of sense-experience and rational processes. This was fundamental with Aristotle, and because Thomas Aquinas followed Aristotle so closely is why he regarded Being—a real existence other than Thought—as the first certainty. Sense and reason call for each other, although in varying degree. There are some types of sense-experience which are so immediate and so coercive that they leave us without any alternative. Our very use of the words we call "nouns" indicates how complete is human agreement as to certain features of the objective world. "This book is one hundred years old" is a statement that might easily divide us as to the alleged age of the book; but as to the fact of the book being a book there could be no doubt. We could not reason at all, unless some things "stayed put." Fixed points there must be if there is to be dependable observation, measurement, inference, and judgment. We must agree that the book is a book before we can begin to talk about its age.

Science assumes fixed points. Rational deduction assumes fixed points. But if we stop at the fixed points, we have neither science nor logic. Logic compels us to advance if we are to complete the chain of reasoning, and while every step may be implicit in the premisses, it still remains that in taking these steps we are expressing our confidence in the reliability of our own reasoning processes. In other words, even in logic we believe in order to know. *Credo ut intelligam.* Science, too, must be factual, but it cannot be purely factual, otherwise there would be no science. The laws of nature, so-called, are scientific interpretations of given facts.⁷ What frequently happens, of course, is that the scientific interpretation seems to be utterly at variance with the facts as declared by the senses. "Sunrise" and "sunset" are perhaps the most familiar cases in point.

But even where science as usually understood is not involved, it is astonishing how much interpretation and imaginative reconstruction enter into our most elementary forms of knowledge. The most any one of us ever saw at a given time of the outside of a house is two sides. Yet we know that a house with only two sides to it is an impossibility. We see the front and one side of the house at one time, and the back and the other side at another time, and in order to get our conception of the house we have to put these together *imaginatively*. To state the case very simply, what we *know* as we stand and look at two sides of the house we have to supplement with what we *remember* or with what we *believe* about the other two sides. When I *know* that the house has a front because I can "see" it, I can only *believe* that it has a back, because I cannot see the back and the front at the same time.

This may appear to be making a very complicated matter out of what is actually something very simple. But that, of course, is just the point. Is it so simple as we make it out to be? Is this certainty of the senses quite so absolute as the rationalist assumes?[8] Knowledge by sense-experience obviously depends upon a process of rational activity—memory, inference, imagination, synthesis, and the like—and this activity is greater or less according as interpretation is needed to supplement the sense-data and to complete their significance.

The man, therefore, who proudly announces that he begins with what he "knows" and rigidly stays by it and by what it may be shown to involve, is under some necessity of considering what this "knowledge" is. When he has reflected a little on what he is so certain that he "knows," he may be willing to acknowledge that there is a mystery equally to the reality which is known and to the process whereby it is known. With this much granted, the way is at least open to consider whether the mystery of existence is not greater than can be grasped by the mystery of knowing; whether there is not an element of the mystery of existence which eludes the mysterious power of knowing; and whether it is not precisely the function of the mysterious power of faith to bring man into actual relationship with that element of existence which knowledge cannot reach.[9] In any event, he might be persuaded to put a question-mark after his rationalistic attempt to reduce the whole of existence and the whole of experience to a neat little cut-and-dried mechanistic formula.

There may be, then, more to existence than the senses are the correlatives of; more truth than reason can discover and comprehend; more certainty than purely rational certainty. This is not to call sense-experience in question, nor is it to call in question the logical understanding. To do either would be absurd. We must keep our feet on the ground. We must tie ourselves to the inescapable. At the same time, we must be true to our total personal equipment. We are not throwing reason under suspicion because we say that it is not omniscient. We are not denying the rationality of existence in the sense of its complete coherence because we say that there are aspects of existence which call for the exercize of the supra-rational faculty of faith. The faith-capacity is of the very structure of personality. We have the right to hold that what is so unmistakably a part of ourselves—our power to believe, our power to trust, our power to act on something less than complete knowledge, our power to achieve a certainty which others may challenge but which we ourselves never can, all that the Scriptures mean by "the witness of the Spirit"—we have the right to hold that this is not so much wastage of equipment, but is intended to relate us to reality in a way not otherwise possible. Man the person, as has been shown in an earlier discussion, is necessarily "bigger" than his known or knowable world. When therefore he interprets his world and himself in suchwise as that some of the most significant aspects of his own being are left totally unaccounted for, the interpretation is somewhere radically defective.[10]

Now the rationalist insists that we are not to go beyond the evidence. We can allow him his point. But there is something that must be said to the rationalist himself, namely, that there is evidence which his own view of things quite overlooks. It is reasonable to ask for evidence: it is just as reasonable to ask for *all* the evidence. Certainly we must say *that the person in his totality* is evidence, and evidence that must be fully used. When fully used, this evidence is our best index to the totality of existence.

Consider again what is involved in the mere experience of knowing. Knowing plainly implies both a knower and a thing known.

Here are three elements: that which knows, the knowing act itself, and that which is known. Knowledge is therefore a complex. A modification of any one of the three elements involves a modification of the total. That is to say, to change the character of the knower (the person) would be to change also both the knowing act and the object as known. Only a person can know in the way a person knows. Only by persons can things be known as persons know them.

This centrality of the knower, or the person, and his determinative character, must never be lost sight of, but they all too often are. The rationalist professes to exercize the coolest detachment in his consideration and estimate of life and his meaning. He has the profoundest respect for logic—which is proper. He would apply ruthlessly the scientific method. He would say that to believe what you cannot clearly demonstrate from what you certainly know is to be guilty of credulity and superstition.

Well, watch him as he goes about his business of knowing and deducing and proving and "concluding." Remember that all that is going on presupposes the working of a human mind. He is dealing, we will say, with a given fact or a given field of observation. As to that, it must be said in the first place that "the given fact," even though it be only a tree, and "the given field of observation," even though it be as much as a wide variety of geological strata, owe something to the mind to which they are "given." They could not be "given" in the same way to the bird that nests in that tree, or to the bear that clambers around in those strata. In the second place, you watch the person as, in true scientific fashion, he begins to "break down" his "given tree" or his "given field of observation" into what he takes to be its ultimate constituents, and then crowns his efforts by stating what he believes is the law or laws according to which these constituents combine to give the "empiric facts" with which he started. What he finds these ultimates to be will depend upon his prevailing interest or purpose, since "we find what we look for," but always what he is seeking is "reals" and their laws. Elements, monads, neutrons, structures, reflexes, psychoses, even values—what is observed and experimented upon and analyzed may be "broken down" until any one of these may be reached, and then regarded as the finality which is being sought, and in whose light existence and experience are then to be regarded.

All this is interesting enough, and valuable enough, and, indeed, for certain purposes indispensable. But at every moment *an observer is at work*, the one tremendous fact which he is quite likely to take for granted and not stop to consider at all, and this observer is a human being, who observes what he observes and in the way that he observes it just because he is a human being and not something else. Not only so, but the elements into which he "breaks down" the "given facts" he started with are elements of *his* experience as a human being, and the farther he gets behind or below his facts, the more imperative it is for him to remember that at every step of the way he is "taking his mind along with him." The result is that when he gets to his stopping-place, his "real," his "monad," his "element," his "—on," his "—id," call it what he will, his stopping-place has become *a pure mental construct*, invisible, intangible, imponderable, immeasurable, and yet, we are assured, so indubitably "real" as to be the most real fact of all existence![11] Yet what is it but the end of a journey so complicated and so mysterious that only a human mind could take it, only a human mind could describe it, only another human mind could repeat it—and certainly only a human mind could possibly overlook its significance!

In a word, the application of the scientific method to "given facts," or any activity of the logical understanding, from which it is customary to say that every least vestige of "subjectivity" is rigidly excluded, turns out to be a combined process of creativity, discovery, and revelation, all depending upon some sort of profound congruity between the nature of the mind that carries through the process and that in which the process eventuates.

It is unfortunate, in the midst of a consideration, aiming to be as non-technical as possible, of "The Christian Revelation," to have to introduce so abstract and, as some would say, so difficult a discussion as the foregoing. Yet the only way to answer the rationalist is according to his rationalism. He must be faced with what is implied in his own method and procedure. And because the naturalist in philosophy is quite likely to be a rationalist in his method and point of view, what answers rationalism also answers naturalism.

Naturalism, which accounts for nature by itself, and which accounts for man by nature, as completely fails to think through all that man is as rationalism fails to think through all that mind is.[12] Just as the most important factor in any science is the scientist, and just as no scientist could ever account for himself in the terms of the science which he constructs; just as the most important factor in any logical series is the logician, and just as no logician could ever account for himself in terms of one of his own syllogisms; so naturalism, when it is offered as a final philosophy, that is, when its principles are claimed to be universally applicable and interpretive, breaks on the fact of the naturalist himself. The best answer to naturalism is the naturalist who puts it together! He claims to study and then to explain experience, but the postulate of the experience is the experiencer: wherefore he, the experiencer, the naturalist, the living man with power to reach into the past and into the future, with power to gather together and to contemplate various fragments of experience and combine them all into a "system," can never be explained either in terms of the experience alone or in terms of what is experienced.

What this all means finally is that the person is *transcendent* to any field of observation with which he may be concerned and which thereupon becomes a form of his experience, and the more deeply he immerses himself in the field with a view to understanding it and interpreting it and reducing it to more simple elements, *the more he becomes immanent in it while yet maintaining his transcendence.* He helps to create what he finds, and the more he considers what he finds the more he indwells it, the more he and it become two inseparabilities, and the more the person and his world achieve "the unity of differences." He is not to be equated or identified with his world, and his world is not to be equated or identified with himself. In no sense is he it, and in no sense is it he, yet notwithstanding the ontological difference neither could be but for the other.

In view of this basic fact (*for it is offered as fact*, as nearly demonstrable fact as anything in philosophy can ever hope to be), what happens to the neat little schemes offered by naturalism as all-explanatory? The mystery of personality is treated as a mere item in the scheme of things instead of as the indispensable postulate of the whole. Can it be that the man who concocts the naturalistic scheme, a scheme, let it now be said, which recognizes highers and lowers, rights and wrongs, facts and values, rationals and irrationals, things beautiful and things ugly, and yet which would reduce all this kaleidoscopic variety to the mechanical operation of one and the same vast impersonal ultimate or groups of ultimates— can it be that he, the man who concocts it, is the stubborn reality upon which the whole scheme breaks like a wave on a rock, because he, the man who concocts it, overlooks the simple but all-important fact that it is *his scheme*! The scheme is a creation, a mental picture, and he is its creator; and while it is inevitable that the creation shall be accounted for by the creator, to account for the creator by what he has created is another matter altogether—*and it cannot be done.*

Yet this impossible thing is exactly what naturalism proposes. It derives the creative, transcendent, and immanent man from that which he helps to create, which he transcends, and in which he is immanent. It can do this with a certain plausibility because of its proud boast that it follows "common sense" and "science" in its view of reality. Therefore it treats the historical process as absolute, and accepts the scientific account of man as an "emergent" or "evolvement" of that process. What can be plainer, asks the naturalist, than the fact that "at one time" man was not, and that "now" he is, and that he is therefore a product of the very system of which he is a part?

The reason why so many people accept this alleged logic of evolutionism is because it is so very simple. They look at the proposal, and they say, "Of course." It is so much easier to say "Of course," than to say respecting the proposal "Of course—*not*!" One can accept readily enough the scientific account of natural processes, and can stand with becoming humility before the long line of specimens in the museum which are shown as climaxing, through the anthropoids, in *man*. It is all so conveniently simple. Man is a descendant. He is a descendant of that which was not man, just as that which was not man was a descendant of something different from itself, and that from something else still different, and so on *ad infinitum*. What a spectacle of growth is here dramatized in a line of specimens!

Yes! But let us push the element of "wonderfulness" a little beyond the point where the naturalist stops for breath. Let us do a
little exclaiming on our own account. Let us, for example, exclaim
—How wonderful that death should give birth to life! How wonderful that that which thinks should be the issue of that which
could not think! How wonderful that that which can recall and
reconstruct the past should be the offspring of the past which it can
recall and reconstruct! How wonderful that that which can ask the
momentous questions, What? Whence? How? Why? Whither?
should be nothing but another "aspect" of that to which it puts the
questions! How wonderful that that which prays should be able to
trace the long pilgrimage by which it came to be "a praying animal"—and yet be able to find nowhere along the way, no, nor yet
anywhere else in that vast frame in which it is now set, any Reality
to which prayer is the inevitable linkage—

> And so the whole round earth be every way
> Bound by lead chains about the feet of Death!

How wonderful, too, that that which, held with strong cords to
love of life, and possessed of imaginative power whereby death is
vested with dread solemnity, should yet on occasion be willing to
die at the behest of a Voice which none but itself ever hears—and
then, having failed of obedience to that Voice, should find that life
itself had lost its joy, and that the death which was shrunk from is
still approaching, only now with an aspect more fearsome than it
ever wore before!

> "And a thousand thousand slimy things
> Lived on; and so did I."

Returning now to our starting-point—the question of knowledge and certainty—we perhaps shall be willing to recognize that
those forms of knowledge which we most readily take for granted,
and which appear to us to be so self-evident, raise a problem of the
most fundamental character. We *do* know, and we *are* certain. But
an analysis of what enters into knowledge, and an analysis of the
grounds of our certainty, at least creates a supposition in favor of
the view that there is more to be known than the normal processes

of knowledge can ever discover, that this other form of knowability may yet be accessible to us through the appropriate means, and that there may arise a certainty in respect of it which is as valid as the certainty arising from other relationships. The limitations we cannot escape bespeak the possibility and one may even say the necessity of revelation. The power of belief which is an element of our rational nature bespeaks that in us by which revelation may make its approach. The power of faith, by which we rest our lives on the reality and truth of what we believe revelation brings to us, bespeaks the possibility of a form of experience arising for us and producing its own type of certainty.

It was said above of the late Lord Balfour that he endeavored in his Gifford Lectures to validate "religious knowledge" by showing that the "uncertainties" which attach to it are attached equally to "scientific knowledge." That is to say, he would put both types of knowledge on the same basis by showing how the sceptic could destroy each. Such a procedure gets us nowhere.[13] It were better to do as has been attempted above, and to show that the very relationship of personality to reality, which makes scientific knowledge a personal achievement based on personal powers to which reality answers, also makes it possible that there shall be nonscientific or religious knowledge. Such knowledge will presuppose its own form of objective reality, namely, God. It will presuppose its own form of personal capacity, namely, faith. And it will presuppose its own form of subjective result, namely, moral certainty. In a word, to destroy that in man with which religious knowledge is so closely implicated is also to destroy that in man with which scientific knowledge is so closely implicated. When we save reality as it is read by faith we at the same time save reality as it is read by reason.

CHAPTER 12

Natural and Supernatural

ONE OF THE SIGNIFICANT DISCUSSIONS OF MODERN TIMES WAS BERG-
son's *Matter and Memory*. Bergson holds that matter can be defined
only in relation to life. Matter is both unfriendly to life and necessary to life. When life reaches the psychic or intelligent level, it is
characterized by memory. Matter has no memory just because it is
the negation of life. Memory is the power by which psychic life
makes the past ever present and assures the perpetuation of the
present into the future.[1]

Much else in Bergson may be open to question, but here at least
is a fact that arrests attention. The past can exist only by becoming
present, and this miracle of continuity is an achievement of man.
We can talk about past existence only as our minds can imaginatively re-capture it, and this brings it into the present. Whatever
else the human mind may or may not be, it is certainly the power
that binds together existence and time. What is existence without
time? What is time without existence? But actual time is always
present time. Past time is time that has ceased to be. Future time
is only a present possibility. In the same way there is no past
existence and there is no future existence: there is only present
existence. The usual picture of the world as a series of events and
facts "strung along" on the line of time like so much laundry hung
out to dry, is naive enough. When existence is considered as something past, the act of consideration is always a present act, or an
act in the present. Therefore the past existence is simply *represented*,
imaginatively re-captured, and by consequence saved from being
swallowed into nothingness.[2]

Such a view will, of course, have to endure the naturalistic re-
tort of being "idealistic," or worse still "non-realistic." But it may
turn out that *this is the only true realism*. Without a doubt, it is

audacious enough to find the ultimate not in what is experienced, nor in the elements to which what is experienced is finally reduced, but in the experiencer himself. The only possible form under which existence can present itself to us, or be represented by us, is the form which is determined by our own nature as persons. That existence may present itself under other forms to other types of subjects—fish, birds, insects, beasts, even angels and demons, if such there be—is a reasonable enough claim; but this does not change the fact that existence can be known only as it is experienced, and that what may be called the "existence-experience-person" combination is a combination *utterly unique* because of the uniqueness of the person by whom the combination is achieved.

Destroy persons, and while you do not thereby destroy existence, you do destroy existence in that form in which alone persons can experience it. When the naturalist says that the human person is "a product of the universe" he quite forgets that the universe about which he is speaking is the universe as he, himself a human person, conceives it. It is impossible, as has already been emphasized, to equate this personalistic universe with the non-personalistic universe.[3] If they are equated, it amounts to saying that *man makes no difference*—which is surely the supreme heresy. Man himself, spiritual transformer, must be set between the two universes in order to explain how the transition is possible from the one to the other. But this necessity leaves us with a postulated non-personalistic universe so utterly barren that it is incredible that man *in his totality* could be derived from it. That it is a *condition* to his appearing is undeniable enough, but that it is the *sole cause* of him—no!

The world of persons, therefore—if the point may be urged once more even to seeming weariness—depends upon persons, and nothing that can be said about the biological antecedents and bases of persons can destroy that fact. My world begins when I begin. My knowledge of my world begins as my consciousness, or power to know and feel, appears. My time begins when I begin, and it ends when I end. I can know nothing of any other world except my world, and I can know nothing of any other time except my time. The reality of existence for persons therefore lies precisely in the reality of the persons. *They* are the ultimates in respect of existence in the only possible way in which they can know anything about it. Genetic psychology and physiological psychology, even behavioristic psychology, may have much to say about the building up of the subject of experience, and about the dependencies of the subject, and about the processes of experience, and the like, and all this is useful and interesting and informing, and it tends to keep us, as William James used to say, "in working touch with reality." But the claim must still be urged—that implicit in all human activity, of whatever sort, and in particular in those higher forms of activity of which civilization, religion, art and science are the expression, is that distinctive and unique and original reality which personality is. Wherefore any view of things which degrades personality, or makes it secondary, or a mere derivative, or a mere aspect of a process, is a gross perversion of the actual situation.

But if what has been set forth gives us the only true realism, it also gives us *the only true humanism*. Evolutionary naturalism usually claims to be humanistic, but it uses the word humanism as a negative of theism. Or if it still retains the word "God," it proposes to empty it of every vestige of its historical meaning, and equate it with "those forces of the universe which support 'the good life.'" The truth of this statement may be seen by anyone who will read Eustace Haydon, *The Quest of the Ages* (which is still one of the most poignant and stylistically perfect defences of non-theistic humanism), especially the chapter, with its references, on "The Passing of the Gods of Old." But if the implication is that the God of the Christian faith no longer has significance for "the good life" or for "the victorious life," as it must be lived under present conditions, the implication is strange indeed.

The simple truth is that humanism can dispense with theism, in particular with Christian theism, only by being less truly humanistic than theism would permit it to be.[4] The human person is not merely a unit in the social whole. He has a transcendent quality which can never be accounted for by making him a mere derivative of a process, much less of a process itself impersonal. Repeatedly the claim has been made in earlier chapters that personality is "bigger" than the world in which it finds itself. For all its admitted dependence, it has a power of mastery over both its heredity and its environment. It obviously needs the world as *milieu*. The attempt here being made to exalt personality does not reduce objectivity to an illusion. The foregoing consideration of "Knowledge and Certainty" was intended to show that personality so transforms objectivity, so illuminates it with the glory of color, and so instrumentalizes its vast silence into living sound, as to more than repay to objectivity any debt owed to it.

But just as surely, this transformation by personality of "givenness" into "meaningfulness," that is, into existence as something now personally experienced and understood, means that it is utterly impossible to account for the person simply in terms of the "givenness." What is "given" must be given to something, and the mysterious and in some respects inscrutable power of personality is at the receiving end of the line. Let it be granted that the "given" is a form of reality. We must stand with Aristotle and Aquinas for the inescapability of Being. But we have come upon insights into the relations of existence as personal with existence as impersonal which even they did not reach. Wherefore we cling to the claim that personality is a form of existence, of reality, which is wholly unique; that it is the function of existence as impersonal to provide the arena for the appearance and activity of existence as personal; that it is the function of existence as personal to bend to its own uses existence as impersonal; and that in the results of this cooperation is found the true purpose of both forms.[5] Coleridge, sojourning in the Hartz Forest, shows that he had caught the great truth when he wrote:

> ". . . For I had found
> That outward forms, the loftiest, still receive
> Their finer influence from the Life within;—
> Fair cyphers else: fair, but of import vague
> Or unconcerning. . . ."[6]

Add a digit to a cipher, and both are benefited. The cipher increases the value of the digit, and the digit transforms the cipher from nothing into something. *The world minus personality and the world plus personality are not the same.* A digit is added to what is otherwise a cipher when personality enters into increasingly intimate relationships with that *milieu* in which alone it can grow. Thus Coleridge again:

> ". . . We receive but what we give,
> And in our life alone does Nature live;
> Ours is her wedding-garment, ours her shroud!
> And would we aught behold, of higher worth
> Than that inanimate cold world allowed
> To the poor loveless ever-anxious crowd,
> Ah! from the soul itself must issue forth
> A light, a glory, a fair luminous cloud
> Enveloping the earth—
> And from the soul itself must there be sent
> A sweet and potent voice, of its own birth,
> Of all sweet sounds the life and element!"[7]

The conclusion, therefore, is that although the natural and the personal are vitally related, it is not possible to treat the personal as a mere derivative of the natural. Neither is it possible, even although the personal so wonderfully transforms the natural in its basic "givenness," to derive the total natural from the personal. Both the natural and the personal point to still something else, which we can only properly describe as the supernatural. Naturalism can do nothing but account for man by nature.[8] It can do that only because it has no proper analysis of either the concept of nature or the concept of man. It treats nature as ready-made, and it treats man as but one more item in this ready-made scheme. Man can be included in nature in the naturalistic sense only as long as he is conceived as simply physiological fact.

But there lies the crux of the situation. The physiological man is no more the whole man than is the economic man or the political man. Conceive man, however, as it has been said above that we should, as a quite unique power of experience, and hence as a form of reality equally distinct in "kind"—do that, and then nature, *as presented in man's experience*, and man, *as the power to apprehend nature in just that way and no other*, are seen to be correlatives, but with the more ultimate significance belonging to the experiencing and apprehending man. To nature in this sense man is transcendent.

Within nature in this sense he is immanent. Of nature in this sense he is the first term, whereby an "existential givenness"—which Baron von Hügel found so undeniable, he said, yet in itself so incomplete—comes to self-fulfillment.[9] Yet it is the very fact that man both appears within and continually needs a "givenness" that yet does not explain him, which leaves the man himself in his most distinctive aspect totally unaccounted for. If we follow naturalism in saying that there is nothing but man and nature, which means finally that "all is natural," and if we follow the view of the relations between man and nature which has been set forth above, then we necessarily come to a complete impasse.

There is no escape from this impasse except as we believe that there is still a third form of reality which stands to man and nature *somewhat* after the fashion in which man, the experiencing person, stands to nature, defined as his experienced world. The analogy, however, is very far from being complete—how far, will be seen to follow from what has before been said about God the Creator. Man is creative only within the limits of a "given": *he does not create his "given."* But because man does not create his "given," and because the "given" is totally unable to account for man, we are led to conclude that both man and his "given" represent the activity of a reality which is creative not in any relative sense but absolutely. Naturalism denies this, and in the same denial digs its own grave.

When naturalism is of the variety which calls itself theistic, it is still true that all it can say about either man or the alleged God is that these are two "aspects" of nature. Wieman, for example, conceives God as an appearance within the naturalistic and unfolding whole, and describes this appearance as "growth of meaning."[10] As to this, many questions could be asked which must now be passed by; but it must at least be said of such a God that "he" (?) possesses not a single one of the powers, qualities, or attributes which Christianity has always assigned to God, and must continue to assign if it is itself to continue.

What may now be called supernaturalism takes the position that man as personal reality is not to be included *in* nature, even although, as already said, he is inseparable from it. A. M. Fairbairn was wont to speak of nature as "constituted in man," and the phrase may be allowed so long as it is not taken to mean that man creates nature, but that man is that complex of qualities through which nature—or, better, existence—reveals potentialities otherwise quiescent. But that in which nature is thus constituted—personality—is no more self-explaining than is nature itself. A supernatural reality is called for which is the common ground alike of that personal reality which is man and of that impersonal reality which man transmutes into his world of experience.[11] From the standpoint of that supernatural, which is now seen to be the absolutely *creative*, both man and nature belong in the category of the *created*.

This gives us three forms of reality: the supernatural, the personal, and the non-personal in all its ranges. The supernatural is self-existent. The personal and the non-personal are not self-existent but dependent. They are only because something else already is. Neither can explain itself and neither can explain the other and neither can dispense with the other and still remain as it is. But while we have these three forms of reality, we need only two categories—the creative and the created. The creative is the supernatural: it is God, and God only. The created is the personal and the non-personal, or man *and* Nature as Nature is usually understood.

It is sometimes suggested that the personal should be included in the supernatural. Nothing but confusion can result from the suggestion. There is only one true supernatural: God the Creator. His creation is distinguishable as the personal, which is "made in his own image," and the sub-personal, non-personal, and impersonal, these being describable as the total necessary *milieu* within which he produces, nourishes, and brings to fruition, the personal. What that *milieu* owes to the human has already been emphasized. Nevertheless, God is God and man is man and nature is nature. Man is other than impersonal nature; nevertheless, even when considered in his most distinctive sense, man is natural when the natural is equated with the created. God is other than impersonal nature, and other than the humanly personal. Impersonal nature and the humanly personal are alike the creatures of God. "It is he that hath made us and not we ourselves."

This gives us not the intangible, illusive, unresponsive God of theistic naturalism, but a God who is a Real Being, prior to his creation, other than his creation, the reason for his creation, ever active in his creation, adequate to the purposes of his creation, exercizing over his creation a providential control, therefore revealed in his creation, in particular in that form of it which is man, and supremely in that which the Christian believes he has done in order to lift the human to that new level of faith and love, of capacity and experience and achievement, which finds both its promise and its power in the Gospel.

Contrast such a God with the God of the various contemporary naturalistic theisms, and it requires only a little reflection to see that whereas this God lightens our darkness and provides an answer to at least our most insistent questions, the God of naturalistic theism does neither. He is no Real Being. He creates nothing, but must be created. He explains nothing, but must be explained. He extends no helping hand. He answers no prayer. He maintains no fellowship. He utters no voice, either of warning or of judgment, either of commendation or of welcome. He pours out no sacrifice of love. He is made in the image of man his maker, but man himself is made in no image.

Such a God is impotent to meet our human situation. He is at a far remove from anything that Christianity has always held God to be. With its God gone, Christianity cannot itself long continue. Naturalism is therefore anti-Christian, and it is that, at least in part, because it is rationalistic. It claims to proceed by the light of reason alone. But it narrowly construes reason because it narrowly construes man. Man is a rational creature, but reason is not all of him. Reason, in the sense of the logical understanding, is but one of a complex of capacities which make up the mystery of human nature, characterized as much by its power to believe as by its power to deduce a conclusion from premises, as much by its power to apprehend as by its power to comprehend, as much by its power to be actively formative as by its power to be passively receptive.[12] There is but one solution of the mystery. It is found in a Creative Supernatural.

Admittedly this is not demonstrable. It is rather a faith, a faith to which we are driven by life itself, a faith to which an alleged revelation so exactly answers and so richly fulfills. In a word, faith that there is a Creative Supernatural is a rational faith. Admittedly, too, what has now been said springs not merely from the feeling of the intrinsic defectiveness of naturalism, considered even as a philosophy, but also and perhaps chiefly from the conviction that what Christianity brings us is capable of being construed into a *Weltanschauung*—a total view of things—to which there is nowhere any comparison. The Christian view, even when not accepted as "revelation," but regarded as solely the result of human reflection, may still be shown to be infinitely more "reasonable" than anything given us by naturalism, vastly more satisfying, and profoundly congruous with man's own deepest nature.

CHAPTER 13

The Supernatural and Christianity

AN ATTEMPT TO PRESERVE WHAT IS TRUE IN NATURALISM AND WHAT is true in supernaturalism is made by those who like to speak of what they call the naturalness of the supernatural and the supernaturalness of the natural. Even so clear a thinker as Borden P. Bowne carried on a polemic against "the undivineness of the natural and the unnaturalness of the divine," which he described as "the great heresy of popular thought respecting religion,"[1] although what he went on to explain was his own view of the question could be accepted without much difficulty. The attempt just referred to, however, amounts in actual fact to affirming in language what it is intended to deny in substance. For it means that the same realities may be called either natural or supernatural, or, better, *both* natural and supernatural.

If language is to have any meaning at all, it is difficult to see how that can be. Why speak of "super" at all, if there is nothing to which it can be "super"? On such a view, there are no longer within the totality of existence any absolute distinctions. It is only by insisting that there are such distinctions that any validity attaches to the verbal recognition of the supernatural.[2] If we are to say of the same reality that it is now natural and now supernatural, it can only mean that we are speaking according to a changing point of view. From *this* point of view, the reality is natural; from *that* point of view, the reality is supernatural. *But either way, it is the same reality*.

The Christian faith does, indeed, recognize a historical reality where this identity exists: it is what is meant by its doctrine of the divinity of Jesus Christ. We believe, says the Nicene Creed, "in one Lord Jesus Christ, the only-begotten Son of God, begotten of the Father before all worlds, Light of Light, very God of very

God, begotten, not made, being of one substance (essence) with the Father; by whom all things were made; who, for us men and for our salvation, came down from heaven, and was incarnate by the Holy Ghost of the Virgin Mary, and was made man." But the very thing that gives this doctrine its significance is the fact of its utter singularity. That singularity is surrendered the moment the normal distinction between natural and supernatural is broken down.

The very life of Christianity is therefore here at stake. It can no more live in an atmosphere of pantheistic monism than it can live in an atmosphere of naturalistic monism.[3] The philosophy "All is one," fascinating as it is to certain minds, has been the bane of the East, and it would fain creep into the West. It haunted the exotic mind of Swinburne:

> "I the mark that is missed
>   And the arrows that miss,
> I the mouth that is kissed
>   And the breath in the kiss,
> The search, and the sought, and the seeker, the
>   soul and the body that is.
>
> "But what thing dost thou now,
>   Looking Godward, to cry
> 'I am I, thou art thou,
>   I am low, thou art high'?
> I am thou, whom thou seekest to find him;
>   find thou but thyself, thou art I.
>
> "I the grain and the furrow,
>   The plough-cloven clod
> And the plough-share drawn thorough,
>   The germ and the sod,
> The deed and the doer, the seed and the sower,
>   the dust which is God."[4]

Better the crudest kind of supernaturalism than a heresy so subtle as that! Yet it is widely-spread, and the philosophers and the poets have helped it on. The popularity of Walt Whitman is not altogether without explanation in this feature of his thought. Whether one follow the style of Democritus, or of Spinoza, or of Hegel; or whether one find oneself caught in the lures of the dreamful mystics; or whether one on more flagging wing seek to keep pace with the daring flights of Goethe or Shelley, the result is likely to be the same, so far as any absolute distinctions are concerned. Our current materialisms and naturalisms, our current secularisms and psychologisms and pantheistic mysticisms, are all singing to an ancient tune.

We can only say again, therefore, that the distinction between the Creator and the creation, and, within the creation, the distinction between the personal and the non-personal, must be steadily maintained and jealously guarded by those to whom the Christian heritage of faith is precious. There is that Being which *is* because it *must be*, and there is that being which *is* only because it *may be*, and because the *may be* has been realized by the action of that Being which *must be*. The supernatural is the *must be*. The natural is the *may be*. The relation between them is therefore the relation of the dependent and the necessary. That chain of effects which is the natural is anchored to that uncaused cause which is the supernatural. The supernatural is that form of existence which in nowise whatever could cease to be or could be other than it is. *This is God.* The natural is that form of existence which is as it is and how it is, not because of anything in itself, but because of God.

Spinoza, the great exponent of Pantheism in the modern West, made no proper place for this distinction—which is what makes him a Pantheist! His one all-inclusive term is Nature (*natura*). Nature is at once an activity (*naturans*) and a passivity (*naturata*). The passivity is but the other side of the activity, and the two together constitute Nature. There are here no creative will or effort and no distinctions. Existence is one whole in its necessary parts, and all the parts are equally necessary, where they are, when they are, and as they are.[5] But this is not Christianity, and it can never be Christianized—as we are now agreed that Schleiermacher discovered. Christianity requires that there shall be "God and—," and it does not matter much how we describe that which follows the "and" so long as we see it as distinct from God himself.

This will be called by some nothing but simple speculation. But it is not simple speculation. If that is all that it is—well, that is all that it is! Speculation is reason's unaided attempt to read the riddle of existence, and the great minds which have come nearest to reading it aright—Plato not least among them—still had no way of judging their own failure or success. Did not Plato himself declare that only if a teacher should be sent to him from the gods could he hope to reach beyond where his mind at last must stop?

The Christian very simply claims that this wider knowledge has been actually disclosed. The Christian believes the things which have been said above, and claims for them more than "simple speculation," because he has put his mind to school to Scripture—to that Scripture in which he dares to find the veritable Word of God. Even as a speculation, it would have its merits, but the truths which make up the body of Christianity were never speculatively arrived at by any man. The man who believes these truths believes them on other than speculative grounds, although once he accepts them as "given," he may be amazed to discover what wings they set to his reason and to what bold ventures of the mind they inspire him. The Alexandrian Theologians accepted their Platonism from Plato himself, regarding him, as we ourselves may still do, as *praecursor Christi in naturabilis*; but they accepted their Christianity as a direct gift of God.[6] Treat the Christian faith merely as a speculation, and it becomes only one of a number of possibilities, between which no man may choose with certainty. Treat it as the substance of the Word of God, and it stands without alternative. We dare agree with Kraemer, that the Bible is to be taken "realistically," by which he means that it is not to be regarded as a book of moral or even religious philosophy, but as a book which sets forth the reality and the character of God, his purpose in creation, his will for men, and what he has done and what men are to do to bring that will to pass.[7]

But it is impossible to accept the Bible message in this realistic sense without at the same time seeking to state it coherently—and it is not stated coherently save as all its essential features are preserved. It is true that there have been endless discussions as to what these "essential features" are, and it is true that even where these are agreed upon men still differ profoundly as to their coherencies. But we may bear in mind Coleridge's observation concerning "that fortunate inconsequence of our nature which permits the heart to rectify the errors of the understanding." One Being, namely God, "Maker of Heaven and Earth," who at various times and in various manners, but in particular in and through the people of Israel, disclosed what manner of God he was, and what manner of purpose he was carrying out in the world, until when the fulness of the time was come he could send forth One whom he called a Son— this is the God whom it is the purpose of Scripture to make us acquainted with.

No intelligent person, reading the record, can possibly misunderstand what in the Hebrew faith at its best and what in the Christian faith always, as it meets us especially in the New Testament, is meant by God.[8] Cultural and philosophical considerations may influence us as we set forth what we find, *but what we find is undeniable.* God is the Eternal Creative Spirit, in whom dwell perfect holiness, perfect righteousness, perfect wisdom, and perfect love. Of his will all things are. Man is the object of his special concern— man who is spirit, and in whom is some reflection of the God who made him. God the Spirit has great business with his creature man, and this is not only affirmed in Scripture, but is the obvious meaning of the whole discipline of life. God would make known to us his will; indeed, has done so and would bring us to accept it.

Unwilling we may often be to submit, even as was Augustine, who wrote of his hesitations: "By believing might I have been cured, that so the eyesight of my soul being cleared, might in some way be directed to thy truth, which abideth always, and in no part faileth. But as it happens that one, who has tried a bad physician, fears to trust himself with a good one, so was it with the health of my soul, which could not be healed but by believing, and lest it should believe falsehoods, refused to be cured; resisting thy hands, who hast prepared the medicines of faith, and hast applied them to the diseases of the whole world, and given unto them so great authority."[9] Often, again like Augustine and many another, we may be stubborn in clinging to our own self-sufficiency, rebellious at the very thought of being under authority. Yet the great goal stands, fixed of the determinate counsel and foreknowledge of God; hitherto unattained by countless numbers yet attainable in God's good time by all; already actually attained by a few, who thereupon become the authentic witnesses, to be overthrown by no sophistry of worldly minds, to the glory of the goal. And not to its glory only, but to the light which shines back from the goal over the long and arduous journey which the believing soul must follow in order to attain. "In his will is our peace." Only those who know it have the right to affirm it. Those who deny it are by the very fact of their denial disqualified from pronouncing.

A not uncommon way of attempting to destroy the distinction of natural and supernatural is by the claim that the distinction is due to the limitations of our knowledge.[10] As we increase in our knowledge—so it is said—we shall find that what we once regarded as supernatural is so no longer. The disappearance of the idea of the supernatural is therefore only a question of time and knowledge, or as some would say, a question of the more rigorous and extensive application of the scientific method.

But the distinction is not at all one having to do with the extent of knowledge. Instead, it has to do rather with the *nature of being*. Admittedly men have often enough confused the "supernatural" with the "superstitious" and the "preternatural," with the "weird," with the "eerie," with the "uncanny," with the merely "mysterious." Rudolf Otto's famous discussion of the "numinous" is not at all points above suspicion here.[11] But no growth in the scientific understanding of things, and no elimination of the superstitious, can destroy the line that divides the Creator and the creature. Human wisdom, "sweeping the heavens with its telescopes," and applying to what it beholds the principles of mathematics, may eventually decide that the universe has limits, and may determine where they are.[12] What of it? The limits of the physical universe are not the limits of existence. Because we may learn where one "kind" of existence stops does not mean that *every* "kind" of existence must stop. It is more likely to mean the opposite. Not *all* can be limitable. There must be one illimitable as the only possible explanation of the many limitables. There is always a Beyond— a Beyond that is Within as well as a Beyond that is Without. Men of the truest wisdom are also men of the deepest humility.

It is more than twenty years now since Leuba published the apparently convincing evidence that the majority of scientific men believed in neither God nor immortality.[13] But within fifteen years the picture had changed. Many of the outstanding scientists of the world to-day affirm a religious faith.[14] Some of these men may not care to use the word "supernatural," chiefly because of the unfortunate connotation which has been attached to it, but their personal statements show that they do believe in that which the word properly stands for. The English scientist, J. S. Haldane, author of the Gifford Lectures on *The Sciences and Philosophy*, and whose little book on *Materialism*, in which he defends what he calls "spiritual realism," would help many a troubled mind, once answered the question of an interviewer as follows: "In ultimate analysis, the universe can be nothing less than the progressive manifestation of God. Nothing but God's existence can impart objective reality to what appears to us imperfectly, first in physical, then in biological, and finally in psychological interpretation."[15]

This is in substance what is being pleaded for here. It involves the distinction between something we know, and something in which we can only believe. But it also involves that no increase in what we know will ever dispense with that in which we believe, or will make it an object of indubitable scientific knowledge. Indeed, finite and infinite become terms with which we cannot dispense. Identify the finite with the created, and this gives us our field within which the triumphs of knowledge may grow from more to more. Identify the infinite with the creative, and we have the field into which faith may take us, but which can never be the object of scientific knowledge. "A scientific knowledge of the Creator" is an utter contradiction in terms: indeed, it savors of sheer intellectual arrogance, to say nothing worse.

It is not enough to say simply that finite and infinite are necessary categories of thought. They are that, but they are more than that. They are necessary distinctions of being. But the distinction involves creation, that is, a creative act, precisely as Christianity requires. There could be no finite if there were not something brought into existence that was not in existence before. The finite exists relatively to the infinite. What is this but another way of saying that the natural exists relatively to the supernatural. The Unmade and the made, the Creative and the created, the Infinite and the finite, the Supernatural and the natural—these are simply so many ways of expressing one and the same distinction. The distinction is rationally defensible. For Christianity it is indispensable, for not only does Christianity itself affirm it, but the distinction constitutes that framework within which alone the great verities of the Christian faith can properly be set.

Creation, then, is revelation. The denial of this in certain influential quarters in the Church to-day is difficult to understand. To minimize the revelation in creation in order to exalt the revelation in Scripture and in Christ is a strange procedure. That Brunner should have separated himself from Barth at this point is a matter for gratitude.[16] To call God Creator, and yet not to see his creation as to some extent his Word, looks like wilful blindness. All that needs to be said in order to give due significance to the revelation in Scripture, and to the supreme revelation in Christ, the Word made alive, is to say of creation that it is, so to put it, revelation in the rough.

Creation—meaning by this the whole course of nature—is anything but an open book, which he who runs may read. Thomas Paine's famous rhapsody: "The creation speaketh a universal language. . . . It cannot be counterfeited; it cannot be lost; it cannot be altered; it cannot be suppressed. It does not depend upon the will of man whether it shall be published or not; it publishes itself from one end of the earth to the other. It preaches to all nations and all worlds; and this Word of God reveals to man all that it is necessary for him to know"—this rhapsody is far enough away from describing the actual situation. It is one thing to read creation in the light of the Christian revelation (which is what Paine all unconsciously did); it is another thing to read it without that light.

Olin A. Curtis, quoting from *The Age of Reason* these words of Paine, comments on them as follows: "The fact is that the more men know about nature, and the more they rely upon nature, the more agnostic and hopeless they become. For one thing, men need to be told a few plain things about themselves, about their origin, about their spiritual condition, and about their destiny. And in nature there is no perspicuous anthropology."[17] Curtis goes on to add that even beyond this lack of clarity as to man himself, nature "nowhere manifests righteousness," and that "from her works alone no person could ever learn that the Creator has any ethical interest."

This can hardly be denied, and it is one of the chief reasons why scepticism is so rife. It would even account for a great believer like Barth altogether discounting the testimony of nature. Much is written on the unfolding scroll of time, and men look at it, and they struggle to make it out, and one reads it in one way, and another in another. It is not that nothing is written, but that what is written is not clear. It is hieroglyphics, and the key is lost.

Or shall we not rather say that the key has been provided, a Rosetta Stone in very truth, but men will not use it. If the Author of Nature is revealed in the Book of Nature, one must know how to read his Book. And it can be truly read only as one uses the light that has been provided for that very purpose.[18] That light is not bare reason. Bare reason—no less a mind than that of Kant being the attest—is precisely the faculty which is so sadly perplexed. So baffled is reason to read the Book that it is not even sure that it is a Book at all! Or that there is an Author!

> "The human spirits saw I on a day,
> Sitting and looking each a different way;
> And hardly tasking, subtly questioning,
> Another spirit went around the ring
> To each and each: and as he ceased his say
> Each after each I heard them singly sing,
> Some querulously high, some softly, sadly low:
> 'We know not—what avails to know?
> We know not—wherefore need we know?'
> This answer gave they still unto his suing,
> 'We know not, let us do—as we are doing.'"[19]

But perhaps there are *kinds* of books, and perhaps there are *ways* of reading, and perhaps there are insights that are *given* rather than discovered. Perhaps men cannot rightly read the book of nature because they do not know the vocabulary and the grammar! Or to change the figure somewhat, assuming that nature is revelation whose import is not clear, then a revelation whose import is clear may be expected, and it will shed its light on every dark fact. God can be known only as God acts. A God eternally solitary is a God eternally unknown. There must be other than he if he is to be known to be, and there can be other than he only as he wills it, that is, only as he acts. But God can act and still not be known, since in order for God to be known there must be those who can so understand his action as that through it they know him.

But whence come these "knowers"? Are they not God's action too? He makes them as they are just in order that they might know him. But knowing means learning, much patient toil in the school of life, acquiring here a little and there a little, but always the sense of bafflement, of unsolved problems, of unattained wisdom, until "the fulness of the time" could come. Eyes and light make one unity, but only slowly can eyes be brought to endure the brightness of the noon-day sun. God withholds *the whole truth* about himself until such time as the revelation of it could be endured and given its proper response. And still there are those who refuse "the good doctrine," as Paul calls it, as being "profane and old wives' fables."

The Christian man, however, believes that the whole truth has been given. He believes that God has revealed himself in the order of natural events; he believes that God has revealed himself in the distinctive nature of man, and in particular in that which leads man on the endless quest of which religion is the universal expression; he believes that God has revealed himself in a way to be called "special" in the life and experience of Israel as these are recorded in the Old Testament, and in a way that can only be called "unique" in the whole fact of Christ and of what he has brought into the world.[20] Hence it is in Christ, if anywhere, that we are given that final truth of God and of his purpose with us men which illuminates the course of all his activities and dealings elsewhere. Here is that Word which interprets all God's other words, that final thrust of his will into the confusions of the human scene which exposes him to us as completely as it exposes us to him.

That this is pure miracle has already been claimed—as truly miraculous as that primal volition of the Creator whence arose the whole frame of nature and its panoramic content. In both cases it is miracle because it is original, that is, not explicable as the mere

relation of consequent to antecedent. What are the antecedents of
the creative fiat? There are no antecedents save the will and purpose of God. What are the antecedents of Jesus Christ? The question is crucial. If he is to be explained as every other man is to be
explained, then he has the meaning which every other man has,
and no more. But if he is not so to be explained, then his meaning is
that of an act of God for which there may be indeed historical
preparation but for which there can be no historical explanation.
He who himself explains history defies history to explain him. We
have here, in Jesus Christ, an irruption, a discontinuity, an action
of the will of God which has its sole reason in his otherwise inscrutable purpose, and the purpose is no longer inscrutable just
because of this action and just because of the light it throws on all
his other action.

And yet what God did in Christ he did in that same stream of
history within which all his other activities fell, and which indeed
alone account for the stream. That is to say, the story of Jesus
Christ is part of our human story. He is a true historical figure. He
appears in the order we are calling natural, only it is the natural in a
new form. The natural both in its totality and in all its parts bespeaks the supernatural, but here is action of the supernatural which
stands solitary, unique, overwhelming, that one action of the creative and redemptive God never to be repeated because it needs no
repetition, never to be duplicated because it needs no duplication.
Perhaps one must ask to be forgiven—as much by the poet himself
as by others!—for quoting Shelley here, yet the words carry true
insight:

> "The Powers of earth and air
> Fled from the folding star of Bethlehem:
> . . . for killing Truth had glared on them."

God has spoken "in a Son," and he speaks no more except to en-
force and apply this one ultimate speech, and this he does by that
Spirit who takes of the things of Christ and makes them known.

You ask for light: here it is. You ask for truth: here it is. You
ask for a way: here it is. You ask for an assurance of God: here
it is. Yes! You ask for an answer to the dark tragedy of man's

sin and sorrow, and here is the answer; you ask for a door of escape, and here is the door; you ask for one sure word that not only affirms God and describes God but puts God forever on your side against every dread foe that life throws up, and here is that word. It is a Living Word, an Indestructible Word, the Eternal Word of God made humanly real: bone of our bone, flesh of our flesh, immersed in our human lot, tried in all points as we are, everlastingly of us, everlastingly for us, everlastingly with us, veritably *Immanuel,* if so be that that and that only is our vehement strong desire.

Where now is that boasted reason which, failing to find God in the pathway of its own searching, concludes that God is but a human dream? In its name, all that has here been written may be denied. Faith exacts a high price, but unfaith exacts a price also.

> "The Sea of Faith
> Was once, too, at the full, and round earth's shore
> Lay like the folds of a bright girdle furled.
> But now I only hear
> Its melancholy, long, withdrawing roar,
> Retreating, to the breath
> Of the night-wind, down the vast edges drear
> And naked shingles of the world."[21]

Faith gives us that by which to live: unfaith at the best gives but a patient Stoical endurance of all the weary weight of a world become unintelligible.

The refusal of what is offered to us in Christ not only denies the rights of man's total nature, compact as it is of intuitions, awarenesses, necessities, hungers, aspirations, which it ought to be the glory of reason to work *with* instead of to *ignore*—it not only does this, but it requires that the highest which has ever been presented to men, the highest which men have shown themselves capable of believing, the highest which men have shown themselves capable of accomplishing just because they so greatly believe, shall be treated as sheer illusion. The Christian faith may not be—indeed, it is not—demonstrable in strict logic: but what *is* demonstrable is the issue which follows alike its acceptance or its rejection. When men, claiming to be strictly and coldly and objectively rational, make an irrational denial of the supernatural, and thereby cut the ground from under belief in God in any adequate sense, and are led to see in Jesus Christ nothing but one more of the world's wistful but frustrated souls, they become as infants crying in the night, and with no father near. That certainly is demonstrable. "You see, we have only ourselves!" and inconsequentially enough one is tempted to add, "Thank God that we have that much!"

But it is not enough, any more than a cage is enough for Shelley's skylark, meant to fly "higher still and higher," until it bursts the gates of Heaven with the liquid melody of its nostalgic song. How much the unbelieving human spirit can crib and cabin and confine itself is evidenced in a dozen contemporary naturalisms, whether they be classified as evolutionary or rationalistic, humanistic or quasi-theistic. No least question is being raised as to the ability, earnestness, and sincerity of the men who adopt these various positions. They rather need our prayers than our frowns. Nevertheless, one who has honestly tried to read and to understand what these men have set forth as their view of the truth of things, can but express himself thus: "Why should I turn away from the glory of the Christian revelation, from the light it sheds where light is most needed, from the answers it gives to the questions that are most insistent—why should I turn away from it *just for this?* It is bread that I want, and I know where to find it: then why offer me a stone, and be surprised that I refuse it? It is a fountain of living waters that I seek and to which I have gone again and again: then why expect me to quench my thirst at your broken cisterns in which no water is?"

May Shelley be quoted again? It is not being forgotten that he was expelled from Oxford for his share in producing a pamphlet on *The Necessity of Atheism;* nor that, years later, he wrote an *Essay on Christianity* which, for all its ethical idealism and its admiration for the character of Jesus, is certainly a long remove from historical Christianity; nor that he remained to the end a Platonic Idealist, for whom there was but one order of reality, of which all else was but ephemeral symbol. But neither is it being forgotten that he wrote *Prometheus Unbound,* concerning which Stopford Brooke commented: "The means employed by Prometheus are the means employed by Christ, namely, enduring love." Nor is it being forgotten that the greatest Roman Catholic poet of our time, Francis Thompson, to whom Christian dogma was not only the stuff of his poetry but the very breath of his life, found in Shelley a kindred spirit, and wrote to him a tribute that will not quickly be surpassed in our English speech. And it was this Shelley who, in one of the songs in *Hellas*, wrote a stanza which, quite apart from the philosophy out of which it may have come, represents an evaluation of Christ which might well be considered not only by the contemporary naturalists, but by that large group of professedly Christian men whose attitude to Christianity and therefore to Christ himself is so unimaginatively rationalistic, so lacking in any large cosmic sense:

"A Power from the unknown God,
   A Promethean conqueror came;
Like a triumphal path he trod
   The thorns of death and shame.
   A mortal shape to him
   Was like the vapor dim
Which the orient planet animates with light;
   Hell, Sin, and Slavery came,
   Like bloodhounds mild and tame,
Nor preyed, until their Lord had taken flight;
   The moon of Mahomet
   Arose and it shall set:
While blazoned as on Heaven's immortal noon
   The Cross leads generations on."

It does not say it all, but is every modern exponent of the Christian Gospel saying even as much as that, and all the far-flung range of truth it seems so plainly to imply?

Christianity as a religion with a supernatural reference is not a logical demand but a great moral appeal. It is a faith to be accepted, not a philosophy to be constructed. It confronts us at a place where the way parts. This is as it should be, for we are men free to respond, not slaves to crouch at the crack of a whip. Then let the appeal be heard again. Choose you must: what will you choose?

Listen you must: to what voice will you listen? Believe you must: what will you believe? Live you must: how will you live? Venture you must: down which road will you elect to go? Build you must: on what will you build? Here is enduring rock; there is shifting sand. "And the rains descended, and the floods came, and the winds blew, and beat upon that house." They have always done that, and they will do it still. But of one building it was said: "It fell not, for it was founded upon a rock."

And for the rest, let the word of Paul suffice: "Other foundation can no man lay than that which is laid, which is Jesus Christ." But he is no enduring foundation for man's building unless he has in himself the quality of the eternal. That he has that quality is the central claim of the Christian faith, and he has it not because with groping hands he reached up into the Infinite Beyond and brought it down, which no man may do, but because he himself issued from that Beyond, his rightful abode, and here among us men so spoke and so acted as that, he being what he was, his speech was the speech of God and his action the action of God.

And by this Word and this Deed we live.

CHAPTER 14

The Supreme Acquiescence: Virgin Birth and Resurrection

IN ALL THAT HAS BEEN SAID ABOVE, THERE HAS BEEN A STEADY IN-
sistence that Christianity is primarily a faith. It is not a groundless
faith, as we have seen. Nor is it a faith that separates itself from life.
What Paul calls the fruits of the Spirit are just as much fruits of
faith. A truly Christian faith is a creative power. It transforms facts
from one category into another. It carries on and completes that
process which is the essence of personal life.

Persons are the means whereby unknown forces are changed
into significant realities. Repeatedly it has been pointed out that
respecting the universe around us we are neither absolute creators
nor merely passive reporters. We help to make what we see, and
we help to make what we hear. The very wonder of mind is in its
being a power to take something "given," and complete its meaning. Until mind has touched it, or until it has touched mind, that
"given" is an unknown somewhat, a mere possibility of experience waiting for the completion of the conditions whereby possibility becomes actuality. All about us, says the physicist, are sound-
less waves of energy and colorless waves of energy. Something
transforms them, in the one case into mighty harmonies, in the
other case into the glorious splendors of the western sky. What
achieves the miracle of transformation? It is achieved by the magic
touch of mind. Mind—at least mind as it appears in man, and as
what man essentially is—is thrown into the infinite ocean of potentiality, and it takes the potentiality and out of it creates the actual world of its experience.[1]

Now the faith that we have been talking about, the faith, shall
we say, that creates all the wonder and wealth of Christian experience, is this same faculty carried to a higher degree and working
upon a given set of facts of a peculiar kind. It is called "higher"

180

because here its law is freedom, whereas elsewhere its law is necessity. All other things being equal, if I look I cannot but see, and by seeing transform stimulating but colorless energies into beauty of form and shade. There is no freedom here, except, indeed, the freedom to open the eyes. Law does the rest, law I can in nowise escape.

But the Christian finds himself confronted with a set of facts, a series of events, to which he is asked to give a meaning, *but which meaning another may refuse to give and still claim to have treated the facts and events quite rationally.* I have no choice about seeing or hearing or feeling, although by these necessary activities I accomplish a miracle of change. But I have a choice about what I do with the Christian facts. I may refuse to transform them. I may refuse to do anything about them except recognize their purely factual aspect, and at some points I may refuse to do even this much. On the other hand, I may give them the meaning they are said to bear. If I do that, I do it of my own free activity. If I refuse to do it, then so far as I am concerned the facts do not bear their alleged meaning. They can bear it for me only on the condition that I make them bear it. That in the divine intent and purpose they do actually have this meaning must, of course, be true: otherwise I am being deceived. But not until I have given them that meaning *for myself* do they undergo the transformation which sets them in their true character as revelations.[2]

Reason, pronouncing on its observations, says that everywhere a great power is at work: faith reads that power as a Personal Will, even God. Reason reports that there is simply a cosmic process: faith sees the cosmic process as the outworking of the purposes of that God, conceived as both Sovereign Will and Holy Love. Reason can go no farther than to say respecting Jesus that he was the Son of Mary: faith adds to his Sonship to Mary the claim of his Sonship to God. Reason, confronted with the Cross, can see nothing there but a broken man, driven to his death by hate and jealousy: to faith, that broken man on a cross is the uttermost judgment on sin of the Holy God and the uttermost expression of his gracious love for sinners—the Lamb of God bearing away the sins of the world. The eyes of reason see nothing but an empty tomb: but to the eyes of faith that empty tomb stands for the miracle of Resurrection. In silent awe, faith marks there the evidence of love's invasion of the last stronghold of sin, to take away its sting, to rob it of its victory, and to turn it into the very gateway of life.

It is not that facts such as these do not already possess this intrinsic significance. We have to believe that they have this significance, however, before they can actually have this significance *for us*. But that they do actually possess it is the testimony of the Word of God.[3] The question therefore becomes again that of our attitude to Scripture. Scripture is a record of facts *and* of what they signify. We can accept the facts and not the meaning; for example, the fact of the Cross and the fact of the Empty Tomb. It must be that they do mean what Scripture says: otherwise is the Christian faith without foundation. But only if we ourselves accept this meaning can the meaning in any vital way affect us. We commit ourselves to the testimony of Scripture, and what is this but our faith? Christian truth is not of human reasoning but of divine revelation: wherefore faith is the only possible organ of its apprehension and appropriation. But in that case, faith is not simply pure subjectivity, an arbitrary act whereby we wishfully assign a meaning where such a meaning does not in actual fact exist. Instead, it is that process whereby objectively given truth becomes tied into the very structure of our life, to accomplish there that redeeming and sanctifying purpose which alone brings life to its fulfillment. We *must* be believers, and here are the truths we are called upon to believe—*if we will*.

It is sometimes said that Christianity is not a question of facts and events, but of truths and ideas, and that these truths and ideas may stand quite apart from any facts or events to which in the past they may have been attached. Kant, for example, attempted this,[4] and he has been widely followed by men who take for granted "the scientific view of the world." Because the scientific view seems to render certain alleged facts impossible, and yet because the related ideas are valuable, it would seem that these valuable ideas could be retained, and the scientific difficulty be evaded, by treating the facts as merely symbolic.

This way of getting rid of awkward facts, however, constitutes a direct attack upon the historical bases of our faith. Abandoning the factual means abandoning the historical, and the very thing that makes Christianity so significant is just the startling events through which it was created.[5] Hegel notwithstanding, there is all the difference in the world between an actual historical Incarnation and the mere God-man *idea* as the synthesizing of the two opposite ideas of God and Man. It is a comparatively simple matter to offer a purely rationalistic interpretation of the Christian facts. But to ask us to surrender the most distinctive features of our faith because these features may be accounted for as to their origin and influence either by psychology or by the study of other religions or by the influence of ancient superstitions no longer to be accepted, is in effect to make non-faith the arbiter of faith. It involves the supposition that there is only one approach to truth, and that all truth must fall into the same pattern. The request certainly assumes that the Church has no rights of its own, no obligation by that which has produced it and by which it must continue to live. It sees the Church as, shall we say, a poor suppliant Lazarus at the gate of the lordly palace of secular wisdom, grateful if it may be thrown a few crumbs from the kitchen table.

Two questions in particular which are affected by this attitude are those of the Virgin Birth of Christ[6] and his Resurrection.[7] Here are two veritable stones of offence, over which men stumble continually, and concerning which we are told that they must be either altogether rejected as having outlived their usefulness, or reshaped in suchwise as that what is so obviously objectionable in them shall be done away. Both claims, impressive enough in a less sophisticated age, have lost their credibility for a scientific age like our own.

As to this, the first thing to say is that neither of these two elements of the Christian faith has anything whatever to do with science. They are not presented for scientific verification. They are certainly not offered as disputing the scientific view of the world— at least, not unless the scientific view of the world is offered as absolutely all-comprehensive and final, and in that case it would cease to be a scientific view, and would have become instead a philos-

ophy.[8] The Christian faith no more asks for scientific corroboration of the Virgin Birth or of the Resurrection than it asks for
scientific corroboration of the Fatherhood of God; or of the Incarnation of the Eternal Son as Jesus Christ; or of the Trinity; or of
the Atonement made for sin in the sufferings and death of Christ;
or of forgiveness as a gift of the grace of God mediated through
Christ on the condition of penitence and faith; or of the Eucharist
as a dramatization of the central fact in divine-human relations,
and an actual participation by the believer in the sufferings, exaltation, and glory of his Lord. If the "truth" of such things depends
upon scientific corroboration, then they can never be held to be
true, because they necessarily lie beyond the reach of "the scientific method," and only where the scientific method is applicable is
a scientific pronouncement possible.

Science as such is equally impotent either to prove or to disprove Christian truth. The area of such truth is the area of faith,
and while what is held in faith must not be in palpable contradiction with what is known to be true in other areas or on other
grounds, the fact of its non-contradictability is also a matter of
very great importance. What cannot be either proven or disproven
at least *may be* true. It will not, of course, follow that every claim
that men can make, of whatever sort, that cannot be disproven, is
therefore to be accepted. We are too familiar with the power of
imagination to say that! But the specific questions before us are not
to be dispensed with as mere imaginations. They are not entirely
wanting in evidence of a kind which even the purely historical
student must respect, but no evidence accessible to us could ever
suffice to lift them beyond the reach of all possible doubt. What is
accepted as a faith can always be denied, but the faith will endure.

> ". . . for on earth
> Who against faith and conscience can be heard
> Infallible?"

The Virgin Birth and the Resurrection, we need to see, do not
stand by themselves. They are parts, and let it here be said at
once, vital parts of the organism of Christian faith, or better, of
the organism of Christian truth. It is at that point that we are to

hold our case. The documentary evidence for the Virgin Birth can always be negatively handled. The records of the Resurrection may be shown to have serious difficulties.[9] It is a comparatively simple matter for historicism, operating from the standpoint of an initial prejudice, to render worthless the evidence for both beliefs. But we should not forget that historicism can get rid of much more than these two. Historicism is the handmaiden of rationalism, by whose postulates it is controlled, and to whose purposes it lends itself. The Christian who supposes he can satisfy the type of mind that makes this approach by giving up the Virgin Birth and the Resurrection, makes a grave mistake. It will never be satisfied until it has seen the Christian religion stripped of everything that even suggests a supernatural reference, and reduced to a comparatively innocuous ethical idealism. It were better that we keep the Christian truth in its entirety, and have something really worth believing in, really worth standing for, really worth living by, than to emasculate it at the behest of alien thought until the perfect round has become a few broken arcs.

As to these two doctrines, one may have considered carefully everything that is to be said against them, the debatable character of the documentary evidence, the similarity to ideas known to prevail in the ancient world, the fact that the original witnesses were never subjected to the sort of rigid examination that could be set up to-day, even the very character of the alleged events themselves—one may have considered all such objections, and yet still say in complete sincerity: "Nevertheless, I believe, and I believe primarily because of the intrinsic nature of Christianity; because ultimately it must stand or fall as an organic whole; because part fits into part with an astonishing exactitude; and because when the living whole is disintegrated, the fragments that are left, useful though they may still be, and acceptable for certain purposes, lack not only the intellectual cogency of the whole, but also, and more seriously, its moral power and its spiritual majesty."[10]

Yet there are still timid believers who would feel so much more secure if these two stones of offence could either be given at least an obscure corner in the architectonics of science, or, failing that, be quietly buried. They even suggest that, after all, neither belief is "essential" to Christianity, and that it is therefore better to drop what has now become an encumbrance, just as other encumbrances have been dropped in the past.

One thing, however, these timid souls should not overlook. There is a way of regarding Jesus Christ which most indubitably *is* essential to Christianity; and the evidence is overwhelming that when men begin to surrender belief in the Virgin Birth and the Resurrection, they are also getting ready to surrender that belief regarding Christ himself which is the vital center of the whole body of faith. There should be no mistake about that. If a person wants a purely humanitarian Christology, well and good; but let him face honestly all that that implies. Let him admit that it changes radically the whole Christian belief as to God. Let him admit that it calls for the surrender of the Incarnation, and of the Atonement, and of Christ as living reality accessible and available here and now. Indeed, it may very well be that the fundamental difficulty is not with the Virgin Birth and the Resurrection at all, but with the historical doctrine of the Person of Christ, and that these two are being let go because they are seen to be serious obstacles to the abandonment of the other.

As to the desirability of some measure, however slight, of scientific support, those who crave it do not seem to realize that the entire Christian case—and in this they are presumably concerned—is so much stronger just because it is not of the sort that can be subjected to direct scientific scrutiny. For all that, they cogitate upon the phenomena of "parthenogenesis" and of "resuscitation," and when they read of experiments in the fertilization of domestic animals, or for that matter of human beings, without organic contact, or of drugs sufficiently powerful to stimulate into action again a heart which had ceased to beat, they become excited over the prospect of scientific proof for the Virgin Birth and Resurrection.

Such scientific experiments have no least bearing on the question at issue. Neither the Virgin Birth of Christ nor his Resurrection from the dead can possibly be a problem for science; they are related rather to the problem of the revelational and redemptive purposes of God, and are offered solely as parts of God's way of meeting that problem. One may believe both or disbelieve both (for to believe in one and not in the other does not help at all), but the real grounds of belief or of disbelief must be the same in each case. Not even Mary herself could have satisfied a group of modern biologists respecting the birth of her Child, nor could John and Peter respecting the Resurrection of Christ. *Neither event was that sort of thing.* Or if it was, then are we impoverished indeed, for we are now deprived of the privilege of faith. We know too much: our increased knowledge has opened one door only to shut in our face another. O foolish Christians, who hath bewitched you! Why do we not see that if to-day, under those conditions of absolute control which science knows so well how to devise, a human mother gave birth to a child in suchwise that all possibility of human paternity was excluded, and thereby proved, what now seems indeed to be actually the case, that parthenogenesis could occur at the level of man, nothing whatever would be proved thereby about the Virgin Birth of our Lord? A modern "parthenogenetic" child would not thereupon be "another Christ"!

The Virgin Birth is not offered as a possibility latent in the race, or as a mere demonstration of what *could* be. We are not talking about *a* virgin birth, but about *the* Virgin Birth, and the differences of expression are significant. Faith is never asked to consider the Birth of Christ as primarily a biological phenomenon.[11] Instead, what is offered is offered as sheer miracle, something that never could be repeated because it was the act of God in pursuit and fulfillment of his age-old purpose to appear among men and accomplish in their behalf that which only he could, and which could be accomplished only in this way. An indubitable parthenogenetic human birth would in actual fact constitute an apologetic handicap, because so many people would then say that it was now possible for them to believe in the Virgin Birth of Christ, while yet they would be believing in it for quite wrong reasons, would be confusing a biological exception scientifically brought about with an inexplicable divine event, and therefore would have given up the only thing which could make faith the morally creative power it must be.

From one point of view, such a monograph, running to four

hundred pages, as that of J. Gresham Machen on *The Virgin Birth
of Christ,* is to be regretted. The book is primarily a defence of the
doctrine on the ground of the documentary evidence, and a more
exhaustive treatment of it has not been made in our time. But the
question can never be limited to that basis. If the *only* reason we
have for our faith is the story in Matthew and Luke, it is little
enough, and uncertain enough. Perhaps the most illuminating
thing that Machen says is that even if belief in the Virgin Birth is
not necessary to every individual Christian, it is necessary to the
completion of Christianity. Insistence on that aspect of the question
is a much wiser procedure than the attempt to transform the
Matthew and Lucan narratives into sworn legal documents which
automatically compel belief.

Much the same position would have to be taken relative to any
attempt to support the Resurrection of Christ by an alleged demonstration of the possibility of "resuscitation." Men have been known
to be buried who afterwards gave signs of life. In such cases, only
one thing could be said: they were buried alive. The recent discovery of a drug able to restore life after competent physicians
have declared life to be extinct simply compels the conclusion that
notwithstanding the diagnosis life still lingered. If a heart that has
ceased to beat should again be stimulated to action, we must infer
that the cessation of the heart-beat is not in every case absolute
evidence of death. Science would admit that in cases such as these
there was every likelihood that, without intervention, death would
actually have occurred; but it cannot admit that where life was absolutely extinct it could be restored.[12]

One must go even farther and say that in the event of there
being controlled experiments for settling this question, resulting in
a person declared by every known scientific test to be dead, and to
have been dead for several days, reviving or having been revived
and thereupon resuming a normal life, even that would have no
bearing whatever on the Resurrection of Christ. We are faced
here not with an example of "suspended animation," or of simple
"resuscitation." The various "theories" of the Resurrection characteristic of a certain type of *Lives* of Jesus in the last century were
so many examples of rationalistic desperation. Even Schleier-

macher once suggested that Jesus did not really die on the Cross at all, but only swooned from the agony, and that the cool air of the rock-hewn tomb revived him.[13] A number of scholars of much less spiritual understanding than Schleiermacher himself, for example Paulus, later took up and elaborated the suggestion; but concerning this even Strauss, avowed enemy of all "supernaturalism" as he was, felt compelled to write: "It is impossible that a being who had stolen half-dead out of the sepulchre, who crept about weak and ill, wanting medical treatment, who required bandaging, strengthening, and indulgence, and who still at last yielded to his sufferings, could have given to the disciples the impression that he was a Conqueror over death and the grave, the Prince of Life, an impression which lay at the bottom of their future ministry."[14]

In the proper view of it, the Resurrection of Christ has no analogy; and so far as its method is concerned it is without explanation, save as we see it as an essential part of the total process involved in the Incarnation of the Son of God. It gets its credibility from one point, and from one point alone. We are asked to believe in it, not as a possibility falling within the order of nature, but as an impossibility in that order as constituted, and yet as an event which actually occurred and could only occur because the subject of it was nature's Lord, "whom therefore it was impossible that death should hold." It is only as such an event, only as such an experience, that it is set forth. Deny that the subject of it was such a One as is presented in the New Testament and as was proclaimed in the earliest Christian preaching of which we have any record, and the credibility of the Resurrection evaporates just as inevitably as does the credibility of the Virgin Birth. Affirm that he was such a One, and what has been called above "The Supreme Acquiescence"— which is the yielding by our stubborn human minds to the miracle of his Birth and the miracle of his Return from Death—becomes a possibility completely sincere.

CHAPTER 15

The Justification of the Acquiescence

IF WE HAVE BEEN RIGHT IN REGARDING BELIEF IN THE VIRGIN BIRTH and the Resurrection as "the supreme acquiescence" of the Christian mind, some further justification of the acquiescence might be appropriate. It should perhaps be said that the acquiescence involved is not of the kind of which Jesus' experience in Gethsemane is the world's most impressive example. A difference should be recognized between the surrender of the will to what is believed to be the will of God for one's life, and the acceptance by the mind of a proffered truth which runs directly across normal human experience. Of course, if one does believe in the Virgin Birth and the Resurrection, it will be because they are taken to be true, and it is always the will of God that truth shall be accepted. For all that, the distinction just drawn is sound enough. Without a doubt, for the typical modern mind the Virgin Birth and the Resurrection are genuine difficulties, belief in which may call for very great effort indeed—shall we say even intellectual travail—such as justifies us in describing the belief as a sheer acquiescence of the mind. And even although in a given case it may not be so, it is always possible that the believer may be described by others as one who has "compelled his mind to accept."[1] The metaphor of "the eye of a needle" has many applications.

It is not necessary to repeat again at length all the reasons that have been urged against the belief in the Resurrection. The outright sceptic goes through much unnecessary trouble to disprove it, as does the rationalistic Christian scholar. Every student knows how widespread was the "solar" myth and the "vegetation" myth in the ancient world, and how the various Mystery Religions were centered in a dramatic representation of the death and resurrection of the god of the cult, symbolic of the purification and of the

190

return to new life of the worshippers themselves.[2] Attempts have been made, supported by an ample show of scholarship, to explain the New Testament story of the Resurrection of Christ as one more example of this dramatization of the victory of the cult-god over the dark powers of the underworld.

In the Mysteries, however, the resurrection drama was never connected with a person so definitely and unmistakably historical as was Jesus of Nazareth, any more, it might be added, than the various stories of the births of half-gods and half-goddesses from human mothers were ever centered in a character even remotely resembling the character of Mary. The Resurrection narratives themselves have been examined with incredibly meticulous care, often with a view to destroying their trustworthiness, especially on account of alleged inconsistencies which the informed believer makes no least effort to deny, since he is fully aware of their presence. In one sense he rejoices in these inconsistencies, for they at least indicate lack of deliberate collusion on the part of the narrators.

What the critics seem steadily to overlook is the fact that long before the narratives were given their present form, there was a Church, daring, resolute, missionary, based upon faith in the Risen Christ and proclaiming him to whomever would listen. We could even admit that certain features may have been added to the narratives to increase their verisimilitude, for example, the "piece of a broiled fish (and a honeycomb)," in Luke 24.42, and the command to the unbelieving Thomas to "touch" for himself the wounded side, in John 20.27—we could admit this, and still leave the fundamental position unchanged.[3] It is not that the documentary evidence is unnecessary or unimportant; it would be foolish to say that. All that is being claimed is that *the documentary evidence is not all that we have to go by.* The origin of the Christian Church itself; the fact that the New Testament is the product of the Church; the fact that when the Church is first met historically it is as a body of believing men to whom the Risen Christ is the most indubitable of all certainties; the fact that the message the Church proclaimed as it achieved its early expansion was just this message of a Christ who having been crucified and buried rose again and made himself known among men, and now "ever liveth to make intercession" —these are the facts that give point to the narratives. The narratives without such facts might very well be held to be suspect: the facts and the narratives combine in a complete congruity.

So that the important question is not, "Do these stories as to how Christ appeared to his disciples agree in absolutely every particular?" But rather is the important question: "Why did men tell these stories at all?" To say that they "invented" them in order to justify themselves in breaking with their own past, in incurring family and social ostracism, in fleeing to distant places, in risking persecution by those in authority—this, to say the least, savors of ingenuousness.[4] Of course the stories do not "prove" the Resurrection: anybody can give good reasons for impugning their evidential value. Of course the facts of the primitive belief and of the primitive Church and of the primitive message do not "prove" it: any informed person can make out an imposing case for "the growth of superstitions in history," and then offer the origin of the Church and its faith as an example of this growth. Of course the disciples may have suffered from "illusions," or have been "sincerely mistaken": it is a simple enough matter to show that people have taken for real what was afterwards proven to have been unreal. All these possibilities may be allowed by the believer himself, without in the least shaking his confidence that there is a *reason* for the Resurrection narratives, a *reason* for the faith of the disciples, a *reason* for the central message of the Church, and that this reason is the one actually given, namely, that Christ, having been crucified and buried, "presented himself alive after his passion by many proofs, appearing unto them by the space of forty days, and speaking the things concerning the Kingdom of God" (Acts 1.3).

The Resurrection does not mean that a dead man walked about again. It means that the episode of death was unmistakably shown not to have been final. The empty tomb and the appearances were "signs" of an overwhelming fact. It is a fact without analogy and without comparison; hence any attempt to describe it can only be approximate. The admixture of "physical" and "spiritual" in the narratives is exactly what we should expect. These men were not concerned with an analysis of their experience so much as they were to bear testimony to an inescapable reality. What their experience of this reality did was to create in their souls a conviction concerning their Lord and his victory over death, which was sufficient to answer all their doubts, utterly transform their estimate of the Cross, destroy the hesitation and uncertainty which had marked their ways, and make out of them a band of men of incredible audacity both in what they said and in what they did. To discount all of this on the ground that it sprang from nothing real in the first place is still any man's right, but the burden of proof lies upon him who would do this, and the burden, in view of the total situation, is heavy indeed.[5] That which meets us at the point of the sudden upbursting of the Christian faith, centered as it is in Christ crucified, risen, and alive for evermore as a redeeming reality accessible to faith and love, constitutes a body of fact not lightly to be pushed aside.

Yet once again it must be allowed that it can be pushed aside by those who wish to do so. For when all is said and done, we are faced with a faith. It began as a faith, and only as a faith can it continue. It is not an irrational faith, because good reasons may be stated in its support. The faith was originally born out of a vast incredulity: Thomas was not the only "doubter" of that little band! Not one of them had any initial expectancy of what finally occurred.[6] Not one of them but could have said:

> "Ye ignorant and idle fishermen!
> Hence to your huts, and boats, and inland native shore,
>   And catch not men, but fish;
>   Whate'er things ye might wish,
> Him neither here nor there ye e'er shall meet with more.
>   Ye poor deluded youths, go home,
>   Mend the old nets ye left to roam,
>   Tie the split oar, patch the torn sail:
>   It was indeed an 'idle tale.' . . ."[7]   *Clough*

Yet the miracle of transformed men occurred, and it ought not to be without significance that the miracle continues to be duplicated wherever the faith is accepted. We can hardly escape here the "either-or." Either Christ rose from the dead, or he did not. Either the empty tomb means miracle, or it means delusion, mockery, and deceit. Either the disciples were the victims of a fantasy—a fantasy from which has sprung a spiritual power infinitely more mighty and more beneficent than any power which has ever sprung from drab reality—or they were confronted with precisely that reality which they claimed, *and which so completely explains everything else.* These are the alternatives, and there is no other.[8] It ought frankly to be acknowledged by the unbeliever that his rejection of the evidence is based on the prior supposition that the alleged event itself could not have happened. Those who believe that it *could have* happened because the subject of the experience was "the Word made flesh" have all the evidence they need to justify their act of faith. They do not say that doubt is impossible. They only say that faith is possible, too.

Where faith is called for, there is necessarily an alternative. Either we know or we believe, and where we believe because we cannot know we recognize that the belief is a venture and may be mistaken. "I believe, help thou my unbelief," must always be our cry. What is belief but unbelief conquered? What is acquiescence but the compulsion of the mind? What is faith but straining doubt held in leash? Browning's Bishop Blougram spoke for others besides himself when he said:

> "With me, faith means perpetual unbelief
> Kept quiet like the snake 'neath Michael's foot
> Who stands calm just because he feels it writhe."

It is no shame to feel clutch at one's heart-strings on occasion the bony fingers of horrific doubt. That is but to know oneself human. The breaking waves were too much for Peter, and he has had his successors. The victory that overcometh the world is not given to those who rest securely in their tents, but to those who, having clothed themselves with the whole armor of God, go forth to the battle, taking with them above all things else "the shield of faith, wherewith to quench all the fiery darts of the evil one." Those "fiery darts" are the insidious voices of doubt, coming from the most unexpected quarters, but without power to injure unless they get by the shield.

> "The sum of all is—yes, my doubt is great,
> My faith's the greater—then my faith's enough."

But this is not all. There is an *experience* besides. We may define experience in this connection as all that happens to a person and all that a person seeks to cause to happen, because he accepts the Christian faith and surrenders himself wholly to it. He takes to be true what he can only believe to be true, but the results of the belief increasingly strengthen his confidence. Experience of the kind referred to can never yield a logical certainty, since a logical certainty admits of no rational contradiction, but it does yield a moral certainty. It has already been said that the point of our greatest necessity is also the point of our greatest risk—the point of choice. There is a *must-be* that we cannot escape, and there is a *may-be* that we cannot escape, and there is a *may-be* that we can escape, but our true measure is in that which we build on a *may-be*. We cease to be slaves driven by compulsion, and become masters exercizing the right of freedom. The right of freedom is the right to be wrong, and there is only one greater right—the right to be right. But the exercize of the right of freedom reveals at once our dignity and our tragedy. It involves dignity, because it means that we are the creators of our character and therefore of our destiny. But it also involves tragedy, because it means that we may treat a false as a true, and a true as a false. In every choice of the right we risk being wrong.

We are therefore under the perpetual danger of being disillusioned. Our rock may turn out to be sand. The star to which we hitched our wagon may turn out to be a Jack o' Lantern. This is the inescapable predicament of free beings. Yet if to avoid the predicament we refuse to venture, we do not thereby escape a choice. The decision not to choose is itself a choice, and because it is negative it is not any the less charged with consequences than it would be had it been positive. Either way there is experience.

It therefore cannot be said that what a person believes about the Resurrection of Christ is a matter of no great importance. A flat refusal of it means that one must choose a view of God and the world, and of the entire structure of Christian truth, congruous with the refusal. One may, of course, assent to it on the condition that every least suggestion of the "miraculous" or of the "supernatural" be eliminated, but what is then assented to is quite lacking in great creative power. The very fact which gives rise to the challenge is no longer there. On the other hand, when one believes in the Resurrection of Christ in the sense of an event completely inexplicable except on the ground that it involves the action of God in a way to which there is no comparison, then one rises to a height of faith which creates an experience not otherwise to be known.

For such an act of God will not be taken as isolated. It will be seen to have far-reaching relationships. It will be seen to require a view of God and of his relation to the world, and a view of Christ and of his relation to God and the whole purpose of God with men, which is exactly what Christianity calls for, and whose acceptance means that the believer is staking his very soul on one audacious and magnificent throw.[9] We must not permit our rationalistic sympathies here to obscure the issue. It does matter, and it matters profoundly, whether we take the Resurrection of Christ as factual or as symbolic or as what is sometimes obscurely described as "spiritual." If by "spiritual" is meant that there was no event transcending the natural order, and if by "symbolic" is meant that the real truth here—the truth which originated the Christian faith —is simply that "no good thing is ever lost," then let it be frankly said that the view means that the Resurrection is not believed in, because there is no indubitable fact for which the word itself stands.

But the surrender exacts a price. It exacts a price in experience. It means that some things are no longer possible. It means that life is again brought within the circle of demonstrabilities. It is "cribbed, cabined, and confined" within a chart of our own making. For those who want it this way, the right so to have it must be conceded. But making that concession does not settle the issue. The alternative still remains, and Christianity means that it is the will of God that the alternative shall be accepted. God has expressed his will in certain great historic realities. But what he has willed *to be* he also wills that we shall *believe*, just as he wills that rich and deep experience which the belief makes possible.

That chain of sequences, however, may always be broken. It belongs to no man to oppose God's will as to what shall *be*, nor to oppose God's will as to the *effects* which follow causes. But it does belong to every man to oppose God's will at the point of *belief*.

God ordains the factual basis of human salvation, and he ordains the method and the nature of that salvation. But while God ordains that belief—more exactly, faith—shall connect the factual basis of salvation with the personal experience of salvation, the act of faith is something that not even God can compel. In the center of every man's being there is an impregnable area, utterly inviolate by any power other than the man himself, where in complete solitariness he must make choice of his ultimate faith. Such a faith cannot be compelled. It is a choice, a free choice, limited only by the proffered alternatives. It is here that the great issues of life are settled, and according to what is here chosen as supremely significant, so will the outcome be. The choice itself—this is ours; but the operation of the choice in the complex web of character, attitude, and destiny, is under a law not of our choosing.[10]

Dissent or assent as respects the total body of Christian truth, including the two elements especially being considered, can never be esteemed a matter of indifference. It is inevitable that results shall be produced, and these results are what is meant by "experience." When a man says, in complete sincerity, "I believe in the Resurrection of Jesus Christ," and "I believe in his Virgin Birth," he is committing himself to much more than these. In the same way, when he denies these, he is denying very much more than these. Involved in the affirmation or the denial, as the case may be, is a total view of things, and a self-commitment to that view. The man who assents to these two truths assents to a quite different view of God and the world from what is assented to by the man who denies them. He denies the absoluteness of naturalistic causality. He believes in a God who not only *can*, if necessary, break his way into the orderly sequences of nature and history, but who has *actually done it*, because it was called for by his purpose with man.

Certainly this can be denied; just as certainly it can be declared. The denial is supported by every objective empiric consideration that can be mustered. The declaration is supported by nothing else than the testimony of the Christian tradition. The sceptic can point to facts; the believer can point only to a faith. It is not an even choice. It takes little enough of will *not to believe*. Yet in believing that for which the evidence is admittedly slight, especially when compared with all that may be said against it, the believer takes a definite stand for a God who can act freely, for a universe in which that free action takes place, and for his own freedom to choose the less probable just because the less probable carries a profounder moral and spiritual significance than is carried by the more probable.[11] He is not blind to what he is doing. He is even willing to admit that there are more palpable reasons for his being mistaken than there are palpable reasons for his being right. But he takes the dreadful chance. He puts himself in the scale against every naturalistic and even rationalistic consideration. He cannot do that without creating for himself what is at times an almost intolerable tension. But at the same time he makes a great discovery, perhaps the greatest discovery the human soul ever can make—the discovery that out of this very tension there is liberated a peace, a power, *a sense of rightness,* which becomes to him the sufficient authentication of his act of intellectual humility in taking sides with truth that might so easily be—and for many is—incredible error.

This discovery of the relation between "tension" and "spiritual life"—a relation of which Rudolf Eucken used to make so much[12]—is tantamount to a confirmation of what has repeatedly been said above, namely, that in respect of Christian things faith is the forerunner of experience. What is usually called "an experience of Christ" is in reality a type of experience made possible because of belief in Christ. In that case, the measure of the belief or faith will have some bearing on the measure of the experience. This is an important fact. It allows for the New Testament distinction between "babes in Christ" and "strong men in Christ." There can be very genuine Christian experience on less than a complete acceptance of the entire body of Christian truth. The first faint venture toward Christ carries an immediate response, which is the beginning of an experience which increases in richness and depth according as the venture becomes bolder and more unqualified. "First the blade, and then the ear, and then the full corn in the ear."

It is this *pari passu* accompaniment of experience and venture which increases the conviction of the believer that he is right because he has found the source of power. If a Christian is one who believes in God through Christ, and who commits himself wholly to Christ in love and devotion, then it is very evident that a person may be a Christian, and may enter very deeply into the secret of Christ, and believe in neither the Virgin Birth nor the Resurrection. It is faith that saves—faith in Christ.

Nevertheless, there is a total body of truth of which Christ is the center, and which without the Virgin Birth and the Resurrection is incomplete. The Church as the Body of Christ is called to bear uncompromising testimony to that total body of truth. The Church is not required to exclude from its membership those who confess intellectual difficulties at this point and that, provided that these persons confess Christ as their Lord and Saviour. But the Church is required to maintain its testimony unimpaired, to bring to bear upon the disciple, through instruction and preaching and song and prayer and ritual and symbolism and sacrament, the whole splendor of its heritage, with the hope that what at one period were stones of offence for the disciple shall become for him a veritable part of the structure of faith. He grows in grace as he grows in the knowledge of Jesus Christ. He sees, or he may see, what is meant by the organism of Christian truth.[13] The Virgin Birth ceases to be a problem and the Resurrection ceases to be a problem, as even the miracles of the Gospel story may cease to be a problem, because all appear as integral parts of that self-consistent whole of truth and reality which is constituted of the Incarnation of the Son of God— who for us men and for our salvation came down, and was born of the Virgin Mary, and was made man, and was crucified, and the third day rose again, and having ascended into heaven for ever liveth to make intercession for us.

There is still no truer way, therefore, of describing Jesus Christ than by calling him Son of God. "He that hath seen me hath seen the Father." The Christian belief as to God is not read out of nature. It is not a merely philosophical deduction. Both the facts which justify it and the truth which they justify are alike "given." Christ is himself God's own "Word," which means that he is not merely a teacher telling us things about God which he believes to be true, but is himself God uttered. God asks us to face the whole fact of Christ, and then to recognize that in so doing we are facing *himself*. The Creator appears within the creation. The essentially Eternal invades the temporal order. What appears *here* is a revelation of what is *there*. One who meets us as Man has all the meaning of God, because he exists for no other reason than just to have this meaning. The *milieu* of man is necessarily different from the *milieu* of God, but when the Son of God exchanges the divine *milieu* for the human, there is a real humiliation, a real sacrifice, a real human experience, while yet the Subject retains an unbroken continuity.

Once this great truth is grasped, the congruity with it of every other Christian truth becomes increasingly clear. The instinct of the Church in clinging to the divinity of its Lord is the instinct of self-preservation, to say nothing more. The attempt to "prove" the divinity—at least as the Church later defined it—by things he said about himself, or to "disprove" it by things that he said or did not say, is quite beside the point. If he had known himself to be what later the Church declared he was, then he could not have been that! The very condition to the Incarnation was in the subjection of the Incarnate One to the law of the human—which precluded that he should have known all that he was making possible. What manner of abnormality would it have been had the Child, the Youth, the Man, known about himself all the truth! *Not the Man knowing the experience of God, but God knowing the experience of the Man*—this is the mystery of the Incarnation. It means therefore that the God of the Christian is a God who knows the human lot, and who within the limitations of that lot accomplished something in which every man could share. Into the very structure of the divine there has been taken up all the fact and meaning of the human. The ontological distinction of the divine and the human has become an ontological identity which, once achieved, remains a permanent fact of existence.

The New Testament may state this chiefly in the form of figures, because the New Testament is a book of religion, not of philosophy. But this is what the New Testament everywhere *means*. "I go unto my Father." "I will send you another Comforter." "A cloud received him out of their sight." "I see the Son of Man standing on the right hand of God." "We must all be made manifest before the judgment seat of Christ." "He hath made us to sit with Christ in the heavenly places." "In him dwelleth all the fulness of the Godhead bodily." "For Christ entered not into a holy place made with hands . . . but into heaven itself, now to appear before the face of God for us." What are these but so many ways of suggesting that the historical Christ is forever integrated with the Eternal God?

Nowhere is this more dramatically done than in the Apocalypse of John. The exiled seer saw "the throne of God *and of the Lamb*," and elsewhere in his vision that Lamb appears as "a Lamb that was slain." It is as though John could not describe God without including in the description all that he means by "the Lamb." He does not mean by this a dualism. He means rather that there is, if the case may be so stated, one Divine Whole of which "the Lamb" is an inseparable part. What is "the Lamb" of the Apocalypse but "the Word" of the Fourth Gospel—a constituent of Deity, the ground of creation, the ground of revelation, the ground of incarnation, the ground of redemption? Just as "the Word became flesh," so "the Lamb was slain to purchase from every nation" a vast company which should be the Church, the New Jerusalem, "the bride of the Lamb." Such daring metaphor is not meaningless. When we put the truth into more sober language, we can but say that it means that he who rules at the heart of the universe is unlike me, *but like me too*. The defeat of God in the first Adam is met by the triumph of God in the Second Adam. It belongs to God eternally to be able to enter our human lot. In and as Jesus Christ he made that entry, and now forevermore he remains the God who did that, who sacrificially created a common center for himself and us men.

Of course we cannot say this in a way that is free from all objection. When the *idea* itself is objectionable, of what use is it to seek to evade the force of the objection by some ambiguous linguistic "re-statement"? It were far better to state the truth definitely, make sympathetic recognition of the numerous alleged difficulties, and yet still insist that this is what the Christian faith really means. In so stating it, we can hardly avoid the paradox. One who was more than man was yet most truly Man; one whose being was eternal nevertheless entered the temporal order by birth and left it by death; one to whom it belonged to uphold all things by the word of his power yet had not where to lay his head; one who was concerned to know and to do the will of God for himself was at the same time giving a new significance to the will of God, and to obedience to it, for all mankind—that all such statements savor of the paradox is undeniable; that objections may be offered to them, objections logical, objections metaphysical, is equally undeniable. Yet it is just as undeniable that such statements must be made if the historical Christian doctrine of Jesus Christ as Son of God and Son of Man is true. Deny the doctrine, and other denials will necessarily follow, but a consideration of what these denials will be might well give us pause. See in Jesus Christ no longer "miracle," and the horizons of reality move in upon us to suffocate our spirits and to restrict our flight. A wall is around us, and from invisible bottom to invisible top there is in that wall no door through which we can pass, no window by which a light that never was on land or sea may fall across our way. It is in the name of all that we believe to be most precious that we declare the fact of such a door, of such a window, and that Christ is it.

The declaration carries with it that Christ should have entered our human lot and should eventually have left it by means that we can only call "supernatural." What has here been written on that question has not been written without full realization of the difficulties involved. Neither has it been written in the interests of mere dogmatic continuity. It has been written because of the demand of the total Christian faith. The miracle of the Person carries with it, by the sheer force of the law of congruity, every other miracle. It is inevitable that the adoption of a purely humanitarian Christology should retire from the thought of men such questions as the Virgin Birth and the Resurrection. If we are to have *these* we must have *him*, and we must have him as in the faith of the Church he has always been held to be—the Son of God Incarnate. But if we do have *him*, then we can have *these* too: indeed, we might say that they take on a certain inevitability. The primary miracle gives verisimilitude to what might be called the secondary miracle. In fact, profoundly speaking there is but the one miracle—the acceptance by the divine of the limitations of the human.

With that much granted, every related event, including Virgin Birth and Resurrection, falls within an order which has already been established. The advance is not from the lesser to the greater, but from the greater to the lesser. What was necessarily first in point of time was last in point of faith's apprehension. The Church had its origin in a circle of indubitable facts—Christ crucified, Christ risen, Christ experientially real. The historical Jesus was understood in the light of the significance he came to have for faith by virtue of the Crucifixion and the Resurrection. For that reason, the doctrine of the Virgin Birth was a late pronouncement. As to what might be called its "informational" basis, we can only surmise. What is not a matter of surmise is that the Church saw in it a fitting capstone to the rising structure of revealed and redemptive truth.

Many a time the individual has found himself following the same procedure. What appeared to be a stumbling-block when placed at the threshold of faith is seen at last to fit into its proper place in the living whole. There will always be those who cannot bring themselves to lay this final stone. They are stayed by the difficulties— documentary, scientific, philosophical. What has here been written has no other purpose than to show that the difficulties are not insuperable. It is admitted that what is called for is an act which is a sheer acquiescence of the mind. Some cannot make it, or think they cannot, and what they miss thereby they do not know, neither do they realize what a radical difference to the view of reality is made by their refusal. Others make the acquiescence, and great though the price of the surrender may at first seem to be, it exerts a liberating influence which none can appreciate save those who know. The acquiescence is, therefore, not dogmatic stubbornness. For the "modern" man it might be one of the most truly free because one of the most truly personal acts of which he is capable. Such an act of acquiescence is surely not without some defence, of the sort that has herein been indicated.

PART III

PERSISTENCE AND RENEWAL

CHAPTER 16

The Changing World-View

MUCH OF THE ADVERSE CRITICISM TO WHICH THE CHRISTIAN REVELA-
tion has been subjected is due to the claim that certain conspicuous
features of it in its historical form are incomprehensible, especially
to minds accustomed to modern modes of thinking. The modern
mind is said to be insistent that what it is asked to believe shall fall
within an acceptable and defensible "frame of reference." Only on
that condition can a proffered belief meet the demand of credibility.
The oft-quoted saying of Tertullian that credibility in respect of
things Christian increases in proportion to their absurdity and impossibility, the modern mind takes to be absurdity indeed.[1] What
can be more completely incredible than to make incredibility the
test of credibility! Anyone who would take the trouble to read the
context in which Tertullian's lines occur would soon learn that the
astute Latin Father was not proposing the substitution of fantasy
for truth. He was carrying on a polemic against the supposition
that human reason understood in the narrow sense is the absolute
measure of existence, both as to actuality and as to possibility.
The polemic was justified then as it is now. Christianity is compelled to challenge the supposition in question, since Christianity
in its most vital aspects must become entirely unintelligible where
the supposition is accepted and where anything that disagrees with
it is denied.

Revolutions in the scientific conception of the world or of given
phases of it, and even in the popular conception, have been frequent,
and are likely to continue to be frequent. Plato long since laid it
down that what is subject to change in itself, namely, the world as
existing in space and time, is always subject to change in the understanding of it.[2] The difference between the physics of Newton and
the physics of Einstein is alone sufficient to raise a question in any-

one's mind as to the absoluteness of Einstein's relativism! No view of the world can be "final" except the view that since it has a history it is in process of becoming, and since it is becoming it must have a cause. Christianity, indeed, accounts for this on the ground of a creative God; but whether one accepts the account or not, it remains that the world is so obviously self-continuous, characterized by change, differences, and the appearance of novelties, yet illustrative of laws and principles apparently permanent, that it is inconceivable that any future view of the world will not include these features.

As to past revolutions in the conception of things, Christianity has shown itself able to survive them, although not without a struggle. The struggle has been due chiefly to the way in which Christianity had become articulated with the conception being replaced. It is neither possible nor desirable to keep religion completely detached from the "ideologies" of the given time and this fact is illustrated in the case of the Christian revelation. The human mind has a diversity of interests, and each interest exerts a modifying influence on the others. The Christian man is truly "a pilgrim of the infinite," but his pilgrimage is through the world at some definite time. He may not *belong* to his "here," but neither can he *ignore* it. A new intellectual epoch is bound to have a disturbing effect upon him. It is never easy for him to sever his faith from what, being familiar, seems to be secure, and to ally it to what seems to be insecure because it is unfamiliar.[3] Yet the fact that an alliance has been made under one set of circumstances indicates the possibility of an alliance being made under a different set. The realization of this possibility is to a large extent what we mean by "the history of Christian thought."

Christianity survived, for example, the Copernican revolution, and it requires only a little imagination to visualize how great that revolution was in its bearing on the usual Christian view of things. The ordinary man found that his most familiar beliefs about the earth and its relation to the rest of existence were being called in question. This was bad enough. Worse still was the fact that the Christian religion was regarded by him as so inextricably interwoven with the view now being challenged that he could not see how it was possible for the religion to live with the new conception.

This accounts very largely for the treatment accorded by the Church to Galileo for his bold defense of the Copernican astronomy. Copernicus himself escaped persecution, partly perhaps because he was already on his deathbed when his *De revolutionibus orbium coelestium* was finally published. The work was actually dedicated by Copernicus to Pope Pius III, who expressed his approval, but this approval may have been due to the fact that Andreas Osiander, of Nuremberg, to whom the publication of the treatise had been entrusted, added a preface of his own, unknown to Copernicus, in which he explained that the theory set forth was offered as a mere interesting speculation, not as a demonstrable fact. This preface of Osiander has often been bitterly attacked. Andrew D. White, for example, writes about it: "Thus was the greatest and most ennobling, perhaps, of scientific truths—a truth not less ennobling to religion than to science—forced, in coming before the world, to sneak and crawl."[4]

Galileo, however, born some twenty years after the death of Copernicus (1543), did definitely suffer persecution at the hands of the Church. His earlier researches brought him considerable popularity, especially among those who saw in them a confirmation of the Copernican theory of the solar system. Somewhat cautiously, he admitted this confirmation. Growing bolder because of the apparent approval of the Church, he undertook to raise the theological issue, although he sought to turn the edge of controversy by showing that Scripture texts could be interpreted agreeably to the new view. This was his undoing. In 1616, it was decreed by the Holy Office that the claim that the sun is a fixed body and that the earth rotates around it was heretical. The Pope, Paul V, forbade Galileo to hold or to teach the condemned view, and Galileo agreed. It is not necessary to repeat the rest of the familiar story. Fifteen years after giving his promise—a promise which should have been neither exacted nor made—Galileo published the *Dialogo*. The work was a manifest violation of the earlier promise; its sale was prohibited; the author was brought before the Inquisition; under a threat of torture, he recanted; and the rest of his life, about eight years, was spent in a seclusion which was virtually imprisonment. *Eppur si muove!*[5]

All this was sad enough, yet in the circumstances quite understandable. It is useless to attack Galileo's condemnation from the standpoint of "modern thought." The only fair thing to do is to stand where the men of the early years of the seventeenth century stood. Both Luther and Melanchthon had condemned the treatise of Copernicus, *De revolutionibus*, on the ground of its contradiction of Scripture. Without a doubt they would have condemned Galileo on the same ground. Roman Catholics and Protestants alike were disturbed by the new theory. Not only was it plain to the senses that the earth did *not* move and that the sun just as certainly did: but the firmness and centrality of the earth were unmistakably a part of "inspired truth." Galileo was plainly deluded. Proceeding on assumptions that to them were so unquestionable, men of the time—although there were noble exceptions, which the critic should not entirely overlook—could hardly have treated Galileo and his new teachings otherwise than they did.

In due time, however, the adjustment was made. The cause which had been championed by Tycho Brahe, Copernicus, Giordano Bruno, Kepler, Galileo, and Newton, whose *Principia*, published in 1687, definitely established the fact and the significance of Natural Law, was seen by an increasing number of men to be the cause of truth itself.[6] Christian men accustomed themselves to the thought that things were not always as they seemed to be. Newton certainly did not draw an anti-religious conclusion from his findings. Boyle may not have been an investigator of the first rank, yet he has his place in both the history of science and religious philosophy as a man who saw the complete compatibility of "the religious view of the world" with the uniformities being detected by the new science. Similarly in the case of Blaise Pascal, who, although primarily a theologian, made very definite contributions to physical science and to mathematics, his mathematical theory of probability being, indeed, but little different from our modern theory of "statistical" laws.[7] It became possible to make the cautious suggestion that the Biblical writers and the Church Fathers had written about matters of scientific import according to the beliefs then prevailing, and that this left Christian truth untouched in its bearing upon the fundamental issues of life.

It even became possible to ascribe to the God of "the new universe" a still greater glory than before, seeing that it was a so much more wonderful universe than had hitherto been realized, and seeing too that many of the superstitious fears of men as to natural phenomena were without foundation. Simpson writes truly: "To many minds in an age that believed that comets were composed of the ascended sins and wickedness of mankind in gaseous form, ignited by the wrath of God, and doomed to return to earth again causing pestilence and other calamities, or were of the nature of fire-balls flung by the hand of an angry Deity, it was something of a relief to be able to understand, with Tycho's aid, how very far off the comet of 1577 actually was, as also something of its real character. So also was it with regard to the common and terrifying interpretations of meteors and eclipses, which were readily associated with such passages as Joel 2.30 or Luke 21.25. The emancipation from fear that has steadily followed in the wake of science is a partial illumination and verification of that supreme word, 'And ye shall know the truth, and the truth shall make you free.'"[8] It would have been even more so if, as Whitehead puts it, there had always been on the part of science and religion alike, a recognition of the duty of toleration as expressed in the words of Jesus: "Let both grow together until the harvest."[9] The failure of so many Christians at this point is described by Whitehead as "one of the curiosities of religious history," although he by no means agrees that in the ensuing controversies science was "always right" and religion "always wrong."[10]

Perhaps a word ought to be said about the quite common notion that prior to the days of Galileo, and long after for that matter, practically everybody in Christendom supposed that the earth was flat, either a disc or having "four corners," this being required by Scripture teaching. Simpson's readable chapter on "Cosmogonies, Ancient and Modern,"[11] or the first two chapters in Dampier-Whetham, *A History of Science*, or the relevant chapters in Andrew D. White's *History*, or *The Earliest Cosmologies* of W. F. Warren, will supply ample evidence that whatever the popular idea may have been, there was at the disposal of men, and had been for centuries, speculations about the structure of the universe which were anything but the crude fancies which are generally supposed. It is true that the curious work entitled *Christian Topography*, written in the sixth century by a monk named Cosmas, surnamed *Indicopleustes* because of his travels, had a certain popularity on account of its defense of the supposedly Scriptural view of the world. He described the earth as a rectangular plane, twice as long as its width, arched by a vault called the firmament, above which was heaven. The plane is surrounded by the ocean. In the north is a mountain around which the sun revolves. Cosmas' view involved the denial of the existence of the antipodes. How, he asked, could "every eye" see the Lord descending from heaven for the last judgment if there were men on "the other side" of the earth?[12]

That the view was even Biblical has often been denied. Warren's discussion of the question is still worth reading. He believed that the ordinary supposition as to the ancient conception of the structure of the universe was entirely wrong. He wrote: "Despite all that the rehearsers of traditional cosmology say, or rather because of what they say, and because of the inconsistencies in which they continually involve themselves, one long-interested student [Warren himself] believes that their attempted reconstruction of the Hebrew and earlier Semitic universe is pitiably mistaken, and that the eminent American astronomer, Newcomb, is far nearer the truth when he pens this deliberate public statement: 'Not enough credit has been given to the ancient astronomers. There is no time within the scope of history when it was not known that the earth is a sphere, and that the direction *down*, at all points, is toward the same point at the earth's center.' If after the word, 'sphere' he had written, 'or other unsupported solid,' he would have stated the exact truth."[13]

In any event, we ought not to forget the theory of the Pythagoreans, who believed that the earth was a moving sphere, revolving not on its own axis but around a fixed point in space, this fixed point being a fire never seen by man, and known as the Altar of the Universe. Both Dampier-Whetham[14] and Whitehead[15] find in the Pythagorean "number theory" of the structure of the universe an anticipation of many modern theories. Shorey, speaking of the Pythagoreanism of Plato's *Timaeus*, includes in this anticipation not only the identification of mathematics and reality, the evolution of the elements, and the theory of the atom as itself a *microcosmos*, but also "the universality and relativity of motion" and "the illustration of relativity by impossible experiments."[16]

When we consider the familiarity of the churchmen of the Middle Ages with Hellenistic philosophy, and especially with Plato and Aristotle, we ought to question the supposition that their view of the universe was purely naïve.[17] That their view was the geocentric rather than the heliocentric is understandable enough. Simple observation called for that, to say nothing of both the Christian tradition and the tradition in cosmological speculation. The geocentric view, however, could be set forth with a certain splendid impressiveness. Reference has just been made to Plato's *Timaeus*. Any of the standard discussions of the famous dialogue— Jowett, Zeller, Grote, Burnet, A. E. Taylor, Shorey—will provide the reader with sufficient background to appreciate the significance of the cosmology presented in it. The view is not Plato's own, but is set forth by Timaeus himself, speaking as a Pythagorean scientist. The result is described by Taylor as "a geometrical science of nature."[18] Timaeus represents the universe as a progressive reproduction under a visible form of a fixed, unchanging, archetypal "model." It is an imperfect because sensible embodiment of its perfect original. This involves a God able at once to "conceive" the original and to "produce" the copy. According to his familiar "mythic" device, Plato allows Timaeus to speak of the universe as "a living being with soul and mind."[19] Every part of the universe is necessary to the being of the living whole. It has a "soul" which is the principle of the perfect ordering of all its parts. It is made spherical, because the sphere is the most perfect figure for fulfilling the purposes of the universe. For the same reason, it moves with a uniform rotation on its own axis.

Much more is said in the dialogue about the rationality of "the cosmic animal"; about the significance of time and how it is measured; about the planets and their revolutions and the causes of them (the planets move in circles, but nothing is said of the theory of Endoxus of Cnidus about the planets being set in revolving "spheres"). Against most interpreters, both Burnet and Taylor interpret Timaeus as teaching that the earth itself is not a fixed but a moving body, and that the motion is "oscillatory" around the center of the universe conceived as an empty space. Taylor regards this as a clear anticipation of the view of Aristarchus of Samos, stated in the third century, which is generally recognized as the first statement of the hypothesis which in the sixteenth century was definitely formulated by Copernicus.

Whether the view set forth in the *Timaeus* was Plato's own or not, and whether he accepted the more common view that the earth makes a daily revolution, like a planet, around an invisible center, is not important for the purposes of this reference.[20] The *Timaeus* is mentioned here simply as evidence that during the Middle Ages there were many Christian scholars who having access to Plato, were familiar with a conception of the universe which they could feel was agreeable to Scripture, and which was at the same time a speculation of great impressiveness. As to the *Timaeus* itself, Shorey says that it gives us "the earliest and grandest statement of the teleological view" of the universe and man's place in it, outside of the Bible.[21]

Similarly with the Aristotelian conception. To the great Scholastics of the thirteenth century, Aristotle was "The Philosopher," and they knew his writings intimately. Movement and sphericity were of the very essence of Aristotle's view of the universe. The view is perhaps too well-known to call for description here, but attention might well be directed to his interesting attempt to show that the only way the universe could be is the way that it is.[22] The argument starts with the claim, indispensable to Aristotle, that God is eternal actuality, that is, being in whom are no unrealized possibilities. He is perfect form, and the heaven or ultimate sphere is his body. Such a body must be eternal, and the only way it can be eternal is by being a rotating sphere. The center of any rotating body is at rest, and this resting-place of the heavenly sphere is the earth. The natural movement of earth is downward. It must have a contrary, which is fire, whose natural movement is upward. Opposites have also intermediates, and the intermediates of earth and fire are air and water. Hence the four elements are implicit in the very structure of the universe. Further, since the presence of contraries in the intermediaries means strife, the contraries seeking to destroy each other, there follow a coming into existence and a passing away. This necessary process of coming into existence involves a circular movement. This calls for another sphere than the first eternal sphere; and it is the fact that the sun and moon belong in this secondary sphere and not the first eternal sphere that gives us the changing seasons and so the possibility of life. There is much more to the same effect. What Aristotle really means is that given the nature of God, all else follows of necessity. Anything is as it is and when it is and where it is because God is as he is.

The whole conception is, of course, speculative and not scientific, but the basic thought is one that men have never been able to escape. Thus a modern scientist like Henderson holds that our solar system must be exactly as it is if there is to be life, the only place in the system where life is possible being a narrow belt at the surface of the earth, and the earth being able to sustain this belt only because of the circumstance of its location in space relative to the sun.[23] And a modern theologian like Brunner can maintain that if God is in control at any one point and at any one time, he must be in control at all points and at all times, because of the fact of universal relatedness and the fact of the absoluteness of the Creative Will.[24]

These apparent digressions have had only one purpose: to show that the persecution of the scientists of the fifteenth and sixteenth centuries for their new world-views does not necessarily mean that the view it was proposed to replace, and to which the Church felt it was committed, was not without a dignity and majesty of its own. Christian theology was not burdened with a weight of cosmological *naïveté*. *The Divine Comedy* of Dante, presupposing as it does the world-view of Thomas, which in its turn very largely presupposes the cosmological speculation of Aristotle, is proof enough of the statement. The world-view may have been scientifically wrong, but it revealed tremendous speculative power, and the fact that Christian thought could so freely make use of it has important implications. It implies the conviction on the part of the Church of some profound congruity between its faith and the facts of existence. And it implies the possibility that what the Christian mind had done once, namely, trace this congruity under one set of beliefs about existence, it could do under another set of beliefs if these should be shown to be valid.

As was said above, this is what actually happened. The new interest in nature which was one of the features of the Renaissance was fostered by Christian men, and although the Church as a whole lagged sadly enough, the heliocentric view of the universe was finally accepted, and the great verities of the Christian faith were seen not to be hindered by the acceptance. Religion thereby demonstrated its power to disengage its own proper ideas, as Whitehead puts it, from "the adventitious notions" which had crept into it because of its association with an earlier but now discredited picture of the world.[25] There was, however, more than a mere disengagement from the old. There was also a power of assimilation of the new, a circumstance of very great significance.

Christianity has more recently repeated this experience in the case of the Darwinian revolution. There are those who hold that the change in thinking effected by Darwin's hypothesis was much less radical than that effected by the theories of Copernicus and Galileo. It is said that the greatest shock civilized man ever experienced was the demotion of the earth from the center of the universe to a mere incident in it. But that idea came to men very slowly. It was born at a time when the means of spreading new truth were very limited. The Darwinian hypothesis, on the contrary, spread itself over the Western world with great rapidity. It had able exponents. Wherever a group of men assembled, it was likely to be the topic of conversation. Moreover, many of those who accepted the hypothesis flatly declared that it spelled the doom of Christianity. The biological theory of the last century made vastly more unbelievers than were made by the Copernican astronomy, and it was opposed with an inconceivably greater vehemence and passion by Christian men. A new theory of the structure of the universe was one thing. The claim that man was blood-kin to the beasts of the field was something quite different. It was bad enough to have seen the earth pushed to one side as of no great account in the universe as a whole. Nevertheless, man was still man, made but "a little lower than the angels," and God viewed him with infinite concern, as was fitting, seeing that it was in his own image that God had made him.

But Darwinism seemed to mean that man must now share the fate of the earth. He too was brought under the scope of natural law. The mechanics which accounted for all things else accounted for man as well. Made from the dust of the earth? Yea, verily, only now without the need of divine inbreathing. Copernicus and Galileo had at least left room for God: all that they had done was to show that God was conducting his universe in a different way from what generally had been supposed. But Darwin, supported by Huxley, Tyndall, and Spencer, had apparently dispensed even with God— certainly with God in any Christian sense. Men were asked to believe that they were no longer children of a Heavenly Father, but instead that they were virtual orphans in a universe which ruthlessly produced and as ruthlessly destroyed. They could, if they wished, still speak of Nature as their Mother, in the fashion of ancient poets.[26] But many felt about that as Francis Thompson has said—

"Nature, poor step-dame, cannot slake thy thirst."

It is still worth while to read the apologetic literature that was produced in the decades immediately following the publication of *The Origin of Species* in 1859. Much of it betrays a quite unnecessary nervousness and anxiety, although that is not surprising when one recalls the assertion of Renan, that Darwinism has sounded the death-knell of religion,[27] and of Feuerbach, that the brain secretes thought in precisely the same fashion that the liver secretes bile: "man is what he eats."[28] Men honestly believed that they were fighting for every precious thing that life contained. They believed that not only was the Christian religion at stake, but even sheer human dignity. The Christian view of God, the Christian view of the world, the Christian view of man—it was felt that all were being called in question. It is not to be wondered at that many Christian people fought as those whose backs were to the wall. A book like Ernst Haeckel, *The Riddle of the Universe*, unbelievably popular as it was in the closing decades of the last century, convinced many people that the new natural science was not only anti-Christian but that it was even anti-theistic. Many gloated over the fact. Many more were aroused to bitter opposition to the science which appeared to lead to such conclusions.

Yet even this radical transformation of the traditional view of man's origin and history was seen to be capable of appropriation by those who found in the Christian revelation a truth which carried its own warrant. Alfred Russell Wallace, indeed, had from the beginning insisted on man's spiritual nature. Tennyson, in *In Memoriam*, raised his voice in behalf of faith in a fashion for which many anxious souls were profoundly grateful. For those who could follow a close argument, the Duke of Argyle, in *The Unity of Nature*, spoke in behalf of religious faith with impressive cogency. Henry Drummond was hardly a great scientist, yet the untold thousands who read his *Ascent of Man*, and especially its great chapter, still a classic, on "The Struggle for the Life of Others," recognized in him a true and competent interpreter alike of science and of religion.

The experience of George John Romanes was anything but unique. Brought up an evangelical, and becoming acquainted with Darwin, he gave himself up to biological science. Beset by doubt, he made a study of Robert Flint's *Theism*, and the book had the curious effect of confirming his doubt. Under the pen-name of "Physicus," he published *A Candid Examination of Theism*, in which he virtually renounced belief in God. But he came to feel increasingly that "reason" could not speak the last word; that Spencer's "Force" detached from "Will" was not sufficient as the "Cause" of all things; and that the spiritual intuitions of the soul itself were not without significance.[29] The religious claims of James Martineau and John Fiske deeply impressed him, and eventually he announced his return to faith.[30] What Fiske, the American historian and ardent disciple of Spencer, did for Romanes, he did for many others—convinced them that evolution was intelligible only on a theistic basis. A reviewer of *The Life and Letters of John Fiske* wrote: "John Fiske's great service was in pointing out that the main outlines of evolution, as laid down by Spencer, were not incompatible with a theistic interpretation of human development or with human immortality."[31] As a matter of fact, Fiske's position on the question was much more positive than is here implied, as may be seen in either his *Idea of God* or his *Destiny of Man.*

It is not necessary to multiply illustrations. What is clear is that after the panic created by Darwinism had somewhat abated, wiser men began to see that the evolutionary hypothesis did not necessarily involve the surrender of religious faith: instead, it had but changed—radically, it is true—the conditions within which faith is to establish and vindicate itself. Christian men recovered their confidence. The number increased of those who realized the reasonableness of such great claims as these: first, that the description of the processes of nature is not at the same time an adequate and final explanation of them; second, that the discovery of the conditions of man's physical origin does not necessarily call for a denial of his spiritual nature and destiny; and third, that if evolution consummates in a creature like man, with such manifest capacities as are his, this does not mean that man is degraded but rather that the natural processes which have this issue are indescribably exalted.[32]

The cause was helped, as it is still being helped, by men of large philosophical interest and power, who were convinced that scientific analysis and religious interpretation were alike legitimate and indispensable activities of the human spirit. Indeed, it would be possible to show that one of the most famous sentences penned in the nineteenth century—that of Hermann Lotze in the introduction to the *Microcosmus*—became the text of which scores of influential works on the relations of science and religion were but so many expositions. Lotze affirmed his purpose to show "how absolutely universal is the extent, and at the same time how completely subordinate the significance, of the mission which mechanism has to fulfill in the structure of the world."

One turns, for example, to Emile Boutroux.[33] He recognized the contrast between science, with its postulate of permanence and invariability, and religion, with its postulate of freedom and growth. He denied that the necessary result was an uncompromising antagonism. He would accept neither the position of the Naturalistic Group, which by destroying all transcendent reference in religion would bring the whole of human experience under the domain of science; nor the position of the Spiritualistic Group—in which he would include the Radical Dualism of Ritschl and the Religious Empiricism of William James—which tended to make such a sharp distinction between the scientific and the religious as must keep them forever apart. Boutroux held that one and the same man could engage himself in both sets of interests, and often did, and that this is an empiric fact to be given due weight. What he called the Scientific Spirit and the Religious Spirit depended alike upon man himself. The man in the laboratory and the man on his knees is the same man, satisfying impulses and needs of which he is the subject, and which existence itself provides for. The two activities are opposites, but they are not contradictories.

The basic characteristic of the Scientific Spirit is a profound sense for fact. The fact is interpreted by the addition to it of reason. The result is a "law," but the statement of the law is not an absolute but a relative affirmation, which is modified according as Nature may refuse to be adapted to it. Any such modification, however, in nowise disturbs the fundamental postulate on which the Scientific Spirit continues to rest, namely, the law-abiding and therefore explainable character of all phenomena.

The Religious Spirit, however, still remains as the evidence to something in both man and existence which does not fall under the formulations of science. There is in man, says Boutroux, a capacity to lay hold upon things otherwise than as they are laid hold upon scientifically. Existence *is* as science knows it to be, but existence is also *more and other* than as science knows it to be. Science works by the rule that "everything happens as if all phenomena were only the repetition of a single phenomenon." Boutroux denies that the whole of life can be conducted by that rule, since life itself calls for discrimination, for evaluation, for the distinction of high and low. This means that man acts in such a fashion as implies that he believes that of the many combinations arising in Nature, some are of more value than others and carry their own imperative.

Boutroux takes this fact to involve *faith*, since there is affirmed the reality of the invisible and the intangible; *an ideal object*, since no matter how much man appropriates of the invisible, he never reaches the condition in which the contrast between attainment and possibility disappears; and *love*, since the very function of the ideal is to lead us to become like it, and we can move toward this identification only as we love. Life lived at this level is what religion essentially is. To say that it is not the highest life qualitatively that man can live is simply wilful blindness. Everything, says Boutroux, including devotion to the purely factual, may go into the making of such a life as this. And when such a life is actually achieved, it becomes entirely justifiable to say that the final purpose both of the complexities of existence and of the complexities of man's own nature, was just that such a life might come to be.

Similarly in the case of Rudolf Otto. Otto is best known for his philosophies of intuition and mysticism, but in his earlier period he made a valuable contribution to the elaboration of the thesis of Lotze.[34] He boldly denied that the proper conclusion from science was naturalism. He argued that such concepts as those of purpose and end, providence and guidance, were indispensable to wholeness of life, and that their denial in the name of science was pure arbitrariness, since it assumed the right of science to speak the last, and, indeed, the only word. Otto held with Lotze that teleological and scientific interpretations were alike necessary, and that the naturalistic approach was incomplete without the religious approach. Not conflict, but mutuality, was what he claimed to be the requirement. Science reveals a vast process. Religion sees in the process meaning and value. No single right of science is interfered with by this evaluating. On the other hand, the evaluating act instantly sees the interconnectedness of things as yielding *a system of means*. Everywhere ends are being sought and attained. Everywhere the mechanistic is seen as the instrumental. The very obedience to law, therefore, that nature so impressively illustrates, so far from destroying the concept of an eternal purpose calls for it and is its strongest proof.

Thus we have, according to Otto, first, the given fact of universal relatedness; second, values emerging from and supported by this system of relatedness; and third, the concept of purpose as best explaining how things are the instruments of values. Teleology in nature validates the religious conception of the world, no matter how much science may change—*and it is continually changing*—in its description of the world processes. Add to this the two other considerations, namely, "the autonomy of the spiritual" and the failure of every effort to show that the spiritual is a mere derivative of the natural as fragrance is of the flower, and then, declares Otto, "we are freed at once from all the petty strife with the naturalistic doctrines of evolution, descent, and struggle for existence."[35]

Those who may refuse to be impressed by Boutroux and Otto because they have to their credit no great scientific achievements could hardly make that excuse in the cases of Joseph Needham and A. N. Whitehead. Needham is one of the world's greatest living bio-chemists. He, too, subscribes to the thesis of Lotze. The very titles of his books are suggestive of his point of view: *Man a Machine*, in which he takes issue with all vitalism, although he argues for "a kind of autonomy in all organisms"; *The Sceptical Biologist*, in which he frankly confesses himself a "neo-mechanist," by which he means that he is as absolutely committed to the mechanistic principle as any of the older mechanists, but that he is not *only* a mechanist; and *The Great Amphibian*, in which he deals with man as a being able to live in more than one "world."[36]

Needham therefore believes that the mechanistic account of reality is true, but that it is not exhaustive. The scientific view is not the only possible view, not the only legitimate view. For the man who can measure—and measurement is of the essence of science—can do other things with what he measures than simply measure it. He can appreciate it or he can criticize it; he can praise it or he can condemn it; he can enjoy it or he can shrink from it.

The capacity to do this is obviously different from that of the scientific. But is it as valid? Is it as defensible? Is it as revelational of reality? Needham himself has no doubt that it is. The same fact, object, or event is susceptible of being regarded either scientifically or religiously, and the same man may do both with equal loyalty to truth. The universal mechanism is also universally instrumental. The mechanistic view of the world is for Needham perfectly valid, applicable even to the phenomena of life; only, it has no ultimate metaphysical value. It is simply "a legitimate

methodological distortion." There are aspects of existence which
escape it—*and no point of view is final under which all things may not
be subsumed*. There are non-measurabilities just as certainly as there
are measurabilities, and both witness to man, "the great amphibian." What is legitimate as scientific method cannot be elevated
to a final philosophy for this very reason that it lacks comprehen-
siveness.

It is in this way that Needham makes a place for religion in a
scientific age. Religion he holds to be a fundamental form of human
experience, characterized by the sense of the holy and by a form of
ethical behavior held to be imposed by that which possesses holiness.[37] He says essentially what is said by Boutroux and Otto, that
the scientific and the religious are states of mind, modes of approach, of one and the same person. Equally fundamental faculties
of man are exercized in a different way, and either way puts the
man in touch with the real. Each, however, must be satisfied to stay
in its own province. If science is not to dictate the conclusions of
religion, neither is religion to dictate the conclusions of science.
Neither field is co-terminous with the whole of reality. If science
were absolutely universal, there could be no religion; if religion
were absolutely universal, there could be no science. Existence is
both factual and non-factual, and man is adapted to both. That is
why, in the view of Needham, man will continue to be both scientific and religious. To neglect either is to impoverish the personality, and to fail of the highest satisfactions.

Whitehead is a distinguished representative of the mathematical
scientists and philosophers. His interest is not in the problems
raised by modern biology but in the problems raised by investiga-
tions into the very structure of existence and by consequence of experience. The principle of relativity and the quantum theory, with
their radical effects on the usual views of time and space, have commanded his attention. He has found it necessary to devise not only a
vocabulary of his own, but also a whole new set of categories, in
comparison with which the schemes of Aristotle and Kant seem
simple enough. His more important works, such as *The Concept of
Nature*, *The Principle of Relativity*, and *Process and Reality*, are
among the most difficult to read of modern books. Fortunately,

Whitehead has given a brief and simplified account of his views in various sections of *Science and the Modern World* and in *Adventures of Ideas*. No one can read even these simplified accounts without being made aware of the fact that recent physics, for those who understand them, have effected a change in the conception of the universe as radical as any change ever called for by heliocentricism, geology, or biology.

What the conception actually is would call for a long explanation not required by the present purpose. Expositions and criticisms are available for those who are interested.[38] The conception is sometimes described as "organicism." It sees every so-called fact as an "event"—a "becomingness" falling within a "process," and consisting of a complexity of "internal relatednesses." The conception is referred to here at all only because of Whitehead's insistence on the fact that it in nowise destroys a true religiousness. The final chapter of *Process and Reality* is entitled "God and the World," and while what Whitehead means by "God" is as difficult to come at as what he means by "World," since to describe God as "The Principle of Concretion" or of "Limitation," the power by which infinite possibility is momentarily focalized as an "event," is to rob God of much of that warmth and intimacy and realness which to most people are undeniable—while this is so, it still remains that Whitehead is an uncompromising defender of religion, understood as the vision of the unchangeably real which lies "beyond, behind, and within the passing flux of immediate things," which man seeks to relate himself to by worship, and by the worship find power, satisfaction, and an incentive to ceaseless effort.[39]

That all this involves a modification of the way in which religion formulates itself, Whitehead does not for a moment doubt. In fact, he insists that such modification is of the very nature of the case. It has happened repeatedly in the past: he does not doubt that it will happen repeatedly in the future. Theology and science alike are subject to development. Each deals with existence, only with existence under widely different aspects. Or, as we have seen the case stated by other thinkers, science deals with those conditions which secure the regularity of phenomena, religion directs itself to those values, moral, aesthetic, spiritual, which the regulated phenomena

are seen to make possible. Religion therefore does not need to be
forever on the defensive. It has its own intrinsic right. Only, it must
exercize itself in the world according as the world is understood to
be at the given time. This calls for adjustment, but never for
surrender.

Nobody will regard this as wholly satisfying the Christian position. That is not why attention has been called to it. What is important, as much with Whitehead as with Boutroux, Otto, and
Needham, is that the right of religious faith is vindicated, irrespective of changing fashions in the scientific conception of things.
Changing world-views leave untouched those distinctive capacities and those deep hungers of the human spirit of which religion is
the evidence.

Modern men who have also accepted the Christian faith have
made free use of such positions as have now been briefly described.
They have achieved a new Christian philosophy. It is a philosophy
which has sought not without success to be true equally to the new
understanding of man's organic relationships with the whole of nature and to that faith which ascribed the vast scheme of things to the
will and purpose of such a God as Christianity had always proclaimed. That the understanding of the creative ways of God
needed radical revision is admitted. But men who were interested
equally in science and in religion have felt increasingly that evolutionary process involved the concept of purpose, and it seemed
to them impossible to have purpose without Purposive Mind, that
is to say, God.

Not only so, but it also became apparent that the very intimacy
of man's relationships with the rest of existence called for the
restoration of man to the place of centrality. The meaning of the
whole movement of life could be—perhaps must be—interpreted in
the light of its highest term, and that highest term was man. The
possibility has appeared that every fundamental Christian claim—
God the Creator; creation as purposive; history as meaningful;
man as at once a sinner and a child of God; the restoration of a
broken relationship as man's supreme need; Jesus Christ as the
means of this restoration; the Holy Spirit as the source of both
light and power; a life of love as the life in which all the powers

find their fulfillment; the Church as a community previsioning and preparing for that final consummation which is the Reign of God fully realized—the possibility has appeared that every such claim could be placed solidly in the new cosmic setting, and the Christian revelation still be seen as the key to the riddle of life as it had been in the days when the riddle seemed more simple.[40]

For it must still be borne in mind that our problem is with the Christian revelation, and how this is to be continued into the ever-changing panorama of thought and action. There are aspects of that revelation which no science can properly command us to surrender. The personality of God; his purpose of love and grace; sin as a distortion of divine-human relations; Jesus Christ as the Incarnation of the Eternal Word; his sufferings and death as an atonement for sin; his present activity as the supreme power in the Christian's life; the right of Christ to universal Lordship; the obligation of the Christian to proclaim Christ everywhere as the means to the highest life—these are not questions falling in the domain of science. We may agree with Whitehead that their formulation must take note of the time in which we live, but that is a different matter from asking science to determine what Christianity essentially is.

The Church may have been slow to move, but that it has moved can be amply attested. The informed Christian has little difficulty in adjusting himself to the findings of astronomy, geology, anthropology, biology, and physics. He knows what is being said about the genesis of consciousness, and about the relation between custom and tradition and the judgments of conscience, and about the inseparability of the individual and society. He knows that the books of the Bible were produced otherwise than was believed by his fathers. He knows that the forms assumed by the early Church bore the marks of the prevailing social situation. He knows that the history of the Church is inseparable from the history of culture in general, and that the history of dogma illustrates the laws of social psychology. All this he knows, and he is prepared to accept its results. He is even prepared to concede that the whole structure of modern society may be entirely revolutionized, and still the Christian revelation maintain itself as bringing to men the deepest truth of life.

But he also knows that there is an absolute element in this revelation which determines the character and the extent of any modification. When it is proposed to deal with Christianity as *nothing but* a historical phenomenon, historically conditioned, and to be understood and explained according to the accepted canons of historical science, then there is but one thing for the convinced Christian to say: "Stand thou on that side, for on this am I."

If it is forbidden to any of the natural sciences to determine what is or is not the essential Christian faith, it is equally forbidden to historical science. Historical investigation may throw light on many of the problems connected with the documents and even with the various doctrinal formulations. What it can never do is to invalidate the faith to which the documents bear witness and with which the formulations were concerned. We can rest secure in the bold judgment of Emil Brunner, that the believer has committed himself to a Christ who must always remain an unsolved problem for both natural science and historical science, and that therefore he knows beforehand, when his faith as to Christ is to be compared with historical and scientific facts, that while the science may assault his faith, "it can never really refute it."[41]

See foreword

CHAPTER 17

The Permanencies of Experience

NO ONE WHO IS IN THE LEAST FAMILIAR WITH THE HISTORY OF thought will need to be told that Christianity is continually faced with the problem of changes in the patterns of thinking. What is too often overlooked is the fact that there is nothing new about this. Few people stop to realize to what an extent the New Testament itself, at least in certain parts of it, is a vast intellectual achievement. A comparatively obscure group of men and women, committed to a view of things which on the face of it seemed utterly incredible, found themselves thrust out into the varied and conflicting thought-currents of the Graeco-Roman world, and out of the necessities which the situation laid upon them there came such great documents as the Epistle to the Romans, the Epistle to the Hebrews, and the Fourth Gospel. Only in one case is there certainty as to the author. In Romans, Paul faced the whole philosophy of Judaism; the Epistle to the Hebrews grapples with a combined Judaism and Hellenism; and the Fourth Gospel is plainly enough written with that form of Hellenism known as Alexandrianism continually in mind.[1] The New Testament is not only the permanent witness to an inherent vitality on the part of the Christian faith whereby it could make the contemporary subservient to its purposes, but it is also the permanent warrant to the Christian to undertake a like conquest as often as circumstances make it necessary.

All that great body of apologetic literature which is the intellectual glory of the Church in the third and fourth centuries has no other significance than this. The achievements of the School of Alexandria alone, born of a Neo-Platonic and Christian contact, made forever illustrious by the names of Clement and Origen, and perpetuated in the noble traditions of a Christian liberalism or, as it may well be called, a Christian humanism, which has continued until this day—these achievements alone are sufficient to show that Christianity, called before the bar of reason newly augmented, is capable of making for itself an impressive case.[2]

It is customary in certain quarters to dismiss as so much sheer incredibility the Nicene Christology, the Cappadocian Trinitarianism, and, to leap several centuries, the Anselmic Soteriology.[3] Too often those who make the dismissal show no synthetic effort in the least degree comparable to those which they so lightly pronounce impossible. They allow the contemporary world-views to force them to abandon the essential Christian position at almost every point, which was the one thing which the thinkers of that earlier day would not do. To an appreciative mind, the way in which the Nicenists took the language of the schools of their time, and made it a vehicle for expressing precisely that truth of Christ which meets us everywhere in the New Testament, must always stand as one of the great landmarks in the Christian conquest of the world.

It hardly needs to be argued that the "makings" of the doctrine of the Trinity are in the New Testament, but it was not until there had been long pondering on the facts by such great minds as those of the Cappadocians, Basil and the two Gregories, assisted by Athanasius and Augustine, that the daring conception was reached that in order to account for the historical and experiential Christian facts the unitary divine essence must be susceptible of a threefold discrimination. The discrimination answered to intrinsic peculiarities in the very structure of deity, which are no more matters of divine choice than is the divine existence itself. These peculiarities are represented by the terms unbegotten, begotten, and proceeding. The second is logically subsequent to the first, and the third is logically subsequent to the first and second, subordination being implied in this logical sequence, but in ontological actuality the three are eternal interdependent mutualities, so that without either the others could not be. When the whole is translated into the language of religion, the unbegotten answers to the Father, the begotten to the Son, the procession to the Holy Spirit— "and these Three are One God."[4]

Nobody will dispute the difficulty of the conception, but the point being urged is that it grew out of the confidence of the Christian mind of the time that the historical and experiential Christian facts were parts of a larger whole of truth, and that the relationship could first be ascertained, and then so stated as to yield a view that was truly comprehensive. Daring these men might have been, but before we chide them too severely for it let us consider whether we are not ourselves more worthy of being chided for our excessive intellectual timidity.

This is not primarily a historical study. If it were, an impressive array of evidence could be mustered in support of the claim which has now been but barely hinted—the claim that in times of great intellectual crisis the Christian faith has not been wanting in followers able to make an appraisal of the new situation; where necessary

> "Strike their finger on the place,
> And say: *Thou ailest here—and here!*"

and on the basis of combined criticism and appreciation, gain for the faith a new cogency from that which for a while had threatened it. The temptation is strong to call attention to the way in which Anselm, asking his great question, *Why Did God Become Man?* answered it in a fashion so completely mastering the contemporary that Shailer Mathews said of it: "The Anselmic interpretation of the death of Jesus is sublimated feudalism."[5] The severe judgment, however, cannot conceal the important fact that Anselm was seeking to do for his day precisely that which we deem to be the task of the modern Christian thinker—the appraisal, interpretation, and appropriation of the prevailing social and intellectual situation.

Why do we so easily forget the accomplishments of other great Mediaevalists who followed Anselm? The sceptic ought to familiarize himself with the fascinating story of how the uncorrupted writings of Aristotle came to the Christian thinkers of Western Christendom in the opening years of the thirteenth century, and set the problem of the relation of Greek science and Christian orthodoxy.[6] This, and nothing but this, explains the great synthesis finally achieved by Thomas Aquinas, who put the crown on the scarcely less significant work of his teacher and friend, Albert the Great, whose scientific achievements were such that, uncompromisingly orthodox as he was, there were not wanting those who suspected him of magic and necromancy. That noble and immortal structure which we owe to the mind of Thomas is in the end his elaboration of the thesis: There are two realms, nature and supernature or grace; man is necessary subject of the first, and possible subject of the second; reason answers to nature, faith answers to grace; the whole is made unitary by one and the same God who is its free Creator and its living bond.

In that thesis, Thomas answered the challenge of the new science to the Christian tradition. It is true that his successors were increasingly unworthy of him, and that Scholasticism was unable to subdue to its formalism the amazing intellectual versatility of the Renaissance. It is true that Christian Humanism, the evidence that faith had again become audacious, found more to its liking in Plato than in the Aristotle who was for Thomas "The Philosopher," so that for many the great scholastic remained under a cloud. But it is also true that during the long deliberations of the Council of Trent, which assured the Catholic counter-Reformation, the *Summa* of Thomas was placed alongside of the Scriptures as the final court of appeal. This was no accidental circumstance, any more than it is an accidental circumstance that in our own time the Neo-Thomistic movement is gathering increasing strength just because of the recognition—by many Protestants as well as by Roman Catholics—that Thomas so clearly comprehended *the problem of relationship as respects the known and the believed*, and so definitely stated the principle of its solution.[7]

It is on the basis of discriminations such as those we associate with the name of Thomas that the modern Christian may still take his stand with complete confidence. Thomas recognized various unities: the unity of being; the unity of revealed truth; the unity of scientific ("natural") truth; the unity of revealed truth and scientific truth—that is, the unity of all truth; the unity of truth and being; therefore the final unity of the whole. That these various unities are theoretical and ideal is true enough; that our conception of the truth in this field and that must undergo continuous revision is also true; but it does not follow that of the things we claim to "know," nothing is absolutely true, or that of the things we can only "believe," nothing is absolutely true. The postulate of being or of existence is a rational necessity, and the postulate of truth is equally a rational necessity, and a third rational necessity is the postulate that being and truth are inseparable. We are equipped to explore the field of natural knowledge, mediated to us through the senses, and the organ of the exploration is reason. But we are also equipped to explore the field which we can only describe as suprasensible, and here the organ of exploration is faith, but not faith as a faculty completely divorced from reason: instead, as a faculty presupposing reason, and reaching certainties which it then becomes the function of reason to correlate with the certainties arising out of the natural or scientific fields.

In a word, while the unity of truth and the unity of truth and being are postulates necessary to account for our intellectual questing, we are still under necessity to show that what we postulate is actually the case; and in a thousand different ways we can trace the relationships of truth, and the relationships of truth and being, and thereby establish the unities. Thus while our understanding of things at this point and that changes continually, there are inescapable permanencies which are the correlates both of our "experience" and of our rational nature, and, as we must believe, correlates also of the nature of God.[8]

Freedom of investigation is both our right and our duty. But freedom here does not mean absence of limitations and absence of restraints. It is impossible to ignore all past experience and all past conclusions. It is impossible to ignore the factual elements falling in the field being considered. It is impossible to ignore the basic elements in which we are constituted rational and spiritual beings. It is impossible to consider any area of existence other than man without continual reference to the fact that already—as required by the postulate of the unity of being, to say nothing more— the area in question and man himself are in fundamental relationship. There is no such thing as complete objectivity, no such thing as complete detachment. The man exists in community, and he experiences in community, and he reflects in community, and he reaches conclusions in community.

In the very act, therefore, of considering the whole or some part of it, the man is the instrument of the whole which he is considering. The fact ties him up to all his fellows in a certain solidarity of experience, and not only that, but also in a certain solidarity of knowledge and of belief. There are certain things that all men must know and certain things that all men must believe, in order to be human. At such points, they have no choice. Their very nature as rational and moral, and the situation in which they find themselves, combine to create these inevitabilities. So we have another unity—the unity of experience, although this is necessarily limited in its range as the others are not. The very meaning of our freedom is that beyond these necessitated uniformities are individual differences of knowledge, belief and experience. It is here that our individuality finds its opportunity; it is here that the necessitated uniformities find their justification; it is here that progress in the apprehension and comprehension of truth becomes possible; it is here, if anywhere, that we make a contribution to the life of the whole.

These reflections are not so remote from the problem of the changing world-view as at first sight they may seem to be. They mean that any world-view must retain certain features. *There are aspects of the world which no thought of man can ever make to be other than they are.* And what is true of the world in its totality—to call it that—is just as true of the world in its parts. It does not matter what the physicist tells us of the composition of fire and water: its phenomenological and experiential features are not changed thereby, and water may still drown us or quench our thirst, fire may still burn us or cook our food. It does not matter what the relativist may tell us about the law of moving bodies: we still have to deal with moving bodies as though they moved, and as though their movement was calculable, and we still have to leap from in front of an approaching car if we want to escape injury. It does not matter what the speculative idealist may tell us about the final identity of thoughts and things: we shall still make the distinction, and we shall still carry on our affairs on the supposition that the act of seeing is one thing and the object seen is another, and that the money we count and the counting of the money are not the same. We shall listen respectfully to the biologist and the anthropologist telling the amazing story of how we came to be as we are, but we shall remind them that, after all, *this is what we are*. We are not *that*, but *this*: therefore *we* never were *that*. But for *that*, we might not have been *this*, but *that* was *that* and *this* is *this*, and neither can ever be identified with the other. How simple it is, and yet how often it is overlooked, and men are measured by what they never were, but by what something else was, and then because of the false measurement the mystery and the glory of what now they actually are fails of recognition.

The differences between the man of wide culture and the illiterate peasant may be very great indeed, but that does not bar them from a certain commonness of experience, and in respect of the great crises which necessarily characterize all human lives their attitudes and their emotions will exhibit a striking similarity. The so-called modern man turns back the pages of history, and always he is conscious of reading the story of beings like unto himself. The situation of those about whom he reads is unlike his own in a score of ways—geographically, socially, politically, culturally, morally, religiously, but again and again, as he reads, all these differences drop away, spirit answers to spirit, essential man speaks to essential man, strange mystic bonds unite this man of to-day with the man of a far distant and far other yesterday. No new psychology, and no new science, and no new theory of the origin and significance of the moral sentiments can prevent a man, as he reads the third chapter of Genesis, from saying at last, with solemn conviction and deep sincerity, "I understand this; I have myself done this; this is my story."

Whatever a man's race or time or creed or place, there are things that speak to him exactly as they speak to every other man, and he makes to them the same response that every other man must make.

> "An intermingling of Heaven's pomp is spread
> On ground which British shepherds tread."[9]

But only for *them*, and only *there*, and only *then*? No. That "intermingling" may be felt—is felt—by everyman, everywhere, everywhen, but by no other creatures except men.

John Keats listened to the nightingale, "light wingéd Dryad of the trees," but he knew that the sentiments aroused in him by the matchless song had been aroused in others since first birds sang and men listened:

> "The voice I hear this passing night was heard
> In ancient days by emperor and clown:
> Perhaps the self-same song that found a path
> Through the sad heart of Ruth, when, sick for home,
> She stood in tears amid the alien corn;
> The same that oft-times hath
> Charmed magic casements, opening on the foam
> Of perilous seas, in faery lands forlorn."[10]

And not only John Keats, and not only haughty emperor and witless clown in a day long since gone, and not only Ruth of the high destiny, and not only the consecrate Hero, awaiting, and at last in vain, the wave-dared visit of her young Leander—not only these; but Matthew Arnold too, out of joint with the world of his time, lover of a world which was dead, heard the same song by "the sweet tranquil Thames," and another heard it with him, and both listened as though between their "fragrant lawn" and "the unfriendly palace in the Thracian wild" time's distancing was suspended. One song; one message; and one, too, every answering soul:

> "Hark! ah, the nightingale—
> The tawny-throated!
> Hark, from that moonlit cedar what a burst!
> What triumph! hark!—what pain! . . .
> Listen, Eugenia—
> How thick the bursts come crowding through the eaves!
> Again—thou hearest?
> Eternal passion!
> Eternal pain!"[11]

Is death any different for the man who lives to-day from what it was for the man who lived at any other time—be the time pre-scientific, superstitious, grossly primitive? Whether it be Bryant exhorting you so to live that you may at last approach your grave as you approach your couch; or whether it be Browning, valiant, yet admitting a fog in his throat; or whether it be Hamlet, soliloquizing, hesitant, since in the sleep of death what dreams may come he cannot tell and dare not guess; or whether it be Spinoza, finding that life is but a meditation of death; or whether it be Boethius, seeking in philosophy some consolation against the approaching hour; or whether it be that "tenderest of Roman poets nineteen hundred years ago" whose unforgettable lament bespoke his unassuageable woe, "Frater Ave atque Vale"; whether it be Socrates, awaiting the hemlock, the while he assures his waiting friends that "no evil can befall a good man, either in this life or in any other"; or whether—if we dare say so—it be Jesus approaching with tears the grave of Lazarus and groaning in himself; or whether it be David uttering his lament for that slain Jonathan to whom his soul was knit with the strong bonds of love—

> "I am distressed for thee, my brother Jonathan:
> Very pleasant hast thou been unto me:
> Thy love to me was wonderful,
> Passing the love of women.
> How are the mighty fallen!"[12]

—whichever of these it be, he does but voice "the burden and the mystery" which are the common lot of men, be they modern or be they ancient, as they contemplate the final dissolution. For some, hope; for some, curiosity; for some, fear—yes! but for none, complete indifference:

> "Life, we've been long together . . .
> 'Tis hard to part when friends are dear. . . .
> Say not, Good-night, but in some fairer clime
> Bid me Good-morrow."[13]

The cynic may ridicule, but his cynicism is not natural, but acquired, and his ridicule is but the evidence that he too cannot escape a doubt as he thinks of the dark cloud into which, in common with all the sons of men, he must sooner or later pass. The cynic's ridicule never can quite conceal the "O that I knew!"

And is it not so that what has been briefly suggested as to persisting rational, emotional, and experiential human stabilities could be illustrated and confirmed in countless other ways? It is not for nothing that men have linked stars with destiny. The stars in their courses fought against Sisera, and perchance they still fight, so interwoven is the web of existence. A blow delivered from the infinite spaces may yet be our earth's undoing! The Wise Men saw a Star in the East, symbol to them of a high significance, and if they saw the Star because already they were wise, they were wiser still because they saw the Star and followed its gleam. Men never knew so much as they know to-day of

> "The spacious firmament on high
> And all the blue ethereal sky."

But has the increased knowledge wrought any least change in the fundamental emotional, and shall we even say, aesthetic attitude of men toward the spectacle of the star-strewn sky when day is done? Was not the wonder expressed by Kant a universal wonder? Nobody ever sang the haunting splendor of the moon as did the ancient Greeks, and they saw her only with the naked eye. We can, if we wish, see her through a Yerkes telescope, but do we really see more than they saw; are we moved more deeply than they were moved; are we teased out of thought at the sight more completely than were they?

One opens such a book as, say, Sir James Jeans, *The Universe Around Us*, and reads again the chapter on "Exploring the Sky," with its comforting conclusion that a stellar collision is likely to occur only once in "a million million million years," which seems little different to the more modest lay mind from saying "never"; or that other chapter on "Stars," in which distances and diameters and temperatures are expressed in figures which the mind simply refuses to accommodate. One reads the book, and doubts not the competence of the astronomer-mathematician. It involves an astounding change in one's world-view.

But does it, after all? Is there any essential difference between more distance and less distance, seeing that the fundamental problem in any case is distance itself? Is there any essential difference between much time and little time, between much heat and less heat, between *maxima* of any kind and *minima* of the same kind? Does the extension of the bounds of being solve the problem of being, or the increase in the grasp of truth solve the problem of truth, or extending the knowledge of being and truth solve the problem of knowledge?

> "When I consider the heavens, the work of thy fingers,
> The sun and the moon, which thou hast ordained;
> What is man, that thou art mindful of him?
> And the son of man, that thou visitest him?
> For thou hast made him but little lower than Elohim,
> And crownest him with glory and honor."[14]

A Hebrew poet wrote that, almost three thousand years ago, and it has adequately expressed the sentiments of uncounted numbers of men and women ever since, as it does still, and the modern astronomer, with all his scientific knowledge, can add nothing to it, and he certainly has no least reason for taking anything from it. That is to say, his scientific knowledge leaves the religious interpretation precisely as it was in the days when the earth was flat and the stars were close and the limits of space were set by a solid sphere.[15] How the comparatively simple cosmogony could move yet another Hebrew poet may be seen in the fortieth chapter of Isaiah:

> "Who hath measured the waters in the hollow of his hand, and meted out heaven with the span, and comprehended the dust of the earth in a measure, and weighed the mountains in scales, and the hills in a balance? . . . It is he that sitteth above the circle of the earth, and the inhabitants thereof are as grasshoppers; that stretcheth out the heavens as a curtain, and spreadeth them out as a tent to dwell in. . . . To whom then will ye liken me, that I should be equal to him? saith the Holy One. Lift up your eyes on high, and see who hath created these, that bringeth out their host by number; he calleth them all by name; by the greatness of his might, and for that he is strong in power, not one is lacking."

Then as now, and now as then, those worlds on worlds retreating "their Great Original proclaim," and much as we may know of the unimaginable processes involved, the proclamation stands unchallenged.

It is true that wisdom is not justified of all her children, and that sometimes one of them in unseemly pride of intellect struts before a ruler of earth to announce that his telescope reveals to him no Ruler of Heaven; whereupon the grand dismissal, "Sire, I have no need of that hypothesis." But the sceptic, like the cynic, is self-produced: he is not the product of the logic of events and of things. And perchance his self-engendered scepticism carries its own self-denial. "I have swept the heavens with my telescope, and I find no God there!" But a God who could be found with a telescope would not be God, and the God who cannot be so found—he is God indeed, the inspirer of the search which fails to find him, and hence the evidence that a wiser search would not have been in vain.

Matthew Arnold may not have said it all, but at the heart of his unfaith there was still a faith, a sense sublime, an indestructible conviction that through all the changes his spirit so deeply deplored there were inescapable and foreordained stabilities, and that these stabilities linked all men together and stamped them as sprung from a common Source and destined for a common goal. And among those stabilities is the way the very world is read—the world within, the world around, the world above:

> "Who can see the green earth any more
> As she was by the sources of Time?"

And as Arnold goes on to answer, in characteristically doleful fashion, his own question, it would seem that modern man had lost the power to see, to hear, and to understand, and that the shore of the river of Time had lost its earlier calm in the confusion of a thousand hoarse cries. But even he is hopeful:

> "Haply, the river of Time—
> As it grows, as the towns on its marge
> Fling their wavering lights
> On a wider, statelier stream—
> May acquire, if not the calm
> Of its early mountainous shore,
> Yet a solemn peace of its own. . . .
> As the stars come out, and the night-wind
> Brings up the stream
> Murmurs and scents of the infinite sea."[16]

Always the stars! Always the sense of cosmic kinship! Always the intuition that the same permanent features of the world speak to the same permanent capacities in the human soul, give rise to like experiences, evoke like responses, and bear upon themselves like meanings. And so,

> "Ye heavens, whose pure dark regions have no sign
> Of languor, though so calm, and though so great,
> Are yet untroubled and unpassionate;
> Who, though so noble, share in the world's toil,
> And, though so task'd, keep free from dust and soil!
> I will not say that your mild deeps retain
> A tinge, it may be, of their silent pain
> Who have long'd deeply once, and long'd in vain—
> But I will rather say that you remain
> A world above man's head, to let him see
> How boundless might his soul's horizons be,
> How vast, yet of what clear transparency!"[17]

Perhaps the point has been over-much labored. Certainly nobody could claim that the analogy held of every phase of our human experience. Change is very real. Some things, be it ever so reluctantly, have to be surrendered. Truth is a severe task-master. There are real losses, said William James, and real losers. Sometimes we lose what we might have kept, and sometimes we try to keep what we ought to give up. There is flux around the stability, but we shall do well to remember that there is stability within the flux, else were neither flux nor stability possible. Heracleitus is right and Parmenides is right only as each recognizes truth in the claim of the other. "All things change." Wrong! "No real thing changes." Wrong! "Things there are that pass, and things there are that endure." Right!

A changing world-view? Yes. But ever amid the change is the spectator, man, and he remains as he always was, and he sees things that other men always saw, and he is swept by the same feelings which have swept all other men, and he thinks the same thoughts which all other men have thought, admits the same deep hungers, is haunted by the same deep questionings, sins the same sins, bows to the same loyalties, commends the same virtues, shrinks from the same spectres—if, indeed, spectres they be and not dire and dread realities—dreams the same dreams, weeps over the same losses, laughs at the same occasions, hates the same shams, utters the same prayers, dies, or would die, for the same cause.

Wherefore is man, the fundamental man, the same yesterday, to-day, and forever. Changed he may be, and changed his world may be, in a thousand ways, but entirely transmuted, so that nothing at all is as once it was—never! Once rational, always rational; once moral, always moral; once religious, always religious. Exceptions there may be, but these are abnormalities: the type itself is fixed.

Then dare we say it: once Christianity was possible, it remains possible forever? The claim would call for careful explanation, and this will later be forthcoming. What is meant by it is that if ever there has been in the world one convinced and utterly genuine Christian, the possibility of Christianity as both a permanence and a universality is established; and that if at any time in his life a man were truly a Christian, he may continue to be a Christian for the rest of his life, irrespective of the influence that may be exercized by historical, literary, and scientific criticism upon the changeable objectivities of his past and present world. That this may be true of other things than Christianity—for example, Buddhism, Parseeism, Mohammedanism—is, of course, obvious. But the point must still be allowed to stand: if there was ever a time when the Christian faith, being what it is, could command a complete assent, that assent is still a possibility, since nothing has ever occurred since which can properly be said to invalidate it. Whether this is also true, however, of the so-called "rivals" of Christianity just mentioned, is another question altogether.

Leaving this for the time being, we consider the view of man himself, as perhaps the best possible preparation for considering the permanence of Christianity. There is definitely a biblical view of man, and this view is indispensable to the total Christian faith.[18] That there are features of it which reflect a naïve psychology is not to be denied, and it is necessary to distinguish between these purely contemporary features and what is central. Man is represented as bearing within himself, in his rational, moral, and spiritual nature, the marks of the God who made him. This is expressed as the kinship of man to God. Of all things that are upon the earth, man is most like the Source. His capacities are reflections, dim though they be, of divine capacities. The Creative God, and the creature man, are bound together by a link of God's own forging. In all this is revealed divine intent and purpose. Man is made to obey God, to know him, to love him, to serve him, to glorify him, "and to enjoy him for ever."

The power to do all these things, however, implies also the power not to do them. In this lies disobedience to the will of God, and the endangering of his purpose. Such a situation means guilt. But men are so constituted that disobedience and guilt cannot be restricted. By reason of the racial origin and the racial law, there is a solidarity of disobedience in addition to specific individual disobedience, hence a solidarity of guilt, hence a solidarity of penalty. This penalty is death, understood in the Bible in both senses of separation from God and a final dissolution which is morally tragic because it means not only separation from God but separation also from all the intimacies and familiarities of existence, to be replaced by none knows what unless God himself shall tell.

But God does not permit his purpose with man to be defeated for want of anything he can do himself. The man whose disobedience evokes the divine wrath is still the object of the divine love. Indeed, the wrath is but an instrument of the love, since in all his dealings with men God seeks their good, devious though the path may be, and almost countless the obstacles to be overcome. Every least movement of man toward God is but a response which God himself has evoked. Prayer is inspired of God, even as it is by God that it is received and answered. But this necessity of man to be continually moved to seek the good by a power not his own is the evidence of how complete is his moral helplessness. So long as he is treated as in the realm of nature, he is in the realm of sin and death. Only as he is made overwhelmingly conscious of the grace of God can there come to him that power and that experience which are prophetic of his final deliverance.

Jesus Christ is the supreme expression of this divine grace. He is sent into the world to accomplish something for God on behalf of men. What he does is meaningful for every man because it is in him, the Eternal Word now become flesh, that every man is originally constituted. An imputed disobedience and unrighteousness which brings every man into a solidarity of sin and guilt and death is met by an imputed obedience and righteousness which creates the possibility of a solidarity of forgiveness, regeneration, and sanctification. There exists the possibility for every man of a new relation to God and a new relation to his fellows, and the dynamic center of this relation is Christ. The center becomes operative in the proportion of the repentance, faith and love. Coming more and more under the control of this love, the man may tap increasingly operative sources of power. He may know in himself the certainty of God. He may become a new creature in Christ Jesus. Fear may be banished. A deep and abiding joy may possess him. Death itself takes on a new meaning, for when the earthly house of his tabernacle is dissolved, a building from God awaits him, a house not made with hands.

The statement could be much enlarged, but it will suffice. The question is as to how this teaching is affected by modern biology and modern psychology.[19] It is simple truth that it is not affected at all—that is, not affected in the sense that biology and psychology compel one to give it up. That there are many who do give it up is, of course, true, but they give it up for insufficient reasons. They give it up because in the Bible teaching they confuse the incidental and contemporary with the essential and permanent, and because in their consideration of biology and psychology they fail to see them as merely descriptive of processes and treat them instead as final ontological and metaphysical explanation.

Man, says the Bible, bears the marks of his Creator. What science can deny that? Man, says the Bible, has fallen below the divine intent. What science can deny that? Man, says the Bible, is involved in a solidarity of guilt before God of which death and its related facts are the penalty. What science can deny that? Man, says the Bible, is being sought by God in a thousand ways—in every good impulse, in every high purpose, in every vestige of remorse, in every bit of sacrificial endeavor for the common good. What science can deny that?

Man, says the Bible, is susceptible of a complete re-organization of his inner life whereby he will escape from his frustration, his bondage, his sense of guilt, his fear; to bring this about is precisely why Jesus Christ came into the world, and this purpose is achieved in the degree in which Jesus Christ is enthroned in the life; in this experience is realized a relation to God which is not only new but is the very relation which God has sought from the beginning, and in the same experience is the promise and the power of a new relation with other men which is also just the relation which ought to be; and the various steps by which this experience is prepared for, the actual experience itself, the nurture of it so that its effects may more and more come to individual and social expression, are all forms of the activity of the Holy Spirit, as God's own means of fulfilling his purpose with men. Consider this Bible teaching, and then ask wherein any scientific view of man, any psychology which is satisfied to remain a psychology and not set itself up as a philosophy, can invalidate it. There is, indeed, a psychology of Christian experience, but in order for that to be, certain conditions are necessary.[20] There must be Christian experience itself; and if there is to be Christian experience there must be acceptance of the Christian faith; and if there is to be a psychology of the experience, it must be built upon a true view of man and his nature, just as much as it must be a true account of the experience and its processes.

The question therefore becomes whether the Biblical view of man, more exactly the Christian view, is true. What has been said above is that it cannot properly be denied by either biology or psychology.[21] This is not to say that denial is not made in the name of both of these. Many people have turned away from the Christian view of man because they have supposed that biology and psychology have made it untenable. If, of course, by the biological view of man is meant that man is simply a higher animal, the product, by the operation of purely self-explaining and impersonal law, of lower levels of life, and that this is a sufficient account of man; and if, by the psychological view of man, is meant that there is no so-called "inner" experience—which means thinking, feeling, judgment, memory, imagination, fear, hope, love, and all the rest—

which is not tied up with the physical organism and the social situation, which cannot be explained accordingly, and which therefore has no other significance than just this—if these are the views of man which are set over against the Christian view, and if these are held to be scientific, exhaustive, final, then the situation for Christianity is serious enough.

But man viewed biologically is not man viewed completely.[22] No Christian will dispute the right of the biologist to his own field, or to the conclusions which his field justifies. It is only when the biologist claims to speak the last word on man that the Christian objects. Similarly with the psychological view. To what extent psychology may be called a science is disputed even among psychologists themselves. But psychology, whether descriptive or normative, has its proper place and its proper field. It also has its proper limits. A purely psychological view of man is no more exhaustive than is a purely biological view.[23] Without a doubt, there is a psychology of the sense of sin, a psychology of the sense of forgiveness, a psychology of the empowered will, a psychology of prayer, and the like. But to set forth this psychology, and then to add flippantly, "That is all there is to it"—that's another matter. Laying bare the machinery of human experience is not saying the last word on all that that experience means.

The reality of conscience and of forgiveness, like the reality of love, of prayer, of divine-human fellowship, is much more than the reality of a discoverable process. The fact and the necessity of the process are undeniable; but just as undeniable is the reality of the type of experience which the process alone can never entirely explain. The instrument is one thing; what is made possible by reason of the instrument is another. The Christian's quarrel with too many psychologists is by reason of their assumption—no, assertion— that when the conditions of human experience are properly charted, the experience has lost its significance as the final and interpretive reason of the whole body of conditions.

The Christian view of man is not concerned primarily with the processes whereby he came to be. It is not concerned primarily with the processes which underlie his experience and give rise to its possibility. It is concerned primarily with what man means now that he is here; with what he is in his fundamental idea and purpose; with the type of experience which is not worthy of him, he being who he is, and with how the unworthy may be replaced by the worthy. It is concerned with the difference between what he is and what God meant him to be; with the causes of that difference; and with the means whereby that difference may be done away. What is here being claimed is that there is nothing in a proper biology and nothing in a proper psychology which requires that this Christian view of man be abandoned. And it is also claimed that there is nothing in the Christian view of man which need prevent the Christian from welcoming and utilizing every bit of light upon man which biology and psychology are able to give him.

Then because biology and psychology do not disprove the Christian view of man, may they be called upon to prove it? No, not to *prove* it. The Christian view of man is ultimately a faith-view. Without a doubt, much that the view involves enters into an experience which may be regarded as self-authenticating. But it is self-authenticating only on the ground that that type of experience is actually what man exists to have. How can he know that? He cannot know it: he can only believe it. Why does he believe it? He believes it for only one reason: because he accepts the finality of the Christian faith.

That is to say, he accepts the Christian revelation. That revelation stands in its own right. It denies no indubitable truth elsewhere. The Christian man sees new truth about man and the world being discovered almost every day through the activity of the gift of reason. He welcomes this truth. He knows that men may draw inferences from it that are a flat denial of his own faith. But he sees that these inferences are not necessary corollaries of the truth. They are determined rather by naturalistic pre-suppositions. He believes that the Bible conveys a truth about man which God himself has given. He believes that he has good reasons for accepting this truth. He takes his stand: *man is a son of God in a natural state of rebellion, and God in Christ is seeking to restore the sonship*. He finds that this gives him light on all the ways of men, gives him light on what he takes to be all the ways of God. The Christian therefore has a principle of evaluation for all other views of man: what denies the Christian view does so only because the proffered view fails to consider all the facts. The Christian view is opposed to no fact about man. It only offers an interpretation of the fact, and it offers it in the name of a view of man which is still the most impressive, the most humbling and the most exalting, the most consonant with every discovered truth about man and his world, which has ever been suggested. This is why the Christian calls it revelation; it is why he admits that it is held in faith; but it is also why he claims that he does not have to perjure himself to accept it, nor to see in it the one sure light as to man which shines amid the encircling gloom.

CHAPTER 18

The Illuminating and Renewing Spirit

FEW QUESTIONS ARE MORE DIFFICULT THAN THAT OF THE MEANING OF the Holy Spirit. The doctrine has been responsible for almost unlimited fanaticism on the one hand, and on the other hand its neglect has been followed by an inevitable spiritual decline. There are those who would make it practically the one all-inclusive truth, as in the case of the Quakers and many of the great mystics, and there are those who would reduce it to nothing more than a form of the activity of the human reason.

That the doctrine, in whatever form it is cast, is an attempt to explain indubitable human experience is self-evident. The question is therefore primarily one of divine-human relationships.[1] God as the source of a certain kind of action; man as the ultimate object of the action—these are the facts which are to be conserved, and whose significance is to be ascertained.

It would be a comparatively simple matter to classify the Scripture teaching on the subject, although not so simple to reduce the Scripture teaching to consistency. Indeed, it is precisely the lack of such consistency which creates one of the chief difficulties.[2] There is an enormous difference between what is said about the Spirit in certain parts of the Old Testament, and what is said in some of the prophets, and especially in what is said in, to use an extreme case, the Fourth Gospel.

If the doctrine of the Spirit, or at least the Christian doctrine, could be derived ..om the Fourth Gospel alone, much difficulty would be avoided, and it might even be that we should have the doctrine in its purest form.[3] "Except one be born of the Spirit, he cannot enter into the kingdom of God" (3.5). "God giveth the Spirit, and not by measure" (3.34). "No man can come unto me, except it be given unto him of the Father" (6.65): that is, the greatest blessing which can come to a man is in a certain relation to God through Christ, and it is assumed that this is a gift of the kind which is Spirit-borne. "The Spirit of truth abideth with you and shall be in you" (14.17). "The Holy Spirit, whom the Father will send in my name, shall teach you all things" (14.25). "The Spirit of truth, which proceedeth from the Father, shall bear witness of me" (15.26). "The Holy Spirit . . . will convict the world" (16.7, 8). "When he, the Spirit of truth, is come, he shall guide you into all the truth . . . he shall take of mine, and shall declare it unto you" (16.13, 14).

These, and similar passages from the same Gospel, are clear enough as to their meaning. They all mean that there is a divine power of a peculiar nature, definitely related to the work of Christ in the world, and which will exert an illuminating, transforming, and vitalizing influence upon those who accept Christ as verily the revealer of God.[4] The words, "The Spirit was not yet given, because Jesus was not yet glorified" (John 7.39), have a definite enough meaning in their own context, but that they are susceptible of another meaning is quite evident. Perhaps the final Christian truth about the Holy Spirit is that he is both the means whereby men are led to "glorify" Jesus in the sense of putting him at the very center of things, and the bearer of the reward, namely, peace and power and insight, which comes to those who thus "glorify" Jesus.

Nor would it be a very difficult matter to review the official pronouncements of the Church on the doctrine of the Holy Spirit. In actual fact, these were few enough, and were usually associated with the doctrine of the Trinity. It was the definitive pronouncement by the Church of the West in the sixth century on the "double procession" of the Holy Spirit (his "procession," that is, from the Father *and* from the Son) that precipitated the controversy which resulted in the division of the Church into Roman Catholic and Greek Orthodox and Catholic.[5] It is a strange comment on *mortalia* that the very doctrine, that of the Holy Spirit, which is offered as the assurance of the unity of the Church should have been the means of its most serious division! No less strange is the fact that belief about the Holy Spirit has repeatedly been associated with so-called "heresy" at other points. Montanism was the conspicuous example of this association in the early Church.[6] In the modern Church it has been illustrated by numerous minor sects, characterized by aberrations of various sorts, but always justifying themselves on the ground of special guidance or empowerment by the Holy Spirit.[7] To review the doctrine historically would not help very much, since it is these very pronouncements which have helped to create the problem for the man of to-day.

There are those who would be satisfied to see in the Holy Spirit nothing more than the objective reference of the mystical experience. There is more than a suggestion of this in Otto's well-known discussion of the "numinous," as also in the chapter in *Mysticism East and West* in which he seeks to find a common theistic foundation for the various forms of Indian mysticism and the mysticism of Eckhart. It is not our purpose to enter into any discussion of mysticism, but it is worth observing that both Paul Elmer More and T. Hywel Hughes agree that the true Christian mystic knows agony as well as joy, and that this is wanting in Indian mysticism. Hughes says flatly that the typical Indian mystic is an "escapist." He refuses to face the grim realities of existence, and seeks surcease in his Nirvana, whereas the Christian mystic takes life for what it really is, faces it, and in the strength of God vanquishes it.[8] Peer Gynt's maxim was: "Do not go through: go around." That is, always take the easier way. But no Christian who has any real understanding of the Holy Spirit could ever do that, since he sees the Spirit as a power of conquest. Conflict with demonic forces may lead to despair, but it may also lead to a greater joy in triumph. "The dark night of the soul" may yet turn to glorious dawn. There is a vast difference, Hughes reminds us, between the stagnation of Hindu passivity and the "peace-with-action" of the true Christian mystic. The fact calls for an appropriate doctrine of God, which in its turn yields an appropriate doctrine of the Holy Spirit.

Again, there are those who do not deny the reality of those experiences which are ordinarily referred to the Holy Spirit as their cause and ground, but who claim that such experiences can be given a simply psychological explanation. Leuba is a conspicuous contemporary example of this tendency, although it is common among that large group of psychologists who have no personal sympathy with the religion which they so carefully scrutinize.[9] Religious experience is reduced to pure subjectivism. What is ascribed by the subject to the action of the Holy Spirit is by the psychologist of this type reduced to a self-induced emotional state.

No one will deny that any human experience, whatever its character, has its own appropriate psychological means. There is a condition to every experience, and a part of that condition is the presence in the human organism of a system of closely articulated nerve relationships whose functioning follows very definite laws. Hocking has described with great clarity this system, its relationships, and its laws, but without falling into the all too common fallacy of supposing that the system itself suffices to explain the experience.[10] The actual operation of the system involves, so to speak, something at either end, sufficient to account for the fact that the system does actually make possible a human experience.

What psychology has really done has been to describe the process whereby a subject is brought into relationship with an object. The statement made by Spinoza, that every *idea* involves an *ideatum*, is in the end only a more formal way of saying that whatever is "other" to a "self" possesses some measure of objectivity, just as, in turn, the very fact of the "other" calls for a "self" to which it is "other." The "self" and the "other" are related by some sort of *media*. When the attempt is made to include the "self" and the "other" in the *media*, or, worse yet, to identify them with the *media*, the result can only be confusion rather than clarity, since to merge in the psychological process itself the self that experiences and the reality which is experienced is to presuppose that very independence of each which it is the purpose of the attempted merging to deny. In a word, when the psychology of experience offers itself as at the same time a metaphysic, transforming needful conditions into reality itself, it is as though a messenger who carried messages back and forth between two persons should be regarded as not only the messenger but also as the person who gave the message and as the person who received it. This would convince nobody; and it is doubtful whether the psychologist who sees in experience nothing but process physiologically described is really convinced by his own theory.

These observations are offered as preliminary to the real issue, which is as to the relation of the Holy Spirit to the Christian revelation, both in the means by which it was first given and the means by which it is apprehended by others, elaborated, propagated, applied, and continually renewed.

What is to be said presupposes much that has already been set forth in connection with "the philosophy of the word." We are to see in God a Being who is able to produce situations. He has not only the power to conceive: he has also the power to carry out his thoughts. That God could conceive and not execute is a permissible view. That in actual fact much that he conceives he never executes would seem to be indubitable. But every actual situation may be said to represent the execution of what God had already conceived. He is therefore not merely the Aristotelian Thinker, who eternally thinks, but who eternally does nothing else. He is also the Hebrew God of Action—the Doer besides the Thinker. The Eternal Word is definable as that constituent of God's nature whereby he can give objective form to his own thoughts. "Without the Word was not anything made which was made." All facts, events, situations, and the like, are therefore so many signs and symbols: they are bearers of meaning.

All this, however, can be said only because we are ourselves the kind of beings who are able to say it! A world without man would not necessarily be a world without meaning, but it would be a world whose meaning remained unknown and unknowable. An unknown meaning can hardly be said to matter! It is only as mind appears that meaning also begins to emerge. Mind is at least a power to ask questions, and what can ask questions can to some extent discover answers on its own account or comprehend them when they are made known.

The function of reason, which is one of man's distinctive gifts, therefore appears. Reason is a power of interpretation. More than this may be involved in it, but certainly not less than this. It may belong to man to apprehend without interpreting. Indeed, awareness may be held to be fundamental. But mere apprehension is not man's highest capacity: such a capacity belongs in some measure to all sentient existence. It is much to know *that* something *is*. It is much more to know *what* something *means*. The meaning of the world as such; the meaning of events; the meaning of human life itself—these surely are questions of primary importance.

That we are able to discover meaning is self-evident. The story of human achievement is the story of applied rationality. Man is forever discovering that *this* means *that*. He is continually discovering that things remote from each other in time and space yet bear the most intimate relationships. He can see how but for one thing another thing could not have been. He knows that in the present an immeasurable past comes to focus, and he knows that this focussed present, which disappears in the very act of coming to be, is to be an item in a new focussing in a future inconceivably distant. He not only lives in a meaningful world, but he knows it. He is not only himself a meaningful creature, but he knows it. He is rational, and he finds his rationality reflected in things. He is conscious of giving his world a completion it would otherwise lack. What otherwise were simply senseless sounds are because of him voices. And what is a voice but an instrument of meaning?

And yet, if the Christian revelation signifies one thing more than another, it is that to the greatest questions man is able to ask he can himself not give the answer. If revelation be an actual fact, it is an evidence at once of man's capacity and of his limitation. There comes a time when man can no longer pronounce: he can only receive.[11] A meaning which he would himself never even suspect is declared to him as the final truth, and he is charged with the solemn responsibility of either accepting it or rejecting it.

Without a doubt, much that is included in the total of alleged revelation bears all the marks of reasonable inference. According to the Genesis narrative, the scale of being which has God as its origin has man as its climax, and to climactic man God has given dominion over all else. The universe is laid under tribute to the very man whom it has served to make possible and in whom it comes to completion. Whatever may be said as to this being in the first place a "revealed" truth, prolonged scientific and philosophical study only serves to confirm it. At least, it confirms this relation of man to the whole, whatever may be said as to an original creative purpose that this should be so.

Man is seen to make the whole universe his servant. True, it serves every other living thing also, but not as it serves man. The universe simply keeps other forms of life *alive*. But in respect of man, the universe is the servant not only of his mere animal existence, but of his mental life, his aesthetic life, his moral life, his political life, his religious life, his whole life of creativity. It compels him to ask questions—and, being who he is and having his distinctive powers, he creates a philosophy. It compels him to investigate relationships—and he creates a science. It compels him to emotional responses—and he creates his various arts. It compels him to seek the help of his fellows—and he creates a society. It compels him to order his societies to seek the good of all—and he creates various political instruments. It compels him to ponder both his own significance and that of the universe which makes him possible—and he creates a religion. That he could not do all this unless he were already something to begin with, is evident: the point is, that these are his activities.

Clearly, they are the activities of a being who is complex enough. He is at least rational; he is at least moral; he is at least social. His distinctive activities are the expression of his distinctive powers. It would all seem to indicate that it belongs to man to gather up in himself and conserve in himself the meaning of the whole process that has made him possible.

But what is the meaning? That still remains the fundamental question. Man can find out very much: his varied history is the evidence of that. But he cannot find out everything: the evidence to that is no less plain. Just as certainly he can do very much, but there is also that which he cannot do, a demand which he cannot escape but which he finds himself unable to meet. The Holy Spirit is to be conceived as the means whereby illumination and power are given to men.

This is a general enough statement. What the ultimate meaning of our life and experience is, and how the meaning may be realized —this combined insight and power represents our urgent and permanent need. We possess as "natural" gifts a power of interpretation and a power of action. But the gifts are under a limitation. The faculty of interpretation is narrower than the range of observation and experience. There are facts and happenings before which reason stands helpless. The faculty of action likewise is narrower than the total human situation. No story of mankind is complete which does not take cognizance of all that which is embodied in the twofold confession: "I cannot understand it," and "I cannot do it."

It would be possible to relate to the Holy Spirit these human capacities operating within even the so-called "natural" limitations. That is to say, man's reason, man's conscience, man's will, may be regarded as evidences of the Holy Spirit. It accords better with what has been written above, however, to regard them as signs bespeaking the action of the Eternal Word. In that event, they could be described as existent conditions making possible the action of the Holy Spirit.[12] That is to say, the work of the Holy Spirit assumes the work of the Eternal Word. There must be a situation before there can be interpretation. It belongs to God, by virtue of the Word, to produce that which is other than himself. In so far as this "other than himself" is man, it belongs to God, by virtue of the Holy Spirit, to provide for the completion of that for whose sake man was produced. Man as bare fact calls for the Eternal Word. Man as fact existing for a purpose which man of himself can neither discover nor carry out calls for the Holy Spirit. There is a divine power which makes creation possible—the Word. There is a divine power which makes redemption possible —that same Word. But there is also a divine power which takes the redemption which is already a possibility and transforms it into actuality—the Spirit.

Creation is of the will of God exclusively. The Incarnation of the Word is of the will of God exclusively. But both creation and incarnation look to a more ultimate purpose. That purpose can never be realized by the will of God alone. There must be divine-human cooperation. The Holy Spirit makes this cooperation possible, and is the promise of its success. Because it is by the Holy Spirit that the purpose of the whole has been made known, as it is by the Holy Spirit that man is empowered to realize a purpose which would otherwise always be beyond him.

The Holy Spirit is therefore the instrument of revelation. Revelation includes at least illumination. It is a disclosure of truth which would otherwise remain at the best only a speculation. Reason has led men to the supposition of a God. Revelation means that God is categorically affirmed, and that he bears a certain character, and is working for certain ends, and what this character is and what these ends are likewise is included in the revelation.[13] God utters his Word, but the meaning of what is uttered is still to be conveyed, and this is the work of the Holy Spirit. Different men observed the same facts, and some saw them as meaning one thing and some saw them as meaning another. Hence there are differences of interpretation. Which one is right?

That is the question of questions. The Christian revelation is in effect an interpretation held to be the true one because it issues from God himself—from God who, through the Spirit, has led men into the truth. It was not enough that God through the Word should *act*: it was also required that God should make known *that* it was his action and *what* the action *signified*. This he does by the Spirit. Revelation by the Word is fundamental, but it is incomplete until it is received into a mind, and it is the Spirit which brings the mind to this apprehension and acceptance. God grants to some men to see beyond what he grants to others. Why this should be so, we cannot say, beyond the general fact that since God needs instruments for his purpose, it belongs to him to select them. But the men to whom he grants it to see come thereby under a responsibility.[14] It is the responsibility of declaration. "That which we have seen and heard declare we unto you also, that ye also may have fellowship with us" (1 John 1.3), states for all time the principle in the case.

The psychology of this illumination it is beyond us to describe. If it could be described in complete detail, we should lose thereby and not gain. We have to allow for the working of a non-rational factor because the result is a non-rational result. He who believes in the principle of revelation thereby affirms his conviction that we need to know more than we can discover, and that this need has been met by a direct word from God himself. That is obviously a matter of faith. The word came by faith in the first place, and it is by faith that others must accept it. All this has been set forth at length in previous chapters. God taught men by the Spirit. It was a new way of teaching. Its method was freedom, not coercion. An alternative to the truth God was seeking to teach was always possible: he who turned from this alternative and accepted what he believed was of God was therefore making a venture on his own account. When he called upon others to make a like venture, he was only calling upon them to do what he had already done himself.

Scripture is one long illustration of what has now been said. Men have always faced the fact of the world. What does the world mean? they have asked. The answers have been many. There is a Scriptural answer: the world means God, and God understood in a very definite sense. Is that just one more guess? If it is, then it is— just one more guess! To believe that answer is true—that the world means God—is to believe that God himself gave it, for only from God himself can there come to man the knowledge of God. "He is past finding out." We must *believe* that God is, which means that we must believe that God has declared himself, or we cannot believe in him at all. Only revelation can save belief from being credulity.

Many similar questions could be asked. The Hebrews believed they were a "chosen" people. Were they right? Moses believed that he was conveying to this people the very law of God, and that God himself had made it known to him. Was he right? The prophets made announcements about God and his purpose, and about the history and experience of the chosen people, and beyond that about all mankind. Were they right? Did Amos read contemporary history aright when he read it as bespeaking a righteous God pronouncing judgment on all the peoples of the earth? When Jeremiah saw the land he loved being over-run by the foreigner, and the people being carried away prisoners, and the very city destroyed which was deemed indispensable to God's purpose, and then declared that not even that destruction, no, not even the destruction of the nation itself, could frustrate God's purpose but rather would subserve it, was he merely a blind optimist, or was he right? Was the Second Isaiah right when he saw in the sufferings of the "Servant of Yahwe" the power by which at last the world would be saved?

To the questions we must answer either "Yes" or "No." If we say "No," very well, but we have only increased our darkness. If we say "Yes," it can be only on the ground that what these men said was being said *by God himself through them*. They were men whose minds had been illuminated. God flashed a revealing beam, and in its light they saw. It was revelation. Revelation through the Divine Word which produces, is completed by the Divine Spirit which makes things clear.

The crucial place, however, is with Jesus Christ and his meaning both for God and for men. From one point of view, he is simple historical fact. Yet the New Testament which describes him in all his matchless human ways also interprets him as the nexus of all God's purpose with men.[15] Jesus Christ and his significance, this significance being to bring God and man together, the reconciliation being possible because he, the Reconciler, was himself the Eternal Word made flesh—this is the burden of the New Testament. The New Testament is concerned not only with factual description, but also with the interpretation of the factual as redemptively intended and redemptively effective. The Cross *means* —the final manifestation of sin and the promise of its destruction. The empty tomb and the "appearances" *mean*—the victory of Christ over the powers of sin, darkness, and death. The events on the Day of Pentecost *mean*—the availability to men of a new power giving rise to a new experience, a new certainty, a new attitude, a new purpose. In a word, Jesus Christ *means*—the salvation of the world. This is manifestly what the New Testament is about, what it everywhere is saying in one form or another. Is what is said actually so, or is it not so?

There can be no more important question. Every one of the events connected with Jesus Christ, as also Jesus Christ himself, can be given a different meaning from the one given in the New Testament. Different men faced the same facts, and saw them differently, as they still do. Christ delivered a man from evil, and the judgment was passed: "He casteth out demons by the prince of the demons." He called himself "Son of God," and many who heard it shrank from him in horror as a blasphemer.[16] He hung on a cross, and the passers-by "railed" and the chief priests "mocked" and the rulers "scoffed": they saw nothing but a crucified criminal. The tomb was found empty, and the authorities said: "A stolen body." In the realization of what they believed was the truth of Christ, the disciples on the Day of Pentecost were held by a great emotional power. "What meaneth this?" some asked. And the answer came: "These men are filled with new wine."

There are conflicting interpretations of Christ therefore in the New Testament. For all that, the New Testament was written primarily to set over against the derogatory interpretation the interpretation which makes Jesus Christ the Son of God and the Saviour of the world, the means whereby is to be fulfilled God's eternal purpose for mankind. The New Testament declares definitely who Jesus Christ was and what he came to do and how his mission was fulfilled. This declaration is not the obvious meaning of the surface facts. From one point of view, all that the New Testament says about Jesus Christ is *absurd*. Yet it is set forth as plain and sober truth. If it is not the truth, "then we are of all men most miserable." But if it *is* the truth, then on what ground could it have been learned by the men who declared it? There is but one answer: *they were taught by the Holy Spirit*. They gave a meaning to facts which reason itself never could have found, and still can not find, in the facts themselves. If what the New Testament says about Jesus Christ is true, it can be true only on the ground that God by the Holy Spirit led men to this truth. Only God can be the guarantor of the New Testament, in what it says about Jesus Christ and his relation to the salvation of the world. We either believe it or we do not believe it, but we have no *right* to believe it unless we also believe that God by the Spirit "revealed" it. And if we do believe that God revealed it, then what else can we do than take the great truth to ourselves?

It is a characteristic of our time to decry all "authoritarian" teaching. In so far as the protest is made in the interests of truth itself, it is commendable. Once error is known to be error, its perpetuation becomes a menace. If new facts are discovered in the field of history or in the field of science or anywhere else, no respect for tradition should hinder their being made known. But it is difficult to see on what grounds the positive teaching and proclamation of Christian truth can be objected to as "authoritarian."[17] That a distinction is to be drawn between Christian truth properly so called and the "wrappings" which from time to time have been thrown around it, has already been allowed: indeed, it would be insisted upon. But if the New Testament as setting forth the truth *of* Christ and *about* Christ is the gift of the Holy Spirit, then it becomes an authoritative source of the Christian faith. If this is not such a source, then we do not have one.

Not only so, but we do not know what Christianity is. The historical Jesus and his meaning for God and men—these are described for us in the New Testament. To deny the description is any man's right, but when he proceeds to a reconstruction on his own account, one which quite ignores what is most unmistakable in the New Testament description, he is simply being arbitrary and subjective. He "makes his own Christianity," which is something no man has a right to do. If Christianity is not such as is presented in the New Testament, then it cannot be anything else that we can discover. The truth of the New Testament is in the reality of the Spirit's guidance. It must either be that, in which case it becomes supremely important and supremely authoritative; or it is something which, being purely imaginary and fictitious, is no longer of vital concern.

If experience is of any value at all in this connection, then we have to say that the condition to a real understanding of Scripture is guidance by the same Spirit under whose influence Scripture was originally produced. This is not to say that one who is content to treat Scripture simply "as literature" will not find in it very much of value. But we have here not merely a book, but a book which represents a profound spiritual movement in human history and experience. It is only as one *yields* to the movement that one begins to see what it all means. All Scripture is because of the inspiration of God. That does not mean that everything that was written was inspired: to say that places upon the mind an unnecessary burden. *It means that men wrote because they were under the inspiration of some divinely-given truth.* As was said in an earlier chapter, there was a complete coincidence of the freedom of the man and the constraint of the Spirit. God enabled the man to see, and under the compulsion of his vision the man then wrote and spoke.

The same Spirit by whose help the truth was given is the Spirit by whose help the truth must be apprehended. This is the unmistakable testimony of experience. "Deep calleth unto deep." There are two ways of reading the Fourth Gospel. One may read it as a critical student, around him all the paraphernalia of scholarship. This is a perfectly justifiable activity, and we cannot be too grateful to the men who have engaged in it. But one may so read the Fourth Gospel, and still miss what is fundamental in it. One must also read the Fourth Gospel on one's knees. One must yield to its testimony concerning Christ. When that happens, the Spirit which gave it becomes the Spirit which illuminates it. Words become bridges. Spirit speaks to spirit, because the Divine Spirit becomes the common possession of both. There was a truth in the contention of the Christian Gnostics that there was a "hidden" meaning in Scripture. What they elicited from Scripture by their peculiar methods of interpretation was often fantastic enough. Nevertheless, there is a sense in which one must be "initiated" in order to understand. "Spiritual things," says Paul, "are spiritually discerned," and did not Jesus himself say that God had hidden some things from the wise and prudent and revealed them unto babes—that is, unto the meek in spirit and the humble in mind?

Then is the gift of the illuminating Spirit an arbitrary act on the part of God? Not arbitrary, but conditional. That God did, indeed, choose men to be the vehicles of his truth to the world seems to be indubitable.[18] But that was a choice to service, and there is a difference between a choice to service and a choice to salvation. He who humbly and sincerely desires to know the truth of God as that truth has already been revealed, has met the basic condition to the illuminating of his mind and the strengthening of his will, which are the gifts of the Spirit. It is true that the situations in which men find themselves are influential factors in determining whether they shall even have this desire. To that extent, there is a determination in respect of Christian truth, but this is a form of that same determination because of which some men must live at one time and place rather than at another. To make this kind of "necessary determination" decisive of salvation would be to impugn both the justice and the mercy of God. The immediate question concerns those persons who have access to Christian truth. For such persons, the possible access may be transformed into actual comprehension, not accidentally and not arbitrarily, but conditionally. We are made free by knowing the truth, but we come to know the truth—*this truth*—only as we open our minds to receive it. Of the Spirit, Jesus said: "He shall glorify me: for he shall take of mine, and shall declare it unto you" (John 16.24). It was as much a promise as it was a pronouncement, and the history of the Church, with all its faults and failings, and the experience of Christian men, with all their imperfections and unworthiness, are so many evidences of the fulfillment of the promise.

That is to say, the Holy Spirit was not only the means whereby the revelation in the Word was enabled to secure a response. The Holy Spirit is also the means whereby the revelation is preserved, the response continually secured, and the fruits of the response established in the lives of men. A survey of the Church of history can be either disquieting or encouraging: it depends on what one looks at. There have been serious divisions. There have been councils characterized by disgraceful scenes and even more disgraceful decisions. The Church has approved activities which were in flat contradiction of its commission. There have been groups within the Church which exaggerated out of all recognition now this feature and now that feature of Christian truth. Defects in the Church have been answered by like defects on the part of individual Christians. All this is so. Yet the fact remains that the revelation has been preserved, the testimony has been proclaimed, a firm conviction of the truth of the revelation has been fostered, and there is sufficient evidence that the Spirit through whom the truth first came has continued to guard and propagate it.[19]

Yet it is not possible for us to reduce the action of the Spirit to definite law. We do not need to doubt that there is such a law, and we understand it in part, but we do not understand it in its entirety. *The Spirit refuses to be mechanized.* "God giveth not the Spirit by measure." From the days of Montanus until now there have been outbursts of new life in the Church. Usually the nucleus of the movement has been in some overwhelming experience on the part of one man, but even that has not always been so. The new life has broken out with apparent spontaneity at various points at the same time. Shall we not say that the Spirit was creating a hunger and then providing for it the satisfying response?

Similarly in the case of individuals. It is a fact that again and again men have found themselves suddenly made aware of the truth of Christ, sometimes for the first time in their lives, sometimes in a new way which made their past insights appear insignificant in the comparison. Not for nothing have men spoken of "The Creator Spirit" and "The Indwelling Spirit" and "The Quickening Spirit" and "The Renewing Spirit" and "The Revealing Spirit." By such phrases they have attempted to suggest and account for experiences of which they were completely certain.

This leads to the important question of so-called "new revelations." In so far as all truth may be said to be revealed, it is self-evident that there are fields of reality from which truth is breaking continually. Not only so, but in the light of the new truth, truth that was once taken to be such is seen to have been error. This necessarily goes with the expanding reach of man's mind. But when the claim is made that the same principle applies to Christian truth, the claim needs careful scrutiny. In what was written in an earlier chapter, the fullest possible recognition was made of what is known as "progressive revelation," as this applies to the Scriptural record. It was allowed that the Old Testament is to be read in the light of the New. But a progressive revelation necessarily means a climactic point. When the Word was made flesh, and when the fact and the meaning of this great truth was brought home by the Holy Spirit to the minds of men, who thereupon set forth, in what we know as the New Testament, all that it had been given them to see and to experience and understand—when that was done, there was created what can only be properly described as "The Christian Standard." The Christian Church is in possession of a body of truth concerning itself—the truth which made it, the truth which nourishes it, the truth which determines its character and sets its purpose—which in the very nature of the case it cannot abrogate. The Church can no more set aside the truth of Christ as that is contained in the New Testament than it determined that truth in the first place. The Church lives by a revelation—by the same revelation which originated it. The Spirit led men to the understanding of the Word of God which Jesus Christ was, but the Spirit will never lead men to the conviction that that original understanding was entirely wrong. Men of great sincerity may repudiate the New Testament interpretation of Jesus Christ, but if they say that they were led to that repudiation by the Holy Spirit, it is evident that all they do is to create an intolerable *impasse*. "He cannot deny himself."

Then are there no "new revelations" of Christian significance? There are, but they lie at the point not of abrogating what has been given, but of deepening insight into it, of more complete submission to it, and of its ever widening application to human life itself. There is a changeless center of an ever-changing movement. The Spirit that set the center, this center being the truth of Christ as we find it in Scripture, and especially in the New Testament, is the same Spirit that inspires the movement, this movement being the effort to bring the life of men more and more within the orbit of experience determined by that changeless central truth.[20] Unyielding loyalty to the center, freedom of action for the loyal soul as it swings in now narrower and now wider circles around that center—these are alike gifts of the Spirit, evidences of the Spirit's control.

Herein lies our permission to talk about the old truth in new ways, to find in it new meanings, and to apply it to the changing life of the world. Some ways of talking about Christian truth are no longer convincing because the "patterns" of thought have so radically changed. But that calls not for the abandoning of the truth but for the furnishing it with more effective instruments. This is the place where, if anywhere, the Church of to-day urgently needs the guidance of the Holy Spirit. But that guidance will never be granted to those who seek to destroy: it will be granted only to those who seek to conserve. How can there be conservation, however, where there is not first possession? Before the Church can be taught how to conserve its heritage, it must learn what its heritage really is. There are evidences that the Church is again going to school to the Holy Spirit. There are evidences that the Church is again becoming aware of the true source of its power. There are evidences that the truth which it is the function of "the Book" to attest is again asserting its power to capture the minds, move the hearts, and control the wills of men.

But that is only one side of our urgent need. It is not enough that we "correct our position" in relation to our standards. There is only one thing that justifies the correcting of the position, namely, a determination to continue the journey in keeping with the correction. This does not need to mean that we shall forget that we are living in the twentieth century and not the eighteenth or thirteenth. There *are* new conditions. There *are* new problems. There *is* the need for new applications. Surely the aroused social conscience is a gift of the Spirit. But just as surely we need the Spirit for the *guidance* of the conscience which has been aroused. In a thousand ways, our world has changed. But the truth of God as revealed in Jesus Christ—this has not changed.

The Church must adjust its impact to the nature of that which confronts it. When it seeks to throw into definite propositions the truth with which it is charged, it must bear in mind the situation which the proposition is designed to reach. The same truth is susceptible of variety of form. The office of the Holy Spirit is a permanent office because the Christian revelation finds itself in a changing world, and the revelation must retain its integrity while performing its illuminating, renewing, and empowering mission according to the conditions of the given time. To lay hold upon new instruments, of thought, technique, and action, while using these instruments in the behalf of a truth which is the same yesterday, to-day, and forever, is the obligation that rests upon the Church of Christ and those to whom its cause is precious. In no other way can that obligation be discharged to-day than it has been in the past—by responsiveness to the Holy Spirit, whose mission it is to create strong desire and then to satisfy it, to smite an open road before the eyes of men and then to lead them along its vistas, and to take of the things of Christ, reveal them to teachable souls, and endue them with meet courage to make them to be teachers in their own turn, according to their time and place.

CHAPTER 19

The Rising Tide of Faith

FEW PERSONS WHO ARE FAMILIAR WITH RESPONSIBLE CHRISTIAN thought in recent years will doubt that there has been a decided swing away from the rationalism of the second and third decades of the century. The characteristics of the so-called Enlightenment of the eighteenth century were very closely duplicated in the opening years of our own. The approach to religion was largely humanistic. Naturalism very generally held the field in philosophy. On every hand, the primary purpose of the Christian gospel was regarded as the improvement of the social order. The term "modernism" was in wide use as describing the new temper. It aroused opposition enough, much of it not too intelligent.[1]

The causes of the re-action from what is now being seen to have been a one-sided emphasis are difficult to classify in any detail. That the emphasis was spiritually impotent became increasingly clear. It was seen to involve a quite cavalier treatment of Scripture. It assumed an optimistic view of human nature: men had but to be taught the truth and put in agreeable surroundings to become all that they should. The emphasis reflected the findings from the comparative study of religions. It treated as suspect the Christian claim of special revelation. The great doctrines of Christianity were explained on grounds chiefly psychological and sociological. A variety of impersonal and finite theisms appeared. The scientific method was treated as universally applicable. Prayer was reduced to a purely subjective exercize. Sin lost its tragic note because it could be so readily referred to environmental influence. The Church itself was looked upon as one more useful social institution.[2]

The awakening to the menace of this situation came to many men as a shock. The order of the spiritual life, indefinitely repeatable, is conviction, repentance, and conversion. There have been

266

those who have gone through that experience in respect of their understanding of Christianity. The evidence to that is all around us. Religious periodical literature, one of the surest reflections of contemporary thought, is revealing enough at this point. The output of significant theological books in the last few years is so much additional evidence, and wherever the leaders of Christian thought assemble to-day, one of the subjects to which they turn their attention as of supreme importance is the rising tide of evangelical conviction.

This interest is not confined to any one land, as may be seen from any of the recent "surveys" of British, Continental, and American theology.[3] It is surely not without significance that at a recent Protestant assembly, a well-known American scholar, speaking of the re-discovery of the theology of the Reformers, the new Biblicism, and Barthianism, as the characteristics of contemporary Continental and especially German theology, should have declared that most modern German scholars in the field of the New Testament are in agreement that "the whole of the New Testament has but one topic, namely, the good news that Jesus Christ is our Lord, and that this theme is displayed in various ways by the different writers." A very similar judgment could have been made respecting British and American scholars in the same field. At the same Assembly, another speaker dealt with "The Revival of Theology in the Roman Catholic Church," directing himself especially to Neo-Thomism. Among other things he said: "On all the more important points that were at issue in the sixteenth century between Rome on the one hand and Wittenberg and Geneva on the other, I am as unalterably opposed to Rome as were our fathers; and yet, as matters stand to-day, I cannot but regard them to a large extent at least, as friends and allies as over against an enemy that would eradicate Christianity, root and branch." The same speaker also declared himself as feeling that "real Protestants have much more in common with Roman Catholics than with Modernists."[4]

The last declaration especially deserves careful pondering. It plainly implies that it is peripheral rather than central matters that divide Evangelicals and Roman Catholics, but that it is these central matters that are challenged by Modernists. If we are to accept this situation as respects Modernists, however, it can only be on the condition that we distinguish modernism and liberalism.[5] Nothing could be more deplorable than that the truly liberal spirit should depart from modern Christianity—unless, indeed, it were that Christianity should become identified with modernism. Any authoritative statement as to what constitutes modernism includes a categorical denial of supernaturalism as usually understood.

Henry Nelson Wieman is a case in point.[6] With undoubted earnestness and sincerity he follows the purely rational approach to the fact of religion, with the result that he rules out all supernaturalness, speaks of God as "growth of meaning,"[7] removes Jesus Christ entirely from the place he has occupied in historical Christianity, and lays down a methodology for religious living which, comprehensive and constructive as it unquestionably is, rests upon a groundwork which one may be forgiven for doubting to be adequate to its task. Wieman's approach to the religious aspect of existence impresses the reader as being of the same cold, impersonal, exact, and analytical type as that of the scientist in his approach to the non-religious aspect. But religion must exist before it can be approached, and devising a method of approach does not carry a guarantee as to religion itself. Positivism applied to religion may much rather be a sign of decay than of growth. If God is no longer "a responding Other," as W. E. Hocking would say,[8] but a purely impersonal function of existence—as Wieman would seem to mean[9]—in that aspect of its structure which bears value and the possibility of more value, then it means that we are no longer to judge value in the light of a God who has already made himself known to us in Jesus Christ; but, having decided for ourselves, by standards of our own devising, what is or is not value, and when meaning has or has not increased, make this the pattern to which whatever God we believe in must conform. Exactly this was the procedure in the ethnic faiths: man created God according to his own standard.

But the very thing that is distinctive of Christianity is its claim that "God became incarnate in Jesus Christ," and that *we do now know* what manner of being God is, and why he made us, and what manner of men he would have us become. This is the theme of

much recent theology, and the fact is the strongest single point in
the evidence that "the tide has turned." It is simple truth to say
that the naturalistic view represented by Wieman is less convincing, less attractive, less acceptable, than it was even five years ago.
A recent symposium on *Revelation* is a signal that cannot go un-
heeded: it is an announcement that the offensive in respect of the
meaning of Christianity has passed from the negative humanistic
and rationalistic to the positive super-naturalistic. Those who par-
ticipated in the symposium make an impressive list: T. S. Eliot
(Anglo-Catholic layman); Karl Barth (Reformed); William Temple (Anglican); Sergius Bulgakoff (Greek Orthodox); M. C. D'Arcy
(Roman Catholic); W. M. Horton (Baptist-American); and Gustaf
Aulén (Lutheran). The editorial preface was written by John Baillie
(Presbyterian). The writers show some variation at the point of
what is usually called "general" revelation, but they reveal an astonishing unanimity at the point of "special" revelation—that is, at
the point of what meets us in the Scriptures and in Jesus Christ and
all he has made possible. The book as a whole indicates that theology is again becoming bold and aggressive, concerned to preserve the Christian heritage in its entirety rather than to trim it
down to meet the prejudices of the hour. It is recovering its proper
task of explicating the revelation of God in Christ, which, in the
language of Horton, meets from on high and by the mercy of God
"man's desperate need of light upon the ultimate meaning and
purpose of his existence."

The contrast between the position represented by Wieman and
the position represented by the participants in the symposium just
referred to could be continued at great length. For example, the
Rethinking Religion of John Haynes Holmes, a straight re-affirma-
tion of the type of religious humanism which Holmes has long
represented, could be set over against the *Revelation and Response*
of Edgar P. Dickie. Dickie sees that the proper correlate of divine
revelation is human responsiveness, and that where the response is
lacking the revealing process cannot be complete. He is not anti-
rational, but he insists that reason as the power to respond to, to
appreciate, and to use, revealed truth, and reason as the power to
discover truth on its own account, are two different things. God

has disclosed to men, and supremely in Jesus Christ, truth which, explore and apply it as we may, is still not of our finding. Revelation, says Dickie, has to do with "a new dimension" of reality, and the purpose of revelation is to relate man to that reality in such a way as to bring him to fulness of life. What Dickie has to say provides also a most effective reply to the *Evangelical Modernism* of C. J. Cadoux. Cadoux writes with a much more profound appreciation of Christianity than can be found in either Wieman or Holmes, but he is hampered by an excessive immanentism which leads him to a view of Christ practically identical with that of Schleiermacher, and which prevents him from seeing in revelation anything more than the interpreting function of reason applied to various historical and experiential facts.

To continue these contrasts is, however, hardly necessary, and it would issue in little more than a collection of book reviews. It might, of course, be said that if contemporary theological writings can be contrasted in this fashion, the claim made above, that modernism is decreasing and that supernaturalism—to use the term which is the most effective negative of modernism—is increasing, can hardly be sustained. But it is not the quantity of the output, but the quality of it, to which attention is being directed, and which is the real basis of the claim in question. Modernism is no longer in control of the field. It is being challenged—challenged by men whose intellectual power and scholarly attainments are unimpeachable. It does not matter if the *number* of men of whom this is true is comparatively small. What matters is their spirit. Gideon's band numbered only three hundred, but that was enough. Notice has been served on the rationalistic, humanistic, naturalistic interpreters of Christianity that they are to have their way no longer.[10]

This does not mean that liberalism is in retreat. It has already been said that the identifying of modernism and liberalism is altogether unjustifiable. There is in Christianity a tradition of liberalism which we can only earnestly pray will never be allowed to perish. Why should it be supposed that open-mindedness to new truth—which is the essence of liberalism—necessarily requires the surrender of those distinctive Christian verities which are admittedly held in faith? Such a surrender is the mark rather of a naturalistic modernism than of a genuine liberalism, a liberalism which is conservative toward the well-tried old and charitable toward the emerging new. One can be a liberal, and reject as utterly inadequate the view of *The Essence of Christianity* which Harnack popularized early in the century. One can be a liberal and even reject the imposing attempt of Troeltsch to bring the whole sweep of Christianity under the scope of social science, an attempt which issued logically enough in Troeltsch's rejection of the "finality" of the Christian religion.

Few men have written more sympathetically and more understandingly of Troeltsch than H. R. Mackintosh, yet Mackintosh said of Troeltsch that the Christianity whose "finality" he denied was a very much "reduced" Christianity;[11] and he added that to those who really understand Christianity because they see it as representing God's uttermost action of love on behalf of needy men, the affirmation of its absolute and final character is the most natural thing in the world. A love greater than the Holy Love of God as revealed in Christ is simply inconceivable. Yet who would dare say that Mackintosh was obscurantist just because he passed this judgment on Troeltsch, or who would dare say that his criticism involved indifference to the profound social feeling so characteristic of Troeltsch?

Mackintosh was unreservedly loyal to the Christian heritage in its totality; he proclaimed it without compromise; he stood resolutely against every attempt to understand and set forth Christianity save in its own light; he said bluntly that if its conflict with "modern thought" were to end, "Christianity would cease to be itself";[12] yet beyond most men Mackintosh was aware of his own time, sympathetic with every great movement that looked to the welfare of men, as practical as he was academic, and intelligently appreciative of every new insight into the facts of life. It is liberalism of the sort that he exemplified—"evangelical liberalism," or "liberal evangelicalism," it has been called—that is coming upon the Church to-day in many lands as the herald of a more vigorous and positive declaration of the Gospel of Christ. "No theologian of the last generation," wrote Professor Henry Bett, "was more splendidly equipped than H. R. Mackintosh with wide learning, with philosophical acumen, and with the gift of spiritual discernment."[13] Yet this is the man who wrote one of the greatest modern expositions and defences of the catholic doctrine of the Person of Christ, and who confessed to his friend, T. Hywel Hughes, that no book he had ever written had given him greater joy in the writing than *The Christian Doctrine of Forgiveness*. He added, says Hughes, "that he thought this was due to the fact that he was dealing with the basic factor in Christianity, the grace of God in forgiveness."[14]

Much the same could have been written about many other men than Mackintosh—men, fortunately, still with us. The number increases of competent scholars and thinkers who find themselves in thrall to the Christian faith in what is truly being described as its "classic" form. To call the roll of the conspicuous names in contemporary theology is to a very large extent to call names which represent the Scriptural, the historical, the positive, the properly catholic. They are of all communions and of all lands. Germans like Barth and Heim, Otto and Sasse, Althaus and Tillich; Scandinavians like Aulén and Nygren, who are worthily carrying on the tradition of the great Söderblom; a Swiss theologian like Emil Brunner, whose *Mediator* and *Divine Imperative* and *Man in Revolt* are among the greatest achievements of evangelical Christian thought in our time; Russian Orthodox like Berdyaev and Bulgakoff; Pryzawara the Austrian Jesuit, who has done so much to make Augustine better known; Kraemer the Hollander, whose brave book, *The Christian Message in a Non-Christian World*, has deeply disturbed those who have been proposing to throw Christianity into the melting-pot with the ethnic faiths, with a view to producing a new universal syncretistic religion; the French Protestant leader Boegner; American Protestants like Niebuhr and Horton, W. A. Brown and John McKay; British Protestants, High Church, Low Church, Free Church, like Temple and Headlam and Quick, Mozley and Barry, Raven and W. R. Matthews, A. B. Macauley and Daniel Lamont, Whale and Oman and Dodd, Flew, Micklem and Vincent Taylor; Anglo-Catholics like Iddings Bell and W. M. Urban, A. E. Taylor and T. S. Eliot; and the Catholic Neo-Thomist group, such as Fulton Sheen and L. J. A. Mercier in America, Belloc and Dawson and Jerrold in England, Karl Adam in Germany, Etienne Gilson, Jacques Maritain and Leon Bloy in France. The names occur to one almost spontaneously, and the list could be duplicated many times.

It is not that these men all think alike at every point. Considering their backgrounds, that would not be possible, nor would it in any case be desirable. All that is being claimed for them is that they are men of the twentieth century, informed as to the currents of contemporary thought, yet frankly accepting the Christian claim as to a revelation of God in Jesus Christ of such a sort as sets Christianity apart from every other religion in the world and confronts man with the conditions both of the richest living here and of his ultimate destiny.

The remarkable interest in the life and writings of Søren Kierkegaard is surely one of the signs of the times.[15] There can be few men who find it possible to follow Kierkegaard at all points. He is so pessimistic, so tempestuous, so utterly paradoxical. His inherited melancholy pervades all he writes, as it distorted most of his relations with his contemporaries. No man more than he was overwhelmed by the tragic sense of life. He saw every man as standing on the edge of a precipice, with "nothing between him and the awful dark" save the undeserved grace of a Sovereign God. Everywhere he looked Kierkegaard saw contrast, nay, more than that, contradiction. Time and eternity, God and man, sin and grace, faith and works, Christ and all others—these stood over against each other with infinite qualitative difference. The prevailing "mediating" theology, dominated as this was by the Hegelian "both-and" philosophy, Kierkegaard opposed with a vehemence amounting almost to frenzy. What could such a theology say about "the existential moment," so real, so concrete, so pregnant of combined despair and hope—that moment when "the solitary individual," the convicted man, stands in utter loneliness before God, seeing in that moment by one and the same revealing flash his own complete sinfulness and helplessness, and the majesty, the sovereignty, the holiness of God, and yet withal his gracious love? And if in that moment the vision of divine love should be withheld, and the sinful man should see in God nothing but a Consuming Fire, whereby he knows himself marked for destruction, and even that he accepts because it is God's will—if that should be, what place is there for such a moment, such a rejection, such a shattering of the soul, such a vindication of the awfulness and the absoluteness of the divine will, in the smooth, all-accommodating, all-explanatory *schema* of the Hegelian metaphysics?

Kierkegaard would have none of it. No "both-and" for him, but a tragic irreducible "either-or." Life is no automatic unraveling of an eternal ball: it is something full of surprises, full of novelties, full of paradoxes. Better stay by the facts in all their naked unrelated and unrelatable tragedy than deny their profound meaning—the absolute will of God—just to make them fit into a man-made pre-conceived pattern without a rough edge of any sort in it. And the more so when, after all, this God—even this God in whose inscrutable will is the destiny of men's souls—has, in the inconceivable and inexplicable miracle of Incarnation, personally appeared among sinful men and as himself a man. "This man is God!" An offence to reason? Certainly. But what of it? What is reason but an instrument of man's bafflement? What is its failure but faith's opportunity? What greater sin than to fail of that faith? That which evokes the faith that, perchance, if God be gracious, may save, is itself an affront to reason. Then let reason be affronted that so man may rise to the height of his supreme achievement in treating as final and absolute truth that which his judgment pronounces to be irrational.

No wonder Kierkegaard was a sufferer. His very reading of the Christian Gospel did but intensify his suffering, yet the very fact confirmed him in his conviction that his reading of the Gospel was right, since suffering is the pathway to redemption—suffering for the Redeemer, suffering for the redeemed.

When one understands Kierkegaard, one begins to understand Karl Barth.[16] It is not right to say that Barthianism has no other explanation than in Barth's discovery of Kierkegaard. Other influences played upon the mind of the young Swiss preacher and theologian. The Great War disillusioned him as to the value of the type of Christianity which he had learned from Herrmann and Harnack. He had been told that the Bible was a record of what men had come more and more to discover about God. He had been told that God was the immanent World-Spirit. He had been told that this God dwelt partly in man, and more completely in Jesus Christ, and that this more complete indwelling represented both the human ideal and the human possibility, provided man knew and observed the conditions to its realization. The work of Christ was to make known these conditions, and thus to promote among men the consciousness of the divine indwelling.

Barth found himself becoming less and less convinced by such teaching. It did not touch the vast human tragedy of which he was becoming increasingly conscious. Kierkegaard spoke to him as his German theological mentors had never done. Dostoevsky also spoke to him, and to much the same effect. The terrible novels of the great Slav, ruthless in their analysis of human nature, engendering the mood of despair respecting anything man can do for himself, pointing to the mystery of the grace of God and all its redeeming action in Jesus Christ—these seemed to Barth to be true commentaries on the Gospel.

He restudied the Reformers, Luther and Calvin; he sounded the depths of Augustine; above all, he steeped his mind in Paul. And a great new truth began to fill out his mind. Immanentism is evangelical poison. God and man are at opposite poles. No man by searching can find out God. The gulf is unbridgeable—from the human side. God on the plane of the eternal, the utterly holy—man caught in the confusions of the temporal, the utterly sinful: how can these two be reconciled? Surely not by anything that man can do. Let him be as religious as he will—his religion is but his own unavailing effort to build a tower to heaven, a tower which must as surely collapse as did that Tower of Babel, permanent symbol of the futility of all human striving. In God alone is man's hope.

But man is not even sure of God—unless God shall make himself known. He can have no communion with him—unless God shall initiate it. He can have no moral peace—unless God shall guarantee it. He can have no indestructible certitude as to his own complete security—unless God shall give it to him. And all this God has done. He has made himself known, in and as Jesus Christ. He has flung a bridge—this bridge—across the yawning chasm. The eternal has entered time and history—paradox enough, yet in this paradox, and the acceptance of it, is the one sure ground of man's salvation. In Christ, God has given himself once and for always.

How do we know? We do not *know*: we *believe*. Failing this belief, nothing can happen: God still remains remote; doubt still reigns; sin is still unforgiven; peace is still wanting; certitude remains impossible. But when the belief exists and the venture is made—this being true faith—the miracle happens. The hidden God becomes the revealed God. The barrier goes down. The moral self-contradiction is solved. The man who can do nothing for himself finds that something has been done for him. It is God who justifies; it is God who sanctifies; it is God who glorifies. Always the means from God's side is Christ, and these means are solely of divine grace, never of human desert; always the means from man's side is faith, *sola fide*, and even this faith is the gift of God, lest any man should boast.

There are concomitants of Barth's position to which serious objection has been taken, especially his dialecticism, his utter separation of God and man, his insistence on the absoluteness of man's moral helplessness, his denial of all extra-Christian revelation, his explanation of Christ as sheer divine intrusion and the like.[17] Yet Mackintosh concludes an unusually discriminating and sympathetic examination of Barth with the assertion that we owe to him "the most serious theological effort of this generation."[18] Barth has exposed the menace of naturalistic humanism. He has shown that Christian life is essentially obedience to the Word of God, and that this Word is not a human discovery but a divine gift, coming from above down, which man must either reject to his condemnation or receive to his salvation. He has brought the sense of "crisis" back into Christian thinking.

Few if any of the men who in one way or another show some sympathy with Barth and his point of view—Thurneysen, Gogarten, Bultmann, Brunner, Heim, McConnachie, Lowrie, Canfield, Pauck, Homrighausen, Reinhold Niebuhr, Hendry—are able to go with him all the way. It is his spirit, his purpose, his emphasis, his protests, his clarifying of the fundamental issues of the Christian revelation in opposition to contemporary naturalisms, rationalisms, and humanisms, that has attracted them and awakened in them an answering response.

Thus Karl Heim, removed from Barth as he is in many ways, has lifted his voice in behalf of the divine transcendence as against the excessive immanentism of the Schleiermacher tradition.[19] He has more confidence in philosophy as such than has Barth, and is in substantial agreement with the endeavor of Heidegger, Buber, and Grisebach to face the metaphysical implications of the doctrine of relativity. Daniel Lamont[20] has endeavored to popularize what is admittedly a difficult body of thought—thought calling for the consideration of such topics as "the boundary question," or the problem of the point or points at which distinctions fall within the whole; the distinctions of reality according to "spaces," "contents," and "dimensions"; the corresponding ways of knowing or apprehending reality; the "person-attitude" and the "observer-attitude"; the differences of "I," "Thou," and "It"; the "time-corridor," the "object-moment," and the like.

Out of his consideration of such questions, Heim draws the following conclusions: that any human standpoint is necessarily relative; that the different dimensions of reality are necessarily apprehended in different ways; that God being that dimension which maintains and pervades all other dimensions, he is not apprehensible by those means by which we apprehend these other dimensions; that this inability is due to a fundamental "distortion" arising out of the very nature of the human will; that the only way therefore whereby God, as *ens realissimum*, and so as transcendent—the term to be taken dimensionally, not spatially—can be apprehended is by "revelation"; and that the human correlative of this revelation is necessarily "faith." According to Heim, therefore, we are so constituted that we need God, cannot escape him, and cannot find him, but are able to respond to his "word," which is his own appointed means of the divine-human reconciliation.

This may sound difficult enough. It is referred to here because it is an example of the attempt being made in our time both to treat seriously the Christian claim of revelation, and to find a basis for that claim not only in the needs of men but in the fundamental structure of existence itself as a structure bespeaking the divine transcendence. Edwyn Bevan's judgment that Barth is the vehement prophet and Heim the calm restrained thinker is true enough;[21] but what Heim's thinking does is to offer a confirmation of Barth's own unwavering conviction that God is not to be equated with some aspect of the world-process, as is the fashion of numerous contemporary naturalistic theisms, but instead that God is always "above," always "other," always therefore inaccessible to men unless he shall by his own act draw near and disclose himself to the one means, faith and love, by which man may know him. That Heim's interest in this question is not merely academic, but that he sees it as the function and purpose of the revelation in Christ to create here and now "the new divine order," he has himself made clear in the little book bearing that title.

A consideration of the relation between the fact of transcendence and the Christian revelation has been undertaken by George S. Hendry in a fashion markedly sympathetic with Barth, but avoiding for the most part the metaphysical problems dealt with by Heim and his group.[22] Hendry holds uncompromisingly to the biblical doctrine of creation. God is first and foremost Creator. Just because God is Creator, he is in nowise to be confounded with his creation. To that extent at least, he is "other." He is himself necessarily of a different "order" of being from anything which he has made: therefore it is impossible for man to advance by natural steps from the creation to the Creator. God is not at the end of a journey which it belongs to man both to undertake and to complete. Reason may argue to the fact and necessity of a First Cause, but Hendry makes the point that causation is not creation. Creation is *sui generis*. The conceptions of First Cause and of God the Creator therefore differ radically. There is no analogue to creation: it is a sheer act of Sovereign Will, something we can neither imagine nor explain, but only believe. No human faculty can discover God as an "object." He remains everlastingly "subject." Any knowledge we have of him is therefore revelation, but revelation means not that the divine "subject" has now become an "object," but that he has made known to us *that* he is, and *what* he is, and what he *requires* of us, and what he has *done* that the requirement, otherwise impossible, may be met.

There is, however, as Hendry points out, a continual temptation to read the revelation in the light of our various forms of knowledge. It might be remarked here, parenthetically, that the reality of this danger is illustrated in even so acute a discussion as that of Jacques Maritain, *The Degrees of Knowledge*, for what Maritain takes to be the highest reach of experience for man, insight into the very nature of that Pure Being which is God, is still presented as a form of knowledge. What Philo attempted to do in amalgamating Israel and Greece has been attempted repeatedly in the Christian Church, but always, says Hendry, this "Hellenizing of the Gospel" has ended in the Gospel being degraded. Luther saw this, and his recovery of the revelation in Christ of the grace of God the Creator marks one of the greatest spiritual epochs in the history of Christianity. The evidence increases that men of our own time are making a like recovery, and precisely this is why we can say that "the tide has turned."

Another illustration of the thesis is in the writings of Nicholas Berdyaev.[23] The last thing anyone would wish to do would be to associate Berdyaev with Barth. The backgrounds of the two men are entirely different. Berdyaev is the recognized intellectual leader of that large group of Russian exiles who have gathered in Western Europe. Feodor Stepun, in *The Russian Soul and Revolution*, has told enough about the early life of Berdyaev, including a revolutionary period and a period in Siberia, to throw light on his return to faith. The faith is Russian Orthodox, with its cult of virginity, its Sophia-philosophy, and its sacramentarianism.

Berdyaev, however, has not simply returned to a dogmatic orthodoxy. He is a bold, independent, and original thinker. The marks of his own tragic experience are upon his thought. "He is quite consciously the heir and debtor of a great succession of thinkers whose interest is mainly ethical, including not only Plato, Jacob Boehme, and Dostoevsky, but even Luther, Ibsen and Nietzsche."[24] So wrote a reviewer in connection with what many will feel is Berdyaev's greatest book, *The Destiny of Man*. The book, which has much in common not only with Dostoevsky, but also with Solovyov, Tuitshev, Chekov, Turgeniev, and many others of like mind, bears some striking similarities to Brunner, *The Divine Im-*

perative, except that the basis of Brunner's ethics is securely laid in the evangelical faith, whereas Berdyaev approaches the problem rather through a highly speculative metaphysics which, though it is theistic and in some respects even biblical and revelational, nevertheless is often more curious than convincing.

The Destiny of Man ought not to be read without a previous familiarity with Berdyaev's earlier works, *Freedom and the Spirit* and *The Meaning of History*. In all his writings he makes use of the conception of primal irrational freedom, which some interpreters insist on identifying with "Nothing," as though God and "Nothing" are the postulates of creation, with the possibility even that "Nothing" is the more fundamental of the two. The interpretation hardly does justice to Berdyaev's *intention*, to say nothing more. It is true that there is a sense in which God finds his creative act is *conditioned*, but that is true of any genuine theistic position.

Berdyaev's conception, however, is a difficult and perplexing one, and is not likely to find very wide acceptance. He regards creation as having been made possible not merely by the will of God, which *alone* could do nothing, but by the fact that an eternal "meonic freedom" consents to the creative act. The term "meonic" is an anglicizing of the Greek *to mē on*, meaning "being which is nothing," and this "being which is nothing" is freedom, the primal irrationality. Through it, the will of God is enabled to create, but this "meonic freedom" not only makes creation possible: it is in itself essential evil, and hence it accounts for the evil which is attendant upon all created existence.

In a word, God cannot, by mere arbitrary will, create the perfect —a profound enough insight. Creation is because of freedom, but then so also is evil because of freedom. In the case of man, this is especially apparent. The freedom in which man has his origin continues to characterize him, and precisely in that fact lies the root of his sin and misery. By creating through freedom (non-being, or the principle of negation), God finds himself confronted with a situation which denies him—a situation in which freedom unrestrained appears as the evil which it is.

Berdyaev regards this as the supreme tragedy, involving alike God, the world, and man. It is as though God created man to be his living companion, and when he had done his work and called man, he found that he had created a rebel. The very freedom in which man had to be made in order to be what God desired is the cause whereby what God desires fails to be. God's creative act provides the opportunity for its own defeat. This is the meaning of "the myth of the Fall"—a Creator powerless before the highest point of his own creation. But God does not accept the defeat. The Creator undertakes to be the Redeemer. The first act is the ground of a second act. God takes upon himself the sins of the world, and he can do that because he already has—and has had from eternity— "the Lamb." So Berdyaev writes: "God in the aspect of God-the-Son descends into the abyss, into the *Urgrund*, into the depths of freedom out of which springs evil as well as every kind of good. This is the only possible interpretation of the mystery of the In-carnation—if we are not to interpret it in the juridical sense."[25] God's sacrifice in Christ is the chosen means—shall we not say the only means—to the great end of subjugating and so sanctifying that very freedom which is the cause of sin and evil but without which there could be no good. God-Creator becomes God-Redeemer by becoming God-Crucifer. The redemption must be achieved from within freedom: to force it from without would be to incur defeat.

This self-end of God sets also the self-end of man. That is to say, just as God, by self-sacrificial love, seeks to subjugate and trans-form that "meonic freedom" which both permits and hinders his purpose, so man, confronted by a like freedom, is called to a like self-sacrificial love. This gives not the ethics of law, and not even the ethics of redemption, in which man is essentially the receiver, but the ethics of creativeness, which Berdyaev insists is the ulti-mate issue of the Christian Gospel.[26] The Gospel is both the call to a new life and the power of it.

Berdyaev agrees with Brunner, however, that this new life can-not be regimented, or identified with any contemporary "ideology" or "social pattern." Therefore he writes: "The absolute revelation of the Gospel about the Kingdom of God cannot be expressed by any social and historical forms, which are always temporal and rela-tive. The truth of the spiritual life cannot be made to fit into the natural life. There never has been and there cannot be any Christian state, Christian economics, Christian family, Christian learning, Christian social life. For in the Kingdom of God and in the perfect divine life there is neither state, nor economics, nor family, nor learning, nor any social life determined by law."[27] The second half of Brunner's great treatise on Christian ethics, *The Divine Imperative*, could truthfully be described as an elaboration of this statement.

This reference to Brunner may very well be the point of departure for a fuller statement of his position.[28] He has manifestly moved farther away from Barth than was the case when he first came into prominence, but while Brunner would prefer to classify himself as a "liberal evangelical," the use of the adjective should not detract attention from the noun and all that it signifies.

Brunner is one of the most effective critics of the various rationalisms which have crept into modern views of Christianity. But he is more than a critic. He is a constructive thinker of great power, and he has thrown the entire weight of a scholarly and penetrating and profoundly Christian mind to the side of Christianity in the evangelical tradition. He charges against the various types of speculative idealism that by their making God and man continuous with each other, all history is made revelational. The conclusion is then drawn that a so-called "special" revelation becomes unnecessary: actually, in the premises it even becomes impossible. The result is a radical revision of the Biblical message, a revision which amounts to a repudiation of practically every distinctive truth which the Bible conveys. Because if there is one thing more than another which Christianity presupposes, it is that a complete breach has occurred between God and man, the cause of which is man's sin.

Brunner is utterly opposed to the ignoring of this indisputable moral fact in the interests of a preconceived theory of ontological continuity. The breach is there, and sin is the cause of it, and sin is of the will of man: therefore nothing that man can do can heal the breach. If there is to be any healing, it must be from the divine side. Jesus Christ is God's means of healing the breach. In that case, he is to be conceived as absolute revelation. He is not to be explained as the flowering of something already immanent in the race. Yet modern theology has to a large extent offered that explanation of him. Why has it? Because it has ignored the Biblical message, has taken its clue from speculative philosophy, and has operated with a non-tragic—which is to say, naturalistic—view of the relations of God and man.

In all his writings, Brunner reiterates his conviction that the true Christian doctrine of man is that he is a sinner, and that any uncertainty at this point involves uncertainty at the point of every other great Christian truth. That we were made in God's image, and that we have fallen away from God—these are two statements to be accepted as facts, irrespective of whether or not we are able to fit them into our picture of reality. Brunner denies that this is a mere religious speculation: instead, he calls it "the one and only serious interpretation of sin."[29] Man, he says, has collectively fallen away from God, and this Fall is "perpetually and inevitably repeated." There is a recognition equally of responsibility and of necessity. Only such a view makes sin fully personal; only such a view at the same time is true to its essential tragedy. And this, and this only, is the Biblical teaching.

This distortion of the original personal relation between God and man can have only one issue—guilt. Guilt can be subjectively significant only because it already has an objective reference. The reference is to God and his will, and because God is holy man cannot be guilty and the fact of his guilt make no difference to his Maker. Brunner bluntly says that the guilt of man means the wrath of God. The moral rent manifests itself in every direction. Existence is distorted because of the sin and guilt of man on the one hand, and the wrath of God on the other.

Brunner is fully aware of how "un-modern" this is, but that, he says, simply means that there is a fatal opposition between the so-called "modern" view of man and the Biblical and Christian view. The Christian view asserts the gulf between God and man as the meaning of revelation, attested, as this actually is, by universal moral experience, which always recognizes a difference between the "ought" and the "can." It asserts that God has bridged the gulf, and that he has bridged it by Jesus Christ, who is therefore the Mediator. He who claims to be conscious of no need of such a Mediator is simply saying that he has never accepted the Christian revelation respecting sin, and grace, and redemption. Men turn to the Mediator only when they see that every other way is barred. Of the fact of Christ, accepted as he is actually presented, there come conviction of sin, repentance for sin, and faith that God will forgive and restore.

Stating the case so baldly as this quite fails to give an adequate impression of the masterly way in which Brunner marshals his material and makes his points. Anyone who may wish to read, in fairly brief compass, an example of his intellectual power combined with a profound spiritual grasp, could hardly do better than to read his discussion of the relation between the Eternal Logos (Word) and the revelation of God in and as Jesus Christ.[30] In this respect, he is like the author of the Fourth Gospel. He begins with a historical fact, the man Christ Jesus, to which faith assigns a certain absolute significance, and then he grounds this historical fact in the very being of God. Without the historical, the metaphysical remains a matter of mere guess-work. With the historical given this significance, we have that living whole of truth of which the various Christian doctrines are simply so many parts. The revelation in Christ is therefore an imperative. It commands us. That is why it is called the Word of God. It is not something that man finds, but something that God gives. The Word calls man back to his true condition. He was created in the Word in the first place, and that is his normal state. But he broke away from it. Only the Word in which he was created can bring him back. The first life is a gift of God in the Word. The second life must be a gift of God in that same Word.

Hence for Brunner the Christian religion is summed up in the claim that the Word, an eternal constituent of the divine nature, the means of all God's self-manifestation, the explanation of prophecy as the burden of the message given to the prophet and constituting whatever authority the prophet had—that this Word became flesh. The Eternal Word appears in history as Jesus Christ. Hence Christ is the personal presence of God among men. To the human reason, this is impenetrable mystery; to faith, it is the ground of salvation. Herein is prophecy fulfilled. Christ was more than a prophet. The prophet spoke for God by the Word, but Christ is God speaking. The Word is the Life—*this* Life. The

Messenger is the Message, and that gives fulfillment of all other revelation, and is itself finality. God no longer speaks *through* somebody, but *as* Somebody.

Brunner admits how wide the repudiation of this claim of the absolute divine self-disclosure in Christ has been, but always the repudiation—whether by speculative idealism, or by mysticism, or by moralism—is made on *a priori* grounds. But Christianity, for him, stands or falls by the claim. Christ is the Mediator, provided solely by God. The Mediator implies the fact of sin, the fact of separation, the fact of judgment, but also the fact of mercy. Briefly, "the fellowship of the Creator with the creature through the Word of the Creator, the real, spoken Word, the Word which is an actual temporal event: this is the revelation of which the Bible speaks, and of which the religious philosophy of Idealism, whether Greek or modern, does not speak."[31]

No one who believes that modernism represented a radical departure from the Biblical revelation and historical Christianity, and who at the same time believes that there is a true liberalism which is every way compatible with the catholic and evangelical faith, can fail to be encouraged by the evidence presented in this brief survey that the tide has turned. The men whose position has been described are not anti-scientific, and they are not anti-critical. They are not living in the past. They are not seeking merely to regalvanize dead dogma, as is so often charged against them. They have recovered or retained for themselves what they believe is the essential character and the inner meaning of the Christian revelation. They believe it is *true*—not true in the sense of the rationally demonstrable, but true as a faith by which life can most worthily be lived, and for which reasons can be given which are not only good reasons, but which become increasingly convincing reasons as experience itself throws more and more light upon the accepted faith. They are not mere Biblical literalists, and they are far removed from so-called Fundamentalism. Barth himself is entirely aware of the critical situation respecting the Scriptures, and Bultmann goes to what can only be called an extreme of critical findings.

The critical use of the Biblical documents and the unreserved acceptance of the revelation to which they bear witness—these are being seen to be perfectly congruous. The application to the New Testament of the principles of the method known as *Form-Criticism* threatened at first to bear very destructive results. But it is being recognized that the fact of the "form" still calls for the truth which it embodies, and this truth is the real problem. The very title of Dibelius' book, *From Tradition to Gospel*, is suggestive both of what was happening, and of the impossibility of explaining the written Gospels apart from earlier fact and faith. It is true that scholars like Loisy and Goguel treat the Gospels in a fashion which creates doubts enough, and that R. H. Lightfoot arrives at conclusions which are sheerly pessimistic. But this is not the whole story. Substantial American scholars like Easton and Grant and Ernest F. Scott, and equally substantial British scholars like Hoskyns and Davey and Dodd and Vincent Taylor, to say nothing of the European scholars who have been considered above, provide all the evidence that is necessary to support the statement that the most complete familiarity with the state of contemporary New Testament criticism does not need to be destructive of a vital faith in Jesus Christ as the New Testament so obviously presents him. It suffices to mention the single example of Vincent Taylor, whose achievements in the realm of technical New Testament scholarship have brought him great distinction,[32] and yet who, in *Jesus and His Sacrifice*, has written one of the great modern books on the Atonement, sound in its Biblical bases, adequate in its historical criticism, reminiscent in its constructive findings of the positions of McLeod Campbell and R. C. Moberly, asserting "vicariousness" in the sufferings of Christ as emphatically as either of these, but going beyond them in his claim of "objectivity."

That there is another side to the question is not for a moment being denied. There are many who have abandoned the naturalistic and humanistic emphases of modernism who do not feel that they are thereby committed to the recovery of evangelicalism. Their sympathies lie rather in the direction of "a new theology" which shall have an undeniable God-reference, but which shall be primarily "society-centered," and which will construe its Christology and Soteriology accordingly. There are, indeed, those who believe that this will eventuate in a distinctive "American" theology.[33] As to this, the future only can tell.

Meanwhile, what is certain is that the tide has turned away from modernism, and is setting definitely in the direction indicated by this survey. What has been written above reveals a growing conviction that Christianity is not to be reduced, in the fashion of nineteenth century rationalism and of twentieth century modernism, to a series of self-evident propositions which reason can easily accept because reason in the first place stated them; but that Christianity is a truth requiring to be set forth according to its own intrinsic nature as a revelation from God, challenging both the sufficiency of reason and the finality of any purely rational view of existence. In a word, Christianity is not to be construed according to some preconceived view of things, as though it were a mere suppliant pleading to be allowed to exist on any conditions that might be laid down; instead, it is to be construed as itself a *datum*; a divine gift, not a human instrument; an apocalypse rather than a deduction; a word, an action, a life, and an experience, proceeding directly from that same eternal source whence came creation itself; an Omega which completes the movement beginning in a primal Alpha.

This can mean nothing else than that Christianity, so far from being required to come to terms with every changing fashion of thought elsewhere, is something to be accepted, experienced, understood, and proclaimed in its own impregnable wholeness. That so audacious a claim may drive many away is to be admitted. But that it is again beginning to assert itself is also clear. God's purpose must often depend upon "the saving remnant." To the wisdom of the world, Christianity always seems "foolishness," but the testimony remains that to them that believe it is "the power of God unto salvation."

CHAPTER 20

The Drama of Man's Deliverance

IF IT BE TRUE THAT THE TIDE OF FAITH RESPECTING THE CHRISTIAN revelation is rising, that is a matter for profound gratitude. The evidence that has been presented is certainly encouraging. But it is not enough that we are able to find here a man and there a man who writes in a way that bespeaks a deep appreciation of biblical and historical Christianity. Besides leaders there must be followers. The insights that are being recovered need to be presented in such a way that others shall be convinced. The Christian revelation can exert no profound influence upon the world unless it can gain acceptance. How to present it so that it shall arrest attention and win allegiance is a pressing contemporary problem.

That there has been a sincere effort in the past generation to "re-state Christianity in modern terms" is undeniable. Anthropology, biology, psychology, sociology, even physics, have been earnestly considered by the Christian apologist with a view to their bearing upon the inherited faith.[1] The whole modern science of criticism has served to render unintelligible many of the traditional phrases, even many of the traditional ideas. There has been a tendency to "strip Christianity to the bone," so to speak, and then to re-clothe it in a dress that shall be unmistakably modern.

Psychology especially has been used for this purpose. Men know the machinery of human experience as they never knew it before. The unity of the human organism is so conceived that we no longer speak of mind and body but of body-mind.[2] At that point at least, Aristotle has again come to supremacy. The sources of motivation have been ruthlessly probed. The laws of behavior have been charted with a scientific exactness. The individual has become a social unit, so integrated with a communal life as to appear to be little more than one of its organs. The genesis and the functioning

288

of the various characteristics of personality have been dispassion-
ately investigated, with the result that there are those who find it
difficult any longer to believe in freedom: for them, a human life is
one more mechanism. The place of the ideal has been considered.
The fears that haunt men have been tracked to their lair and shown
to be irrational. Both moral sanctions and religious feelings have
been subjected to a like analysis, too often with the result that they
have been robbed of any absoluteness and of any permanent objective reference.[3]

Many have given themselves to the effort to "adjust" Christianity to what psychology has brought to light concerning human
life. Much of the work has been eminently constructive. There is
probably more *intelligence* as to Christianity today than there ever
was. "Religious education," which one could wish were more often
"Christian education," is being carried on by the use of a methodology of marked precision.[4] Public worship has been brought under
the scope of the movement, and not without reason. "Methods of
private devotion" have been devised in keeping with the new psychological insights, and there is reason to believe that they are ex-
tensively used.[5]

All this is so. For all that, there is an uneasy feeling abroad that
the Christian faith is losing ground. It is losing ground at the point
where it has always been strongest; namely, among "the common
people."[6] These are the people of whom it is said that "they heard
Jesus gladly," and these are the people from whom again and
again the Church has received new life and power.

It would be impossible to state all the reasons for this widespread indifference. Some of them, especially those which are more
purely intellectual in their character, have been referred to in earlier
chapters. But the question may well be raised whether in the attempt to "re-state Christianity in modern terms" a very important
fact has not been overlooked. It is well to seek precision in respect
of Christian truth, but when Christian truth is dealt with *scientifically* rather than *religiously*, inevitably it is being robbed of power.
The great truths with which the Christian revelation deals can at
best only be *suggested*.[7] It is impossible to state them as one states a
mathematical or chemical formula. Exactitude is the first require-

ment in the expression of a scientific truth, but it is not so in the expression of Christian truth, because Christian truth is not truth of reason but truth of faith. We are moving now in the realm of belief. Our necessity is to make belief vivid and compelling. We have to bring into the present something from the beyond. We have to be made to realize that we are more than creatures of the here and now. Existence is not limited by what we can chart of it. Beyond the limits that we can reduce to law is yet other reality, and it is with that reality that we have to do just as much as we have to do with that which lies on this side of the boundary—perhaps even more so![8]

For this reason, we are to give proper place to the qualities of imagination and emotion, and it is here that there has been serious failure. It is a curiously deficient psychology that has supposed that Christianity could be entirely intellectualized without any loss. For the philosopher or theologian concerned simply with "the system of truth," this intellectualizing might be well enough, but Christianity is first a religion, not first a philosophy or a theology, and certainly not first a psychology. The Christian revelation has the most far-reaching ethical and social implications, but it is primarily neither a system of ethics nor a social theory. It is primarily a religion, which means that it has a supernatural reference. Because of this supernatural reference, it cannot be brought under the scope of any purely rational *Weltanschauung*. That the supernatural reference is intended to re-act on the natural is profoundly true—so true, indeed, that he who does not see it does not see what Christianity really means. But the revelation has made known to us great over-historical, over-social, over-natural, over-rational truths, and while these truths are intended to bear their fruitage in this world of space and time just because they have to do with human life whose habitat this world is, they can fulfill their purpose only as their peculiar origin and their peculiar nature are continually recognized.

The most effective way to assure this recognition is by treating the Christian truths imaginatively, and by frankly admitting that this is being done. In so treating them, not only "the common people" but also the so-called "intelligentsia" are likely to be impressed. It is when Christianity is confined to a hard and fast literalism, from which all poetry, all imagination, all symbolism, all myth, all emotion, have been ruthlessly excluded that the common people are left cold and the scientific mind is antagonized. Plato employed the myth. He made no pretence that the myth in itself considered was true. He used the myth to illustrate, convey, or suggest a truth which was too elusive to be compressed within the limits of precise philosophical terminology.[9] He does, in fact, instruct us more effectively and move us more profoundly by his myths than by some of his arguments, although argument and myth have the same purpose. It is the myth—that is to say, the appeal to our imagination by the use of his own—which thrusts back the horizons, creates the sense of spaciousness, makes us aware, if only dimly, of the vast issues which wait on life, and causes to shine a light that never was on land or sea.

The Christian revelation loses its appeal when it is dealt with prosaically, when it is reduced to a set of "concepts" and "thought-patterns" thrown into a definite scheme. This is what we have seen happen in our time.[10] We have been afraid of emotion, and we have discountenanced the use of imagination on the supposition that the imaginative is necessarily the unreal. In so far as we have done this, we have been blind to Christian history. It is well enough to "tidy up" our thinking, but Christian thinking, or, rather, thinking on Christian things, which is so "tidy" that it has around it no aurora is lacking at just the crucial point. For the purpose of the Christian revelation is to bring the whole of a man's life under one great commanding central control. That can never happen where the emotions are not touched, and nothing touches the emotions like a great truth imaginatively presented. To say what is not actually so because only in this way can what actually is so bring its full impact upon the total life—this is not only legitimate, but it is indispensable if the glow of the greatest truth of existence, which is the truth of God and man in Jesus Christ, is to be captured, and the truth itself achieve its full result in the experience of men.[11]

Scripture itself is the evidence of this. There is much in Scripture that is to be understood exactly as it is expressed. But there is much more that is simply ruined if it is treated in this literalistic fashion. The story of the Fall is not literal history. It is psychological truth imaginatively set forth.[12] The experience of Moses at the burning bush, or of the boy Samuel in the temple at Shiloh, or of Elijah in the cave at Horeb, or of Isaiah in the Temple, and the like, are told in a fashion to make them vivid. Even the set discourses of some of the Hebrew prophets are expressed in language which touches the emotions, the very sources of action, by kindling the imagination. The prophet would make men *feel* by making them *see*. That all the furnishings of the Temple of Solomon and all the paraphernalia of the sacrificial system were intended to create in the mind truths which lost something of their power when expressed in prosaic words, goes without saying.[13] In the Old Testament there is the language of apocalyptic. It is a language of bold color, of daring metaphor, of images which stagger us by their sheer audacity.[14] What is literally untrue becomes the vehicle of what is true indeed. The Second Isaiah described the way in which the chosen people would eventually come into their own, and for the purpose he used all the resources of one of the world's most opulent imaginations.[15] Nothing of the sort ever happened in the way he described, yet the truth he was concerned with, the truth that God's purposes will eventually prevail, is made the more effective by the very boldness of the expression.

Doubtless the truth of the book of Jonah could have been stated in a much more simple and matter-of-fact way than it was. Yet how much does it owe to its vehicle? Is the book of Daniel "true"? If the question means, "Was the book written when it purports to have been written; did the events described happen in just that way; was there actual anticipation of the various empires dealt with, and of their experiences?"—if this is what the question means, then one can only say that few modern scholars would answer that the book was "true." For all that, they would say that it was one of the truest books in the Old Testament, true in its insight, true in its grasp of the significance of history, true in its declaration of providential control, true in its assertion that right is not forever on the scaffold nor wrong forever on the throne, true in the note it sounds that steady defiance of the powers of darkness will eventually prevail.[16]

In the same way, the New Testament is a book of religion. This is not to say that it does not contain genuine historical fact, nor that it nowhere deals with demonstrable truth. To say that would be absurd. But because it is a book of religion, it deals with the overtones of existence. Its concern is with realities which are not accessible to leaden-footed literalism, with its tender regard for syllogistic logic. Matthew is often blamed for his fondness for relating events in the life of Jesus to passages in the Old Testament, but Matthew may be wiser than his critics. Is he not thereby suggesting that the life of Jesus is integrated with the whole sweep of history, and that there belongs to him a cosmic significance?[17] The Birth and Infancy narratives in Luke may properly be called "mythic," if "mythic" be understood as at the other extreme from "scientific." But to say that the non-scientific is "not true" is purely gratuitous. Indeed, if it comes to that, the scientific account of many a common fact is true only from the standpoint of that particular science. From the standpoint of the ordinary life of men, it is not true at all. If Eddington's account of a table is correct, we ought not to be able to sit at it, nor even to see it. How can one "sit at" such a table, and how can one "see" it? Yet we do both. What does it mean but that "truth" is of many kinds?[18]

Hence religious truth is truth expressed in a way to make it religiously significant, or significant for life in its religious aspect. Without a doubt, the psychologist could show that Jesus' temptation following his baptism was entirely subjective.[19] Yet how much more graphic it is when described objectively—yes, and how much more true! Did the Transfiguration occur exactly as described, or does the description represent an attempt on the part of the Evangelists to perpetuate the memory of an overwhelming experience? What is meant literally by "a voice from heaven"? Yet he who denies that a great reality is meant by it serves not truth but error. "This is my beloved Son." Literalize that, and what happens? Deny that it has any meaning at all, and again what happens? "The Son of Man came . . . to give his life a ransom for many." Incredible crudities of thought and statement have been inspired by that great saying, so much so that other men, in an understandable repulsion, have gone to the opposite extreme and reduced the saying to innocuousness.[20] The Resurrection narratives represent the result of employing language framed in connection with the level of ordinary experience to describe an event and an experience which were not ordinary but, to speak restrainedly, extraordinary.

So also with much that meets us in the Epistles. Repeatedly the language employed by Paul, John, and others for describing Jesus Christ, the work he did, and his significance for human life, is the language of metaphor.[21] The great saying, "The Word became flesh," is part of a total conception of things which supposes that there is both a creative and a created, and is intended to suggest that what meets us in Jesus Christ is a mysterious intermingling of both, a revelation of the higher appearing within the lower. If one is so inclined, one may take grave exception to such terms as "propitiation," "reconciliation," "adoption," "our High Priest," "peace with God," "remission of sins," "delivered from the Evil One," "the free gift," "dead with Christ," "new life in Christ," "the image of his Son," "grieve the Spirit," "Christ our righteousness," "Christ in you," "Christ for you," "Christ sacrificed for us," "victory through Christ," "a new creature in Christ," "every man perfect in Christ Jesus," "the eternal purpose in Christ," "redemption through his blood," " a lamb . . . foreordained before the foundation of the world," and so on almost endlessly.

Without a doubt, what these various terms stand for could be expressed in some other way. The question is whether any other way would be quite so effective, and even whether it would be quite so true. Conceivably the New Testament could be re-written, and the fact of Christ and his work and his meaning be set forth, in language of prosaic literalness. But in many places, the result of that would be to turn truth into untruth. It is only on condition that we leave the metaphor, the symbolism, the poetry, the imaginativeness, that we can leave with the New Testament revelation its proven power to expand the minds of men by its great vistas, move their hearts, and quicken the springs of action.

There are evidences that this view of the matter is coming to increasing recognition. It has received suggestive treatment at the hands of Reinhold Niebuhr.[22] In a discussion of Paul's words, "As deceivers, yet true," he says frankly that Paul wrote many things that were not literally true because in no other way could he bring to bear upon his readers' minds the impact of the truth he was concerned with. The Christian teacher and preacher has to deceive in one respect in order to make effective the truth in another respect. No one will deny that it is dangerous to admit this, but it is dangerous only because it may so easily be misunderstood or perverted. Always there are two considerations to be borne in mind— the one, to express Christian truth in a way that shall least do it violence; the other, to make effective its appeal to the minds of men.

It is a question whether there is still any better and any truer way to express the content of the Christian revelation than the way which might be called dualistic. Dualism supposes opposites, and it supposes conflicts, and where there are opposites and conflicts there is always the possibility of defeat or victory. And if there is anything of which the ordinary man is most keenly aware, it is just this fact of opposites and conflicts. He might be a theoretical monist, but he never talks monistically when he is talking about the deepest aspects of his experience.[23] One might almost say that the language of dualism is man's natural language, and it is his natural language because it agrees so exactly with what is forced upon his attention every day, both within his life and without it.

For it is everyday experience that life does not follow an even tenor. The history of life on the earth is the history of struggle. Streeter has written a suggestive chapter on "Creative Strife."[24] Bergson speaks of "Creative Evolution," but he does not describe the process as automatic: everywhere the *élan vital* meets opposition.[25] The great dramatists have been under no misapprehension as to the possibility of man becoming the unwitting victim of a malign power. The problem raised in the book of Job is a perennial problem. The story of King Oedipus is pure and undiluted tragedy: it ranks with the story of Beatrice Cenci[26] and of Othello and of King Lear as a true transcript of human life. One watches with equal fascination the progress of "Childe Roland" toward "The Dark Tower" and the increasing intensity of "The Temptation of Saint Anthony." The story of human saintship is the story of perpetual overcoming. The road to *Paradiso* lies, if not always through

Inferno, certainly always through *Purgatorio*. The pilgrim must wade through many a Slough of Despond and he must resist the seductions of many a Vanity Fair and must feel upon his face the foul breath of many a horrific Apollyon, before he gains sight of the Celestial City. It is "by great tribulation" that man enters the kingdom.

It is so respecting the larger movements of history and society. The history of civilization is the history of conflict.[27] Whole masses of men seem suddenly to have become inspired by an insane frenzy. Hence war, rapine, conquest, enslavement. Every proposed social good has found its enemies, and still finds them. Let a legislator introduce a bill that will tend to ease the burdens on human backs, and at once powerful interests combine to defeat his measure. It is not so much that men are intrinsically bad. Bad they may be, but oftentimes they do worse than they are. They find themselves the victims of all sorts of pressures. Surveying the scene, men find it difficult to reduce it all to a unity. The philosopher may discourse all he wishes about "ontological monism," but the ordinary man is much more likely to believe that great and perhaps fundamental divisions run across the very face of existence. "Life is a struggle against odds": this is his dictum. There is always an enemy. He may not be sure as to what Berdyaev means by "meonic freedom," or Paul Tillich by "demonism," or Brightman by "The Given," but in so far as these terms represent the recognition of an opposing element in life and an attempt to account for it and its dire consequences, he would be in entire sympathy with them.[28]

Significantly enough, this is precisely the point of view of Scripture, and in particular of the New Testament. Speaking generally, we may say that the New Testament presents man as the seat of a conflict; that this conflict extends beyond man into the very arena in which he finds himself; that it permeates even "the invisible world"; that God himself is involved in it; that the evils of life, especially that moral evil which is sin, result from the triumph of the negative element in the conflict; and that Jesus Christ came into the world as God's own representative, agent, embodiment, personal presence, both as the evidence that God was on the side of man in the struggle, and as the means whereby victory could be achieved.[29]

Again and again in the New Testament, this is the "thought-form" with which one is confronted. It is not the only "thought-form," but it may properly be called the prevailing one. Christ is the divinely-sent Champion of men against a dire evil. For our sake he throws himself into the conflict. The powers of darkness and death resist him as they resist us. At last they overwhelm him even as they overwhelm us. His death is the victory of the demonic forces. But he could not be holden of them. He took from the grave its sting and from death its victory. His Resurrection is not only his triumph, but it is God's and it is ours.

Gustaf Aulén calls this "the dramatic view" of the work of Christ.[30] He claims that it gives us the essence of the New Testament. He finds it in the Fathers of the Early Church. What historical students know as "the ransom theory of atonement," the view, that is, attributed to early Christian thought, that Christ offered himself to the devil on condition that men should be released from bondage, and that after the devil had agreed to the condition he found himself unable to retain his hold upon "the pure soul of Jesus," hence turning out to be the loser on both counts— this view, Aulén says, although sadly caricatured in most of the presentations, is essentially an attempt to retain the dramatism of the New Testament. His discussion of Irenaeus in this connection is one of the great achievements of modern historical scholarship.[31] He does not ignore the fact that in Irenaeus and other Fathers there are crude metaphors about the Cross as a "mouse trap for Satan" and as a "hook baited with the flesh of Christ to be gulped down by Satan as by a great fish," and so on.[32] But it is Aulén's point that the metaphors are only metaphors. The responsible thinkers of the Early Church were not a group of incompetents. They were a body of men keenly aware of the moral struggle. In their own experience they had known the need of deliverance, and they had found in Christ their deliverer. They knew how Christ and his work was described in the New Testament, and they described it in similar terms. They are not concerned so much about a final philosophical *rationale* as about an effective presentation. How can we best understand Jesus Christ? How can we help others best to understand him? These were their questions.

They answered by setting him against the vast background of cosmic strife on the one hand, and in the very center of man's own strife on the other hand. He is therefore Saviour, Deliverer, Champion, Helper, Guarantor. In him and by him God smites his own foe and the foe of men.[33] He smites successfully. Wherefore it follows that although the final victory be long in coming, it has been assured. God is on the side of man.

Aulén further shows that although, for reasons not needing to be entered into here, this view of the matter was obscured for a thousand years, it was recovered by Martin Luther, who confessed his obligation to Irenaeus, and it was by him made central in his revitalized evangelical theology. Aulén admits that the Lutheran theologians failed to continue the emphasis, chiefly because they remained under the influence of the "juridical" type of theology associated with Anselm and most of the great Scholastics. But he leaves us in no doubt as to Luther conceiving and proclaiming the work of Christ in essentially "dramatic" terms.[34] Luther speaks of mankind as beset by enemies, by tyrants. The tyrants are sin, law, death, wrath, and the devil. Christ, the gift of the grace of God, goes out to meet them. There is a dreadful conflict, but grace wins the victory, because the grace is the grace of the omnipotent God. Aulén quotes Luther's *Shorter Catechism*: "Christ has delivered, purchased, and won me, a lost and doomed man, from all sins, from death and from the devil's power." Or again the *Greater Catechism*: "He has redeemed me from sin, from the devil, from death and all woe . . . Those tyrants and gaolers are all crushed, and in their place is come Jesus Christ, a Lord of life, righteousness, all good and holiness, and he has snatched us poor lost men from the jaws of hell, won us, made us free, and brought us back to the Father's goodness and grace." Or again the *Commentary on Galatians*, at 3.13: "Christ, who is God's power, righteousness, blessing, grace, and life, overcomes and carries away those monsters, sin, death, and the curse . . . When therefore thou lookest upon this person, thou seest sin, death, God's wrath, hell, the devil, and all evil, overcome and dead. In so far therefore as Christ by his grace rules in the hearts of the faithful, there is found no more sin, death, and curse; but where Christ is not known, they still remain . . . This is the primary article of Christian teaching."

There is much more to the same effect. Luther frequently speaks of the Law as a tyrant attacking Christ. When Christ died, it seemed that the Law had conquered, because death is an instrument of the Law. But it was an unjust victory, since the victim, having broken no law, was guiltless, and undeserving of death. The apparent victory of the Law was therefore its defeat. In himself perfectly keeping the Law while yet being treated as though he had not, Christ robbed the Law of its terror and its power, and made manifest the grace of God for men. The very wrath which man's sin evokes in God is itself done away by something in God which is deeper than wrath, namely, love and grace. While the Curse and the Wrath express God's will respecting men, at the same time they oppose it, because God's ultimate will is that men shall be his sons. If men remain under the Wrath, God has failed in his creative task. But in Christ he goes forth to battle. In the name of love, he meets and destroys the power of that sin and death which come of disobedience to Law and which reveal Wrath.

What is this but a statement of the work of God in Christ in dramatic terms and against a dualistic background? Exactly as in the New Testament, exactly as in the early Fathers, there is a daring delineation of divine conflict and divine victory. It is true that Luther was fond of bold colors.[35] He paints with a wide brush. But this alone is not a sufficient explanation of what and why he writes. He has himself become vividly aware of the moral struggle. He knew it in his own life. He sees it in the world around him. Everywhere is the clash of elemental forces—God and the devil, sin and holiness, love and hate, life and death, law and grace. Are the powers of darkness doomed? Is God on the side of man? Can hope of victory be entertained? He believes the answer has been given, and the answer is Jesus Christ, by whom God seeks to accomplish the deliverance of mankind from their chains.[36]

Obviously this is not cold and calm philosophizing. This is not dispassionate analysis of human experience. This is not reducing the order of life to a syllogism. A skeleton of thought does indeed underlie it, but the skeleton is clothed with flesh and blood and it glows with life. Too often has theology achieved such a perfection of rationality as to lose all power of emotional appeal. Men read it or listen to it, and their only comment is, "What of it?" That is because the great truths of the Christian revelation are so presented as to be detached from life itself. They lose their power of appeal. What came to men in the first place in the midst of moral conflict, and was therefore clothed in the language of their own experience, has again and again proved its effectiveness when it was presented in its original form.

The Gospel of Christ is not primarily a philosophy: it is primarily a religion. It is true that it involves a philosophy, and in these pages some attention has been given to what that philosophy is. But when it is presented simply as a philosophy, it is strangely impotent. This attempt to present "a philosophy of the Christian revelation" therefore ends with the assertion that while it is well for the purposes of intellectual satisfaction to ascertain what that philosophy is, the appeal of the revelation is most effective when it is clothed in language which kindles the imagination and moves the heart because it answers to the everyday experience of moral conflict.

Consider then the Gospel story itself from this point of view. If there is one thing that that story makes real more than another, it is that Jesus Christ was the unrelenting foe of the evils of life. In order to appreciate this, no backlying question of his relation to God needs first to be raised, although when that question finally is raised it makes the fact the more significant.

For one thing, Jesus saw evil in the human heart. This is fundamental. "He knew what was in man." He may not have said anything about Original Sin, but he knew well enough that the roots of sin were in human nature. He saw sinful deeds as the result of something that lay deeper than the deeds. Some of his Sayings are perfectly ruthless in their exposure of the heart of man.[37] "For from within, out of the heart of men, evil thoughts proceed, fornication, thefts, murders, adulteries, deceit, lasciviousness, an evil eye, railing, pride, foolishness: all these evil things proceed from within, and they defile the man" (Mark 7.21). Jesus knew that a man was his own worst enemy. He knew that the moral struggle was won or lost within. No one understands him who does not see him in connection with his purpose to help men win that struggle.

Again, Jesus was the enemy of the evils that afflict the bodies of men. It would be a serious mistake for any man to discount the healing activity of Jesus because of some difficulty with the idea of miracle. If Jesus was against sin, he was also against physical suffering. Not only did he say to the palsied man, "Thy sins be forgiven thee," but he also said to him, "Take up thy bed and walk." Not only did he call himself the Bread of Life, but he also fed the hungry. There is something startling in the fact that in a day when most men took pain and disease for granted,[38] Jesus gives every evidence of hating them, and of regarding them as abnormalities—something having no intrinsic right in God's universe, something indicative of a still deeper disturbance, and something therefore which must be eradicated. "An enemy hath done this." Jesus could very well be the patron saint of the medical and every other humanitarian profession.[39]

But there is also evidence that Jesus was aware of the presence and action of a mysterious power of evil which was continually disrupting human plans and disturbing human relationships. One hesitates to talk about this because it can so easily be misunderstood. Yet we cannot altogether discount the apocalyptic and eschatological descriptions which are put on the lips of Jesus. It is as though he conceived a cosmic power of evil, mysterious, elusive, malign, which manifests itself in all sorts of unexpected ways, with which he himself will have to grapple, which it will take even all of God's resources to overcome.[40] The best-laid plans go wrong. Men combine to destroy some great evil, only to find that they have made another possible. The very social necessities which serve human good become the means of evil. It is not that men intend this—at least, not always. *It happens.* That good comes in the same unintended fashion is also true, but this does not change the other fact. Jesus continually assumes, even asserts, a dualism. He sees the world as the seat of a conflict. A battle is proceeding, and it is a battle to the death.

Doubtless in much of his expression Jesus is dramatizing the

situation. But that is just the point. He dramatizes it, not only because there is a real conflict, but because he wants to make it vivid.
Sometimes he speaks as though the Kingdom of God comes by
natural processes,[41] but again and again he speaks of it as *cata-
clysmic.*[42] For him, the question of evil is much more than a question of making the hearts of men right with God. It is a question of
guaranteeing the destruction of the very cause of evil. There is an
enemy alike of God and man—*and that enemy is why he was here.*
He came to give himself a ransom. He would come to a death-
grapple with the elemental evil—slay it as mythic heroes slew
the great dragon.

On occasion, he spoke as one who was conscious of the opposition of a veritable kingdom of evil spirits. Did he not say that
the attempt to turn him from his chosen path following the Temptation was due to some malign power? Did he not say that he must
bind the strong man before he could despoil him of his goods?
When he announced that he must go to Jerusalem to be crucified,
did he not treat Peter's protest as inspired by that very demonic
power which he was going to Jerusalem to meet in its most dreadful form?[43] He was under no misapprehension about that journey to
Jerusalem being a journey to Armageddon. The evil powers from
which he came to deliver men were going to overcome him. For
their malign purpose they would use as instruments the disloyalty
of friends, the hatred of his fellows whom yet he loved, unspeakable
mental anguish, excruciating physical pain, at last death itself.
Perchance he previsioned not only Gethsemane but that still darker
moment when the cry of dereliction should burst from his lips
because even the Father seemed to have vanished.

But it was as he had said: he must enter the realm of the Strong
Man if he would bind him—and the Strong Man would be waiting
for him! Calvary was the meeting-place of the elemental powers of
existence—and if anyone wants to say the Hosts of Heaven and the
Hosts of Hell, he has New Testament warrant for doing so. *The
daring language represents metaphysical reality.* Jesus is no longer as
the Good Samaritan, dealing with results. He would deal with the
cause. He was now as the apocalyptic Rider on the White Horse,
his eyes like a flame of fire, his garment sprinkled with blood,

behind him the armies of heaven. He was looking for the Beast.[44] Only when the Beast itself was chained, would the days of the brood of the Beast be numbered. He met the Beast in the Beast's own den—and the Beast came out licking its chops, leering its horrid triumph, so that it seemed to Matthew that the earth must have quaked and the sun itself have hidden its face. Incarnate Love met Incarnate Hate, and when the sound and fury of that decisive clash had ceased, all that was left to mortal sight was a Cross against the sky, and on it a broken form, mute evidence of the defeat of Love. Drama, you say? No: tragedy—*unless!*

For that Cross is not final, although many make it so. They make it so because they are blind. They make it so because Resurrection has no place in their world-view, and a world in which Resurrection has no place means a world in which death speaks the last word. And the whole meaning of the Christian revelation, express it soberly or express it dramatically, is that the last word belongs not to death but to life. The Cross is rightly read only in the light of the Resurrection. The evil that destroyed Perfect Love thereby inflicted upon itself its own death-blow. For the Resurrection is the evidence of God's domination, but it is an evidence which could not have been given save for the Death which went before.

Yet too often men rhapsodize over the Cross and keep silence over the Resurrection—chiefly, one suspects, for philosophical reasons—and they do not see that if the Cross is not answered by Resurrection, that which led Jesus to the Cross is without final authentication. What we instinctively feel is the greatest is defeated by what we know is the less. The Resurrection is the dramatizing of the finality and indestructibility of self-giving love. It is a way of saying, in one overwhelming and inescapable divine word, that victory belongs to the cause with which Jesus Christ is forever identified. In the name of love he submitted to the powers of darkness. But in their victory was their defeat. "He could not be holden." "He led captivity captive." For all time and to all men the word has been spoken—that the triumph of Christ is the promise of a universal triumph.

Can this be made to mean anything to our time? It will mean very much if men can be made to see that what meets us here is *the deepest truth of existence made alive.* God in Christ has spoken to men in a fashion that leaves no doubt as to the issue of life for those who will accept what he has said and done. The Christian revelation understood as consummating in the victory of Christ, is the one sole justification of moral optimism. We must continue to live in a world of conflict. We must continue to know that life is full of danger. We must continue to contemplate the possibility of good and holy things being destroyed. The demonic power has not been done away: it has only been shown to be limited, to be defeatable, to be under an ultimate doom. But the nature of things is on the side of the man who has faith in such a God as God has shown himself to be, and who pays the price of that faith.

But the price must be paid. It is in part intellectual and in part practical. It involves both a philosophy and an activity. Implied here is a radical reconstruction of the view of existence. If we seek to fit existence into a neat little scheme of categories, a scheme so complete that nothing escapes it, the glow and the richness and the warmth and the vitality of the Christian faith will fade away. It cannot be reduced to a mechanical exactitude. It demands of men a certain recklessness. Audacious adventure is of its essence. It finds the key to life in self-giving love. This was the secret of the life of Jesus, and in Jesus the Word is made flesh. This is but to say that the secret of the life of Jesus is the secret of the life of God. But self-giving love is love in conflict with that which is hateful and dark. It is because God loved that he gave himself. It is because Christ loved that he gave himself. And the self-giving triumphed. The Cross that love accepted became the means to a more abundant life. Love walked through death to life, and became immortal.[45]

And this law of the life of God, disclosed in the Christian revelation, what is it but the law also of the life of man? The evils of life call for self-giving love if they are to be subdued. For self-giving love will not be only an emotion. It will be an activity. It will guide intelligence. It will devise instrumentalities. It will seek to pit concrete measures against specific forms of evil. In the deep conflict of forces which life essentially is, self-giving love, the Cross, the Resurrection, stand in organic relationship. The price of triumph must be the willingness to accept defeat. The pathway to domination must be suffering. The way up is by the way down. "In that he ascended, what is it but that he first of all descended." Love stoops to conquer. Christ is God stooping, but Christ is also God rising as otherwise not even he could have risen.

All this happened in such a world as this. Its immediate subject was *a Man* immersed in the stream of history. That God was involved in it too, yes!—but this is that in which he was involved, by which he spoke, by which he made known the ultimate truth of things. The great battle was fought and won under such conditions as are common to our humanity. The earnest of our own possible victory took place in the arena in which we all have to fight. This greater David who met a yet greater Goliath was bone of our bone and flesh of our flesh. In him the inevitable universal conflict stands in supreme representation. On him God stakes his cause, and the cause of God is the cause of man. How Jesus Christ fought and won is how God fights and wins, and is how man must fight and win. The history of Jesus Christ, from the Annunciation to the Ascension, is a dramatic representation of the conflict which lies at the very heart of existence, and of the principles and processes by which alone the conflict can issue in divine and human triumph.

It is incredible that when the truth is so presented it will leave men cold. Men know that life is a struggle. They know that they are opposed by dark and dreadful forces. Even those who accept a purely mechanistic philosophy cannot escape the feeling that contending powers are all about them and within them. The social field today is shot through with antagonism. Ruthlessness is being embodied in political instruments. The hearts of many are in danger of failing for fear. Rightly understood, the Christian revelation conveys a message of hope to every man who is conscious of the burden and the mystery, and of what otherwise is but the weary weight of an unintelligible world.

The Church will do well to keep its treasure in that vessel which has always best held it. The message that is dramatized in the Christian sacraments and in the great festivals of the Christian year, especially Christmas, Good Friday, Easter, and Whitsunday (Pentecost), loses its potency when it is expressed in unimaginative and purely prosaic language. What was dramatically conveyed to men in the first place waits on dramatic presentation, because in no other way can all its nuances be preserved, all its suggestion of cosmic background be conveyed, and all its power of emotional appeal reveal itself. Those who are called to leadership in the Church of Christ, whether they preach or whether they teach or whether they write, or whatever they do, will be wise in proportion as they clothe the skeleton of truth with the beauty of pulsating life. Always must the Word become flesh.

NOTES
AND
REFERENCES

CHAPTER 1

1. See H. R. Mackintosh, *Types of Modern Theology*, pp. 277 f., for a defence of what Barth means by a denial of natural revelation. Cf. Barth's comment on Rom. 1.20 in the *Römersbrief*, quoted in Lowrie, *Our Concern with the Theology of Crisis*, pp. 114–117. Lowrie (footnote, p. 115) refers to Otto's interpretation of Job 38, in *The Idea of the Holy*, pp. 80–83, as an example of the alleged natural revelation to which Barth so vehemently objects.

2. See the searching examination and criticism of Speculative Idealism from this point of view in *The Mediator*, chaps. 2 and 3.

3. Cf. Oman, *Vision and Authority* (sec. ed.), chap. 4, on "The Divine Teacher."

4. Westcott, *Christus Consummator*, although published more than half a century ago, is still worth reading on this question. See espec. pt. II. See also Orr, *Christian View of God and the World*, lect. 7; Fairbairn, *Philosophy of the Christian Religion*, bk. I, chap. 1; bk. II, pt. 2, chap. 2.

5. Matthews attempts the re-instatement of the teleological argument. He treats man as "not an alien in the universe," but as "the revelation of its nature," the creature in whom "the universe discloses itself in its real inner being" (p. 127).

6. All genuine Idealism, from Plato on, is based on this assumption. For a clear modern statement, see Pringle-Pattison, *The Idea of God*, lect. XI, pp. 207–216. Cf. H. H. Farmer, *The World and God*, chap. 4, on "The World as a Symbol."

7. See the whole of pt. IV, and espec. chaps. 17 and 22.

8. So Browning in *Cristina*, third stanza.

9. The case is argued in Plato, *Parmenides*. For a summary, see the closing paragraph of Jowett's introduction to the dialogue. Taylor, however, in *Plato*, chap. 14, treats the dialogue as "an elaborate *jeu d'esprit*," and insists that any interpretation must bear this ironic spirit in mind (p. 351). Cf. Whitehead, *Adventures of Ideas*, chap. 11, on "Objects and Subjects," and his remarks on the inadequacy of language, *ibid*, p. 178.

10. See *Normative Psychology of Religion*, by H. N. Wieman and Regina Westcott-Wieman, chap. 3. Cf. review in *Religion in Life*, Winter Number, 1936.

11. See p. 323. Since writing the paragraph in the text, the present writer has observed, in *Normative Psychology of Religion*, an anticipation by Wieman of the objection that growth of value in the world is not God, but only the work of God (p. 60). He seems to think the distinction is not important; the parenthesis quoted from the later book may therefore be significant.

12. R. L. Calhoun, in his chapter on "Plato as Religious Realist," in *Religious Realism*, ed. D. C. Macintosh, has no least doubt that Plato be-

lieved that "mind is ground of the whole," and that "this supreme νοῦς is itself ensouled" (p. 243). "For if Living Mind at its best be really dominant in the universe, then the hope of the *Phaedo* and the exultant proclamation of the *Republic*, that good is the supreme end of all, are not without rational foundation" (p. 245). See also A. Fouillee, *La Philosophie de Platon*, II, livre deuxième. Fouillee interprets Plato to mean that *"la vraie réalité ne peut donc se concevoir que sous la forme de l'esprit, et l'absolue réalité est la perfection spirituelle ou l'Esprit pur"* (p. 675).

13. *Religious Thought in the West*, p. 2.

14. *Towards a Religious Philosophy*, chap. 4.

15. See the discussion in Rogers, *Morals in Review*, pp. 178 ff.

16. *Op. cit.*, p. 67.

17. One of the best accounts of the movement is Hiralal Haldar, *Neo-Hegelianism*.

18. J. H. Stirling, *The Secret of Hegel*, is still the most impressive exposition of Hegel, for those who will take the pains to master it. Stirling describes what he calls "the germ of Hegel" as follows: "The universe is but a materialization, but an externalization, but a heterization of certain thoughts: these may be named, these thoughts *are*, the thoughts of God. To take it so, God has *made* the world on these thoughts. In them, then, we know the thoughts of God, and, so far, God himself" (*Secret*, sec. ed., p. 85). There is an interesting account of the *Secret* in chap. 10 of *James Hutchison Stirling*, by his daughter, Amelia Hutchison Stirling.

19. Andrew Seth (Pringle-Pattison), *Hegelianism and Personality*, lect. V, on "Hegel's Doctrine of God and Man," offers a brief but searching criticism. See also his *Philosophical Radicals*, pp. 268 ff.

20. See Whitehead, *Science and the Modern World*, chap. 9, and *Adventures of Ideas*, chap. 9, both on "Science and Philosophy"; Eddington, *The Nature of the Physical World*, "Conclusion"; and for a convincing argument by a modern philosopher, Urban, *The Intelligible World, passim*, but espec. chaps. 9, 10, and 11. Cf. Smuts, *Holism and Evolution*, chap. 5, on "General Concept of Holism," and chap. 9, on "Mind as an Organ of Wholes."

21. *Any Saint.*

22. This is what W. R. Matthews means when he says that we cannot deal with "the place of mind in nature" without dealing also with "the place of nature in mind" (*Purpose of God*, p. 106).

23. See W. R. Sorley, *Moral Values and the Idea of God*, pp. 290–293; 496–500, and elsewhere.

24. The qualification, "within the circle of the natural," is important, since it still leaves open the question of the extent to which man can of himself "know" that to which he prays. The fact that man can pray bespeaks his kinship with a transcendent, but it does not preclude that any adequate knowledge of the transcendent comes to him only "by revelation."

25. John 14.9. The verb used for "see" here (ὁράω) means more than mere physical beholding. Other verbs in the context, "know" (γιγνώσκω and οἶδα) and "show" (δείκνυμι), likewise call for the deeper interpreta-

tion. It was as though Jesus said: "In understanding me aright, you at the same time rightly understand God."

CHAPTER 2

1. *Growth of the Idea of God,* chap. 8. Mathews thinks that we are justified in describing as "God" these productive cosmic activities (p. 226). A reviewer wrote of Mathews' conception: "It will not satisfy the convinced theist because it holds that ascribing personality to God is only a pattern convenience, answering to no independent ontological fact" (*The Christian Advocate,* New York, Nov. 26, 1931).

2. Cf. Galloway, *Philosophy of Religion,* p. 27.

3. This is the truth in Otto, *The Idea of the Holy,* chaps. 1–4, but Lyman, *The Meaning and Truth of Religion,* p. 73, points out the limitations. Cf. Otto, *Mysticism, East and West,* chap. 4.

4. Evelyn Underhill, *The Mystic Way,* speaks of "The Instinct for Transcendence"; see chap. 1, sect. 1, and the closing section on "The Inner Mystery," pp. 351 ff.; cf. T. Hywel Hughes, *The Philosophical Basis of Mysticism,* chap. 2.

5. *The Coming Religion,* pp. 24–27; cf. chap. 12, on "Religion in the Future."

6. See espec. chap. 2, sect. 5, on "Meaning of Completion," which answers the question, "What kind of completion does man seek?" (p. 42).

7. *The House of Life,* Sonnet LXXIII.

8. Any of the discussions of ethical theories will make this plain, e.g., H. Rashdall, *Theory of Good and Evil,* 2 vols., or James Martineau, *Types of Ethical Theory.* Cf. C. Gore, *The Philosophy of the Good Life,* chap. 8, sect. 3.

9. From *Songs in Absence,* Arthur Hugh Clough.

10. The thought appears in all of Berdyaev's writings, but espec. in *Freedom and the Spirit* and *The Destiny of Man.* See the discussion of Berdyaev below, Chapter 19.

11. Arthur Hugh Clough, *Hope Evermore and Believe,* first stanza.

12. *The Idea of God,* lect. V. Cf. the remarks on Evolutionary Naturalism in Urban, *The Intelligible World,* pp. 303 ff.

13. C. C. J. Webb, *Pascal's Philosophy of Religion,* p. 110, quotes the correct form: "*Console-toi, tu ne me chercherais pas si tu ne m'avais trouvé; tu ne me chercherais pas si tu ne me possedais. Ne t'inquiète donc pas,*" and reference.

14. *Saint Thomas Aquinas,* p. 164.

15. E. S. Ames, *Religion,* is a conspicuous example of this social emphasis, an emphasis which is the proper logic of the idea of God presented, namely, "The reality of a social process belonging to the actual world (p. 176). . . . the order of nature including man and all the processes of an aspiring social life" (p. 177).

CHAPTER 3

1. It is doubtful whether Karl Barth has anywhere stated his case for the Scriptural revelation any more clearly and effectively than in *Das Wort Gottes und die Theologie*, translated by Douglas Horton as *The Word of God and the Word of Man*. See espec. chap. 2 and chap. 7, pp. 249 ff. His plea is for the recovery of "the scriptural principle," but this, he says, involves that "we shall need to think through the category of *revelation* again" (p. 250).

2. On the question whether the final interpretation of Scripture rests with the Church (the Catholic view) or with the individual (the more extreme Protestant view), see Hagenbach, *Hist. of Doctrines*, sect. 240, notes (7) and (8), and references there cited.

3. This was apparent to even a literary critic like George Saintsbury, who offers some devastating comments on *St. Paul and Protestantism* and *Literature and Dogma*. "The child-like fashion in which Mr. Arnold swallowed the results of that very remarkable 'science,' Biblical criticism, has always struck some readers with astonishment and a kind of terror. . . . Mr. Arnold does not exactly offer us a stone for bread, but he does, like the benevolent French princess in the story, offer us a piecrust." See *Matthew Arnold* (Modern English Writers), pp. 133, 136.

4. How close Luther came to this conception may be deduced from the discussion and references in Seeberg, *Lehrbuch der Dogmengeschichte*, IV. 1, §75, 2. Cf. Neander, *Hist. of Christian Dogmas*, vol. II, "Luther's Views of Inspiration," pp. 638 f., and the discussion in K. Fullerton, *Prophecy and Authority*, chap. 6.

5. See McClure's discussion in chap. 6.

6. See Eric North, *The Book of a Thousand Tongues*, commemorative of the work of the Bible Societies, and full of fascinating information about "The Book of Books."

7. One of the classical examples is William Robertson Smith; see the biography by Black and Chrystal. For an example in America, see H. G. Mitchell, *For Benefit of My Creditors*. Cf. Peake, *The Bible, Its Origin and Significance*, chap. 8, on "The Story of Old Testament Criticism."

8. See Barton, *The Religion of Israel*, chap. 4, on "Moses and the Covenant with Yahweh."

9. For graphic description of outstanding men of the period, and their relation to the contemporary life, see Kittel, *Great Men and Movements in Israel*, chaps. 2–7. Wallis, *God and the Social Process*, throws much valuable light on this question of social relationships. Less radical is W. C. Graham, *The Prophets and Israel's Culture*.

10. For somewhat detailed consideration of the question, see Driver, *Intro. to Literature of O. T.*, the chaps. on 1 and 2 Sam., 1 and 2 Kings, and Chronicles. For simple statements of the principles involved, see *Abingdon Bible Commentary*, the introductory sections to 1 and 2 Sam., 1 and 2 Kings, and Chronicles.

11. As in Kittel, *op. cit.*, under note 9.

12. See the whole story, 1 Sam. 18–30.

13. See Edghill as cited, pt. 2, sects. 4 and 5; cf. Oesterley, *The Evolution of the Messianic Idea.*

14. The literature on the prophets is endless. See W. R. Smith, *The Prophets of Israel*; Batten, *The Hebrew Prophet*; A. B. Davidson, *O. T. Prophecy*; in Loisy, *La Religion d'Israël* (troisième ed.), chap. 4, 5; Duhm, *Die Theologie der Propheten*; Knudson, *The Beacon Lights of Prophecy*; Gordon, *The Prophets of the O. T.*; Skinner, *Prophecy and Religion.* An excellent brief account of O. T. religion is H. Wheeler Robinson, *The Religious Ideas of the O. T.*

15. The case is well stated by E. P. Dickie, in *Revelation and Response*, chap. 2, on "Revelation or Discovery?"

16. See Peake, *op. cit.* (note 7), chap. 18, on "The Old Testament and the New."

17. Peake, Driver, and G. A. Smith have all written excellent books on Jeremiah, and they deal sympathetically with this phase of his thought. Somewhat more popular are Longacre, *A Prophet of the Spirit*, T. C. Gordon, *The Rebel Prophet*, H. Wheeler Robinson, *The Cross of Jeremiah*, and C. E. Jefferson, *Cardinal Ideas of Jeremiah.* Chaps. 5 and 6 in the last-named are effective examples of homiletical interpretation.

18. See Ezra 9 and 10; Nehemiah 13.23–31.

19. See the exposition of "Jonah" by W. C. Graham in the *Abingdon Bible Commentary*, pp. 787 ff.

20. Gal. 4.4, 5; Heb. 1.2; John 1.14, 18.

CHAPTER 4

1. There is in Jewry a growing recognition of Jesus. The appreciative views of such distinguished Jewish scholars as C. G. Montefiore, Israel Abrahams, Joseph Jacobs, and Joseph Klausner, are simply and briefly described in T. Walker, *Jewish Views of Jesus.* See also E. R. Trattner, *As a Jew Sees Jesus*, and Emil Ludwig, *Son of Man.* Books such as D. Philipson, *The Reform Movement in Judaism*, and M. H. Farbridge, *Judaism and the Modern Mind*, indicate an increasing awareness of the need of change in Jewish thought and practice. On the other hand, the voluminous work of Robert Eisler, *The Messiah Jesus*, is largely an attempt, based on a study of early non-Christian and anti-Christian sources, to discredit the supposed historical origins of Christianity.

2. Of the many recent defences of this witness as historically true, one of the best is C. H. Dodd, *The Apostolic Preaching and Its Developments.*

3. This case is nowhere better stated than in Brunner, *The Mediator*, chap. 7, on "The Divine Word."

4. Cf. the little book by H. S. Coffin, *The Portraits of Jesus Christ in the N. T.*

5. See Vincent Taylor, *Formation of the Gospel Tradition*; B. H.

Streeter, *The Four Gospels*; and E. F. Scott, *The Validity of the Gospel Record*.

6. J. A. Findlay, *Jesus Human and Divine*. Cf. the discussion in L. W. Grensted, *The Person of Christ*, chap. 11, and C. E. Raven, *Jesus and the Gospel of Love*, espec. chaps. 13, 14, and 15.

7. The interpretation of the κενῶσις passage in *Lightfoot, Comm. on Philippians*, is still a classic. Pfleiderer, *Paulinism*, vol. I, pp. 146 ff., represents the older rationalistic interpretation. Dorner, *System of Christian Doctrine*, vol. III, sects. 100–106, attempted to work into systematic theology the "impersonal" view, namely, that "the pre-existent Christ" stands for "the divine principle of *objective* revelation." Beyschlag, *N. T. Theology*, vol. II, chap. 3, sect. 10, practically repeats the position: he describes Paul's assertion of the pre-existence in verse 6 as "enigmatic" (p. 77). Porter, *The Mind of Christ in Paul*, seeks to evade the force of the passage. He asserts its complete difference from the Logos Christology of Col. 1.15–17, whose Pauline authorship he questions, partly on the ground of this difference. He writes of the passage: "As a story about a divine being and his choices and actions in times and in places which are entirely out of reach of our human knowledge, the story must be called mythical" (p. 205). Quite characteristically, R. H. Lightfoot (*not* the Bishop Lightfoot of the great *Commentaries!*), *History and Interpretation in the Gospels*, pp. 210 ff., finds no value in the passage. For a more objective interpretation, see Holzmann, *Neutestamentliche Theologie*, II, Erst. Kap., 6.4, and cf. I, Erst. Kap., 6; Anderson Scott, *Christianity According to St. Paul*, pp. 270 ff.; and Stevens, *Theology of the N. T.*, pp. 396 ff. Cf. the brief statement in C. H. Dodd, *The Meaning of Paul for To-Day*, pp. 88 ff., and the theological application in Curtis, *The Christian Faith*, pp. 237 ff.

8. See the discussions in references under note 5, above.

9. See *Abingdon Bible Commentary*, intro. to "Matthew," pp. 953 f., by J. Newton Davies, for a note on these omissions, additions, and differences.

10. See note 7, above, for title. Lightfoot passes severe strictures on the Fourth Gospel, in which, he says, "we are seldom, if ever, walking on firm ground" (p. 224); and of the attempts of the other three Gospels to describe and interpret Jesus Christ, he says that they "must be regarded as provisional and tentative" (p. 218).

11. The reading of Huck's *Synopsis* (of the three Gospels) should alone suffice to settle this question for an open mind.

12. It was the conclusion he reached in *Das Messiahgeheimnis in den Evangelien* (1901).

13. Cf. Dodd, note 2, above.

14. See Brunner, *The Mediator*, chap. 6, on "The Christian Faith and Historical Research."

15. Paul never *abandoned* eschatology in the sense the term bears in much modern N. T. interpretation, *e.g.*, the "crisis" theology. Of 1 Thess. 4.13–18, H. T. Andrews wrote: "This passage contains Paul's earlier and

cruder view, and we must not regard it as the final statement of his position" (*in loco*, Peake, *Comm. on the Bible*, p. 878).

16. Cf. E. F. Scott, *N. T. Idea of Revelation*, and Chapter 18 below, on "The Spirit."

17. There are few finer expositions of Galatians than W. M. Mac-Gregor, *Christian Freedom*. The Galatian situation is dealt with as illustrating "the tyranny of a tradition," namely, that the institution has a right to dictate to the individual, which the author sees as a modern danger, and a denial of true "freedom in Christ."

18. The review in Schweitzer, *The Quest of the Historical Jesus*, of the history of Gospel criticism "From Reimarus to Wrede," is relevant to this point. Cf. Weinel and Widgery, *Jesus in the 19th Century and After*, espec. chaps. 2 and 7.

19. The author fully realizes that these are precisely the points of issue, but he regards them as of the essence of the revelation—which is the chief reason why this book is being written.

CHAPTER 5

1. The limitation is important. How many of those who had personally known Jesus afterwards became his followers, we have no means of knowing. If Jesus visited Jerusalem at three Passovers (as John intimates) or at only one (as the Synoptics seem to mean), he would have been an object of interest to great numbers of people from distant places. The knowledge thus acquired would not, however, be very intimate. He did, of course, attract much attention at his last Passover, and Peter in his sermon on the Day of Pentecost plainly charges that many of his hearers (Acts 2.22, 23) were involved in the closing scenes. The figures given in Acts 2.41; 4.4, are probably only approximate. There is no doubt that beyond the Twelve was a large circle of less intimate followers of Jesus—those who had been the subjects of his healing ministry, those who had been impressed by his teaching in various ways, and persons especially mentioned, such as Zacchaeus, Nicodemus, Joseph of Arimathaea, Mary, Martha, Lazarus, Cleopas, "the Seventy" (Luke 10.1, although there is a critical problem here), the women "and many others" mentioned in Luke 8.2,3 (cf. 23.49—"all his acquaintance and the women"), and the "many disciples" who "went back, and walked no more with him" referred to in John 6.66 (cf. 6.60 ff.). It is probable that many members of the primitive Church were recruited from these. Certain it is, however, that the rapid expansion of Christianity brought within the movement great numbers who in no way at all had known Jesus "after the flesh." This would be especially true after the persecution following Stephen's death (11.19), and even more true after Barnabas and Saul began their definite missionary travels (13.2 ff.). And as the years passed away, the numbers would naturally increase of those whose knowledge of Jesus was through the testimony of others.

2. In Hebrew thought, Satan (or "the Satan") seems to have had the

function of an agent of God sent to entice men, not because God desired them to fall, but because he would learn how stedfast they were. This is manifestly so in Job 1.6–12. See Peake, *Problem of Suffering in the O. T.*, chap. 5, espec. pp. 84, 85, 101, 102. The "devil" of Jesus' temptation (Matt. 4.1 ff.) has the same function. Jesus here calls Peter "Satan" (Matt. 16.23) because the disciple who has just confessed the Messiahship is playing exactly the same rôle as that played by the tempter in the wilderness: he is trying to persuade Jesus to follow some other than his destined path.

3. R. W. Dale, *Atonement*, appendix, note D, which deals with the cry of dereliction from the Cross, quotes medical authority in support of the claim in the text (closing pages of lect. III) that the actual cause of the Death of Christ was a broken heart, due to the sense of being deserted at last, not only by his friends, but even by God.

4. *Summa*, I, quaest. XIX, art. 2. The conclusion is stated as follows: "*Cum ad perfectionem voluntatis spectet ut bonum quod quis habet, aliis communicet, hoc divinam praecipue voluntatem decet ut se et alia velit; se ut finem, caetera vero ut ad finem ordinata, id est propter se; quo condecet ejus summam bonitatem alia eam participare.*" Cf. Gilson, *The Philosophy of Saint Thomas Aquinas*, pp. 140 f.

5. *Microcosmus*, vol. II, bk. IX, chap. 7, sect. 7. "The only thing that is really good is that Living Love that wills the blessedness of others" (p. 721).

6. The thought is frequent in Coleridge's prose writings, but is nowhere better expressed than in the closing lines—pathetically addressed to his "babe so beautiful"—of the poem, *Frost at Midnight*:

> ". . . so shalt thou see and hear
> The lovely shapes and sounds intelligible
> Of that eternal language, which thy God
> Utters, who from eternity doth teach
> Himself in all, and all things in himself.
> Great Universal Teacher! he shall mould
> Thy spirit, *and by giving make it ask.*"

7. The discussion of the Resurrection in Arthur Weigall, *The Paganism in Our Christianity* (chap. 9), makes its strictures on the assumption that "the original Christians" believed that Jesus' "dead body had come to life again."

8. P. 264. For a much more restricted view, see the article by W. J. Sparrow-Simpson, on "The Constitution of the Church in the N. T.," in *A New Comm. on Holy Scripture*, ed. Gore, Goudge, and Guillaume.

9. See Oliver C. Quick, *Doctrines of the Creed*, for a recent attempt to deal with the *essentials*. Cf. the "modern apology for the Apostles' Creed," *Christian Fundamentals*, by A. C. Baird. Chas. Harris, *Creeds or No Creeds?* is a polemic in behalf of the *creeds*, chiefly with reference to a negative modernism.

10. *Jesus and the Gospel* (2nd ed., 1909), pp. 397 ff. The symbol should be read not only in the light of Denney's own elaboration, but also in the light of what he has written on p. 49. Christ, he says there, "stands on

the divine side of reality, and is the channel through which all God's power flows to men for their salvation."

11. The suggestion was made by J. H. Bernard, in *Studia Sacra*, chap. 4. Cf. the comment *in loco* in Peake, *Comm. on the Bible*, p. 715.

12. Cf. the scholarly volume of C. C. McCown, *The Genesis of the Social Gospel*.

13. The classical account is Edwin Hatch, *The Influence of Greek Ideas and Usages upon the Christian Church* (Hibbert Lectures, 1888). Cf. Harnack, *History of Dogma*, vol. II; Tollinton, *Clement of Alexandria*, 2 vols.; and McGiffert, *A History of Christian Thought*, vol. I.

14. *The Divine Imperative*, chap. 25. Cf. R. Niebuhr, *An Interpretation of Christian Ethics*, chaps. 5 and 6, and *Moral Man and Immoral Society*; Garvie, *The Christian Ideal for Human Society*, pt. IV, chap. 7; Wm. Temple, *Christ and the State*, lect. 4, and *Essays in Christian Politics*. For the situation in Europe, see A. Keller, *Five Minutes Before Twelve*, and Wm. Teeling, *Crisis for Christianity*.

15. This distinction is questioned by many High Churchmen. See C. Gore, *The Holy Spirit and the Church*, note B to chap. 1.

16. Cf. Origen, *Against Celsus*, bk. VI, chap. 48: "We say that the Holy Scriptures declare the body of Christ, animated by the Son of God, to be the whole Church of God, and the members of this body—considered as a whole—to consist of those who are believers; since, as a soul moves and vivifies the body, which of itself has not the natural power of motion like a living being, so the Word, arousing and moving the whole body, the Church, to befitting action, awakens, moreover, each individual member belonging to the Church, so that they do nothing apart from the Word" (*Ante-Nicene Fathers*, Edinburgh ed., American Reprint, 1926. Quoted from vol. IV, p. 595).

17. *Op. cit.* (note 14), chap. 13.

18. The "integrating" power of Christian faith is to-day widely recognized. James, *Varieties of Religious Experience*, is still a classic. See also A. D. Nock, *Conversion*; L. D. Weatherhead, *Psychology and Life*; P. G. S. Hopwood, *The Religious Experience of the Early Church* and *A Testament of Faith*; Norborg, *Varieties of Christian Experience*; E. M. Ligon, *The Psychology of Christian Experience*. For a different emphasis, cf. J. R. Oliver, *Psychiatry and Mental Health*; MacMurray, *The Structure of Religious Experience*; Jung, *Psychology and Religion*.

19. Striking contemporary evidence of this was afforded by "The Madras Conference" (World Missionary Conference, 1938), at which "The Younger Churches" expressed a desire to be left with greater freedom to develop their Church life according to the genius and culture of their respective nationalities.

CHAPTER 6

1. See Bertrand Russell, *Why I Am Not a Christian*, and the reply by H. G. Wood, *Why Mr. Bertrand Russell is Not a Christian*. Cf. C. F. Rogers, *The Case For Christianity*; C. L. Drawbridge, *Common Objections*

to *Christianity*; K. Ingrams, *The Unreasonableness of Anti-Christianity* and *Why I Believe*; and Chas. Harris, *Pro Fide* (4th ed., rev., 1930).

2. See Jacques Maritain, *The Degrees of Knowledge*, chap. 5, on "Mystical Experience and Philosophy." Cf. W. P. Montague, *Ways of Knowing*, chap. 2, on "Mysticism"; and Oman, *Vision and Authority* (2nd ed., 1929), chap. 9, on "The Unity of Experience."

3. Much relevant material may be found in H. O. Taylor, *The Mediaeval Mind*, 2 vols. (4th Amer. ed., 1927); H. Rashdall, *Universities of the Middle Ages*, 3 vols.; G. R. Owst, *Literature and Pulpit in Mediaeval England*; P. T. Forsyth, *Christ on Parnassus*; E. C. Moore, *The Story of Instruction*; Karl Vosser, *Mediaeval Culture*, 2 vols.

4. A great modern like Paul Elmer More, espec. in his volumes on *The Greek Tradition*, has dealt adequately with this relationship.

5. Lewis Browne, in *Since Calvary*, has not hesitated to point this out, apparently with some pleasure, as also H. Elmer Barnes, in *The Twilight of Christianity*; but C. L. Brace, in an old but still useful book, *Gesta Christi*, has told the other side of the story.

6. Letters of Samuel Rutherford, ed. Andrew A. Bonar, letter CCCLXIV, p. 707.

7. *Pragmatism*, p. 296.

8. Josiah Royce, in *The Problem of Christianity*, vol. I, states the case according to his philosophy of loyalty. For a briefer statement, see his *Sources of Religious Insight*, chaps. 5 and 7. Cf. J. E. Turner, *The Revelation of Deity*, chaps. 8 and 9, and W. E. Hocking, *Human Nature and Its Remaking* (rev. ed.), chaps. 45 and 46.

9. See Evelyn Underhill, *The Life of the Spirit and the Life of To-Day*. Rufus Jones, *Studies in Mystical Religion*, quotes the familiar words of Tauler: "One man can spin, another can make shoes, and *all* these are gifts of the Holy Ghost. I tell you, if I were not a priest, I should esteem it a great gift that I was able to make shoes, and I would try to make them so well as to be a pattern to all" (p. 281; see Jones' entire chap. 13 on "The Friends of God"). Cf. Inge, *Philosophy of Plotinus*, vol. II, lects. 14–16; Wm. Temple, *Christ the Truth*, chap. 6.

10. *Philebus*, 59–66. Cf. the comment in Taylor, *Plato*, pp. 431–434; also Martineau, *Types of Ethical Theory*, vol. I, 2nd ed., pp. 48–51.

11. The writer once heard the story told of a famous black and white artist of the closing years of the last century, but he has not been able to verify it.

12. Cf. J. A. MacCulloch, *The Harrowing of Hell*, espec. chap. 20, on "The Permanent Value of the Descent Doctrine." MacCulloch writes: "The old legend of Christ's carrying his Cross to Hades and leaving it erected there after he had rescued souls and spoiled the spoiler of his prey, witnesses to a profound truth. The Cross, the Crucified Saviour, is active in the Other World as on this earth. The love of God is not limited to earth and time" (p. 325).

13. Gustav Aulén, *Christus Victor*, has definitely released the Fathers from much of the opprobrium long attached to them for their supposed

"ransom to Satan" view of the work of Christ. See the quotations given in Grensted, *A Short History of the Doctrine of the Atonement*, pp. 36–45.

CHAPTER 7

1. One of the "paradoxes" of the "crisis" theology is in the claim that Christianity confronts mankind with a "historical absolute." It is this question with which Kierkegaard struggled in the *Philosophical Fragments*. See Eng. trans. by D. F. Swenson, espec. the moving paragraph on p. 25. The sense in which Troeltsch, espec. in *Die Absolutheit des Christentums* and *The Historical Standpoint and Its Problems*, attempted to conjoin the "historical" and the "absolute" in respect of Jesus is set forth in Sleigh, *The Sufficiency of Christianity*, chap. 4. (Sleigh gives a complete bibliography of Troeltsch, pp. 27, 28.) More critical of Troeltsch, and of other historical relativists, than Sleigh is Bouquet, *Is Christianity the Final Religion?* See espec. his chapter entitled "Synthesis." Von Hügel, *Essays and Addresses on the Philosophy of Religion*, 2nd series, writes at length on Troeltsch, both appreciatively and critically. See also H. R. Mackintosh, *Types of Modern Theology*, chap. 6, on "The Theology of Scientific Religious History."

2. Of the volume by T. J. Thorburn, *The Mythical Interpretation of the Gospels* (1916), James Denney wrote in a *British Weekly* review: "It is no compliment to the common sense of mankind that a book like this should be thought necessary, but if it was to be written at all, it could not be done more courteously or conscientiously than it is here by Dr. Thorburn." The "mythical" idea, however, persists in reappearing, and it has recently drawn from H. G. Wood another reply in *Did Christ Really Live?*

3. *The Growth of Religion* (with W. M. Horton), p. 346. Cf., however, H. S. Box, *The World and God*, chap. 25, on "Creation."

4. *The Christian Message in a Non-Christian World*, p. 68.

5. See Lotze, *Microcosmus*, vol. II, bk. IX, chap. 1. "To ask by what device [the world] has been made, or how it has been brought about that there is any coherent world whatever, instead of none at all, we hold to be a wondering flight of fancy that shoots beyond the mark" (p. 586).

6. See W. R. Matthews, *The Purpose of God*, pp. 76 f. Matthews makes the point that evolution *within* nature necessarily presupposes that system of relations which nature really is, and such a system cannot be explained by the "evolution" which presupposes and requires it.

7. For a brief but clear statement, with the references, see Windelband, *History of Ancient Philosophy*, sect. 41, pp. 257 ff.; cf. W. D. Ross. *Aristotle*, pp. 167–178.

8. *De Principiis*, bk. II, chap. 3; cf. bk. III, chap. 5. See Hagenbach, *History of Doctrines*, sect. 47, notes (7) and (9).

9. *Ethics*, pt. I, prop. XV. For a discussion of this proposition and the related ones, see de Burgh, *Towards a Religious Philosophy*, chap. 3, pts. 3 and 4.

10. *Space, Time, and Deity*, 2 vols. For a discussion of Alexander, see Rogers, *English and American Philosophy Since 1800*, chap. 8, sect. 2, espec. p. 428. Cf. Urban, *The Intelligible World*, pp. 446 ff., and p. 231. Alexander distinguishes between "God" and "Deity." Both are always "out in front." "Deity" is that toward which the universe is irrepressibly moving. "God" is the form in which "Deity" is represented at a given time. The realization of this representation would be the end of the movement were it not for the fact that the realization only results in the discovery that "Deity" is *still* "out in front." In a word, "God" is forever in the making, ceasing to be in the moment of coming to be. He is the nexus between two worlds: one dead, the other striving to be born.

11. See Martensen, *Christian Dogmatics*, sect. 59. "In a certain sense one may say that God created the world in order to satisfy a want in himself; but the idea of God's love requires us to understand this want as quite truly a *superfluity*" (p. 114). O. A. Curtis, *The Christian Faith*, is more emphatic than Martensen, whom he yet follows: "The will of God is *not driven into creation*. God creates because he *would* and not because he *must*" (p. 508).

12. See Barth, *The Knowledge of God and the Service of God*, lect. III, on "The Majestic, the Personal God."

13. Cf. A. M. Fairbairn, *The Place of Christ in Modern Theology*, bk. II, div. III, chap. 2, on "The Fatherhood and Soteriology." Fairbairn writes: "God conceived as Godhead is a Being with life in himself, communicable and ever in process of communication; Christ conceived as the Incarnate Son is a Person so possessed of the communicable life of God as to be the inexhaustible medium of its communication to man" (p. 471).

14. *Søren Kierkegaard*, p. 33.

15. The evidence is impressively stated in Dark and Essex, *The War Against God*. See also Visser t'Hooft, *None Other Gods*, and M. Spinka, *Christianity Confronts Communism*; but cf. B. C. Plowright, *Rebel Religion* (see the discussion in MacFarland, *The Christian Faith in a Day of Crisis*, chap. 10), and M. M. Black, *The Pendulum Swings Back*. Black undertakes to show that in our time the "pendulum" is swinging from materialistic mechanism applied to every phase of existence back to "The Great Tradition" which sets in the center the purposive God and the free and responding man.

CHAPTER 8

1. See P. T. Forsyth, *The Person and Place of Jesus Christ*, lect. XI, the closing paragraph: "God has done things for his own which it has not entered into the heart of man to conceive. It is the miracle behind all miracles. All detailed miracle was but its expression. It is the miracle of grace. And it can be realized (little as it can be conceived) only by the faith that grace creates, that answers grace, and works by love" (p. 320).

2. The literature is endless. For an impressive statement, comparable

in its way to J. S. Mill's essay on *Nature*, see Proudhon, *De la justice dans la révolution et dans l'église.*

3. See E. Lewis, *Jesus Christ and the Human Quest*, chap. 5, on "The Facts of Life" (with references), and cf. chap. 6, *ibid.*

4. In *Dialogues Concerning Natural Religion.* For a discussion, see Pringle-Pattison, *Idea of God*, lect. I; cf. C. W. Hendel, *Studies in the Philosophy of David Hume*, lects. XI–XIII.

5. Two serious modern attempts to deal with this problem are Tennant, *The Concept of Sin* (see also his earlier work, *Origin and Propagation of Sin*), and N. P. Williams, *The Ideas of the Fall and of Original Sin.* In lect. VIII, Williams attempts a "re-interpretation" of "original sin," with special reference to recent psychology (cf. Barbour, *Sin and the New Psychology*); and in lect. VIII he offers a metaphysical view which has some affinities with Coleridge's idea of "a fall of the race-soul." For a still more highly speculative view, see N. Berdyaev, *Destiny of Man*, chap. 2. The evangelical view is well stated in Brunner, *The Mediator*, pp. 139–152.

6. One of the best discussions, exhaustively documented, of the difference between the two men and their points of view is in E. Jauncey, *The Doctrine of Grace*, chap. 5, on "The Pelagian Controversy." See also B. B. Warfield, *Studies in Tertullian and Augustine*, art. V, on "Augustine and the Pelagian Controversy," and cf. R. S. Moxon, *The Doctrine of Sin*, chaps. 3, 4, and 5.

7. Cf. Kierkegaard, *The Sickness unto Death*, the synopsis in Lowrie, *Kierkegaard*, p. 612, and the extracts on pp. 86 ff., 124, 126 f.

8. See the discussion in Brunner, *The Divine Imperative*, chap. 14, on "The Threefold Meaning of the Law."

9. Cf. N. Berdyaev, *Freedom and the Spirit*, chap. 6, sects. 5–9, espec. pp. 213, 215, 226–228, and observations on the difference between the Biblical myth of the Fall and the myth of Prometheus.

10. One who describes himself as a "layman," but who is among the farseeing minds of our time, W. MacNeile Dixon, in his discussion of "The Mighty Opposites," in *The Human Situation* (Gifford Lectures, 1935–1937), chap. 10, has come very close indeed to describing, in a quite fresh and novel way, what the theological doctrine of depravity is *feeling after.* See also W. E. Hocking, *Human Nature and Its Re-Making*, chap. 20, on "Sin as Status."

11. See E. Lewis, *A Christian Manifesto*, chap. 6.

12. *Religion Coming of Age*, p. 229.

13. A. Eustace Haydon, in both *The Quest of the Ages* and *Man's Search for the Good Life*, puts the case with great power. Similarly Walter Lippmann, in *The Preface to Morals* and *The Good Society.*

14. *Op. cit.* (note 10), chap. 27, on "Ideals and Their Recommenders."

15. See H. A. Overstreet, *The Enduring Quest*, for an impressive statement of this general conception. The view is characteristic of the various philosophies of "emergence," as, *e.g.*, Lloyd Morgan, in *Emergent Evolution* and in *Life, Mind, and Spirit.*

16. *The Life of Jesus*, chap. 25, the closing paragraph.

17. Lotze goes further than this. He criticizes the supposition that there can *first* be unrelated existents which *afterwards* become related. Hence, "in point of fact, reality contains nothing that is or could be isolated in its own pure existence, and out of all relation. If then there *is* nothing that is unrelated, we are entitled to say that it belongs to the notion and nature of *existence* to be related." *Microcosmus*, vol. II, p. 587. See also bk. IX, chap. 1, sect. 3.

18. *The Sceptical Biologist*, p. 86.

19. Even in so excellent a book as R. H. Strachan, *The Authority of Christian Experience*, there is a tendency to over-emphasize the "subjective" at the expense of the "objective." See espec. pt. I, chap. 3, and pt. II, chap. 5.

CHAPTER 9

1. See B. B. Warfield, *Calvin and Calvinism*, pp. 23 f., for a brief statement of what Calvin really meant by the divine sovereignty. See the same author's *Studies in Tertullian and Augustine*, pp. 127–130, for a brief account of Augustine "as a religious genius."

2. "Comparative" studies of religion often suffer from either too much or too little objectivity, but on the statements in the text see Gore, *The Philosophy of the Good Life*, or Horton's section, chaps. 1–5, in Wieman and Horton, *The Growth of Religion*.

3. Gal. 1.15, 16. See Lightfoot, *Comm. on Galatians, in loco*; G. S. Duncan, *Galatians, in loco* (Moffatt N. T. Commentary); and cf. W. M. MacGregor, *Christian Freedom*, chap. 5.

4. *Metaphysics*, bk. IV, chap. 2.

5. 2 Peter 3.9.

6. See Bowne, *Metaphysics*, chap. 4, for a consideration of the metaphysical basis of this inter-relatedness. Cf. Knudson, *The Philosophy of Personalism*, pp. 198–202; Buckham and Stratton, *George Holmes Howison*, pp. 262–306, the article by Howison on "The Harmony of Determinism and Freedom"; and in the same volume, "The entire world of spirit . . . God creates only through the creative spirit of man" (p. 352).

7. Cf. J. S. Huxley, *Religion Without Revelation*, the interesting chapter 4, entitled "Personalia." Many of the personal statements in *Contemporary American Theology*, 2 vols., ed. V. Ferm, have much the same significance. Practical and emotional habits, engendered in early life in connection with a definite body of beliefs, may still continue when the beliefs have been changed for others which there is no guarantee would have created the attitudes in the first place.

8. The three possibilities of explanation concerning the course of one's life are chance, necessity, and providence. "Providence" allows for the mutuality of objective "control" and subjective "freedom," but in the end it is necessarily a doctrine of personal faith. "My times are in thy hands" is not something to be proved but to be confessed. See C. F. D'Arcy, *Providence and the World Order*, chap. 8, on "The Providential

Order"; Bushnell, *The Moral Uses of Dark Things*, espec. chap. 15, on "The Mutabilities of Life"; and E. Griffith-Jones, *Providence Divine and Human*, vol. I, bk. I, "The Christian Theory of Providence," chap. 2. Griffith-Jones writes: "Thus the normal relation between the human will and the divine is one of subordination, co-operation, and fellowship in the pursuit of the moral ends for which the world exists. The divine will, being creative and directive, is ideally supreme; the human, being created and subordinate, is ideally obedient and co-operant" (p. 108).

9. Tennyson, *Morte d'Arthur*.

10. See W. N. Clarke, *An Outline of Christian Theology*, pp. 389–395: "The elect of the New Testament, like the elect of the Old, are chosen and called of God that he may use them for the good of other men. . . . The elect are elect for the sake of the non-elect" (pp. 393 f.).

11. Cf. Berdyaev, *Freedom and the Spirit*, chap. 5. The *term* is not especially present in Berdyaev's discussion, but the *idea*, that it is the very effort of good that gives evil its greater opportunity, is everywhere being stressed.

12. D. G. Rossetti, *Mary's Girlhood*, stanza 2.

13. See below, Chapter 19.

14. See Barth, *The Knowledge of God and the Service of God*, lect. 5, on "The Way of Man."

15. Kant deals with the question in the *Metaphysics of Morals*, the *Critique of the Practical Reason*, and *Religion Within the Limits of Reason Alone*. For discussion, cf. R. Otto, *The Philosophy of Religion*, chaps. 8 and 9; John Watson, *The Interpretation of Religious Experience* (Pt. First: Historical), lect. 8, on "The Critical Philosophy," espec. pp. 278–281; Pringle-Pattison, *Idea of God*, lect. II, espec. pp. 31–37; and Kronenberg, *Kant: Sein Leben und seine Lehre* (6ste Aufl., Munich, 1922), Teil II, Kap. 8, seite 249–266.

16. Chap. 13.1, 2, ed. O. W. Wright, 1875.

17. From a review of R. Niebuhr, *Beyond Tragedy*, printed in *Religion in Life*, Winter Number, 1938, pp. 137 f.

18. Bk. I, chap. 12, par. 5.

19. *Ibid*, chap. 13, par. 2.

20. Cf. W. MacNeile Dixon, *The Human Situation*, chap. 14, on "The Laws of God, and the Laws of Man." The chapter is hardly a defence of Rousseau's saying that the good are without sense if there be no God, but it seriously raises the question as to how long ethics can continue without the support of religion. See the same author's *From Morality to Religion*.

CHAPTER 10

1. The position is characteristic of modern philosophical idealism in general, although it had its antecedents in the eighteenth century Enlightenment. See Leslie Stephens, *English Thought in the Eighteenth Century*; Caldecott, *Philosophy of Religion*, chap. 12, sects. 1, 2, with special reference to the Deists; lect. III on "English Deism and Butler's *Analogy*"

in John Oman, *The Problem of Faith and Freedom*; and the examination of idealism and general revelation in Brunner, *The Mediator*, chaps. 1, 2. John Caird, *Philosophy of Religion*, chap. 8, on "The Speculative Idea of Religion," is an excellent example of the type of thinking which it represents. Cf. Henry Jones, *A Faith That Enquires*, lect. XV, on "The Absolute and the Natural World," and Haldane, *Pathway to Reality*, bk. III, lect. 6.

2. See the striking argument sustained by Alfred Noyes, in *The Unknown God*. Cf. C. H. Dodd, *The Authority of the Bible*, chap. 13.

3. For an example of the older rationalism, see Pfleiderer, *The Early Christian Conception of Christ*. For examples of the more recent type, see Arthur Weigall, *The Paganism in Our Christianity*; the numerous comments on the N. T. text in G. L. Clark, *Fundamentals of Early Christianity*, some of them sheerly incredible, *e.g.*, pp. 85, 114, 164–174, 506, 509–510, 681; Kirsopp Lake, *Stewardship of Faith*; Loisy, *The Gospel and the Church*.

4. *E.g.*, the statements by A. F. Gilmore, J. H. Holmes, J. H. Dietrich, E. S. Ames, and Brown Landone, respectively, in *My Idea of God*, ed. Joseph Fort Newton.

5. See Bruce Barton, *The Man Nobody Knows*.

6. Cf. Wieman, *Normative Psychology of Religion*, chap. 8, on "Sin and Forgiveness," and R. S. Moxon, *The Doctrine of Sin*, chaps. 7, 8. For a discussion, see Barbour, *Sin and the New Psychology*, chaps. 3, 4, 5.

7. For a modern philosopher's attempt to retain the idea of the Trinity, see the article on "The Trinity" by W. Pepperell Montague, in *Religious Realism*, ed. D. C. Mackintosh, pp. 495 ff.

8. The paragraph gives the substance of much that may be found in John Dewey, *A Common Faith*. Cf. the discussion in D. S. Cairns, *The Riddle of the World*, chap. 2, on "Humanism."

9. W. G. Ballantine, in *The Basis of Belief*, describes with engaging clarity the place of observation, the varieties of induction (distinguished as primary, secondary, and mixed), resemblance, co-existence, causation and succession and wherein these differ, hypotheses, fallacies, and proofs. Newman, *The Grammar of Assent*, is still a classic for its statement and defence of "the illative sense" (chap. 9). Balfour, in *A Defence of Philosophic Doubt* and *The Foundations of Belief*, defends the thesis that since science and religion alike rest on "assumptions," a rejection of religion on this ground calls for a rejection of science (at least of scientific certainty) as well—an argument which Pringle-Pattison, *Idea of God*, pp. 59 ff., regards as dangerous. The "Conclusion" (chap. 12) in A. Campbell Garnet, *Reality and Value*, sums up an able defence of the value-certainty of our experience. Oliver Quick, *The Ground of Faith and the Chaos of Thought*, discusses in chap. 2 "Two Types of Argument for Belief," with which cp. chap. 4, on "Two Ways of Knowledge" in B. H. Streeter, *Reality*. W. P. Montague, *The Ways of Knowing*, is helpful for its distinction and evaluation of the "ways." Hume concludes his *Dialogues Concerning Natural Religion* with a recognition of the fact that there can be religious faith only as there is scepticism. A great modern like Paul Elmer

More, in *The Sceptical Approach to Religion*, is an impressive illustration of the truth of Hume's principle.

10. See E. Lewis, *The Faith We Declare*, chap. 1.

11. Cf. John Macmurray, *The Structure of Religious Experience*, chap. 3, on "The Reference of Religious Ideas."

12. See John Oman, *Vision and Authority*, (rev. ed.), bk. II, chap. 1, on "The Religious Society."

13. There are many aspects of "modern thinking" which are friendly to the Christian view, as is made plain in various parts of this book. The present reference is to those which are clearly inimical. For a brief examination of some of them, together with adequate bibliographies, see the "Supplementary Chapter, 1930," prefixed to Chas. Harris, *Pro Fide*, (4th ed.), pp. xiii–lxxix.

14. See Brunner, *The Divine Imperative*, chaps. 7 and 8, and the same author's *God and Man*, chap. 2. Cf. Royce, *Studies of Good and Evil*, chap. 4; Niebuhr, *Beyond Tragedy*, chap. 8, on "Christianity and Tragedy," espec. pp. 165–169, and *An Interpretation of Christian Ethics*, chaps. 3 and 4. In the latter book, Niebuhr writes: "Original sin is not an inherited corruption, but it is an inevitable fact of human existence, the inevitability of which is given by the nature of man's spirituality" (p. 90).

CHAPTER 11

1. The chapter (V) in Jacques Maritain, *The Degrees of Knowledge*, which deals with "Mystical Experience and Philosophy," takes the essentially Thomistic position concerning the knowledge of the super-sensible. That the super-sensible is knowable is not for a moment to be doubted, nor is any doubt to be thrown on the reality of the mystical experience. It still remains, however, that sense-coercion supported by social verification leaves us no alternative, and that an alternative is possible in respect of any other alleged experience of the objective. This is why in the text attention is being directed rather to "kinds of certainty" than to "kinds of knowledge."

2. The Thomistic insistence that truth and being are mutualities, and that man as intelligence is constituted relative to both, is the only alternative to scepticism. See Etienne Gilson, *The Philosophy of Saint Thomas*, chap. 17, and notes, and the same author's consideration of "La Doctrine de la Double Vérité," in *Etudes de Philosophie Médiévale*.

3. One of the most useless pieces of intellectual ingenuity is that which undertakes to show that we have, and can have, no dependable knowledge of the external world. One wonders what this "external world" *is* to the doctrinaire who is seeking to dispense with it! It seems hardly worth while to "prove" that what "is not there" is not there! *What* is it that is "not there"? See Bowne, *Metaphysics: A Study in First Principles*, chaps. 2–5, and his epistemological view in *The Theory of Thought and Knowledge*. Cf. the discussion of Bowne as a "Transcendental Realist" in F. J. McConnell, *Borden Parker Bowne*, chap. 6. Bowne, fol-

lowing in the tradition of Lotze, and avoiding the scepticism of Kant, held unflinchingly to the principle that the way in which reality was given in the experience of a personal self was the only kind of reality in which the self could be interested, as it was also reality in the one form which the self could not deny.

4. This is the truth, and the only truth, in Barth's categorical denial of "general" revelation. H. R. Mackintosh, *Types of Modern Theology*, suggests that the denial has certain qualifications, and is very close to what Chalmers meant when he said, "Apart from Christ, I find that I have no hold of God at all" (pp. 277–278). He quotes Barth: "Knowledge of grace in point of fact destroys the idea of an indirect revelation in Nature, in History, or in the consciousness of our own existence." Brunner, however, certainly supposes that Barth denies "general" revelation, and just as certainly Barth supposes that Brunner affirms it. Hence Barth's emphatic pamphlet, *Nein!* The question of the relation of the two men is discussed by David Cairns, in the Introduction, pp. 18 ff., of Brunner, *God and Man.* In his "apology" for accepting an invitation to deliver the Gifford Lectures, which limit the lecturer to a topic in "Natural Theology," Barth frankly says that he does not even believe in "Natural Theology," and that he intended to use his opportunity to set forth that "Revealed Theology" with which the Gifford Foundation was not concerned! See *The Knowledge of God and the Service of God*, pp. 3–7.

5. The remark in note 1 above is only intended to point out that an almost unavoidable ambiguity attaches to the word "knowledge" as used not only by Thomists but by most religious thinkers.

6. See the reference under note 8, Chapter 10, above. There is an excellent discussion in J. H. Beibitz, *Rationalism and Orthodoxy of To-day.* See also F. E. England, *The Validity of Religious Experience*, chap. 8, on "The Nature of Apprehension," and cf. H. R. Mackintosh, *The Christian Apprehension of God*, chap. 2, on "The Special Character of Religious Knowledge." Mackintosh writes: "We know the facts of the physical world in one way, those of the spiritual world in another. In both instances, however, we have real knowledge" (p. 54). See note 1 above.

7. See the discussion on "law" in Eddington, *The Nature of the Physical World*, pp. 237–246. "The mind has by its selective power fitted the processes of Nature into a frame of law of a pattern largely of its own choosing; and in the discovery of this system of law the mind may be regarded as regaining from Nature that which the mind has put into Nature" (p. 244).

8. The single case of what is the meaning of "the present moment" is sufficient to suggest the whole complicated question. For a readable discussion, in the spirit of J. W. Dunne and Karl Heim, see Daniel Lamont, *Christ and the World of Thought*, chap. 6, on "The Present Moment."

9. Cp. the observation of A. N. Whitehead that faith in reason is trust in "the ultimate nature of things" as intrinsically harmonious, that science rests on faith in the order of nature, and that this faith is "a particular example of a deeper faith." *Science and the Modern World*, p. 27.

10. See S. S. Laurie, *Synthetica*, vol. I, Meditation XIX; vol. II,

Meditation II. Laurie completes his first volume with the words: "Strange it would be if a being could emerge on the surface of one of innumerable worlds, asking questions and projecting infinite possibilities to which the only response was the brutal and stupid answer of The Grave."

11. It is customary in some quarters to dismiss these considerations by lightly exclaiming, "Idealism!" Idealism undoubtedly is involved, but it is at least a *critical* idealism, and it does as much justice to the *assumed* subject in the subject-object relation as it does to the *asserted* object, and this is not too often done in theories claiming to be "realistic." Garnett, *Reality and Value*, is a suggestive recent attempt to do justice to both factors. See also J. E. Turner, *A Theory of Direct Realism.*

12. Pringle-Pattison calls this "lower naturalism" in distinction from (his own) "higher naturalism." *Idea of God*, lect. V.

13. See note 9 to Chapter 10 above.

CHAPTER 12

1. See the discussion in Chevalier, *Henri Bergson*, chap. 5, on this book of Bergson. Chevalier says of it: "It contains within it enough to shatter into fragments a whole false science and lay bare the rock upon which, as upon an impregnable base, metaphysics can enthrone a rational belief in spirit, and in the immortal destiny of man" (p. 175).

2. A different view of the question may be found in Karl Heim, *God Transcendent*, sect. 21, pp. 146 ff.; in S. Alexander, *Space, Time and Deity;* and J. W. Dunne, *An Experiment with Time.* Dunne regards time as "an infinite series of dimensions," and not as one dimension only. Lamont, who is largely influenced by Heim, offers an illuminating discussion in *Christ and the World of Thought*, chap. 5, on "Time." Whitehead considers the question in his own distinctive way in *The Concept of Nature*, chap. 3, and in *Science and the Modern World*, chap. 7, on "Relativity," in which he lays stress on the *endurance* of the objective, as "the repetition of the pattern in successive events" (p. 183). In *Process and Reality*, he speaks of his "philosophy of organism" as an attempt to do justice, among other notions, to the notions of "time as perpetual perishing" and "endurance as re-creation" (p. 196). J. E. Turner in *A Theory of Direct Realism*, chap. 18, offers what he calls "A Realistic Theory of Time," much of what he says turning on the distinction between "the actual temporal characteristics of reality" (unknown to us) and "the aspects which these assume in perception" (known to us). But must we not talk about the unknown in terms of the known? Is not the only time we *know* the "Now-time"? Is not "Now-time" inseparable from an experiencing self? Which is the burden of what is being said in the text. See also F. H. Brabant, *Time and Eternity in Christian Thought.*

3. It will be difficult to find the case stated more clearly than in chaps. 5 and 6 of Bowne, *Personalism.* Cf. W. M. Urban, *The Intelligible World*, chap. 7.

4. See Lawrence Hyde, *The Learned Knife*, chap. 10, on "Humanism

328 *A Philosophy of the Christian Revelation*

and Religion." Cf. the striking "Introduction" to *Belief in Man*, by
P. S. Richards; the numerous writings of Paul Elmer More, especially
vol. III, *On Being Human*, of "The New Shelburne Essays"; and Lynn
Harold Hough, *Vital Control* (Forest Essays, first series), Essays I, III,
and VIII.

5. See Knudson, *The Philosophy of Personalism*, pp. 225–246.
6. *Lines Written at Elbingerode.*
7. *Dejection: An Ode*, stanza 4.
8. For a statement, see R. W. Sellars, *Evolutionary Naturalism*.
9. See *Essays and Addresses on the Philosophy of Religion*, I, pp. xiii,
xiv, 56, 57.
10. *Normative Psychology of Religion*, pp. 51–52, 60, 137.
11. See *The Philosophy of the Christian Religion*, bk. I, chap. 1, sect. 2,
parag. 1, pp. 27 ff. "If we eliminate Personality from Nature—either objectively, as interpretable; or subjectively, as interpreted—we are left
without a Nature we can regard as intelligible. . . . The Personality
which makes Nature was not made by the Nature it makes" (p. 30).
12. Cf. D. C. Macintosh, *The Reasonableness of Christianity*, espec. his
use of the term "reasonable," pp. 17 ff.

CHAPTER 13

1. *The Immanence of God*, preface.
2. The treatment of the distinction in John Oman, *The Natural and
the Supernatural*, chap. 5 (d), pp. 69 ff., agrees with what is meant in the
text, if it is read in the light of Oman's book as a whole. Cf. his chaps.
15–17. See also the argument in J. E. Turner, *Personality and Reality*,
offered as "A Proof of the Real Existence of a Supreme Self in the
Universe."
3. See the criticisms of Pantheism and so-called Semi-Pantheism in
Chas. Harris, *First Steps in the Philosophy of Religion*.
4. *Hertha*, stanzas 5, 7, 8. W. S. Rutland, in *Swinburne: A Nineteenth
Century Hellene*, regards *Hertha* as the poem in which most definitely
Swinburne identifies himself with Blake's dictum, "All deities reside in
the human breast" (p. 146).
5. *The Ethics*, pt. I, prop. 29, proof and note. Pollock's longer work
is still the best book in English on Spinoza. See his more recent short
monograph, *Spinoza* (Great Lives Series). Cf. Joseph Ratner, *Spinoza on
God*, chap. 2, and H. Höffding, *Spinozas Ethica: Analyse und Charakteristik*.
6. See Chas. Bigg, *The Christian Platonists of Alexandria*; Patrick,
Clement of Alexandria; Tollinton, *Clement of Alexandria*, 2 vols.; and
for an excellent and sympathetic short study, Westcott, *Religious Thought
in the West*, the chapter on "Origen and the Beginnings of Christian
Philosophy," pp. 196 ff.
7. *The Christian Message in a Non-Christian World*, pp. 63–68.
8. See W. R. Matthews, *God in Christian Experience*, chaps. 2, 3, 4.
9. *Confessions*, VI, 6.

10. This is really the claim that lies at the root of Comte's Positivism. See some of the astonishing statements in Wiggam, *The Decalogue of Science*, chapters on "The Tenth Commandment," described as "The Duty of Philosophical Reconstruction."

11. *The Idea of the Holy*, chaps. 2, 3, 4, 5. Otto's view has provoked endless discussion. Short and readable discussions are Robert Mackintosh, *Values*, chap. 9, and John Baillie, *The Interpretation of Religion*, pp. 246–255.

12. See Jeans, *The Universe Around Us*, pp. 68–81, for the present status of the question. The Aristotelian theory of a "bounded" universe was a pure speculation arising chiefly from his idea that perfect motion was motion in a circle: hence there is an outermost heavenly rotating sphere within which the "world-all" is included, and inclusion means limitation. See *Physics* III, 2, 5.

13. See Belief in *God and Immortality*, a questionnaire, with analyses and conclusions.

14. See the symposium edited by Colton, entitled, *Has Science Discovered God?* The symposium included Kirtley F. Mather, Robert A. Millikan, Heber D. Curtis, Edwin G. Conklin, Albert Einstein, William McDougall, and Michael Pupin.

15. As reported in *The British Weekly*, March 3, 1932.

16. See note 4 to Chapter 11 above.

17. *The Christian Faith*, p. 107.

18. The idea of God held by E. S. Brightman, namely, that God suffers from "restrictions within his own nature," described as "The Given," and that these restrictions, God's own "problem," are the reasons for the imperfections of the world, arises in part from his regarding as "a radically mistaken view" the Christian belief that "there has been revealed in Scripture a complete and adequate idea of God." See *The Problem of God*, chap. 5.

19. Arthur Hugh Clough, *The Questioning Spirit*, first stanza.

20. The distinction is employed by W. M. Horton, in his article in *Revelation*, ed. John Baillie.

21. Matthew Arnold, *Dover Beach*.

CHAPTER 14

1. It ought to be apparent that mind has this function whether the "theory" of mind be that of the most absolute Idealism at one extreme, or of the crudest Behaviorism at the other. Bergson, Morgan, Dewey, S. Alexander, Holt, Spaulding, Sellars, Watson, Russell, equally with Kant, Lotze, Bowne, Pringle-Pattison, Hocking, have to deal with mind as the *sine qua non* of human experience, irrespective of their understanding of the process as to how mind came to be, or even of their understanding of what mind essentially is. Cf. Hoernlé, Studies in *Contemporary Metaphysics*, chap. 8, on "Theories of Mind." Even Whitehead describes his realistic philosophy of organism as an attempt to describe "how ob-

jective data pass into subjective satisfaction," and he defines an "object" as a "potentiality" able to become "a component in feeling" (*Process and Reality*, pp. 135–136). But the "feeling" in question is admittedly subjective; the "potentiality" is admittedly objective; and while Whitehead repeatedly declares that he is at the opposite pole from Kant, it is difficult to see that under his elaborate terminology there is anything else than the ancient truth that knowledge of the world is a function of mind and that mind exists to make that knowledge possible.

2. See Garnett, *Reality and Value*, chap. 5, on "The Self and the World." Garnett distinguishes between "sensa" and "values." On the view in the text, the "sensa" *compel* response, the "values" *may* be responded to.

3. Feuerbach, in *The Essence of Christianity*, may be said to have anticipated the contemporary use of "wishful thinking" as accounting for religious faith. See Oman, *The Natural and the Supernatural*, chap. 3, on "Theories of Religion as Illusion." Oman quotes Jodl's comment on Feuerbach: "The specific quality of the religious outlook is phantasy winged by human desire" (p. 35). A complete demonstration of the objectivity of the "facts" mentioned in the text is impossible: they depend upon testimony and its acceptance, *i.e.*, on "a venture of faith."

4. As long ago as 1793, in *Religion Within the Limits of Pure Reason*.

5. See C. H. Dodd, *History and the Gospel*, and cf. H. G. Wood, *Did Christ Really Live?*

6. Even so convinced an evangelical as Brunner confesses to difficulty with the Virgin Birth, and regards the idea as a "burden" which is "apt to obscure the meaning" of the truth of the Incarnation. See *The Mediator*, pp. 322–327. The Commission which prepared the statement on *Doctrine in the Church of England* would retire the doctrine to the periphery. The impatience of the rationalists is quite understandable, once their assumptions are granted. On the other hand, such an elaborate monograph as Machen, *The Virgin Birth of Christ*, throws the doctrine out of perspective, because it does not recognize either the *real* difficulty or the *real* basis for faith.

7. The treatment in Goguel, *La Foi a la Résurrection de Jesus*, is amazingly exhaustive and moves everywhere on a high level, as the reading of the *Préface* alone will suffice to indicate, but the conclusion, dealing with "*L'Evolution de la Foi et des Récits*," is essentially negative so far as concerns any proper "objectivity" answering to the original "individual experience" of the disciples. *La foi* may be explained as due to the operation of known laws of religious experience which transformed "*une expérience extatique et mystique*," and limited to individuals, into a definite statement of a historical and objective fact made an article of faith for the entire Church. "*Le caractère de la croyance à la résurrection a changé. Au debut, elle a été une conviction individuelle dérivant d'une expérience personelle. A la fin, elle est devenue la reconnaissance d'un fait objectivement établi. Elle n'a plus été l'aboutissement de la foi; elle en est devenue le point de départ*" (p. 455). The cautious treatment by G. H. C. MacGregor, *The Growth of the Resurrection Faith*, two articles in *The Expository Times*, February and March,

1939, is in the nature of a *via media* which many would find possible of acceptance. For a more "psychological" treatment, see Berguer, *Some Aspects of the Life of Jesus*, chap. 9.

8. Cf. Hoernlé, *Studies in Contemporary Metaphysics*, chap. 2, on "The Idol of Scientific Method in Philosophy."

9. See Klausner, *Jesus of Nazareth*, pp. 232 f., pp. 356 ff.; Lobstein, *The Virgin Birth*; Loisy, *Les Evangiles Synoptiques*; Thompson, *Miracles of the N. T.*

10. See Quick, *Doctrines of the Creed*, chaps. 14 and 15, and the whole movement of thought in such books as Temple, *Christ the Truth*, Bell and Deissmann, ed., *Mysterium Christi*, Grensted, *The Person of Christ*, Rawlinson, *The N. T. Doctrine of the Christ*, and L. S. Thornton, *The Incarnate Lord*.

11. Yet this is what Brunner seems to suppose. *The Mediator*, p. 325.

12. Cf. E. R. Micklem, *Miracles and the New Psychology*, pp. 128 f. Micklem says that a modern physician who was convinced that a person was actually dead, and learned afterwards that the person was "re-animated," would simply conclude that he had been mistaken in his original conviction.

13. This, however, was in the posthumously published, *Leben Jesus*, a book which Weinel and Widgery, *Jesus in the* 19th *Century and After*, think must not be taken too seriously. Schleiermacher is much more definite in the discussion in *Der Christliche Glaube*, sect. 99, although he never felt that the Resurrection was *necessary* to the theological construction of the Person of Christ. See Mackintosh, *Types of Modern Theology*, p. 87.

14. *A New Life of Jesus*, vol. I, p. 412.

CHAPTER 15

1. Cf. Wm. James' essay, *The Will to Believe*, and also *Pragmatism* and *The Meaning of Truth*. There are obvious limitations on James' central principle of "voluntarism" in respect of belief: it does not justify us in believing "whatever our whim suggest," or in supposing that "judgments are *constituted* true by their satisfaction of desire." See Rogers, *English and American Philosophy Since* 1800, pp. 371 ff.

2. For standard discussions, see Kennedy, *Paul and the Mystery Religions*; Angus, *The Mystery Religions and Christianity*; Clemen, *Primitive Christianity and Its Non-Jewish Sources*; Legge, *Forerunners and Rivals of Christianity*, 2 vols.

3. There is general agreement that the words, "and a honeycomb," are a late addition. A common interpretation of the incident is that it represents either the "materializing" of an experience originally more spiritual (See W. Manson, *The Gospel of Luke*, Moffatt N. T. Commentary, *in loco*), or an attempt to confute the so-called Docetic heresy, which held that Jesus' body was a mere phantasm (H. D. A. Major, in *The Mission and Message of Jesus*, ed. Major, Manson, and Wright, p. 295). On the "touching" by Thomas, see Wright in his section of the

same volume, pp. 942 ff. Cf. the same author's comments on the Fourth Gospel as "the dramatized essence of Christian theology" in *The Meaning and Message of the Fourth Gospel*, pp. 98 ff. See also Bernard, on *St. John*, 2 vols., in the International Critical Commentary, pp. 681 ff. Bernard makes the point that there was no *actual* touching, only Jesus' *invitation* to touch, which Thomas did not need to accept, because the *seeing* convinced him.

4. Even Klausner draws the line at "deliberate imposture," which, he says, "is not the substance out of which the religion of millions of mankind is created." His reference is to the charge that the disciples had stolen the body of Jesus. *Jesus of Nazareth*, p. 357.

5. See Quick, *The Doctrines of the Creed*, chap. 14, on "The Incarnation and Historical Criticism." Quick protests against the critic demanding "proof" of the resurrection such as "science or the law courts would call cogent" (p. 150). Auguste Sabatier wrote: "It is absolutely chimerical to expect of science the establishment of any miracle whatsoever." *Outlines of a Philosophy of Religion*, p. 78.

6. That the disciples had such an expectancy is often affirmed, but even Klausner (*op. cit.*, note 4) denies this (p. 358), offering as evidence the fact of the visit of the women to the tomb to anoint the body.

7. Arthur Hugh Clough, *Easter Day*.

8. Berguer is mistaken when he says that the choice is between "God bringing a corpse back to life," which he regards as an impossible view, but the one held by many Christians, and his own "psychological" view. See *Some Aspects of the Life of Jesus*, p. 292. There is a third possibility—the one set forth in the text, which allows for the "psychological" but affirms a real "objectivity." This "objectivity" was a fact which we are not able exactly to describe. The empty tomb was incidental to the fact, and was even required by it, but in what happened to the body is precisely the point where the "miraculous" element enters, and it is something on which we cannot pronounce.

9. See H. R. Mackintosh, *Doctrine of the Person of Christ*, pp. 368 ff. Mackintosh says of the Resurrection that it marks a vast expansion of the activity of the Son to a point where he becomes practically indistinguishable from the Father (p. 370).

10. Cf. H. B. Alexander, *Truth and the Faith*, chap. 2, on "The Parable of Vision." Alexander says that there are two worlds, each of which we are equipped to apprehend, but in a different way.

11. See Galloway, *Religion and Modern Thought*, chap. 10, on "Religion and the Supernatural."

12. See *Life's Basis and Life's Ideal*, pp. 110–215. Cf. W. Tudor Jones, *An Interpretation of Rudolf Eucken's Philosophy*, chap. 9, on "Characteristic Religion."

13. The older theologies made much of this "structural wholeness" of Christianity as a body of truth. See Martensen, *Christian Dogmatics*, sects. 29–36, pp. 57–71. Cf. Curtis, *The Christian Faith*, chap. 13. Curtis says: "Doctrines are all interlocked at the root. Between them there is an underlying philosophical connection. This philosophical connection must

be revealed. Not only so, but the connection must be brought out in such a way as gradually to exhibit the Christian faith as one mighty organic whole" (p. 183).

CHAPTER 16

1. *On the Flesh of Christ*, bk. V.
2. *Timaeus*, 29. Cf. Taylor, *Plato*, pp. 440 f.
3. Cf. the notes of "The Pessimism of Scepticism" in James Orr, *Christian View of God and the World*, appendix to lect. II, espec. the extract from Theodore Jouffroy, p. 69.
4. *A History of the Warfare of Science With Theology*, vol. I, p. 123.
5. See Draper, *The Intellectual Development of Europe*, vol. II, chap. 8.
6. See J. Y. Simpson, *Landmarks in the Struggle Between Science and Religion*, chaps. 6 and 7.
7. See Dampier-Whetham, *A History of Science*, pp. 153 ff.
8. *Op. cit.*, pp. 135 ff.
9. *Science and the Modern World*, pp. 267 f.
10. *Op. cit.*, p. 261.
11. *Op. cit.*, chap. 3.
12. See Whitehead, *op. cit.*, p. 261. Cf. Beazley, *The Dawn of Modern Geography*, vol. I, for an account of Cosmos' work.
13. *The Earliest Cosmologies*, pp. 24 f.
14. *Op. cit.*, pp. 19 f.
15. *Op. cit.*, pp. 41 ff.
16. See *What Plato Taught*, p. 342.
17. For this familiarity, cf. H. O. Taylor, *The Mediaeval Mind*, vol. II, 4th Amer. Ed., chap. 37, and espec. chap. 38.
18. See *Plato*, p. 441.
19. *Timaeus*, 30–37.
20. Cf. A. E. Taylor, *op. cit.*, pp. 450 f.
21. *Op. cit.*, p. 345.
22. *De caelo*, II, 3.
23. See *The Fitness of the Environment*, and cf. introductory chap. to his *Order of Nature*.
24. See *The Mediator*, chap. 11, espec. paragraphs 6 and 7.
25. *Op. cit.*, pp. 270 f.
26. Cf. Ovid, *Metamorphosis*, bk. I, 348–415, where he tells the story of Deucalion and Pyrrha, and their repeopling the earth, after the Deluge, from "the bones of their mother," which turned out to be the stones (*saxa=ossa*) of the earth (*terra=mater*).
27. See Wm. Barry, *Ernest Renan*, chap. 2, on "The Eclipse of Faith," espec. pp. 32–35, and the comment, p. 62, on Renan, *The Future of Science*.
28. See Ueberweg, *Geschichte der Philosophie*, III, Neuzeit, §31. *"Feuerbach treibt dann diesen Naturalismus auf die Spitze in dem Satze:*

der Mensch sei nur das, was er esse, und sagt sich von jeglicher Philosophie los" (Seite 405).

29. Cf. Caldecott, *Philosophy of Religion*, pp. 333 ff.

30. In a little book, *Thoughts on Religion*, edited by a no less stalwart believer than Charles Gore.

31. *The Yale Review*, July, 1918.

32. Cf. J. Y. Simpson, *Man and the Attainment of Immortality*, chaps. 11 and 12.

33. What follows is based chiefly on the closing chapter of Boutroux, *Science and Religion in Contemporary Philosophy*. Cf. also his *Contingency of the Laws of Nature*, pp. 150 ff.

34. See his *Naturalism and Religion*, espec. chaps. 3, 9, 10, and 12.

35. *Op. cit.*, p. 84.

36. The general thesis of all of these books of Needham may be read in the closing lines of *The Sceptical Biologist*, p. 86.

37. *Ibid.*, pp. 240 f.

38. See, *e.g.*, Stallknecht, *Studies in the Philosophy of Creation*, part III, chap. 2, on "Whitehead's Philosophy of Organism"; D. M. Emmett, *Whitehead's Philosophy of Organism*; and R. Das, *The Philosophy of Whitehead*.

39. *Science and the Modern World*, p. 275.

40. See such recent works as Streeter, *Reality*; H. H. Farmer, *The World and God*; W. R. Matthews, *The Purpose of God*; Wm. Temple, *Nature, Man, and God*; de Burgh, *Towards a Religious Philosophy* and *From Morality to Religion*; and D. S. Cairns, *The Riddle of the World*.

41. *The Mediator*, p. 170.

CHAPTER 17

1. See Kennedy, *Philo's Contribution to Religion*, and cf. W. F. Howard, *The Fourth Gospel in Recent Criticism and Interpretation*, chap. 4, on "The Background of Thought."

2. Few historians have stated the case with finer feeling than A. V. G. Allen, *The Continuity of Christian Thought*, the section on "The Greek Theology."

3. See Hugh M. Scott, *The Nicene Theology*. Scott represents the older orthodoxy, but he says much that is still relevant. For a more modern and less sympathetic view, see McGiffert, *A History of Christian Thought*, vol. I, chaps. 10–15.

4. See I. A. Dorner, *System of Christian Doctrine*, vol. I, sects. 28 and 29.

5. *The Atonement and the Social Process*, p. 108.

6. See any of the standard histories of philosophy, the section on the Middle Ages; also the writings on the period of H. O. Taylor, G. G. Coulton, Étienne Gilson, Maurice de Wulf, espec. his *Philosophy and Civilization in the Middle Ages*. Cf. the relevant chapters in *The Legacy of Rome*, ed. Cyril Bailey, and *The Legacy of Greece*, ed. R. W. Livingstone.

7. See J. S. Zybura, *Present-Day Thinkers and the New Scholasticism;* J. L. Perrier, *The Revival of Scholastic Philosophy;* J. J. Walsh, *High Points of Mediaeval Culture;* E. I. Watkin, *The Philosophy of Form;* and G. Bruni, *Progressive Scholasticism.*

8. Cf. Gilson, *The Philosophy of Saint Thomas Aquinas,* chap. 2, on "Faith and Reason," and his *L'Esprit de la Philosophie Médiéval,* espec. chaps. 1 and 2.

9. Wordsworth, *Lines Composed Upon an Evening of Extraordinary Splendor,* stanza 2.

10. *Ode to a Nightingale,* stanza 7.

11. *Philomela,* the closing lines.

12. 2 Samuel, 1.26, 27.

13. Mrs. Barbauld, *Life.*

14. Psalm 8.3–5.

15. Cf. W. R. Inge, *God and the Astronomers.*

16. *The Future,* from last two stanzas.

17. Matthew Arnold, *A Summer Night,* from last stanza.

18. See the excellent brief statement in H. Wheeler Robinson, *Religious Ideas of the O. T.,* chap. 4, on "The Idea of Man." On what follows, see also his *Christian Doctrine of Man.* For a more "theological" statement, see Brunner, *The Divine Imperative,* chap. 15.

19. W. E. Hocking, *Human Nature and Its Remaking,* is in effect a restatement in terms of a modern psychology of the biblical teaching concerning man and how he may be "born again." Cf. the same author, *Thoughts on Death and Life.*

20. One of the best is C. H. Valentine, *Modern Psychology and the Validity of Christian Experience.* A book quite worthy of consideration is S. P. Juergens, *Newman on the Psychology of Faith.* See also A. D. Nock, *Conversion;* E. M. Ligon, *The Psychology of Christian Personality;* and an article by T. Hywel Hughes on "The Psychology of the Oxford Group Movement," *Expository Times,* July, 1938.

21. The case should also be stated positively. The literature referred to above—which could be greatly extended—is the evidence that both biology and psychology may be used to *subserve* the Christian revelation.

22. This was always the claim of the eminent biologist, the late Sir J. Arthur Thomson. See, *e.g., Science and Religion* and *The System of Animate Nature,* 2 vols., and cf. the references in Chapter 16 above to the works of Needham.

23. The growing realization of this fact is one reason why J. B. Watson, *Behaviorism,* is now almost forgotten. Cf. Wm. McDougall, *Body and Mind,* and W. Brown, *Mind and Personality.*

CHAPTER 18

1. See the discussion in W. A. Brown, *Christian Theology in Outline,* chap. 22, pt. 1. "The simplest view is that which regards the Spirit as a

term expressive of God's activity in the soul of man, as distinct from his outward manifestation in nature and history" (p. 398).

2. See Davidson, *The Theology of the O. T.*, chap. 4, pts. 1–4, for the O. T. teaching. Davidson admits the diversity of the O. T. teaching, but claims that it all bears the one common meaning that God in his self-communication exerts upon man a "dynamical" influence (p. 128). Cf. E. F. Scott, *The Spirit in the N. T.*, chap. 1, on "The Spirit in the O. T." Stevens, *The Theology of the N. T.*, pt. IV, chap. 9, considers the teaching of Paul, but can only conclude that "Paul's language, when taken as a whole, does not furnish us with the materials for a precise definition of the Spirit" (pp. 443 f.). As to the *work* of the Spirit, however, Stevens shows that Paul is explicit enough. For a very full discussion, see Birch Hoyle, *The Holy Spirit in St. Paul*, and E. F. Scott, *op. cit.*, chap. 5, on "The Pauline Doctrine of the Spirit."

3. For a different view, cf. E. F. Scott, *The Spirit in the N. T.*, pp. 205–208.

4. See Stevens, *op. cit.*, pt. II, chap. 5; E. F. Scott, *op. cit.*, chap. 6, sect. (2); T. Rees, *The Holy Spirit*, chap. 6, on "The Logos and the Spirit"; A. Sabatier, *Religions of Authority*, bk. III, chap. 3, on "The N. T. the Charter of the Religion of the Spirit." Cf. Rufus Jones, *Studies in Mystical Religion*, chap. 1, on "The Mystical Element in Primitive Christianity." John's thesis, says Jones, is that "spiritual life is the result of the incoming of God into human life," (p. 17). The relation between love (ἀγάπη) and the Spirit is discussed in Nygren, *Agape and Eros*, vol. I.

5. The so-called *"filioque"* clause was added to the Nicene-Constantinople confession in 589 A.D., at the third synod of Toledo. The synod pronounced an anathema against all who did not believe that "the Holy Spirit proceedeth from both the Father and the Son." See Hagenbach, *History of Doctrines*, vol. I, sect. 94, and cf. W. A. Curtis, *History of Creeds and Confessions of Faith*, p. 74.

6. See McGiffert, *A History of Christian Thought*, vol. I, chap. 9, on "Montanism."

7. See W. W. Sweet, *The Story of Religions in America*. Cf. Kellems, *Alexander Campbell and the Disciples*, chap. 8, on "The Work of the Holy Spirit"; Elmer T. Clark, *Small Sects in America*.

8. *The Philosophic Basis of Mysticism*, pp. 53 f.

9. See Leuba, *The Psychology of Religious Mysticism*.

10. In *Human Nature and Its Re-Making*, pt. II, the section on "The Natural Man."

11. It is the thesis of Wm. Temple, in *Mens Creatrix*, that the four distinctive human activities are knowledge, art, conduct, and religion. These represent so many converging lines, but the lines never meet. All that philosophy can do is to offer a general conception of "the kind of fact which would constitute the point of their ultimate convergence" (p. 298). In the Christian revelation, there is actually declared to be, as historic fact, precisely what philosophy recognizes to be needed, if men are to be saved from an ultimate scepticism. Hence the title of Temple's chapter (21), "The New Start."

12. Cf. T. Rees, *op. cit.*, chap. 6, and W. R. Inge, *The Philosophy of Plotinus*, vol. II, lects. XIV-XVI, on "The Spiritual World."

13. See the article by M. C. D'Arcy, in the symposium *Revelation*, ed. John Baillie.

14. Cf. John Oman, *Vision and Authority*, (rev. ed.), bk. I, chap. 7, on "Seeking Truth," and the exposition of "Isaiah's Call and Consecration" in G. A. Smith, *Isaiah*, vol. I, chap. 4.

15. Even Schweitzer, notwithstanding his radicalism at so many points, leaves us in no doubt here. See *The Quest for the Historical Jesus* and *Paul and His Interpreters*.

16. Matthew 26.62–68; Luke 22.66–71.

17. There are many excellent suggestions in the chapter (6) on "Faith and Belief" in Wieman, *Normative Psychology of Religion*, but the reader is always left with the feeling that "authority" *per se* is no proper ground for belief. One could agree with the principle that "propositions that cannot be tested should not be believed" (p. 123), but it is obvious that a proposition must be presented before it can be tested. If the testing supports the proposition, it still remains to ask whence came the proposition in the first place. It is true that the authoritative must pass over into the experiential, but the experience does not *create* the authority: it only serves to *validate* it.

18. Cf. Glover, *Paul of Tarsus*, pp. 236 f., on God's "choice" of Paul.

19. C. E. Raven, *Jesus and the Gospel of Love*, passes some severe strictures upon the Church of history, but the closing chapters (13–15) express a profound conviction as to the persistence and re-discovery of the essential Christian revelation.

20. The modern "social" emphasis in Christianity is a clear case in point. Nothing new has been added thereby to the revelation in Christ. Rather has the Church been led to a new understanding and a new application of what it had always possessed. See A. E. Garvie, *The Christian Ideal for Human Society*; Bennett, *Social Salvation*; Stanley Jones, *Christ's Alternative to Communism*; F. Ernest Johnson, *The Church and Society*; Josiah Stamp, *Christianity and Economics*; Wesley Bready, *England Before and After Wesley*; Christopher Dawson, *Religion and the Modern State*; Fanfani, *Catholicism, Protestantism, and Capitalism*; and for a more individual emphasis, Douglas Jerrold, *The Future of Freedom*.

CHAPTER 19

1. Cf. the statement in E. E. Aubrey, *Present Theological Tendencies*, chap. 2, on "Modernism"; also G. B. Smith, *Current Christian Thinking*; R. Niebuhr, *Reflections on the End of an Era*; S. Mathews, *The Faith of Modernism*.

2. The two volumes, *Contemporary American Theology*, ed. Vergilius Ferm, represent a wide range of opinions, but enough is included to justify the statements in the text. See also E. A. Burtt, *Types of Religious Philosophy*, chap. 8, on "Modernism."

3. See W. M. Horton, *Contemporary English Theology* and *Contemporary Continental Theology*. Cf. the three volumes of C. S. MacFarland, *Contemporary Christian Thought* (1936), *Trends of Christian Thinking* (1937), and *The Christian Faith in a Day of Crisis* (1939). In these three volumes, Dr. MacFarland reviews approximately a hundred recent theological books. The books are admittedly "selected," but even a cursory glance at the titles will indicate the appearance of a more positive trend.

4. As reported in *The British Weekly*, August 25, 1938.

5. How necessary this distinction is may be inferred from the fact that in a recent volume, *The Quest of Religious Certainty*, by H. A. Bosley, the various books of the eminent English Congregational scholar, Sydney Cave, are referred to as exemplifying "the modernistic approach" (p. 28, footnote). Cave's "approach" may be "modern" in the methodological sense intended by the author, but Cave's *conclusions* are a long remove from what most persons would regard as "modernistic."

6. See *The Growth of Religion*, by Wieman and Horton, pt. II, Wieman's section.

7. But cf. the reference to Wieman in Chapter 1 above.

8. *The Meaning of God in Human Experience*, pt. IV, on "How Men Know God." See espec. chaps. 16, 21, and 22. Cf. chap. 46, on "The Divine Aggression" in *Human Nature and Its Re-Making*.

9. Cf. his earlier book, *The Wrestle of Religion With Truth* (1927), pt. II, on "The Concepts of Religion," and espec. chaps. 11–13, in which Wieman deals sympathetically with Whitehead's "Concept of God."

10. Comparable in significance to the symposium on *Revelation* already referred to is the collection of "Essays in Explanation and Defence," ed. W. R. Matthews, and entitled, *The Christian Faith*. The writers are Sydney Cave, J. K. Mozley, W. R. Matthews, G. S. Duncan, A. E. J. Rawlinson, N. Micklem, J. S. Whale, H. Wheeler Robinson, Edwyn Bevan, Francis Underhill, F. R. Barry, and Percy Dearmer. It is true that these are all British theologians, and that due regard must be paid to what Horton (in *Contemporary Continental Theology*, pp. 232 f.) and Aubrey (in *Living the Christian Faith*, chap. 4) say about the desirability of a distinctively American contribution to theology. As to the suggestion, see the volume of essays, entitled *Affirmations*, by Seven American Anglo-Catholics. The seven writers are B. I. Bell, W. A. Orton, W. M. Urban, F. A. Pottle, T. O. Wedel, Frank Gavin, and R. A. Cram, and the names are significant. Yet each of the seven men represents the "historical" position. The authors of the British essays referred to stand in the front rank of recognized Christian scholars, and every one of them is emphatic in his support of the distinctive claims of historical Christianity. Indeed, Bishop Rawlinson, who writes on "The Christian Belief in Christ," affirms the historic view that "in Jesus Christ we have to do, not with a human being who was deified, but with a Divine being who became man" (p. 152). And the article by J. S. Whale, on "Sin and the Need of Redemption," is as uncompromisingly "evangelical" as anything being written by Barth or Brunner.

11. Mackintosh's actual language is that following the Great War and its anguish, Troeltsch gave expression to a version of Christianity which was "gravely and even fatally diluted" (*Types of Modern Theology*, p. 216).

12. *Op. cit.*, p. 189.

13. *The Methodist Recorder*, May 27, 1937, (p. 8).

14. *The Congregational Quarterly*, p. 142, April number, 1938. Cf. the Memoir by A. B. Macaulay, prefixed to the volume, H. R. Mackintosh, *Sermons* (1938).

15. See *The Journals of Kierkegaard*, ed. and trans. Alexander Dru; Swenson's introduction to his translation of the *Philosophical Fragments*; Steere's introduction to his translation of *Purity of Heart*; Theodore Haecker, *Søren Kierkegaard*, a brief essay, but a classic; the two studies of Kierkegaard by E. L. Allen and J. A. Bain respectively; L. M. Hollander, *Selections from Kierkegaard*; the chapter on Kierkegaard in H. R. Mackintosh, *Types of Modern Theology*; and the voluminous study, *Kierkegaard*, by Walter Lowrie. Lowrie includes much of Kierkegaard's own writings, and adds an appendix consisting of a synopsis of all of Kierkegaard's writings, as also a select bibliography including Danish and German titles besides English.

16. Walter Lowrie, *Our Concern with the Theology of Crisis*, pp. 19 f., gives a bibliography of the so-called Barthian group up to the time of publication (1932). There should be added *Credo*; the answer to Brunner, entitled, *Nein!* the translation of *The Church Dogmatic*, *I*; the article in *Revelation*, ed. John Baillie; and the Gifford Lectures, *The Knowledge of God and the Service of God* (1939); besides volumes of sermons. Lowrie's bibliography of English expositions could be supplemented by McConnachie's second volume, *The Barthian Theology and the Man of To-Day*; H. Rolston, *A Conservative Looks to Barth and Brunner*; A. Keller, *Karl Barth and Christian Unity*. Lowrie's own book is written manifestly *en rapport*, and is one of the best English studies. See also Aubrey, *op. cit.*, chap. 3, on "The Dialectical Theology." For a short exposition, however, combining sympathetic understanding, clear insight, warm appreciation, and sound critical estimate, there is nothing better in English than the chapter on "Karl Barth: the Theology of the Word of God," in H. R. Mackintosh, *Types of Modern Theology*.

17. Cf. D. S. Cairns, *The Riddle of the World*, pp. 154 ff., pp. 180 f., footnote, and Appendix B, pp. 364 ff., much of which is directed against Barth's denial of "general" revelation.

18. *Op. cit.*, p. 317.

19. The books of Karl Heim in English are *The New Divine Order*, *God Transcendent* (a translation of the first volume, entitled, *Glaube und Denken*, of a proposed series), *Spirit and Truth*, and *The Church of Christ and the Problems of the Day*. The introduction to *God Transcendent* is by Edwyn Bevan, who includes some useful information on Heim's intellectual and spiritual experiences. See also in T. S. K. Scott-Craig and R. E. Davies, *Germany's New Religion*, the article by Heim on "Responsibility and Destiny," and the introduction by the translators.

20. The first eight chapters of Lamont, *Christ and the World of Thought,* are in effect an exposition of Heim's philosophy.

21. Introduction to *God Transcendent,* pp. v, vi.

22. In *God the Creator,* the Hastie Lectures in the University of Glasgow, 1935. Cf. the article on Hendry and his book by John Baillie in *The British Weekly,* March 25, 1937. Baillie describes the author as "A Scottish Barthian."

23. In addition to the books mentioned in the text, are *Man and the Machine, The End of Our Time, Fate of Man in the Modern World, The Bourgeois Mind, Christianity and Class War, Dostoevsky,* and (most recent) *Solitude and Society.* In the last-named volume, Berdyaev refers to a book he wrote some twenty years ago, entitled *The Meaning of Creation,* in which he defined "Existential Philosophy," although without using the term (p. 51). See also, in the same volume, p. 65, his reference to *The Meaning of Creation.*

24. Review of *The Destiny of Man* in *The Church Times* (London), April 30, 1937.

25. *The Destiny of Man,* p. 34. Cf. *Freedom and the Spirit,* chap. 5, on "Redemption and Evil," espec. sect. 3, pp. 171–179.

26. *The Destiny of Man,* pt. II, chap. 3, on "The Ethics of Creativeness."

27. *Ibid.,* pp. 160 f.

28. For bibliography, see Lowrie, *Our Concern With the Theology of Crisis,* p. 19. *Der Mittler* has been translated as *The Mediator.* Needful additions to Lowrie are *The Theology of Crisis, The Divine Imperative, Our Faith,* and *God and Man.* The last-named contains a valuable introduction by David Cairns, including an interesting "Personal Note" on Brunner. An important work of Brunner, not yet available in English, is *Wahrheit als Begegnung.* His exhaustive Christian anthropology, *Der Mensch im Widerspruch,* has been translated as *Man in Revolt.*

29. *The Mediator,* p. 147.

30. *Ibid.,* bk. II, chap. 7, on "The Divine Word." Cf. *God and Man,* pp. 122–130; *The Theology of Crisis,* chap. 2.

31. *The Mediator,* p. 214.

32. See *The Formation of the Gospel Tradition.*

33. See, *e.g.,* E. E. Aubrey, *Living the Christian Faith.* Cf. note 10, above.

CHAPTER 20

1. Some typical titles are G. B. Foster, *Christianity In Its Modern Expression;* P. Gardner, *Practical Basis of Christian Belief;* Eucken, *Can We Still be Christians?* James Marchant, ed., *The Future of Christianity;* S. Angus, *Essential Christianity;* F. R. Barry, *Christianity and the New World.*

2. See Wm. McDougall, *Body and Mind.*

3. See especially the writings of James Leuba, of whom Wieman, in

Formative Psychology of Religion, p. 44, flatly says that his psychological studies have tended to deal with religion as illusion.

4. For an excellent statement, see Vieth, *Objectives in Religious Education*.

5. Wieman, *Methods of Private Religious Living*, reveals a side of the author's thought not too apparent in his later writings.

6. Such books as Visser t'Hooft, *None Other Gods*, and A. Keller, *Five Minutes to Twelve*, can be ignored by no earnest Churchman.

7. For an example of what is meant, see Marc Boegner, *God, the Eternal Torment of Man*.

8. The writings of Rufus Jones reveal this quality, e.g., *Studies in Mystical Religion*. See also von Hügel, *Essays and Addresses on the Philosophy of Religion* (First and Second Series), and espec. his *Mystical Element of Religion* (2 vols.), based on Saint Catherine of Genoa.

9. Cf. the chapter on "The Myths of Plato," in Westcott, *Religious Thought in the West*.

10. This seems to the writer to be the case with Wieman, espec. in *Formative Psychology of Religion* and his section of *The Growth of Religion*. His autobiographical chapter in *Contemporary American Theology*, ed. V. Ferm, First Series, is revealing at this point.

11. Cf. Bushnell's discussion of "Sacrificial Symbols and Their Uses," in *The Vicarious Sacrifice*, vol. I, pt. 4.

12. See Peake's discussion in his *Commentary on the Bible*, pp. 138 ff.

13. Without a doubt, it was the furnishings and ceremonies in the Temple which originated the process of thought in the mind of Isaiah consummating in his vision. See Isa. 6.

14. E.g., Isa. 9, 33, 59; Jer. 25.15–28; Ezek. 1, 17; Dan. 10; Joel 2; Amos 8; Nahum 3; Zeph. 1.14–18; Zech. 4, 5, 14.

15. Cp. Isa. 55 and Ezra 8.

16. See Montgomery, *Daniel*, in International Critical Commentary, espec. sects. 19 and 22.

17. Matt. 1.22 f.; 2.5 f., 15 f., 17 f.; 3.3; 4.14 f.

18. *The Nature of the Physical World*, pp. ix–xii.

19. The three forms of Jesus' temptation were forms of contemporary messianic speculation—the Reformer, the Wonder-worker, the Conqueror. See Matt. 4.1–10.

20. As in Rashdall, *The Idea of Atonement in Christian Theology*, pp. 29 ff., and note beginning on p. 49.

21. Cf. E. Lewis, *Jesus Christ and the Human Quest*, pp. 257 ff.

22. In *Beyond Tragedy*, chap. 1. See review in *Religion in Life*, Winter Number, 1939.

23. The writer himself believes that it is possible to recognize a "cosmological dualism" while still retaining an "ontological monism." That is, dualism is inseparable from the creative process, but "prior to" the creative process there is only one.

24. In *Reality*, chap. 6.

25. See the summary statement in *Creative Evolution*, p. 251: "matter" is defined as "the inverse of the life movement."

26. The story has been dramatized by Shelley.

27. See Spender, *The Decline of the West;* and for a discussion less depressing, B. Kidd, *The Science of Power.*

28. The relevant respective titles are *Freedom and the Spirit* (Berdyaev); *The Meaning of History* (Tillich); *The Problem of God* (Brightman).

29. This is the order of Paul's argument in *Romans,* and is implicit, though less logically presented, in the *Fourth Gospel.*

30. See *Christus Victor.*

31. *Ibid.,* pp. 33 ff.

32. For a collection of these metaphors, see Grensted, *Short History of Doctrine of Atonement,* chap. 3.

33. *Op. cit.,* p. 47.

34. *Ibid.,* chap. 6, espec. p. 138. See p. 129 for what Aulén calls "the nerve of the whole."

35. Aulén quotes on p. 120: "For Christ sticks in his [the devil's] gills, and he must spue him out again, as the whale the prophet Jonah, and even as he chews him the devil chokes himself and is slain, and is taken captive by Christ" (from *Works,* Weimar ed., xx, pp. 347 f.).

36. Luther, says Aulén, "retains throughout the dualistic outlook, and therefore regards God himself as engaged in the work of redemption" (p. 132).

37. Jesus spoke about sin in the Sermon on the Mount fully as drastically as anything written by Paul in *Romans.* See Matt. 5.21 ff.

38. Cf. John 9.1 ff.

39. See the chapter on "Supernatural Healing" in Karl Heim, *The New Divine Order.*

40. See Matt. 24 and 25.

41. Cf. the relevant parables in Matt. 13.

42. See Mark 13.

43. "Get thee behind me, Satan!" Matt. 16.23.

44. See Rev. 19.11–16; 13.1–18.

45. A famous poem, the *Rubaiyat* of Omar Khayyam, which has nowhere a Christian sentiment, yet contains one stanza which expresses a universal desire:

> "Ah Love! could I and thou with Fate conspire
> To grasp this sorry Scheme of Things entire,
>   Would we not shatter it to bits—and then
>   Re-mould it nearer to the Heart's Desire!"

With which compare Browning's *Rabbi ben Ezra,* supposedly a reply to Edward Fitzgerald's translation of the Persian poem. Browning could write:

> "I see the whole design,
> I, who saw power, see now Love perfect too;
> Perfect I call thy plan:
> Thanks that I was a man!
> Maker, remake, complete—I trust what thou shalt do!"

umph, 303; and the Word, 64 f.; as a word, 69

Resuscitation not resurrection, 188 f.

Re-union of Christendom, 65 f.

Revelation, and authority, 259 f.; bases of, 154 f.; and certainty, 145 f.; the Christian, 16 f., 30; and Church, 62 f.; as conditioned, 52 f.; continuance of, 263 f.; and creation, 94 f., 172 f.; and documents, 45 f.; and faith, 256 f.; one final, 32; form and substance, 140; and freedom, 141; general, 3 f., 113, 132, 145 f., 282 f.; and history, 34 f., 42 f.; instrument of, 256; man the presupposition, 174; and modern thought, 225 f.; and the N. T., 47 f.; and the O. T., 30 f.; process of, 40 f.; and reason, 111 f., 253 f.; and religion, 18 f.; response to, 269 f.; and scepticism, 132 f.; and Scripture, 168 f.; and signs, 8 f.; special, 3, 113, 132 f., 145 f., 174, 282 f.; and the Spirit, 252 f.; and the supernatural, 290; a symposium on, 269; and transcendence, 277 f.

Riddle of existence, 28, 103, 253 f.

Roman Catholicism, 267 f.

Russian Orthodox Faith, 279

Salvation, election and, 261 f.; its meaning, 87 f.

Satan and Christ, 90

Scepticism, 236, 239; and Christianity, 123 f.; inevitable, 143; and revelation, 132 f.

Scholasticism, 230 f.

Science, and Bible, 243 f.; and change, 207 f.; and creation, 96 f.; and God, 171; and immortality, 171; and intelligibility, 14; limitations of, 293; and origins, 92 f.; and reason, 147 f., 150; and religion, 208 f., 211 f., 215 f., 218 f., 219 f., 223 f.; and Resurrection, 183 f.; and the scientist, 24; and Virgin Birth, 183 f.

Scientific method and Christianity, 135 f.

Scripture (see also Bible), authority of, 34 f.; and criticism, 34 f., 140, 285 f.; God in, 257; imagination in, 291 f.; and inerrancy, 55; inspiration of, 34 f., 260 f.; purpose of, 30; and revelation, 168 f.; the Spirit in, 248 f.

Securus judicat, 71

Sense-experience, 147 f.

Servant Songs, 42

Signs and revelation, 8 f.

Sin, conviction of, 127; and freedom, 142; and man, 283; and modernism, 136; original, 104, 108 f., 129 f., 142; and society, 110

Socialization and religion, 20

Society and sin, 110

Sociology and Christianity, 70

Sola fide, 276

Solar system, and God, 215

Sovereignty of God, 120

Space and time, 237 f.

Spinozism, 11

Spirit (Holy), 248 f.; the, and Church, 31, 262 f.; descriptions of, 263; in Fourth Gospel, 261; and the good, 86; and human nature, 255; and New Testament, 50, 54, 58; and Old Testament, 45; permanent office of, 265; and revelation, 58, 252 f.; and Trinity, 249 f.; and the Word, 255

Spiritual, autonomy of, 222

Stars and destiny, 236 f.

Subjectivism and values, 137 f.

Suffering, and nature, 103 f.; and redemption, 274

Summa Theologica, 231

Supernatural, and Christianity, 70 f., 165 f.; as creative, 162 f.; and knowledge, 170; and man, 27 f.; and natural, 156 f.

Symbols, 3 f.; and revelation, 8 f.

Synoptics, 49, 52, 54 f., 92

Temporal and eternal, 10, 12

Temptation of Jesus, 293

Testimony, and Christianity, 62 f.; of Church, 74 f.

Theism, and evolution, 218 f.; and humanism, 158 f.; modern, 136; and naturalism, 93; and Spinoza, 11

Theocratic ideal in Israel, 37

Theologians, contemporary, 272 f.

Theology, modern trends, 267 f.; necessity of, 221; and science, 224 f.; "society-centered," 286 f.

Thomism, 230 f.

Time, and existence, 156; and space, 237 f.

INDEX OF PROPER NAMES

Luther, Martin, 33, 210, 279, 298 f., 342
Lyman, E. W., 311

Macauley, A. B., 272, 339
MacCulloch, J. A., 318
MacFarland, C. S., 338
MacGregor, G. H. C., 330 f.
MacGregor, W. M., 315
Machen, J. G., 188
Macintosh, D. C., 328
Mackenzie, Kenneth, 66
Mackintosh, H. R., 92, 209, 271 f., 276, 326, 332
Mackintosh, Robert, 329
Mahomet (Muhammed), 7, 74, 134, 178
Manson, W., 331
Maritain, Jacques, 279, 325
Martensen, H., 320, 332
Martineau, J., 218, 311
Mathews, Shailer, 18, 230
Matthews, W. R., 5, 310
McClure, J. G. K., 32
McConnell, F. J., 325 f.
McCown, C. C., 317
McDougall, W. M., 335
McGiffert, A. C., 334
McKay, John, 272
Melancthon, Philip, 210
Mercier, L. J. A., 272
Micah, 39
Micklem, E. R., 331
Micklem, N., 272
Milton, John, 184
Mitchell, H. G., 312
Moberly, R. C., 286
Moffatt, James, 33
Montague, W. P., 318, 324
Montanus, 250, 262
Montefiore, C. G., 313
Moore, E. C., 318
More, P. E., 11, 250, 324 f.
Morgan, Lloyd, 321
Moses, 7, 35, 133, 257

Narcissus, 7
Neander, 312
Needham, Sir Joseph, 115, 222 f.
Nehemiah, 43 f.
Newcomb, Simon, 212
Newman, J. H., 324
Newton, 19, 207, 210
Nicaea, 229
Nicoll, W. R., 124

Niebuhr, Reinhold, 294 f., 317, 325
Nietzsche, F., 279
Nineveh, 44 f.
Noah, 7
Nock, A. D., 317
North, Eric, 312
Noyes, Alfred, 324
Nygren, Anders, 272, 336

Oedipus, 295
Oesterley, W. O. E., 313
Oliver, J. R., 317
Oman, John, 309, 328
Origen, 94, 317
Orr, James, 309
Osiander, Andreas, 209
Otto, Max, 5
Otto, Rudolph, 6, 170, 221 f., 250, 309, 311
Overstreet, H. A., 321
Ovid, 333
Owst, G. R., 318

Paine, Thomas, 172
Parmenides, 240, 309
Pascal, Blaise, 25, 121, 126, 210
Pauck, Wilhelm, 276
Paul, 7, 49 f., 51, 57 f., 120
Paulus of Heidelberg, 189
Peake, A. S., 312, 316
Pelagius, 106
Perrier, J. L., 335
Peter, 49 f., 51
Pfleiderer, O., 314
Phaedo, 10
Phaedrus, 10, 103
Philemon, 59
Philipson, D., 313
Philo, 279
Philomela, 7
Pietists, 71
Plato, 10, 20, 86, 103, 117, 132, 168, 207, 213 f., 231, 279
Plowright, B. C., 320
Poe, E. A., 39
Pollock, Frederick, 328
Porter, F. C., 314
Pringle-Pattison, A. S., 12, 24, 309, 310
Prometheus, 178
Proteus, 7
Proudhon, P. J., 321
Pryzawara, E., 272
Pythagoreans, 212 f.

Quick, O. C., 316, 324, 332

Rashdall, Hastings, 64, 311
Raven, C. E., 314, 337
Renan, Ernest, 111, 217, 333
Republic, 10
Richards, P. S., 328
Ritschl, A., 220
Robinson, H. Wheeler, 313, 335
Rogers, A. K., 310
Romanes, G. J., 218
Rossetti, D. G., 19, 323
Rousseau, J. J., 23, 109, 323
Royce, J., 11, 318
Russell, Bertrand, 5, 317
Ruth the Moabitess, 43 f., 235
Rutherford, Samuel, 83

Sabatier, A., 332
Saintsbury, George, 312
Samuel, 36
Santayana, George, 11
Sasse, 272
Satan, 315 f.
Schleiermacher, F. W., 11, 167, 189, 331
Schmidt, N., 19
Scholastics, 231
Schopenhauer, Arthur, 115
Schweitzer, Albert, 62, 315, 337
Scott, Anderson, 314
Scott-Craig, T. S. K., 339
Scott, Hugh M., 334
Seeberg, R., 312
Shakespeare, 86
Sheen, Fulton, 272
Shelley, P. B., 39, 167, 175, 177 f.
Shorey, Paul, 11, 213
Simpson, J. Y., 211
Sleigh, R. S., 319
Smith, G. A., 33
Smith, G. B., 337
Smith, W. R., 312, 313
Smuts, J. C., 310
Socrates, 10, 236
Solovyov, Vladimir S., 279
Sorley, W. R., 310
Sparrow-Simpson, W. J., 316
Spencer, H., 218
Spinoza, B., 11 f., 94, 114 f., 167, 236, 251
Stallknecht, Newton P., 334
Stamp, Sir Josiah, 337
Stephens, Leslie, 323

Stepun, Feodor, 279
Stevens, George, 336
Stirling, J. H., 310
Strachan, R. H., 322
Strauss, D. F., 18, 136, 189
Streeter, B. H., 295, 324
Sweet, W. W., 336
Swenson, D. F., 339
Swinburne, A. C., 166
Synoptists, 49 f., 54 f.
Syrinx, 7

Tauler, 318
Taylor, A. E., 11, 213, 214, 309
Taylor, H. O., 318
Taylor, Vincent, 286, 313
Temple, William, 11, 269, 336
Tennant, F. R., 321
Tennyson, A. L., 154, 218
Tereus, 7
Tertullian, 115, 207
Thomas Aquinas, 25, 64, 108, 147, 159, 230 f.
Thomas Didymus, 191, 193
Thompson, Francis, 15, 20, 24, 114, 178, 217
Thomson, J. Arthur, 335
t'Hooft, Visser, 123
Thorburn, T. J., 319
Thurneysen, E., 276
Tillich, Paul, 296
Timaeus, 10, 213
Trattner, E. R., 313
Troeltsch, Ernest D., 271, 319
Tuitshev, 279
Turgeniev, Ivan S., 279
Turner, J. E., 327, 328
Tyndall, John, 217

Unamuno, Miguel, 11
Underhill, E., 311
Urban, W. M., 272, 310, 311, 320

Valentine, C. H., 335
Valjean, Jean, 105 f.
Virgil, 103
Von Hügel, Baron, 161, 341
Vosser, Karl, 318

Walker, T., 313
Wallace, A. W., 218
Wallace, W., 12
Wallis, Louis, 312